The Complete Foundations of Soul Astrology

The Complete Foundations of Soul Astrology

A deeply fascinating, yet amazingly simple course in Soul Astrology to support your journey of spiritual awakening

Ruth Hadikin BSc.

First Print Edition © 2019 Ruth Hadikin. All rights reserved.
This book or any portion thereof may not be reproduced or used in any manner whatsoever without the express written permission of the publisher except for the use of brief quotations in a book review.

ISBN-13: 978-0995559349
ISBN-10: 0995559341

Published by Ruth Hadikin Associates
Contact info@RuthHadikin.com

Cover design ©Ruth Hadikin Associates 2018
Background image: Blue Sunrise. View of Earth from space. Photo 33660001 © Rfischia - Dreamstime.com

Dedication and Acknowledgement

This book is dedicated to all my teachers. I have been extremely fortunate to meet knowledgeable, wise, and skilful teachers throughout my whole life, from even before I started school when my mother and grandfather taught me to read. Right up to the present day there have been countless teachers, too numerous to mention, to whom I am deeply grateful. In particular I would like to thank Master Astrologer Alan Oken for generously sharing his insight and wisdom, especially in the refined art of astrological delineation, which has greatly facilitated my own skill at interpreting the mandala that is our birth chart. I am also grateful to Esoteric Astrologer Candy Hillenbrand for her succinct descriptions of the Soul Purpose of each sign, which have inspired my own writing, and which I have quoted often.

My good friend and mentor, Master Visionary Intuitive Anya Sophia Mann deserves a special mention for her major contribution to my understanding of the energetics of astrology, and my ability to describe them. It is very rare to meet someone with such an exquisite ability to discern and describe subtle energies, who is also a master teacher and facilitator. Above all not only has she has taught me how to discern subtle distinctions in the quality of energy, but she has also given me the precise language to describe those distinctions.

I am deeply grateful to her for her kindness and generosity in sharing her unparalleled skill of discerning energy and her precision of language in describing subtle energetic distinctions. Her teaching and support is invaluable as I continue learning to identify, define and understand the energies of astrology more deeply and precisely. I aspire to be able to discern and describe energy to the degree that she can. Her influence has not only changed the outcome of this book, but in fact without her input it probably would never have been written.

Ruth Hadikin
December 2019

Contents

Introduction

1. Soul Astrology As A Spiritual Path

2. Personality-Soul Fusion

3. The Twelve Zodiac Signs

4. Your Soul's Purpose

5. Understanding Energy: by element, modality and polarity

6. The Planets

7. The Soul Centered Meaning of The Signs

8. Houses: Mansions of The Soul

9. Navigating the Depths of Karma

10. The Sun

11. The Moon

12. The Moon's Nodes

13. Aspects

14. Esoteric Astrology

15. Mercury's Sacred Path to The Rainbow Bridge

16. Venus and The Law of Attraction

17. Mars, The Pulse of Life

18. Jupiter and The Emergence of God Consciousness

19. Saturn, Catalyst for Self-Mastery

20. The Dweller on The Threshold

21. Uranus, A Sacred Rebellion

22. Neptune, The Luminous Nature of Being

23. Pluto, Emptiness and Clear Light Wisdom

24. The Angel of Presence

Further Reading

Index

About The Author

Introduction

The chapters in this book were written as a series of articles: *The Foundations of Soul Astrology*, to support the further study of Soul Astrology as a tool to support spiritual awakening. The series was first published through my email newsletter *Life's Greatest Adventure*.

All twenty-four articles are presented here in their entirety as a complete system to support you in going deeper in your journey of self-exploration by using Soul Astrology as a tool for understanding yourself and your Soul's journey. Although you can read it as a stand alone, it is primarily intended to support students of Soul Astrology so you will find many references to the book *Soul Astrology* throughout.

The purpose of this volume is to cover some of the material that was first introduced in *Soul Astrology* in more depth, and also to include astrological principles that were not addressed, such as aspects and the soul-centered meaning of the planets through the signs and houses. In chapter seven I have included a quick reference table for each sign so you can distinguish between personality and soul-centered expressions at a glance. I hope you find this helpful. Although we cover some complex esoteric topics it is my hope that this has been done in such a way that it has simplified the subject matter, so that it is easier to grasp and apply as a practical tool in bringing a more spiritual perspective to understanding your horoscope.

It is still the simple combination of your Sun, Moon and Rising Sign that will tell you the most about your Soul's Journey and your purpose in this incarnation. It is my sincere wish that this simple approach to understanding your horoscope will support you in your journey of spiritual awakening.

For those of you who are new to Soul Astrology below is a short introduction to the principles that underpin this unique approach to self-exploration and spiritual awakening.

---

[1] Hadikin, R. (2016) *Soul Astrology: How Your Rising Sign Reveals Your Soul Path and Life Purpose.* Ruth Hadikin Associates. Order online at https://soulastrologybook.com

Your birth horoscope (birth chart or natal chart) is like a snapshot of your own energy field taken at your birth. Although it seems to be about things that are outside of you, like planets and Zodiac signs, they are really just reflections of who you are as a spiritual being.

Ultimately you are not separate from the Universe. You are part of a continuous flow of Divine Energy having an individual expression. We can think of this individual expression of Divine energy as your Soul.

According to *Esoteric Astrology*[2] your Soul's journey begins in the first Zodiac sign, Aries, as "a point of light in the mind of God" and travels on a journey through each of the twelve Zodiac signs culminating in the twelfth sign of Pisces. Some astrologers believe your Soul spends up to eight lifetimes in each sign.

At the time of your birth, the Zodiac sign that was rising on the horizon (in astrology this is called your Rising Sign or Ascendant) created a window of opportunity, a kind of 'portal' for you to beam in on, because it was a vibrational match for the current stage of your Soul's development.

So if someone has Cancer Rising for example, it's because they are a Cancer Soul that they were able to incarnate when Cancer was rising on the horizon. It was their time. The prevailing energy matched their Soul's vibration and so it was the perfect time for them to incarnate into this life.

This is why I refer to the Rising Sign as your *Soul Sign*. Throughout this book, it is important to remember that whenever I refer to your Soul Sign I'm talking about your Rising Sign.

Your Soul Sign represents your subtle Soul light (your Rising Sign), your Sun Sign indicates how you flow your prana or life-force energy, and your Moon Sign indicates how you flow your emotional energy. So we could say that your Soul Sign is showing you what you came to do, while your Sun and Moon are showing you how you will do it.

---

[2] Bailey, A.A. (1951) *Esoteric Astrology: Volume III, A Treatise on The Seven Rays.* Lucis Publishing Company, New York. Lucis Press Ltd, London.

You might also find it very helpful to read the free eBook *Your Essential Guide To Soul Astrology*. You can get your copy by signing up for my free newsletter *Life's Greatest Adventure*[3].

As with *Soul Astrology* once again I have made numerous links to Wikipedia and would remind you that these are merely to serve as a springboard for your further studies. Wikipedia articles can be a helpful starting point but they can also be biased and limited. They can never be relied upon as a final authority on any subject, so you are always wise to do further research of your own.

In writing this volume it was my intention to re-iterate and expound upon some of the concepts first introduced in *Soul Astrology*. For readers who are new to Soul Astrology as a subject I have repeated some important basic principles. For those who are already familiar with Soul Astrology and my work it is helpful to revise these specific points before expounding on them, to deepen your understanding.

You will notice that I have also once again repeated many quotes that I feel deserve deep contemplation. This is intentional on my part.

At the intellect stage of our journey (I say more about these stages later in this book) our ever-seeking "monkey mind" likes to rapidly devour information and then look for more. This keeps us in a constant state of 'searching' that is not conducive to the realization of spiritual truth.

It is more helpful to sometimes pause and quietly contemplate the subject matter, so deeper insights can arise in your own mind, before proceeding. So wherever there is repetition of profound quotes, salient points and deeper insights, rather than giving in to the tyranny of your monkey-mind, relax into the moment and view them as an invitation to go deeper in your study and contemplation.

Some quotes that first appeared in Soul Astrology are repeated again here, sometimes at the beginning of a chapter, and then later again in the same chapter. The intention is that after digesting the information within the chapter, you will then have a deeper understanding of their meaning.

---

[3] You can sign up for my newsletter on my website at https://ruthhadikin.com

One thing I have learned from the Tibetan tradition, is that even the greatest spiritual masters will apologize upfront for any errors and omissions in their work. Again I would like to continue in that vein here by pointing out that each of us, myself included, is interpreting spiritual teachings according to our own level of consciousness. In this book I am merely sharing my own insights and impressions, and in so doing apologize for any errors or inaccuracies there may be due to my own ignorance, misunderstanding, or lack of consciousness. Each student on the path is encouraged to keep going deeper in their own spiritual journey and to trust their own intuition and insights first and foremost, above all else.

Finally I hope you enjoy your journey with Soul Astrology and that it inspires you to go even deeper into your own journey of spiritual awakening through Self-exploration.

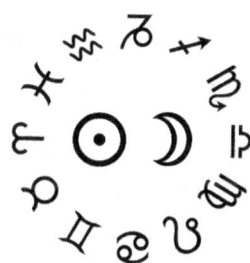

1. Soul Astrology as a Spiritual Path

Soul Astrology provides a language that can be helpful in understanding your experience and your path. To follow your Soul path in everyday life you also need to be able to 'listen' to the energy of your Soul, and to know where it is guiding you, so that you can follow. This insight comes through self-observation, awareness, and your own experience. In the book, *Soul Astrology*[4], we introduced the idea of karma as *everything we have ever learned in this and past lives*.

In those spiritual traditions with a concept of karma, there is also the concept of *dharma* which goes hand in hand with karma. Dharma in a sense is our life purpose. It is what we have come to do in the world. The word dharma is a Sanskrit word that originates in the Indian spiritual traditions such as Hinduism and Buddhism.

There is no single English word that correlates to dharma but it has been translated variously as *right living* and *cosmic law and order*[5].

---

[4] Hadikin, R. (2016) *Soul Astrology: How Your Rising Sign Reveals Your Soul Path and Life Purpose*. Ruth Hadikin Associates. Order online at https://soulastrologybook.com

[5] *"In Hinduism, dharma signifies behaviors that are considered to be in accord with Rta, the order that makes life and universe possible, and includes duties, rights, laws, conduct, virtues and **"right way of living"**. In Buddhism, dharma means **"cosmic law and order"**, and is also applied to the teachings of Buddha."* Online document at: https://en.wikipedia.org/wiki/Dharma Accessed December 6th 2019.

So we might think of dharma as living in accord with the natural rhythms and laws of the Universe.

Not everyone is born to be a great warrior, president or celebrity, but every single living being has a unique purpose according to the rhythms and laws of the Universe. You have your place in the grand scheme of things just as much as a president or an ant, a great soprano or a butterfly. In a bee hive, each bee has it's own purpose: some are worker bees, some are warrior bees, and then there is a queen.

Every living thing in existence is exactly where it is supposed to be, serving its purpose, and that includes you. So how do you know if are you a worker bee, a warrior or a queen? Well we can look at your horoscope (your birth chart) for clues!

Your horoscope is a symbol of your energy field and if we know where to look it can tell us a lot about the energy you were born with. While there isn't exactly anything in your chart that says precisely 'you are a plumber', we can look at some of your predispositions, tools, and talents, and kind of figure it out from there!

Your Rising Sign

One of the first things we can look at is your Rising Sign because that is telling us about your Soul's energy and, more importantly how it wants to flow into the world. For example, if you have Leo Rising you are here to express Divine Will and purpose in the form of heart-centered leadership. But that's pretty esoteric, how do we then take that statement and translate it into everyday life?

Your Sun and Moon

Look next to your Sun and Moon signs because they will tell you much about how your Soul energy is being channeled into the world. Maybe your Sun is in Gemini so you could be a heart centered leader (Leo Rising) who uses your words and communication (Gemini) to convey your message.

Maybe your Moon is in Libra, so in addition to having a primary 'MO' (modus operandi or 'way of being') of 'using words and communication', you also respond to others emotionally (the Moon) with tact, charm, diplomacy and a sense of fairness and justice (Libra).

Your Midheaven

You can also look to your midheaven (MC) to tell you something about your public, or outer image: how others see you and how you like to be seen (or not) out in the world. With Leo Rising you may have Aries on the midheaven, which means you may be an innovative, bold, courageous leader who takes inspired action in the world.

Equally you could have Taurus on the MC which means you would take a more considered approach and may want to be seen as more conventional yet patient, and hard-working.

There are some traditional houses to look at too. Conventionally the Tenth House is the house of 'career' but this isn't always the case. It is more accurate to call the Tenth House the house of vocation or, since that's what we're talking about today, let's call it the house of dharma!

The Tenth and Sixth Houses

Esoterically the Tenth House is associated with our masters and guides, and our spiritual lineage. So it is saying a lot about where you are in terms of your spiritual development and what you are bringing to the planet in this existence.

If you are really living in alignment with your soul, and doing work that you truly love, knowing it is what you are here to bring to the world, then yes, the Tenth House will reflect your 'career'.

However if you are in a 'career' because your parents thought it was a good idea, or you're just working to pay the bills but you really feel that you were here to bring something else to the planet, then your 'work' will show up in the Sixth House, while your true vocation, your dharma, will be reflected in the tenth.

For example if you have Cancer on the Sixth House cusp, you could be working to pay your bills in a retail store. You may excel at sales because you really understand people's needs (Cancer), but you may be working your way through college to graduate as a psychologist because with Scorpio on the Tenth House cusp you know deep inside that your real 'life's work' is to support people's inner transformation and healing in a much deeper way than retail allows you to do.

Your Lunar North Node

You could also take a look at the *lunar Nodal Axis*[6], which tells you something about your role in the society into which you were born.

In particular, the lunar North Node is pointing to a path that may be unfamiliar to you, but if you follow it, it can support you in your Soul's growth, and fulfill your role in society.

If you are uncertain about your life purpose, here are the basic starting points:

1.   Your *Rising Sign* is telling you what energy your Soul has come to embody and express into the world in this lifetime.

2.   Look at the condition of your *Sun and Moon*, which signs they are in, which houses they are in, and which planets they have aspects to.

3.   Look at the condition of your tenth and sixth *Houses*: which signs are on the cusp, and if any planets are there.

4.   Look at the condition of your *Midheaven*[7]: which sign is there, and study any planets that are there.

5.   Look at the *lunar Nodal Axis*: in particular your lunar North Node.

6.   Put it all together and (while it won't say 'you're a plumber') it will give you a very good sense of what you came here to do, and how you will do it!

All the above points are covered in depth in later chapters. As you continue reading, refer back to this list, take notes, and meditate on each of the above points in relation to your own horoscope. This will deepen your understanding of Soul Astrology, and clarify your Soul Path and Life Purpose.

---

[6] See chapter twelve, *The Moon's Nodes*.

[7] The midheaven is one of the four angles of the horoscope. It can be found near the top of your chart, usually marked by the letters MC. It represents your public image, how the world sees you and how you want to be seen, and often your position in society.

Once the goal is clearly seen (your own true nature) your path becomes clear. Your spiritual path then becomes a practice of simply letting go of what you are not, all that is false, so that your true inner nature can shine forth.

The Soul is a vehicle for spiritual energy, and so your Soul Sign indicates your innate core essence. It is the essence of who you really are, and your true nature as a spiritual being, but this all remains latent while you are identified with, and driven by, the needs of the ego-personality.

Your spiritual awakening involves realizing this core energy and expressing it into the world, while releasing all that is NOT you (your karma or conditioned behavior), thereby becoming a fully Soul-Centered individual.

In this volume it is my intention to cover the foundations of Soul Astrology in more depth and weave it all together so that you can see how it works as a powerful tool for you in your spiritual journey. You might find it helpful to keep a copy of *Soul Astrology* and your Birth Chart to hand. I will also offer suggested fieldwork to support those of you who wish to go deeper in your studies of this fascinating topic.

Suggested Fieldwork:

- Download and read *Your Essential Guide to Soul Astrology*[8] (if you haven't read it for a while, read it again to refresh your memory).
- Get two notebooks. Use one for your study notes (what you are learning about astrology); and use the other as a reflective journal where you write your deeper insights, self-observations and realizations about YOU that arise from your study and meditation.
- Self-observation is essential. If you don't already do so, start a regular meditation practice. It can be a sitting or an active meditation, whichever works best for you, to support you in practicing self-observation and cultivating self-awareness.

---

[8] Free eBook with Ruth's email newsletter *Life's Greatest Adventure*. Available on my website https://ruthhadikin.com

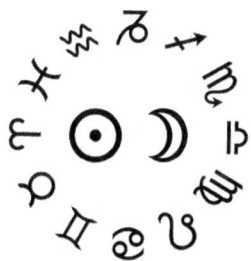

2. Personality-Soul Fusion

One of the fundamental principles of Soul Astrology is the concept of personality-Soul fusion, so it's worth checking in with yourself often to clarify your understanding by asking, "What is it really about?"

This brings you right back to the core questions of who you are, and why you are here. What do we mean by personality? ...and what do we mean by Soul? Let's explore...

At a fundamental level, we are beings of light. Our whole energy field is made up of different frequencies, or vibrations, of light. All spiritual traditions, no matter what their differences, have at their core a message of light. Science is now also finding evidence that confirms this fact, that at our very deepest essence we are beings of light. That being the case then, what do we mean by personality and Soul?

"We now know, today, that man is essentially a being of light."[9]

- Dr. Fritz Albert Popp, Biophysicist

Essentially there is no separation - there is only a difference of experience based on frequency - or vibration. At the denser end of

---

[9] Vey, G. *Are Humans Really Beings of Light?* Online document at http://viewzone.com/dnax.html Accessed December 6th 2019.

the spectrum light is matter, at the lighter (finer) end of the spectrum, matter is light:

> *"there is no difference between energy and matter
> except for the rate of motion ...
> Matter is spirit vibrating at it's slowest
> and spirit is matter vibrating at it's fastest"*
>
> - H.P. Blavatsky[10]

As the finer light of your Soul (represented by your Ascendant) incarnates into physical matter, it changes vibration. It is really more accurate to say that your physical form IS a slow-motion expression of your Soul, but for the sake of simplicity we can use the analogy of a crystal prism to help us understand more clearly.

As light shines through a prism it is refracted which allows us to see the colors of the rainbow that make up the light. In a similar way we could say that the light of your Soul (Your Ascendant) is refracted through the lens of your personality (mainly your Sun and Moon signs), which gives us the myriad expressions of human diversity.

Before the prism, light is one 'whole' experience. We aren't aware that it is made up of the different colors of the rainbow until the prism allows us to see the different parts that make up the light.

Likewise as our Soul-light is 'refracted' through the 'lens' of our personality signs we get to see our many rainbow colors of humanity.

This is part of the reason for our lives, the purpose of our journey in a physical body, so we get to experience the multidimensionality and diversity of human experience, and expression.

We get to see all the myriad expressions of humanity through our own unique individual expressions, before we return to oneness, before our rainbow 'disappears' back into the light.

So if we are all 'one' in light, what do we mean by Soul?
What is our personality?
... and how are we having individual experiences?

---

[10] Quoted by Alan Oken in his *Metaphysics of Money* webinar series. Available online at https://alanoken.com

What is Soul?

Your Soul can be thought of as your individualized expression of Divinity. If the whole of existence (seen and unseen; physical and non-physical) were an ocean, then you may consider your Soul to be like a glass of water taken from that ocean.

It is still part of the ocean, it still has all the qualities of the ocean, it will eventually return to the ocean, yet for a short time it is having an individualized experience, as you.

> *"The Soul is our individual link to the essential substance of the Creative Source... Astrology is a system that seeks to interpret the nature of the Universal Life Force as It moves, shapes, and creates human life and all events.*
>
> *The planets, signs, and houses, are not the causal elements of manifestation. They are, rather, the reflections of a transcendental synchronicity manifesting through the rhythms and timing of a cosmic clock."*
>
> - Alan Oken[11]

What is Personality?

Your personality, somewhat ironically, is a little more difficult to explain and understand because so much human behavior seems to be so far removed from the light!

On one level (keeping it simple) you can understand personality as everything you have ever learned: all of your behavior from this and past lives, that now exists as 'seeds' in your consciousness. Some are actively expressed while others lie 'dormant' awaiting for the right conditions in order to ripen.

For a deeper understanding you can think of your personality and Soul as being on a spectrum of frequency or vibration.

In essence there is no separation between personality and Soul, you only experience a sense of separation when your attention is focused solely on the drives of the personality.

---

[11] Oken, A. (2008) *Soul Centered Astrology. A Key To Your Expanding Self*. Ibis Press, Florida.

A Spectrum of Consciousness

Many contemporary spiritual teachers describe our spiritual journey in terms of a journey 'from fear to love'. This can be thought of as a spectrum of vibration, like the musical scale, that ranges from 'lower vibration' emotions such as guilt, shame, and fear to 'higher vibration' emotional states such as love, joy and peace. Dr. David Hawkins describes this as a *spectrum of consciousness* and there is a very helpful diagram of this in his book *Power vs. Force*[12].

In *Esoteric Astrology* The Tibetan explains that there are fundamentally six zodiac signs and that we experience them as twelve signs due to our *dualistic mind*[13]. Interestingly this is similar to a concept known as the Six Lokas in some Tibetan Buddhist traditions.

In the theory of the Six Lokas, or six 'realms', our lower emotions correspond to higher states of consciousness. So anger, for example, is thought to be a lower frequency of love and through prayers and spiritual practices anger will be transformed into love. They are thought to be simply different 'vibrations' on the same spectrum. So we can take heart in this fact because it means that if we have a lot of anger, it means we also have a huge capacity for Love - we just need to learn how to shift the vibration.

The Six Lokas

Anger = Love

Greed = Generosity

Ignorance = Clear Wisdom

Jealousy = Openness

Pride = Peacefulness

Laziness = Compassion

---

[12] Hawkins, D. (2014) *Power vs. Force: The Hidden Determinants of Human Behavior.* Hay House.

[13] The dualistic mind separates reality into component parts using labels, for example me, you, a tree, a car, a cat etc. In contrast, a nondual mind percieves reality as whole: one complete neverending dance of activity and energy, without separation.

> *"our anger obscures our capacity to love,*
> *our sadness obscures our joy,*
> *our prejudice obscures our equanimity, and*
> *our greed obscures our compassion"*
>
> - Tenzin Wangyal Rinpoche[14]

We mentioned above how, in *Esoteric Astrology* The Tibetan explains that there are fundamentally six zodiac signs and that we experience them as twelve signs due to our dualistic mind. Early in the relationship between the Tibetan and Alice Bailey he simply introduced himself as "The Tibetan" and said he was the Abbott of a monastery in Tibet.

If so, the Tibetan would have been very familiar with the concept of the Six Lokas, which is said to be thousands of years old. I often wonder if there is a correlation between the Six Lokas and the six 'polarities' in astrology!

Just as a reminder, the six polarities are:

Aries-Libra
Taurus-Scorpio
Gemini-Sagittarius
Cancer-Capricorn
Leo-Aquarius
Virgo-Pisces

Our personality and Soul are not separate but can be thought of as two ends of a spectrum of vibration or frequency, with a variety of expressions in-between. Our personality can therefore be thought of as simply a lower vibration expression of our Soul light. This is why, to keep things relatively simple, in some of my articles I speak about the personality as the 'fear-based' expression and the Soul as the 'love-based' expression. However we can see that the entire energetic spectrum is really much richer than that.

The beauty of speaking in terms of a spectrum, is that it reminds us that there really is no separation. Essentially, while there is no difference between us at our essence, any one of us can be at any point along the spectrum at any time. The 'seeds' of both the 'lower'

---

[14] Wangyal, T (2011) *Awakening The Sacred Body: Tibetan Yogas of Breath and Movement.* Hay House.

and 'higher' vibration expressions exist in us all, and can 'ripen' in different circumstances.

This is whole basis of astrology. When we look at a natal chart we can see all the potential 'seeds' - both 'negative' and 'positive' in our stream of consciousness. As we become more self-aware, we are more able to navigate the spectrum for ourselves and choose higher expressions of our Soul Light.

Your Fantastic Journey

You take a fantastic journey in your exploration of who you are... and what do you find? That you really are a fantastic being of light, with a myriad different expressions. You also discover this fact for yourself through the simple power of your own self-awareness. You don't have to take anybody's word for it. It is your own inner treasure, simply waiting to be discovered - by YOU!

There really is no separation, however your perceived separation is part of an illusion generated by your social conditioning and your brain. The solution is to cultivate your awareness to the point where you perceive reality as it really is: a complete, whole, and unified 'hologram' of intermingled, intertwined, dancing energy and light. This holistic field of perception IS personality-Soul fusion. The very thing that makes you whole is pure awareness. Awareness is therefore the key to your personality-Soul fusion and the method for cultivating awareness is meditation.

Self-awareness allows you to make your own inner journey of light, where you discover the simple truth of your being for yourself. Soul Astrology gives you a language and tools to describe the energy dynamics that you become aware of, as you continue your journey to oneness through personality-Soul fusion.

Suggested Fieldwork

Meditate on the energy of your Sun, Moon and Rising Sign. What higher quality (or combination of qualities) is your Soul wanting you to express in this lifetime: Love, Generosity, Clear Wisdom, Openness, Peacefulness and/or Compassion? Write your insights in your reflective journal.

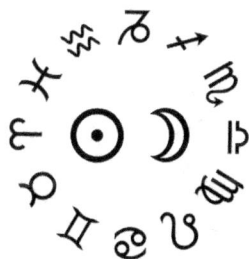

3. The Twelve Zodiac Signs

Fundamental to any study of Western Astrology are the twelve zodiac signs. The term Zodiac comes from the Ancient Greek word *zodiakos*, which literally meant circle *of little animals*. The modern word *zoo* shares the same origin. In ancient times people lived and worked more directly with animals, so the symbology of the zodiac allowed people to understand specific energetic patterns.

Earlier we mentioned that according to *Esoteric Astrology* our Soul's journey begins in the first Zodiac sign Aries as *a point of light in the mind of God* and travels on a journey through each of the twelve Zodiac signs culminating in the twelfth sign of Pisces. We also pointed out how some astrologers believe we spend up to eight lifetimes in each sign[15]. So a good understanding of the energy patterns represented by each sign is essential to a thorough understanding of your Soul Astrology, especially the energy of your Sun, Moon and Rising Sign.

The Twelve Zodiac Signs in order as they appear throughout the year are:

Aries - cardinal, fire, positive

Taurus - fixed, earth, negative

---

[15] Weiner, E. (1991) *Transpersonal Astrology: Finding The Soul's Purpose*. Element Books Ltd.

Gemini - mutable, air, positive

Cancer - cardinal, water, negative

Leo - fixed, fire, positive

Virgo - mutable, earth, negative

Libra - cardinal, air, positive

Scorpio - fixed, water, negative

Sagittarius - mutable, fire, positive

Capricorn - cardinal, earth, negative

Aquarius - fixed, air, positive

Pisces - mutable, water, negative

Each sign is described in terms of its 'modality' (cardinal, fixed and mutable), polarity (positive or negative) and element, which describe more specifically how the energy flows with each sign. We will cover this in more depth later in this book, but by way of an introduction here is a short description:

The Modalities

The beginning of each season, spring, summer, autumn and winter is marked by the four cardinal signs: Aries (spring equinox), Cancer, Libra (autumn equinox) and Capricorn.

The peak of each season is marked by the four fixed signs: Taurus is the fullness of spring, Leo is the height of summer, Scorpio the peak of autumn and Aquarius marks the depths of winter.

The mutable signs mark the changing season, where one season rolls into the next - In Gemini spring rolls into summer, in Virgo summer rolls into autumn, in Sagittarius autumn rolls into winter and in Pisces winter rolls into spring.

A good way to begin understanding the energetics of our own horoscope is to observe ourselves through the changing of the seasons.

The Elements

A basic understanding of the dominant elements in your own chart will give you a simplified 'snapshot' of your own ego-personality. For example, generally speaking:

• Air signs (Gemini, Libra, Aquarius) think their way through life;

• Water signs (Cancer, Scorpio, Pisces) feel their way forward;

• Fire signs (Aries, Leo, Sagittarius) focus on action and energy, while

• Earth signs (Taurus, Virgo, Capricorn) approach life practically, organizing physical resources and putting infrastructures in place.

The Polarity of A Sign

Each sign is also described in terms of being 'positive' or 'negative'. This is not about one's outlook (optimistic or pessimistic) but describes the flow of energy. Positive signs are said to be 'electric' in that they radiate energy outward, while the negative signs are said to be 'magnetic' in that they attract, or pull energy inward.

The combination of modality, element and polarity gives each zodiac sign it's unique energetic signature. For example, even though they both possess fixed energy, Aquarius - the fixed air sign (positive) uses energy quite differently from Scorpio, the fixed water sign (negative).

The Blended Six

A fully Soul Centered individual is one who is fully integrated. This means they have completed the process of Personality-Soul Fusion, integrated their Soul and personality, and can now access and fully express the highest octave of each sign. They will no longer experience polarity, so they can express the highest octave of Aries-Libra, Taurus-Scorpio, Gemini-Sagittarius, and so forth.

As we journey through this process together, eventually the whole of humanity will collectively shift towards wholeness. The twelve Zodiac signs as we currently experience them will then become what the Tibetan refers to as the blended six:

> *"The 12 opposites must become the blended six, this is brought about by the fusion in consciousness of the polar opposites. Pause and consider this phrasing. The opposites eternally remain from the point of view of human reason, but to the initiate who's intuition is functioning they constitute but six great potencies, because he has achieved "the freedom of the two" as is sometimes called.*
>
> *For instance, the Leo subject who has an initiated consciousness preserves the individuality developed in Leo, as well as the universality of Aquarius; he can function, if he so chooses, as a fully self-identified individual, yet possess simultaneously a fully awakened universal awareness; the same thing can be said of balanced activity and consequent fusion in all the signs. This analysis constitutes in itself an interesting and far reaching field of speculation."*
>
> - The Tibetan, *Esoteric Astrology*

Because the blending of opposites is such a fundamental concept in Soul Astrology it is vitally important to have a thorough understanding not only of your own Sun, Moon and Rising Signs, but also their opposite signs, and the energetic dynamics between them. It is worth taking some time here now to go deeper in our exploration of the Six Polarities.

The Six Polarities

The Zodiac is made up of twelve signs arranged in a circle. Each sign therefore has it's polar opposite on the other side of the circle. So although we have twelve signs, they are grouped into six pairs of opposites. These are called the six polarities.

The six polarities are:
- Aries-Libra
- Taurus-Scorpio
- Gemini-Sagittarius
- Cancer-Capricorn
- Leo-Aquarius
- Virgo-Pisces

Because of the illusion of separation, we tend to think of them as separate, but it is important to remember that they are inherently connected. In Soul Astrology, not only are they connected but they are an important key to unlocking your spiritual journey: your healing journey to wholeness and personality-Soul fusion.

> *"We may break a piece of magnetized steel as often as we like, we shall never be able to separate the positive from the negative pole; each fragment will always have both. This shows that polarity is an aspect of unity, not an arbitrary duality but an inseparable whole"*
>
> – Lama Anagarika Govinda

Opposite signs can be thought of as two 'poles' (two ends) of one continuous energetic spectrum. Understanding the totality of this spectrum can lead us out of a sense of duality into a more complete experience. The opposite pole of any sign can therefore be considered as a spiritual "gateway" in the sense that it opens us up to the higher spiritual potential of our own sign. By embracing the energy and character of the opposite sign, we energetically create an evolutionary loop (like the figure-eight infinity symbol) that enables a quantum leap to a higher Soul vibration.

To understand this we have to remember that in Soul Astrology we are always talking about energy and the movement of energy. Studies in quantum physics have shown that matter can act as a particle or a wave depending upon how it is observed. In other words it can appear like a solid object or it can be more like a fluid wave of energy. Essentially there is no separation. There is only a difference of experience based on frequency or vibration. At the denser end of the spectrum light is matter, while at the lighter (finer) end of the spectrum, matter is light:

> *"there is no difference between energy and matter except for the rate of motion ... matter is spirit vibrating at it's slowest and spirit is matter vibrating at it's fastest"*
>
> - H.P. Blavatsky

Because we are creatures of habit, we tend to 'solidify' at one end of a polarity. Through our social conditioning and brain wiring we will tend to have a default set of behaviors and psychological patterns.

Polarization Happens Through Habitual Patterns

The process of polarization was explained in depth in *Soul Astrology* but it is so fundamental to our understanding that it is worth repeating here. Our default patterns are reflected in our Zodiac signs (especially our Sun and Moon). We are born under our particular Zodiac signs because that is the energetic patterning that we are already resonating with as our default way of being. As we repeat habitual, comfortable patterns throughout our lives, our brain becomes wired for that behavior so we become more prone to repeat our familiar habits and less adaptable to change. We become 'polarized' and our behavior tends to 'solidify' at our preferred end of the pole.

We can be so identified with our end of the 'pole' that we fail to recognize the qualities of the opposite sign in ourselves. We may even be attracted to someone with Sun, Moon or Rising Sign in our opposite sign because they appear to possess qualities we think we lack.

Although this can be a very comfortable relationship it can also keep us stuck in terms of our own spiritual growth. The 'honey trap' is that we might always rely on the other person to provide those qualities in the relationship and fail to develop them in ourselves.

For example if we are a practical, methodical Capricorn, and our partner is a loving, nurturing Cancerian, we might always rely on them to provide the emotional strength and they might always rely on us to be practical, down-to-earth, and resourceful. So we remain polarized and never recognize or develop these qualities within ourselves. If we don't develop the qualities of our opposite sign, we miss an important opportunity to move towards wholeness.

When we develop the qualities of our opposite sign in ourselves, we move toward the center and bring ourselves to harmony and balance. This breaks our habit of 'solidifying' at one end of the spectrum and elevates our consciousness to a new level. It's not that one end of a polarity is dense and the other more light: at the level of ego-personality both can be equally dense, but once we begin to move toward the other pole, we generate movement which naturally elevates our consciousness. Thus in moving toward the center we arrive at a lighter level of consciousness than is experienced at either pole.

Dr. Noel Huntly explains how this happens in terms of quantum theory and vibration. At lower levels of consciousness we are vibrating at a slower rate and matter is denser. Matter therefore appears as particles that can appear to oppose one another.

As we generate movement we increase the vibration and the particles can begin to aid one another rather than opposing. They can move to a harmonious state where they begin to synchronize and harmonize:

> *"the opposite nature of this oscillation on the lower levels gradually converts to a cyclic 'oscillation' in which the two poles are assimilated, unified, and in effect rotate around in a vortex action--- now 'aiding' one another rather than opposing ... In addition, in this ascension process, separate vortices become more in phase with one another. Undivided wholeness (for example, a quantum state) is created by putting its parts into phase (into harmony, resonance, 'on the same wave length')."*
>
> - Dr. Noel Huntly Ph.D[16]

You can use this information to consciously accelerate your spiritual growth in two important ways:

• by embracing the polar opposites of your personality signs (predominantly your Sun and Moon signs) you expand your perception, and can detect and perceive your more subtle Soul-sign qualities more easily.

• by embracing the polar opposite of your Soul Sign you raise your frequency, elevate your consciousness, become aware of more subtle energies, and can therefore express the lighter, more subtle, frequencies of your Soul in your everyday life.

Consciously embracing the qualities of your opposite signs moves you toward greater degrees of synthesis and wholeness and thereby accelerates your spiritual journey, your individual process of personality-Soul fusion.

Ultimately you become a fully integrated individual through Personality-Soul Fusion: in other words you are fully Soul-Centered and experience no separation between personality and Soul.

The Nature of The Six Polarities

Aries-Libra

The Aries-Libra polarity is about the initial impulse to exist, and then the natural balancing of that impulse as all 'things' find their right relationship to one another in the manifest universe. For individuals this comes down to finding the balance between our

---

[16] Huntly, N. (1998) *The Meaning of Beyond Duality*. Online document at http://www.users.globalnet.co.uk/~noelh/Duality.htm Accessed December 7th 2019

individual will and right relationship with each other.

Taurus-Scorpio
The Taurus-Scorpio polarity is all about overcoming our human tendencies for desire and attachment - both of which lead to suffering when taken to extremes. When these energies are 'tamed' they become powerful catalysts for spiritual advancement.

Gemini-Sagittarius
The Gemini-Sagittarius polarity is about integrating the esoteric paths of idealism, knowledge, wisdom and love, to arrive at the true state of Divine Union, which The Tibetan called *Love-Wisdom*.

Cancer-Capricorn
The Cancer-Capricorn polarity teaches us about how to manage and appropriately use the most precious resources of all: our spiritual resources, such as empathy, caring, love, compassion, and our abilities to engineer light to illuminate the darkness and create heaven on earth.

Leo-Aquarius
The Leo-Aquarius polarity teaches us a lot about the importance of individuality, and higher group consciousness. Mastery of this polarity is about integrating the heart-centered leadership of Leo, with the higher group consciousness of Aquarius, so that we realize that we are both connected as one, and within that we have an individual experience. We are one body of humanity, each having an individual experience.

Virgo-Pisces
The Virgo-Pisces polarity teaches us a lot about love and connection: how we use discernment to keep our attention on flowing Divine Love through the heart, and then by so doing, we awaken the Sacred Heart of Humanity, which eventually ends all suffering.

In studying the twelve zodiac signs and especially your Sun, Moon, Rising Sign (and their opposites), never lose sight of the fact that you are always studying energy patterns. Astrology is simply a way of giving language to describe the underlying energetic reality of the Universe, and your natural place, at home, within it.

> *"I cannot too strongly reiterate the constant necessity*
> *for you to think in terms of energies and forces,*
> *of lines of force, and energy relationships...*

*The whole story of astrology is, in reality,
one of magnetic and magical interplay
for the production or externalization of the inner reality..."*

-The Tibetan, *Esoteric Astrology*

Suggested Fieldwork

•   Self-observation is essential. If you don't already do so, start a regular meditation practice. It can be a sitting or an active meditation, whichever works best for you, to support you in practicing self-observation and cultivating self-awareness.

•   Meditate on the energy of your Sun, Moon and Rising Signs, and their opposites, so you become very familiar with them. How does their energy show up in your daily life through your life-force energy (prana), daily activities, thoughts and emotions? Write your insights in your reflective journal.

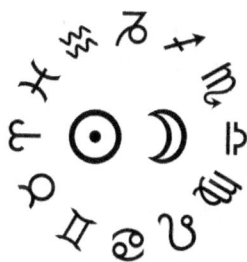

4. Your Soul's Purpose

Your soul is indicated by your Rising Sign (Ascendant). This is the sign that was rising on the horizon at the time of your birth and, as the dawn of your life, it is considered by soul-centered astrologers to be the most important sign in astrology, precisely because it indicates your soul's path, purpose and expression.

> *"The soul is the reality lying behind the persona, the mask of the soul. It is the soul or higher self that comes first, as does the Rising Sign. The Rising Sign, the soul and the soul's purpose are therefore one and the same"*
>
> - Errol Weiner[18]

Your soul is on an unfolding journey in which it eventually passes through each sign. Your journey through the twelve signs of the Zodiac is described by The Tibetan in *The Labours of Hercules*[17]. At each 'stage' we can see that the soul is growing and developing.

Some astrologers[18] suggest that the soul spends up to eight incarnations in each sign, in which case we can see that it would take

---

[17] Bailey, A.A. (1974) *The Labours of Hercules: an astrological interpretation.* Lucis Press Ltd.

[18] Weinor, E. (1991) *Transpersonal Astrology: Finding The Soul's Purpose.* Element Books Ltd.

the soul up to eighty-four incarnations to complete one cycle through the Zodiac. As we shall see later in this book, when we explore the nature of time, it's not as simple as a linear progression from A to B, the soul's journey is much more complex than that, but for now to support our understanding it's a good analogy.

Your Rising Sign can give you a sense of what your soul has come to do in this lifetime:

ARIES RISING: THE ARIES SOUL

If you have Aries Rising you are here to inspire others with Divine ideas. Your challenge is to tame your mind, cultivate your intuition and cultivate self-awareness to the point where you can distinguish Divine inspiration from the needs and drives of your own personality.

TAURUS RISING: THE TAURUS SOUL

If you have Taurus Rising you are here to release personal attachment and develop your senses for their highest purpose: to lead you to freedom, liberation, illumination and eventually enlightenment. Because Taurus resonates with peace, you tend to relax once you have all your creature comforts around you. Your biggest challenge is to not become complacent, and stay awake!

GEMINI RISING: THE GEMINI SOUL

If you have Gemini Rising you are here to teach right human relations. To do this you have to 'marry' the head-mind and the heart-mind and deeply understand relationship as the interplay of light.

Because Gemini is so curious you are interested in everything, so your biggest challenge is to stay focused on your soul path and not become distracted by mundane affairs.

CANCER RISING: THE CANCER SOUL

If you have Cancer Rising you are here to find your inner light, keep it lit, and flow greater degrees of compassion into the world. Because Cancer is the sign of mass consciousness, you feel the fear of the masses.

The biggest challenge for you is not succumbing to fear but to allow it to move through you and become transmuted into compassion.

LEO RISING: THE LEO SOUL

If you have Leo Rising you are here to usher in an era of heart-centered leadership. Your biggest challenge will be to not become identified with your actions. You are NOT what you do. There is a real self, and a false self, and it is your job to figure out which is which. Once you do this you align with your soul purpose and your life becomes an expression of Divine Will.

VIRGO RISING: THE VIRGO SOUL

With Virgo Rising you are here to be of service by flowing pure Divine love into the world through your work. Your biggest challenge is to not become discouraged and disheartened by the imperfection of the mundane world, which could leave you feeling anxious and critical. The perfection you seek is the perfection of the soul. Let go of ideas of how things 'ought to be' and flow your love anyway.

LIBRA RISING: THE LIBRA SOUL

If you have Libra Rising you are here to bring in greater degrees of harmony and balance into the world through right relationship. In your case this comes from a deep understanding of the relationship between all things: including people and the beautiful planet we live on.

Your biggest challenge is finding the balance between self and other in your own relationship. You matter as much as others. Not more, not less. Finding the point of balance that honors both is part of your life's work.

SCORPIO RISING: THE SCORPIO SOUL

If you have Scorpio Rising you are here to transform darkness into light through your own journey. I've never met a Scorpio soul who had an easy life. You are learning about energy and how to flow energy in ways that are beneficial to all concerned. It often feels like your life is one big struggle, but it is a struggle which makes you stronger, and comes at the appropriate time. Like a chick pecking it's way out of an egg, it's time now to hatch.

Your biggest challenge is to not get caught in confrontation but to transmute the energy of any potentially volatile situation, which transforms you and lifts you to your highest potential.

SAGITTARIUS RISING: THE SAGITTARIUS SOUL

If you have Sagittarius Rising you are here to uplift humanity through the revelation of truth and wisdom. To do this you have to know truth for yourself, the deeper spiritual truth that lies beyond mind and mental concepts. Since Sagittarius is the sign of the philosopher you love to think and formulate philosophies to guide our way of living. Your biggest challenge is to release all man-made mental concepts, go beyond opinions and philosophy, and discover the underlying truth of your existence.

CAPRICORN RISING: THE CAPRICORN SOUL

If you have Capricorn Rising you are here to express your vocation for the greater good1. Our 'vocation' is our spiritual calling, you are here to listen to your spiritual calling and make the sacred manifest in the world. At the highest level the Capricorn soul is an engineer of light, you have an innate knowing of alchemy and how to manifest heaven on Earth. Your biggest challenge is to use your talent and energy for spiritual purposes: to aspire to spiritual heights rather than becoming lost in the trappings of worldly wealth and achievement.

AQUARIUS RISING: THE AQUARIUS SOUL

If you have Aquarius Rising you are here to flow the dual waters of love and life into the world in ways that benefit humanity. Your biggest challenge will be to get out of your head and into your heart. The spiritual energy of which we speak flows through the heart and, as the fixed air sign, Aquarius is very much a sign of the mind. It is too easy for you to be lost in ideas. When you access the power of your heart you will use your mind as the vessel, the vase of Aquarius, through which you steadily direct the love and light that flows from your heart.

PISCES RISING: THE PISCES SOUL

If you have Pisces Rising you are here to flow universal love into the world. The biggest challenge for you is to create appropriate boundaries, and not take things personally. Because you can feel what others feel, it is easy for you to take on other people's feelings. It is important for you to realize that everything you feel isn't yours, and that other people are responsible for their own feelings. Allow others to learn their own lessons, and stay in the place of love. This way you become a 'spiritual pacemaker', striking a heart-tone that others can follow.

Your Soul's Purpose   **27**

What you are here to do and how you will do it...

So above, we just summarized *what* you are here to do! *How* you will do it, depends upon other factors in your chart, in particular your Sun and Moon signs.

For example if you are a Cancer Soul with a Gemini/Leo personality (Gemini Sun/ Leo Moon) *what* you are here to do is *to flow compassion into the world* (Cancer Soul). *How* you do it is through writing, speaking, communicating (Gemini) and creative self-expression (Leo).

Whether you will experience and actualize the full spiritual potential of your Rising Sign or not, depends upon your level of consciousness. If you are spiritually asleep, you will naturally experience the qualities of your Rising Sign as an inherent part of your personality.

As you awaken to your spiritual purpose you will feel a quickening, experiencing the subtle stirrings of your soul's calling, through your Rising Sign. The Rising Sign bridges the worlds between sleep and awakening.

Your Soul Keynote

In *Esoteric Astrology*, The Tibetan gives a soul 'keynote' for each sign. It can be helpful to meditate often on the keynote for your Rising Sign.

Some are quite esoteric and their meaning is not immediately apparent. They aren't meant to be figured out intellectually either (which could be misleading), it's not a puzzle! They are best used simply for meditation, then notice what deeper insights arise in you, from your Soul.

This can help to awaken your Soul's resonance, and support you in aligning with your Soul Purpose in this lifetime. Below are the Soul Keynotes for each of the twelve signs - remember to meditate on the one for your Rising Sign (not your Sun sign). I'd also be curious to hear your experience - let me know!

ARIES:

"I come forth and from the plane of mind, I rule."

TAURUS:

"I see and when the Eye is opened, all is light."

GEMINI:

"I recognize my other self and in the waning of that self, I grow and glow."

CANCER:

"I build a lighted house and therein dwell."

LEO:

"I am That and That am I."

VIRGO:

"I am the Mother and the child. I, God, I, matter am."

LIBRA:

"I choose the way which leads between the two great lines of force."

SCORPIO:

"Warrior I am and from the battle I emerge triumphant."

SAGITTARIUS:

"I see the goal. I reach that goal and then I see another."

CAPRICORN:

"Lost am I in light supernal, yet on that light I turn my back."

AQUARIUS:

"Water of life am I, poured forth for thirsty humanity."

PISCES:

"I leave the Father's home and turning back, I save."

Your Main Motivation in Life

Have you ever noticed where you put most of your attention in your life? Is it home, family, learning, relationships, self-discovery, personal advancement, business growth, something else? Whatever it is, your main motivation and where you place much of your attention is likely to be connected to your Rising Sign, and can be a vital clue to your Soul's purpose for this lifetime!

This can be in contrast to your Sun, which indicates your vitality, or your life-force energy. You will most likely invest a lot of time and energy in the area of life indicated by the house where your Sun is, and express this energy in the manner according to your Sun sign - your 'style'. But your underlying motivation, your reason for doing whatever it is that you are doing, is very likely to be associated with your Rising Sign (ascendant) and that is where to look for deeper clues about your Soul purpose in this lifetime.

It is important in your self-observation to keep checking your underlying motivation as you go through your day to day activities. This will give you important information about your Soul's path and purpose. For example if you have Cancer Rising, a main underlying motivation for you may be the urge to nurture.

Signs of Preparation, Crisis, and Service

In addition to the twelve 'stages' of our Soul's development, the Tibetan also groups the Zodiac signs into three major stages of development which he calls *preparation*, *crisis*, and *service*. This helps us to understand the overall picture and get a sense of what is actually unfolding. As you read this remember your ascendant is the indicator of your Soul's journey and some astrologers believe we have the same Soul sign for up to eight incarnations. So that gives a sense of perspective in terms of your Soul journey.

Preparation: Aries, Taurus, Gemini, Cancer

That said now let's take a look at these three stages of preparation, crisis and service. The first four signs are said to be signs of preparation: Aries, Taurus, Gemini and Cancer.

Perhaps it's because of my background in midwifery but I can really relate to this idea of stages. In all aspects of our growth and development, there is a stage of preparation. In which we must simply wait, experience, and grow. This is a vitally important stage when much is happening to prepare us for who we are becoming. I think of the embryonic stage of development in the womb.

During the embryonic stage something very amazing and miraculous happens. It is a process of cell division and definition. What I mean by that is that following the initial sperm and egg coming together, not only do the cells multiply fast, but they take on form appropriate to purpose. At first it's difficult to tell the difference between the embryo of a fish, a puppy, an elephant or a human! In those very early stages they are all similar, but it is during the first twelve weeks of pregnancy that the embryo defines itself. It's cells not only grow and multiply but they become distinctly human.

This is not a matter of conscious awareness or thinking about doing anything: it is a process that is guided by the Soul that began before the incarnation, and unfolds naturally. The incarnating entity is in blissful ignorance of what he or she is about to become! So it is with our Soul's development in the first four signs. We may or may not be consciously pursuing a spiritual path. We may be in blissful ignorance. However, at a Soul level we are still taking form and shape: in preparation for who we are to become as fully awakened beings of light.

Crisis: Leo, Virgo, Libra, Scorpio

Then we come to the signs of crisis: Leo, Virgo, Libra and Scorpio. The word crisis is very interesting. We often think of a crisis as something traumatic, or bad, happening. However, one dictionary defines crisis as "*A crucial or decisive point or situation; a turning point.*"[19]

Indeed our modern word crisis has it's origins in the Greek word krinein which means 'to decide' and refers to a 'decisive point'. So a crisis forces us to act or to move. It pushes us into the next stage of our development that is necessary for our growth. Imagine our infant growing nicely in the Mother's womb. He or she can't stay in there forever! Soon the day of 'crisis' will come, when that decisive turning point arrives and it is time to be born into the next phase of our existence outside the womb.

It's appropriate that the first sign of crisis is Leo: because our first

---

[19] https://www.thefreedictionary.com/crisis

'crisis' is the crisis of individuation. Our journey of independence and individuation begins with birth. So it is at Soul level, when one has Leo Rising, one's whole life is about the journey of individuation. Indeed this theme of individuation continues through Virgo and Libra until we reach the final stage of crisis in Scorpio, where we undergo another major transformation.

The Tibetan says we 'do battle' in two signs: Leo and Scorpio. In Leo we battle for our individuality, in Scorpio we battle for our Soul. Scorpio brings a crisis between the temptations of our lower personality and the higher calling of our Soul, which 'pushes' us into the final stage of our development.

Service: Sagittarius, Capricorn, Aquarius and Pisces

The final four signs, Sagittarius, Capricorn, Aquarius and Pisces, are said to be the four signs of service. As a result of the experiences and development through the stages of preparation and crisis, the Soul now has capacity. The preparation is done, and the Soul is now 'fit for purpose'. So what is this capacity and purpose? It is the capacity to bring greater degrees of light into the world through the body of humanity, for the purpose of evolving consciousness, through the evolution of human consciousness. No small task!

So if you were feeling at any point as though you don't matter, remember you are on a very important journey. Even though you may not be aware of it, you ARE a being of light, and your journey IS unfolding in perfect, Divine, timing!

Your Chart Ruler

> *"wherever your chart ruler goes, so do you!"*
> - Alan Oken

In astrology we are always talking about energy and how energy flows. After looking at the basics of your horoscope - your Sun, Moon and Rising Sign, the next thing to study if you really want to understand how the energy of your horoscope is playing out in your life, is your 'ruling planet'.

First of all, let's look at this term 'rulership' as it is used astrologically. Rulership is a very old term from the days back when the king or 'ruler' was the custodian of his land and his people. We can't really relate to this in our modern era where we see the effects of malevolent 'rulership', dictators, war and power games every day in the news, but this is not what is meant in the astrological sense. It is not something or someone that has power over us, but rather something that supports us in our growth- much like a loving gardener who knows exactly what conditions are necessary not only for the plants to survive but to thrive and reach their highest potential. So in this sense the 'ruler' is more like a guardian or custodian.

Our ruling planet is showing us the major theme of our life and helps to create the conditions for growth. If (as we mentioned a couple of weeks ago) the Earth is the stage upon which the play of our life is being acted out, then the ruling planet is showing us the main storyline in the script. How do you know what your ruling planet is? Your chart ruler is the planetary ruler of your Rising Sign (ascendant).

Always remember, in determining your chart ruler, to look for the planet ruling your Rising Sign. Here are the conventional planetary rulers for each of the twelve zodiac signs:

Aries is ruled by Mars

Taurus is ruled by Venus

Gemini is ruled by Mercury

Cancer is ruled by the Moon

Leo is ruled by the Sun

Virgo is ruled by Mercury

Libra is ruled by Venus

Scorpio is ruled by Mars and Pluto

Sagittarius is ruled by Jupiter

Capricorn is ruled by Saturn

Aquarius is ruled by Saturn and Uranus

Pisces is ruled by Jupiter and Neptune

You can see that some signs are ruled by more than one planet, and some planets rule more than one sign. They will have different expressions as their energy is colored by the quality of the sign. For example while Mercury always relates to our mental processes, language and communication, his expression is different in airy Gemini than it is in earthy Virgo.

Once you know your chart ruler you can see the 'story of your life' in your chart by looking where it is in terms of sign and house position, and any aspects to other planets. This is something you can keep returning to as the story of your life unfolds, and you become accustomed to using your horoscope as a compass and guide in your life (Of course when I say horoscope I mean your actual natal chart which is symbolic of your energy mandala, not the so-called 'horoscopes' that appear in the press)!

You will have a wealth of information at your fingertips, before you even take into account another layer - what your Soul ruler is! In Soul Astrology we consider the conventional ruler to be the 'personality' ruler, and we also have a 'Soul' ruler. Once we know both we can see the higher and lower expressions of our Rising Sign.

Now we'll look at the Soul rulers for each of the twelve signs and if you'd like to go even deeper into this fascinating subject, I highly recommend Alan Oken's excellent book on the subject: *Rulers of The Horoscope*[20].

Understanding the flow of energy is key to understanding astrology because, after all, astrology is simply a language of energy and light. Your Rising Sign is the key to your chart because it is the sign that was rising on the horizon at that point in time and space when you were born.

If you've ever experienced a sunrise, you'll understand that each new dawn has a very special feel to it. There is a unique energy signature. It brings a new energy into the day and carries that energy forward. Likewise the sign that was dawning at the point of your birth was bringing in the energy of your Life and Soul that you are carrying forward.

This is why the Rising Sign is considered the most important sign in

---

[20] Oken, A. (2008) *Rulers of The Horoscope. finding your way through the labyrinth.* Ibis Press, Florida.

Soul Astrology - it is carrying the energy signature of your Soul. As we can see, looking at the planetary rulers in your chart can indicate the story, or main theme, playing out in your everyday life. When we also look at the *Soul Rulers* of that same sign, we can see the theme that your Soul is wanting to develop in this lifetime.

The Soul Rulers for the twelve signs are:

ARIES: Mercury

TAURUS: Vulcan

GEMINI: Venus

CANCER: Neptune

LEO: The Sun

VIRGO: The Moon

LIBRA: Uranus

SCORPIO: Mars

SAGITTARIUS: Earth

CAPRICORN: Saturn

AQUARIUS: Jupiter

PISCES: Pluto

By understanding the soul and personality expressions of your chart rulers (the planets ruling your Rising Sign) you can clearly see the 'story of your life' (as in the everyday theme that is unfolding) and the 'story of your Soul', in other words what is also wanting to happen for your Soul's growth and development!

Tracking Your Chart Ruler

If you really want to track your chart ruler, you need to see where it 'goes'! This means looking at *transits and progressions*. Transits show us where the current planetary positions are interacting with your birth chat, while progressions show us how the planets have moved on - or progressed - from your birth chart.

You can track transits of your chart ruler by looking at the current position of the planet and seeing how that relates to your chart. For example if your Rising Sign is Gemini or Virgo your chart ruler will be Mercury. Next you look to see the current position of Mercury. On my website is a table in the sidebar where you can quickly check the current position of any planet.

If you keep a journal, and note what is going on in your life, and also note what is happening with your ruling planet at the same time, you can really take your self-exploration to the next level through Soul Astrology.

Recommended Further Reading:

- *"Rulers of The Horoscope: finding your way through the labyrinth"* by Alan Oken

- *"The Labours of Hercules: An astrological interpretation"* by Alice Bailey

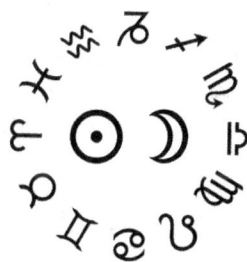

5. Understanding Energy: by element, modality and polarity

The Elements

In the Tibetan tradition, it is said that everything manifests from the *dharmakaya* (wisdom body) realm, via the *sambhogakaya* (energy/light body) realm into the *nirmanakaya*[21] (physical body) realm.

> *"the Spirit of God moved upon the face of the waters"*
>
> - The Tibetan, *Esoteric Astrology*

In other words, from the Divine formless realm of pure awareness there is first a movement into subtle form: a thought, an impulse, which then translates through the elements into a gross physical form (earth), action (fire), emotion (water) or written or spoken word (air).

The Tibetan tradition teaches that forms manifest from the formless realm through the elements in a specific order: that as consciousness arises from the pure wisdom realm it creates movement or wind (air), this gives rise to heat (fire), which condenses into water and finally creates earth.

---

[21] *Trikaya: The Three Bodies of Buddha.* Online document at https://www.learnreligions.com/trikaya-three-bodies-of-buddha-450016 Accessed December 7th 2019.

At the time of death it is said that the reverse happens:[22]

- the energy of earth dissolves in water
- the energy of water dissolves in fire
- the energy of fire dissolves in wind (air),
- the wind energy dissolves into consciousness,
- and the consciousness dissolves into the base of all (pure, formless, awareness).

The elements are thereby considered the most basic foundation of our experienced reality.

Five Wisdoms

Also in the Tibetan tradition, the five elements[23] are associated with five *disturbing emotions* AND *five wisdoms*. The point is that the elements can take on *either* a positive or negative expression as they manifest into form, depending upon our consciousness. Because they arise from consciousness itself we can use the power of our own conscious awareness to influence their expression.

Tenzin Wangyal Rinpoche describes the qualities of the five elements in great detail[24], including how to recognize where you have an excess or deficiency, the 'wisdom' associated with each element, and which exercises you can do to balance your elements.

Here is a brief overview of the qualities of each element, according to Tenzin Wangyal Rinpoche:

Earth: heavy, solid, connected, secure, gravity.
Water: comfort, fluid, contentment, cohesion.
Fire: creativity, intuition, enthusiasm, joy.
Air: change, curiosity, learning, intellect.
Space: tolerance, spaciousness, awareness, clarity.

---

[22] Keys, K. (2005) *Bardo: Dying Days*. Online document at https://kaykeys.net/spirit/buddhism/bardo/0days.html Accessed December 7th 2019.

[23] Earth, water, fire, air and space.

[24] Wangyal, T. (2002) *Healing with Form, Energy and Light: The Five Elements in Tibetan Shamanism, Tantra and Dzogchen*. Snow Lion.

When we become really good at self-observation we can recognize when we have imbalances of the elements within ourselves, and can even correct the imbalance at an energetic level before this leads to problems manifesting in our everyday reality. Clearly this takes some skill and expertise, so I can't emphasize enough how important self-observation is so that you become familiar with the dynamics of your own energy field.

Identifying Imbalances in Your Elements

This takes skill and practice but to begin with, make sure you are familiar with the qualities of each element as described above. Make sure you can recognize the solidity of earth, the soothing feeling of water, the enthusiasm of fire, the movement of air and the clarity of space in your own body. Set some time aside and meditate upon each one so that you can clearly recognize and connect to them as real energies within you.

For this knowledge to be helpful to you in your spiritual journey it is essential that you have practical, real, experience and that this is not just an intellectual exercise. So practice the exercises mentioned above, and in Tenzin Wangyal Rinpoche's books, to make sure that you have a real, felt, experience of the elements. This in turn develops your somatic awareness (felt-sense in the body), your sensing capacity, and your capacity to perceive and detect more subtle spiritual energies.

Once you are familiar with how the elements feel when they are balanced, you can call upon them to correct imbalances. The following are some notes I made whilst reading *Healing With Form, Energy And Light*.[25] There is much more detail in the book. I have been experimenting with this myself and invite you to do the same to really become familiar with the energy of the elements within yourself.

Imbalances of Air

When your air element is off balance you can feel anxious. You may feel jittery, fidgety, and unable to concentrate. You may talk too much and/or feel unsettled. You can correct this by connecting to Earth. Feeling grounded, solid, and stable. Now you may think that

---

[25] Wangyal, T. (2002) *Healing with Form, Energy and Light. The Five Elements in Tibetan Shamanism, Tantra and Dzogchen.* Snow Lion.

fire would be the solution but if your air is imbalanced, fire feeds air, and this may lead to agitation!

Imbalances of Fire

When your fire is off balance you can feel agitated. You may feel hot, flustered, and irritable, frustrated or angry. You can correct this with the soothing effect of water, allowing yourself to feel calmed, soothed, 'cooled' and comforted. Literally 'taking the heat' out of a situation.

Imbalances of Water

When your water is off balance you can feel stuck, confused, lack direction, weepy, emotional, tired, depressed and/or bogged down in self-pity. You can correct this with the warmth of fire. Connecting with the warmth and joy of the Sun for example, supports the nurturing, comforting quality of balanced water.

Imbalances of Earth

When your Earth is off balance you can feel "*dull, lazy, and dim. Too solid. Unable to move*"[26]. You can correct this with the movement of air. Connect with new thoughts and ideas, or connect and communicate with people, and this will get your energy circulating again.

This is only a very brief introduction. To really integrate the elements into your spiritual practice (and to learn about imbalances of the fifth element - space) you are recommended to read *Healing With Form, Energy And Light*[27] for yourself and apply the exercises so that you become familiar with how the elements play out in your own energy field.

Observe Yourself

Pythagoras and many spiritual masters before him advised their

---

[26] Wangyal, T. (2002) Healing with Form, Energy and Light: The Five Elements in Tibetan Shamanism, Tantra and Dzogchen. Snow Lion.

[27] Wangyal, T. (2002) *Healing with Form, Energy and Light: The Five Elements in Tibetan Shamanism, Tantra and Dzogchen.* Snow Lion.

students to practice self-examination[28], in other words: observe yourself. This means (if you don't do so already) taking up some form of meditative or mindfulness practices whereby you learn to go within. You learn to observe your thoughts, feelings, motivations and actions as you go through your day. Notice what moves you. Notice what motivates you. Notice what energies drive your behavior, and your day. Start noticing (at first) which element they relate to.

When you're driving a car, you have to keep your eyes on the road, no matter what else is happening. You might be talking to passengers, and/or thinking about where you are going and what you need to do when you get there, but nevertheless you can't take your attention and your eyes off the road, not even for a second.

With a little practice self-observation can easily be integrated into your day in much the same way. No matter what else is happening, keep your eyes on 'the road' - and the 'road' is YOU. No matter what you are doing, always keep some of your attention on you. Buddhists call this 'mindfulness' (watching your body, speech, and mind), but it is essentially the same practice of self-examination that Pythagoras advocated in his mystery school in ancient times.

The Elements and Personal Mastery

At the most basic level the elements point to something we are here to learn and master in this lifetime:

- Fire signs are about mastering our energy through our actions.
- Earth signs are about mastering our physical resources (including our physical body).
- Air signs are about mastering our thoughts and speech.
- Water signs are about mastering our emotions.

Your Soul is on a fantastic journey through each of the twelve signs of the Zodiac. It is a journey of self-exploration, self-discovery, self-knowledge, self-understanding and adventure. Most of all, it is a fantastic journey of light! Ultimately you are on a journey of discovering your own true nature as a being of love and light, in

---

[28] Calter, P. (1998) *Pythagoras & Music of The Spheres*. Online document at https://www.dartmouth.edu/~matc/math5.geometry/unit3/unit3.html Accessed December 7th 2019.

physical form. In its deepest sense Soul Astrology is the study of love and light, expressed as you.

> *"The energies represented by the four elements*
> *are ultimately the fundamental realities of life*
> *that are being analyzed with astrology"*

– Stephen Arroyo

On your Soul's journey you pass through the many different terrains of the elements in the expression of your personality signs:

- You understand the element of water by experiencing the highs and lows of emotions, from deserts to waves of tsunamis and to great bliss. This is the path of awakening awareness through mastery of emotions, which leads to the highest experience of compassion.

- You understand the element of fire through the experiences of your heart, from the deep fires of passion to the clarity of intuition. This is the path of awakening awareness through mastery of action, creativity, and passion, which leads to the highest experience of heart-centeredness, love and intuition.

- You understand the element of air through the experiences of your mind, from navigating the dense, fear-based, labyrinth of lower thought to the infinite vastness, wisdom and clarity of Universal Mind. This is the path of awareness through mastery of mind, which leads to the highest experience of wisdom.

- You understand the element of earth through the experiences of physical form, from meeting the everyday needs of the physical body to deep somatic awareness (body awareness). This is the path of awareness through mastery of physical form, which leads to the highest realization of 'emptiness', meaning that all forms are not solid but are also expressions light.

As your Soul continues through many physical incarnations, you get to experience all of the elements in their various forms of expression. Most of us are a blend of two or three elements, which dominate our personality experience in this lifetime. Some people have an equal balance of all four while others may only have one or two, which indicates a specific focus on those elements in this lifetime.

Eventually you will experience every element, which will contribute to your wisdom and your Soul's awakening.

The Elements and Your Personality

On your Soul's journey, through which you reach your full potential as a human being, you will pass through the stage of ego. This stage of your process has been described by many spiritual traditions in different ways. For example, the Indian mystic OSHO spoke of seven 'doors' in childhood development where your 'ego' becomes established[29]. So as usual it is important to take a look at what we mean by ego or ego-personality.

Ego is not some terrible disease that you need to be rid of, but is rather a natural *illusion*[30] in which you become identified with your mind, while losing sight of your spiritual and energetic reality. This 'ego-illusion' arises naturally as part of your normal healthy intellectual development and, as you grow in your Soul awareness, you reach a point where you release identification with the illusion, and re-align with your essence. In psychological terms we might think of ego as your *personality* (ego-personality).

> *"You live in illusion and the appearance of things.*
> *There is a reality, but you do not know this.*
> *When you understand this, you will see that you are nothing,*
> *and being nothing you are everything.*
> *That is all."*
>
> - Kalu Rinpoche

Your ego-personality can be thought of as a collection of drives, traits, talents and impulses, that result from your conditioning in this and past lives. It is very possible that character traits and behaviors which appear at an early age, like Mozart playing the piano when he was two, are skills that have been learned in past lives and are still held as memory in our energy field. Many of our fear-based reactions could have been established in the same way. In astrology, we use our natal chart as a two-dimensional symbol of our pre-

---

[29] The Fragrance of Nothingness. Online document at http://www.oshosearch.net/Convert/Articles_Osho/The_Heart_Sutra/Osho-The-Heart-Sutra-00000005.html Accessed December 7th 2019

[30] *"An illusion is a distortion of the senses, which can reveal how the human brain normally organizes and interprets sensory stimulation. Though illusions distort our perception of reality, they are generally shared by most people"* from https://en.wikipedia.org/wiki/Illusion

existing energy field, our personal 'mandala'. Learned behavior from past lives will show up in a natal chart as character traits and predispositions, largely indicated by our most personal planets: the Sun and the Moon.

Astrology is a vast topic, yet you can begin very simply if you know which element your Sun and Moon are in. Once you know this, by observing your thoughts, words and actions closely, you can relate those qualities to your own life. The elements are the foundation of astrological understanding. Before scientists discovered physics, chemistry and created the periodic table[31], ancient people understood the world by thinking of everything in it (including us) as a combination of four or five elements. Western astrology uses four elements: fire, earth, air and water, while eastern astrologies such as Tibetan Astrology include space or ether as a fifth element.

A basic understanding of the dominant elements of your chart can give you a simplified 'snapshot' of your own ego-personality. For example, generally speaking:

- Air signs (Gemini, Libra, Aquarius), think their way through life;
- Water signs (Cancer, Scorpio, Pisces) feel their way forward;
- Fire signs (Aries, Leo, Sagittarius) focus on energy/action and
- Earth signs (Taurus, Virgo, Capricorn) approach life practically, organizing physical resources and putting infrastructures in place.

Few of us will be dominated by one element (although some people are). Most of us will be a mixture. We can already see the combinations of ego-personality types that are possible. For example if our Sun is Gemini and Moon is Cancer, we will basically be a thinking-feeling type. The combinations are many depending upon the various Sun-Moon signs, such as thinking-thinking; thinking-feeling; feeling-action; action/practical and so forth.

Similar to OSHO, we might also think of the four elements as 'doors' through which our ego-personality becomes established and

---

[31] *"The periodic table, also known as the periodic table of elements, is a tabular display of the chemical elements, which are arranged by atomic number, electron configuration, and recurring chemical properties."* from https://en.wikipedia.org/wiki/Periodic_table

is maintained. In this volume we'll look at the elements at a fundamental level, relating the elemental qualities to our own personal development, and see how they can assist us in understanding and transcending our own individual ego-personality.

The Fire Ego: I Am Me

In astrology the element of fire is the one most associated with ego-personality, yet interestingly it is also closely associated with spirit, which indicates that ego itself has an important function in the journey of spirit into matter. Ego forms an essential foundation for the individuation process in this current stage of the evolution of human consciousness.

According to *Esoteric Astrology* we are collectively passing from instinct, through intellect, to intuition. Within the intellectual or 'mental' stage, that which we call ego is actually the arising of a mental concept of 'me' or 'I'. Animals don't think of 'me' or 'mine'! This is a capacity of human intellect.

Our ego-mind creates this illusion of a false self, through an ongoing process of identification, which is evident in our continuous 'story of me', 'myself', 'I' and 'mine'. We have an innate ability to experience life through our five senses. As soon as we open our eyes, seeing happens. We don't have to do anything in order to see, it happens anyway. Yet our ego-mind immediately takes the credit by thinking "I see". There is an assumption that there is an "I" who is 'doing' the seeing, but if we look closely we cannot find this "I" or "me" anywhere, other than in our thoughts.

> *"Egoism, the limiting sense of 'I', results from the individual intellect's attributing the power of consciousness to itself"*
>
> - Patanjali

In our everyday lives we can become identified with many things including thoughts, feelings, actions/roles, possessions, which all contribute to our sense of self. So if we feel sad we may identify with being 'a sad person' or if we have a role in society we may become identified with our position. When circumstances fit our idea of ourselves we may think "this is really me", and when they don't we may think "this isn't me" or even "I'm just not myself".

One of the functions of mindfulness is to observe how this idea of 'I' arises in our daily lives. This requires observing those thoughts, feelings and activities that generate a strong sense of 'I'. If we have personal planets in any of the fire signs we may notice a strong sense of 'me' or 'I' arises in association with action - when we are doing something. This can include a role or career, for example if we are a Mother or a Manager our sense of self can be so interwoven with that identity that if we lose the role we feel we are no longer 'ourselves'.

Twelve Archetypes: Twelve Egos

The twelve signs of the Zodiac are human archetypes, which means they can also be thought of as twelve types of ego-mind, in other words twelve *stories of ME*!

Each sign has a key phrase that sums up it's dominant 'ego-story' in the form of an "I" statement, which we will transcend as we align with our higher consciousness. For example, in terms of the fire signs: for Aries this key phrase is "I am", for Leo "I will", and for Sagittarius "I seek".

As we practice mindfulness and become more aware of our true nature we will gradually begin to drop the ego story so Aries will experience pure existence without "I" getting in the way. This will be a higher, clearer, purer octave of Aries energy, unobstructed by any story. Likewise Leo will experience pure creativity, unimpeded by any erroneous ideas of a creator, and Sagittarius can experience seeking in total freedom without the added hindrance of a seeker.

Few of us are dominated by one element. Most of us are a mix of at least two or three, which makes life interesting! As you go through your day, notice where your attachment to your 'story' is strongest, and how it relates to the elements of your personality signs. With practice you can drop your story and allow your energy to flow freely and naturally. It gives new meaning to getting out of your own way!

The Earth Ego: I Am What I Own

If you have a predominance of earth in your personal planets you might find your sense of 'me' connected to the practical, tangible, physical world. Your status or worldly position, your home base, your income and possessions, and even your physical body. You may derive your identity, your sense of 'who I really am', and especially your sense of value and self-worth from these things. Ego arises with the mental concept that if there are possessions, there must be a 'possessor' of these objects.

The Air Ego: I Am My Thoughts

If you have a predominance of air in your chart you may find your sense of 'me' attached to thinking. This concept is encapsulated in the famous quote by the French philosopher René Descartes "I think therefore I am", as though your ability to think is evidence of your existence. Yet there is so much more to you than your ability to think. When you delve a little deeper into your being you realize there is also awareness. Awareness of thinking. Ego arises with a mental concept that if thinking is present, there must also be a thinker. Yet if you look closely you will never find any evidence of this thinker, beyond an idea of its existence. What you find is awareness.

> *"I think therefore I am."*
>
> - René Descartes

The Water Ego: I Am My Feelings

If you have a predominance of water in your charts you may find your sense of 'me' attached to your feelings and emotional experience. This is encapsulated in phrases such as "I feel great!" or "I don't feel like myself today". Your sense of self is affected and influenced by your moods and feelings. Your sense of 'who I really am' is attached to a feeling state. Ego arises with a mental concept that if there are feelings there must be a 'feeler', there must be a person inside who is experiencing the feelings. Yet again, if you look really closely, you will find no such experiencer beyond an idea of its existence.

Three Modalities

Within each element there are three 'modalities', or ways through which the energy expresses: cardinal, fixed and mutable. Modalities tell us something about the way energy moves, or flows. The three modalities are: Cardinal, Mutable and Fixed.

- Cardinal energy has a creative quality to it. It is the energy of spring and creation and its purpose is to initiate and make manifest.
- Fixed energy has a stabilizing quality to it. It is the energy of summer and its purpose is to act as a place-holder to stabilize creations for the duration of their lifespan.

- Mutable energy has a dissolving, changing, quality to it. It is the energy of autumn and its purpose is to dissolve creations and release the energy so it may be re-used by cardinal energy again in the next cycle.

Cardinal Energy

Think of a tree. The first green shoot that fights it's way purposefully through the rocks and the earth towards the light of day, is driven by cardinal energy: the energy of creation, evolution and new beginnings. Cardinal energy is a driving force that pushes life onwards and upwards.

Fixed Energy

Now think of the trunk of the tree. That is fixed energy: the energy of a placeholder, containing and holding the energy within a fixed form or structure. It will stabilize the tree within a structure for the duration of its life so it can fulfill its purpose. Fixed energy is a stabilizing force that supports and sustains life.

Mutable Energy

Now think of the end of the life cycle when the tree dies. The leaves die and drop off, the trunk will eventually break down, and the matter will decompose and transform into compost. This breaking down, changing and dissolving of form is mutable energy. The energy can then be re-used (in the form of cardinal energy) once again for the beginning of a new life-cycle. Mutable energy is a destructive force that allows continuity of life through death and rebirth.

In the modalities we see the three essential energies that comprise the cycle of life: cardinal (creation), fixed (stability) and mutable (destruction). There are three signs in each element, one corresponding to each modality:

FIRE:
Aries is the cardinal fire sign.
Leo is the fixed fire sign.
Sagittarius is the mutable fire sign.

EARTH:
Taurus is the fixed earth sign.
Virgo is the mutable earth sign.

Capricorn is the cardinal earth sign.

AIR:
Gemini is the mutable air sign.
Libra is the cardinal air sign.
Aquarius is the fixed air sign.

WATER:
Cancer is the cardinal water sign.
Scorpio is the fixed water sign.
Pisces is the mutable water sign.

Cardinal Signs

Cardinal signs are the initiators in life. When it comes to change they are right there at the beginning getting things started. Like the ignition of the car, they give a burst of energy, impulse and enthusiasm at the beginning to ignite any project or practice. The challenge for cardinal signs lies in following through. Once a change becomes established as habit or routine, cardinal signs can become restless again and seek something new to capture their interest. This can lead to starting one thing after another without sticking at anything long enough to establish it and reap rewards.

Fixed Signs

Fixed signs create structure and stability. They find a deep sense of security in established routines and are happy to continue plodding on exactly as they are. They are very reliable but often resistant to change. It can be very challenging for them to create space in their lives to do something different, but if and when they do they will likely continue until it becomes firmly established and achieve the results they desire.

Mutable Signs

Mutable energy is the energy of change. They change all the time and have probably tried every form of meditation, yoga and everything else in between, just for the experience of it! Often a practice can be dropped before it even gets started because they have done all the research, read about every possible spiritual practice, maybe dabbled a little, failed to experience any results, concluded that it therefore mustn't work, and moved on. Their challenge lies in applying something long and deep enough to get at least some preliminary results.

Cycles of Time

When we place the twelve Zodiac signs in order throughout the year - each cycle begins with a cardinal sign, which flows into a fixed sign, which flows into a mutable sign and then another mini-cycle is initiated with another cardinal sign.

The full Zodiac year begins with cardinal sign Aries and ends with mutable sign Pisces. So we can see the patterns - cardinal energy initiates a cycle, fixed energy sustains it and mutable energy dissolves it into the next cycle.

The Twelve signs in order as the appear throughout the year:

Aries - cardinal
Taurus - fixed
Gemini - mutable
Cancer - cardinal
Leo - fixed
Virgo - mutable
Libra - cardinal
Scorpio - fixed
Sagittarius - mutable
Capricorn - cardinal
Aquarius - fixed
Pisces - mutable

Cardinal is always first, followed by *fixed* energy, followed by *mutable*. So we can begin to see how life operates through cycles within cycles! Each cycle begins in a cardinal sign, is carried forward in a fixed sign, and is completed and dissolved in a mutable sign. If we apply this to the year, we can see that each season begins in a cardinal sign.

The four seasons, spring, summer, autumn and winter are marked by the four cardinal signs: Aries (spring equinox), Cancer, Libra (autumn equinox) and Capricorn.

The peak of each season is marked by the four fixed signs: Taurus is the fullness of spring, Leo is the height of summer, Scorpio the peak of autumn and Aquarius marks the depths of winter.

The mutable signs mark the changing season, where one season rolls into the next - In Gemini spring rolls into summer, in Virgo summer rolls into autumn, in Sagittarius autumn rolls into winter and in

Pisces winter rolls into spring. One of the best ways to understand the energies involved is to observe ourselves through the changing of the seasons.

Sign Polarity

Generally in Astrology the polarity of a sign is whether it is considered 'positive' or 'negative' (this is different from the 'six polarities' that we speak of in Soul Astrology). This is often misunderstood, because the tendency in modern times is to equate 'positive' with 'good' and 'negative' with 'bad' as the popular expressions 'positive thinking' or 'negative thinking' reflect, but the polarities in astrology are nothing to do with moral judgements of good or bad, but are specifically referring to how we flow energy.

For example, you wouldn't think of a positive electrical charge as 'good' and a negative charge as 'bad', they are simply the labels we have chosen to describe the differences in how energy flows! Likewise, in astrology, when we use the term positive and negative, we are referring to the polarity of a sign. In other words, *the direction in which the energy flows*.

Everything in nature has cycles. Nature breathes in, and breathes out. We cannot breathe out continuously and forget about the in-breath, yet that is what we try to do on a daily basis! Our modern lifestyle has become about 'productivity': doing, action, creating, production, putting out, putting out, putting out, in other words breathing out.

Yet the most effective part of any exercise system, whether it be a training program at the gym or a regular yoga practice, happens when we stop and allow ourselves to receive the benefit. This is why in any yoga practice 'resting' postures are built into the plan. The key to health is balancing the output, with the input. We expend energy, and then relax and allow ourselves to receive the benefits of that expenditure. The correct balance between "breathing out and breathing in" is the key to our health, well-being, and spiritual growth!

Positive signs are considered to be electric, in the sense that they are *sending energy outwards*. They are active, radiant, enthusiastic, and are traditionally associated with masculine or 'yang' energy. These are all just different ways to describe energy that radiates or emanates outwards away from itself.

Negative signs are considered to be magnetic in the sense that they are *receiving energy inwards*. They are passive, attractive, reflective, and are associated with feminine or 'yin' energy. These are all just different ways to describe energy that magnetizes, or attracts in towards itself.

These labels have nothing to do with male and female in gender terms. It is perfectly possible for women to have a dominance of positive signs and for men to have a dominance of negative signs. Most of us have some planets in both polarities, although one polarity will be dominant, while in some people there will be an equal balance of both.

Are You Electric or Magnetic?

To see whether your energy is mostly positive (electric) or negative (magnetic) take a look at your birth chart and count how many planets you have in each polarity. Only count the personal and social planets: The Sun, Moon, Mercury, Venus, Mars, Jupiter and Saturn, together with the Ascendant (AC) and Mid-heaven (MC). Add up the points to see which (if any) is dominant in your chart.

Positive "Electric" Signs:

All the fire signs: Aries, Leo, Sagittarius;
All the air signs: Gemini, Libra, Aquarius;

Negative "Magnetic" Signs:

All the earth signs: Taurus, Virgo, Capricorn;
All the water signs: Cancer, Scorpio, Pisces.

As you go deeper into your self-observation, and become aware of more subtle energy, you will notice that it isn't really as simple as merely 'active' or 'passive', although that's a good description to get started.

However once you become more aware, you will realize that active implies effort, or doing something. Whereas, in reality, the positive signs don't need any effort to radiate energy outwards. Like the Sun it is just a natural energy, a heat, that emanates from the core.

Likewise we will also see that the negative signs aren't entirely 'passive', because there is a subtle activity involved in the process of attraction. Like radiance, attraction is an active process, but one that doesn't require effort so much as awareness.

If you have a dominance of positive signs you need to be careful not to get caught up in too much 'doing' where you can burn yourself out. Finding the easy place of simply 'being' and allowing your energy to radiate will be helpful to you.

If you have a dominance of negative signs you need to guard against becoming too passive and slipping into dullness. Finding the place of being alert and softly focused within the active yet delicate process of attraction will be very helpful to you.

Remember, we're not talking about 'good and bad' but the direction of energy flow. Like the + and - poles of a magnet, a battery, or electricity. Neither one is better than the other, they are just different, like the tide coming in or going out. Like breathing in, or breathing out.

Positive signs are more electric. Their energy is naturally pushing out. Radiating. Negative signs are magnetic. They naturally pull things towards them. Receiving.

If you have a balance of planets in positive and negative signs then you should find it relatively easier to strike a good balance between rest and activity although in our modern society you will still have to buck the trend of 'constant doing' to weave in some downtime and really rest deeply enough to replenish yourself!

If you have a dominance of magnetic (-ve) signs then you may need more rest than others. Rest for you is when you draw in the energies of the Universe, nurture, replenish, and rejuvenate yourself. However, in order to take in a good deep, breath, we need to breathe out fully! So for you, even though you are naturally good at magnetizing energy towards you, the balance comes in doing enough of the right kind of activity (breathing out), to maximize the benefits of your 'in-breath'.

It is also vital that you find the time for quality rest involving some yoga or meditation-type practice that maximizes the benefit of your ability to draw in vital pranic energy to yourself.

Watching TV or playing games doesn't cut it, that's still essentially 'doing', and you may find such activities drain you even further by cutting you off from your vital source of natural prana!

If you have a dominance of electric (+ve) signs, ironically, you might have to work harder at 'resting'. Like a Duracell bunny you do seem to have an infinite innate source of energy, and you may feel as though you need less rest, which is partly true. But then you may have periods were you feel totally burned out. Even a fire needs oxygen to keep on burning.

Doing some kind of active meditation, where you regularly 'do' your resting as part of your lifestyle, is essential to maintain a healthy balance, connect with your spirit, and help you to avoid periods of exhaustion and burn out.

Once you understand how your energy flows it can support you in staying healthy, balanced and using your energy in the most effective way to support you on your journey of spiritual awakening through self-exploration.

Recommended Further Reading:

- *Healing with Form, Energy and Light: The Five Elements in Tibetan Shamanism, Tantra and Dzogchen* and

- *Awakening The Sacred Body* by Tenzin Wangyal Rinpoche

- *Learn to Meditate: a quick start guide to meditation for beginners*[32] by Ruth Hadikin

---

[32] Hadikin, R. (2015) *Learn to Meditate: a quick start guide to meditation for beginners.* Kindle Edition. Ruth Hadikin Associates.

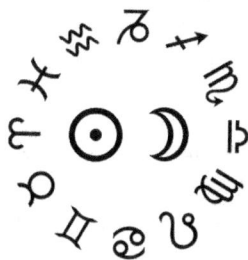

6. The Planets

In the previous chapter we talked about the Tibetan tradition, where it is taught that forms manifest from the formless realm through the elements in a specific order. We saw that, as consciousness arises from the pure wisdom realm, it creates movement or wind (air), this gives rise to heat (fire), which condenses into water and finally creates earth.

So from this spiritual perspective we can see that planets, are formed *from consciousness itself*, and therefore must by nature *contain the consciousness that they emerged from*. Each planet is therefore a formation of energy that holds a *unique field of consciousness*. We could say therefore, that planets are embodied consciousness holding a specific vibration, frequency, or field of awareness.

What, How, and Where

When we have astrological connections with certain planets, and especially if we can make a conscious connection with that planet, they become important spaceholders for our journey of awakening, because of their capacity to hold a specific vibration, experience, or field of consciousness, for us to experience.

This is why when we first learn astrology, we say that the planets represent *what*. For example the Moon represents emotions, so *what* we're talking about when we look at the Moon in your chart, is some aspect of your emotional energy. The zodiac sign describes *how* that energy expresses itself, and the house describes *where* (in terms of which area of your life is involved).

For example, take a Moon in Leo in the Second House: the Moon is *what*, Leo is *how* and the Second House is *where*. Leo is the sign of creativity and the Second House is the area of your inner resources and finances, so with a Leo Moon in the Second House you could gain emotional security and satisfaction by creatively drawing upon your own inner resources to generate income.

It is said of Pythagoras that he could *hear the music of the spheres*.[33] This means he had the capacity to connect with the frequency of each planet. You can not develop this capacity merely by reading about it, because holding mental concepts and ideas in your mind keeps you tuned in to the frequency of intellect, and actually blocks your capacity to perceive higher frequencies.

To connect to the planetary frequencies in the way that Pythagoras could, you need to develop a daily practice whereby you clear your mind of everyday thoughts and concerns and allow yourself to experience what the Tibetans call the *mind of clear light*:[34] the pure, clear, light of awareness that is beyond thinking. This is why your daily meditation practice is so vitally important on your journey of spiritual awakening through self-exploration.

The Two Truths

In Tibetan Buddhism there is the concept of the two truths. First there is *conventional truth*, which we can all experience and agree upon. It is true by *convention and labeling*. For example I am sitting on a chair. If you could see me you would agree that is true.

Secondly there is *ultimate truth*, which refers to the truth of our ultimate reality. So even though conventionally I am sitting on a chair, quantum physicists could go deeper and declare that there is actually no chair there at all: only empty space and atoms. Mahayana Buddhists could go deeper and deeper into self-exploration and

---

[33] Calter, P. (1998) *Pythagoras & Music of The Spheres*. Online document at https://www.dartmouth.edu/~matc/math5.geometry/unit3/unit3.html Accessed December 7th 2019.

[34] *"The fundamental innate mind of clear light is considered to be the nature of mind, or the ultimate root of consciousness"* Definition from https://www.rigpawiki.org/index.php?title=Clear_light

declare there is no "I" there either. Not even a trace! So even though *conventionally* we would all agree that *I* am sitting on a *chair*, ultimately *nobody is sitting on anything*!

In order to be able to understand the planetary energies like Pythagoras did, we have to first be familiar with both the conventional understanding of the planets and then move towards ultimate truth through our own experiential knowledge (knowledge and understanding gained from our own experience). Each planet supports us in our journey of awakening, by facilitating a shift from a conventional expression of our nature to a higher spiritual quality that is more in alignment with ultimate truth.

A Spectrum of Conventional and Ultimate Characteristics of The Planets:

The Sun - from ego to radiance
Moon - from emotional attachment to receptivity
Mercury - from mental concepts to pure intelligence
Venus - from romantic attachment to Divine Love
Mars - from aggression to Divine Will
Jupiter - from greed to generosity
Saturn - from limitation to authenticity
Uranus - from disruption to awakening
Neptune - from addiction to compassion
Pluto - from destruction to emptiness

The Evolution of Human Consciousness

In *Esoteric Astrology*, The Tibetan taught that as a collective, humanity is evolving from *instinct to intellect*, from *intellect to intuition*; and from *intuition to illumination*. This not only describes the evolution of human consciousness, but it also describes our individual path of spiritual awakening because as we awaken individually, we will each experience these unfolding 'stages' of consciousness. Indeed it is the awakening of individuals that is at the spearhead, driving the collective evolution of consciousness.

As we look at each of these stages in turn, and their planetary associations, remember that we are talking about the evolution of human consciousness AND your individual path of spiritual awakening at the same time: for they are one and the same. I would also like to add one final stage: emptiness.

So our complete path is as follows:

instinct > intellect > intuition > illumination > emptiness

What do I mean by 'emptiness'? Emptiness is pure presence, awake awareness, without mental concepts. There is an important distinction between illumination and emptiness. In illumination we become full of light. We can experience great bliss and have an experience similar to nirvana, yet we can still be in duality. When we arrive at 'emptiness' we have pure, non-dual awareness. In the Tibetan tradition the highest wisdom of all is the wisdom realizing emptiness. I will explain more about that in a later chapter.

Now let's look at the planets as spaceholders and how they relate to each of the evolutionary stages above. First of all, what do we really mean by the term 'rulership' as it is used astrologically? Rulership is a very old term from the days back when the king or 'ruler' was the custodian of his land and his people. Rulership doesn't seem like a good thing to us in our modern era where we see the effects of malevolent 'rulership', dictators, war and power games every day in the news, but this is not what is meant in the astrological sense.

Rulership is not something or someone that has power over us, but rather something that contributes to the conditions that support us in our growth - much like a loving gardener who knows exactly what conditions are necessary not only for plants to survive but to thrive and reach their highest potential. So in this sense the planetary 'ruler' is more like a guardian, or custodian, creating the conditions that support our Soul's growth.

We speak of planetary 'rulers' (or spaceholders) on many levels in astrology. You will have your overall chart ruler, this is the planet which usually has the most power and influence throughout your lifetime (see my earlier newsletter on tracking your chart ruler) by providing the conditions for your Souls growth.

In addition to your chart ruler each house in your chart will have a planetary ruler: we take into account the natural ruler (for example Mars is the natural ruler of the First House) and we take into account the actual ruler.

For example if you have Libra on the Fifth House cusp then Venus (as the ruler of Libra) would be the planetary ruler of your Fifth House. I don't want to get sidetracked with specific house rulerships here, I just wanted to present the idea that all the planets are spaceholders in your life, not just your ruling planet.

In terms of the evolution of human consciousness, and your individual path of spiritual awakening, the planets are creating conditions for you that support definite stages:

Instinct: Sun, Moon, Mercury, Venus, Mars.

Intellect: Jupiter, Saturn.

Intuition: Uranus

Illumination: Neptune

Emptiness: Pluto

These stages are not rigid, but serve as a general guide. You will often experience overlap, for example when you experience transits of Neptune you will be having experiences that can ultimately lead to greater illumination. You could also be experiencing a powerful transit of Mars at the same time. In this case the 'illumination' of Neptune can support you in transforming the instinctive aggression of Mars into conscious assertiveness.

Below you can see how the interplay of planetary energies create the perfect conditions to support you in your journey of spiritual awakening.

The Planetary Spaceholders

The Sun creates the conditions for life itself to exist. We live in a solar system, and the consciousness of the Sun is the major 'spaceholder' (see last week) for the perfect conditions for life to exist. At the physiological level the Sun is prana: the very life force that animates and breathes 'life' into physical forms.

The Moon creates the conditions for life to take shape and form. The Moon is said to be the 'Mother of all forms', and influences the shaping of form in physical matter. We might say that the Moon provides the magnetic attachments (emotional and otherwise) that hold forms together. This links us closely with Karma, as our magnetic impulses (instincts) propel us from one life to the next.

Mercury creates the conditions for the development of mind, mental processing, and communication appropriate to our group and species. At the physiological level Mercury governs the nervous system and cellular communication.

Venus creates the conditions for us to recognize and attract what we need for the continued survival of the species. Through Venus we recognize beauty, harmony, and cultivate personal magnetism.

Mars creates the conditions for us to assert ourselves as an individual and to move forward into the world to get what we need. Physiologically Mars rules the blood, sexual activity and your body's inflammatory responses. At the instinctual level Mars is all about protect and survive.

Jupiter creates the conditions for us to expand our minds beyond our immediate self-consciousness. Through Jupiter we expand our learning, give and receive education, and distribute knowledge. Through the conditioning influence of Jupiter we are able to reach out to our fellow human brothers and sisters and connect with them, not as adversaries, but as our larger human family.

Saturn creates the conditions for us to build structure and organize systems. As we become part of larger groups and societies, some kind of structure and organization becomes a necessity if we are to succeed.

Through the conditioning influence of Saturn that we realize that life simply does not expand continuously, and that in our evolution we also need to embrace limitation and death.

Uranus brings freedom from oppression, so we are free to explore our individuality. Then through exploring our individuality we discover our intuition and prepare ourselves for the illumination stage of our development.

Neptune 'spiritualizes' through a three-step process of illusion, disillusion, and finally illumination. Before we arrive at the exalted state of spiritual illumination and bliss, we have to navigate a long unfolding process of illusion and disillusion.

Pluto is the great revealer. Pluto reveals that which is hidden, lurking beneath the surface, the darker side of our own nature. In this way Pluto show us what we have to change if we are to transform darkness into light.

By studying the deeper meaning of the planets in your own horoscope you will understand how the interplay of planetary energies have created the perfect conditions to support you in your journey of spiritual awakening.

Suggested Fieldwork

- Deeper Self-observation. Take out your own horoscope (natal chart) and in your Soul Astrology journal -make a note of what sign and house each planet is in. If you didn't do so already begin your daily meditation practice. In your meditation begin attuning to the energy of each planet. Take your time, you can spend a week or more on each planet. Take as long as you need to, to build a strong connection. Write your experiences in your journal.

- The Planets Suite. Composer Gustav Holst had an interest in astrology. He composed the Planets suite to try and capture the essence of each planet, as he experienced it. (It isn't known why he never composed movements for the Sun and Moon, and Pluto was not yet discovered at the time of his composition).

Following your own meditations you may wish to listen to the movements composed by Holst[35]. How do they compare with your experience? Ultimately, as you fine-tune your intuition, it is important to trust your own experience and not be influenced by anyone else's impression.

- Further Reading: In your copy of *Soul Astrology*[36] study and meditate on *Chapter five: The Planetary Spaceholders*

---

[35] The full Planets Suite can be found on YouTube at https://www.youtube.com/watch?v=UmOTMkoCCkM and on Soundcloud at https://soundcloud.com/jaqob-jackson/gustav-holst-the-planets-suite

[36] Hadikin, R. (2016) *Soul Astrology: How Your Rising Sign Reveals Your Soul Path and Life Purpose*. Ruth Hadikin Associates. Order online at https://soulastrologybook.com

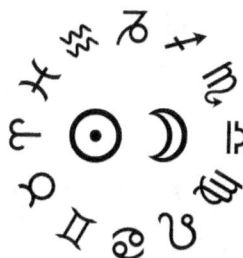

7. The Soul Centered Meaning of The Signs

In contrast to the planets, zodiac signs aren't actually physical things at all: they are fields of energy or, more accurately, they are *fields of awareness* or Divine Intelligence.

In the previous chapter we introduced the *what, how, and where* of astrology and saw that the planets represent *what* energy is present. In the same vein, the zodiac signs describe *the style or manner in which that energy is expressed,* in other words, *how.*

The Zodiac Sign tells us something more about *the energy of the planet in question.*

So, for example, an Aries Moon would be very different from a Cancer Moon. While the basic qualities of the Moon remain the same, it will always be some form of emotional experience, the zodiac sign will always give us more of the bigger picture about an individual's instinctive or emotional nature, telling us more about *how* that emotional energy is being expressed (or not).

Your Soul Sign

In chapter four we discussed how your soul is indicated by your Rising Sign (Ascendant). This is the sign that was rising on the horizon at the time of your birth and, as the dawn of your life, it is considered by soul-centered astrologers to be the most important sign in astrology, precisely because it indicates your soul's path, purpose and expression.

Personality and Soul Signs

In Soul Astrology we are often speaking on two levels. It is important to understand the difference between the ego-personality expression of your Soul Sign and its higher, Soul-Centered expression. The twelve Zodiac signs represent twelve Divine Intelligences.

In their purest form these energies carry a high vibration and Divine Purpose. By the time this energy has filtered its way through a foggy, confused and conditioned, egoic human mind, its original "tune" is distorted somewhat.

This 'distorted' expression of the energy is your ego-personality and once you have fully 'healed' by clearing your conditioned behavior you are said to be fully integrated. In other words the process of personality-Soul fusion that we talked about in chapter two is then complete. You can then fully express the Soul Centered vibration of your Soul Sign AND your personality signs.

Each sign has a higher vibration (or Soul-Centered) expression and a lower vibration (personality) expression. If we think of the octaves of the musical scale, we can get an idea about the lower and higher vibrations of each sign. The lower octaves are fear-based and come from externally imposed ideas about how we ought to be, while the higher octaves are love-based and arise purely from within our own heart.

This is an important point, not only for understanding the lower and higher expressions of each sign, but for knowing how to shift from lower to higher expressions for yourself. The shift is from fear to love, but this is meaningless until you experience the shift in perspective that comes from navigating the octaves on the spiritual spectrum. When you come from a place of love within, you will naturally express the highest octaves of your sign.

Your Personality Signs

As mentioned above your Soul's journey is indicated by your Rising Sign, so what of the planets?

The planets are indicating embodied patterns that you carry in your energy field from this and past lifetimes. In other words they reflect what Western Psychology would refer to as your 'personality'.

This is especially the case with the Sun and Moon, since they are the most personal planets, but also Mercury, Venus and Mars will also play a significant part in shaping your personality. Whatever signs your personal planets are in, are your personality signs. The light of your Soul, indicated by your Rising Sign, is focused through the lens of your personality. So you could say that your Soul Sign indicates *what* you came here to do, while and your Sun and Moon signs show *how* you will do it.

The Soul-Centered Meaning of The Signs

The Soul Centered meaning of each sign is it's highest vibration and expression. In Soul Astrology Zodiac signs not only tell you something about your own energy field (your horoscope reflects your own personal energy field - the energy you were born to express in this lifetime) but (through your Soul Sign) they also tell you something about the journey of your Soul, as developmental stages, from Aries through to Pisces. At Soul level each sign not only brings deeper awareness, realization and understanding for us as individuals, but also a greater capacity for us to benefit humanity and progress towards our collective spiritual awakening.

Below is an overview of the twelve signs to give you some sense of the Soul-centered meaning for each Zodiac sign, which can serve as a basis for your own meditation, observation, and deeper contemplation:

Aries

At the Soul level Aries is the sign of existence itself and in *Esoteric Astrology* it is said to be the sign that is 'closest to God'. The highest vibration of Aries is Divine Inspiration, initiating Divine life force energy itself, pouring into existence from a single point (or source).

Some Personality and Soul Centered expressions of ARIES	
Personality:	**Soul:**
Bold	Vitality
Courageous	Intuition
Arrogant	Clear Knowing
Spontaneous	Presence
Impatient	Cosmic Awareness
Reckless	Inspire others with Divine Ideas

Taurus

At the Soul level Taurus is about revelation and illumination. It is a very mysterious sign, associated with the opening of the third eye. The highest vibration of Taurus is full spiritual awakening, in other words enlightenment.

Some Personality and Soul Centered expressions of TAURUS	
Personality:	**Soul:**
Practical	Release personal attachment
Stubborn	Path of The Buddha
Affectionate	Opening of Third Eye
Loyal	Path of Inner Peace
Calm	Developing Senses for Higher Purpose
Possessive	Illumination and Enlightenment

Gemini

The energy of Gemini both creates and dissolves polarities in the Universal dance of Creation, which was known to the Ancient Rishis of India as the "breathing in and out of Brahma." The highest vibration of Gemini is sacred communion with the Divine.

Some Personality and Soul Centered expressions of GEMINI	
Personality:	**Soul:**
Intelligent	Teaching Right Human Relations
Communicative	Marriage of Head and Heart
Objectifying	Interplay of Light
Sociable	Path of Love-Wisdom
Jittery	Union of self and other
Unreliable	Union of polarities

Cancer

At the Soul level Cancer is associated with emotional intelligence, empathy and Love. The highest vibration of Cancer is the highest Love of all: Compassion.

Some Personality and Soul Centered expressions of CANCER	
Personality:	**Soul:**
Caring	Love as Compassion
Supportive	Fine-tune intuition, recognise inner light
Sensitive	Recognition that All Humanity is Family
Tenacious	Understanding Messages of Emotions
Neurotic	Mastery of Sensing Capacity
Moody	Love as Spiritual Nourishment

Leo

At the Soul level Leo is about power, purpose, creativity and the expression of Divine Will. The highest vibration of Leo is the ultimate Self-Realization (in which we fully realize our own true nature).

Some Personality and Soul Centered expressions of LEO

Personality:	Soul:
Grand	Path of Individualisation
Generous	Open Hearted Leadership
Egocentric	Namaste (God in me, sees God in you)
Loyal	Divine Will as Creative Self-expression
Creative	Self-awareness
Attention-seeking	Path of Self-realisation

Virgo

At the Soul level Virgo is about bringing spiritual energy into physical matter. The highest vibration of Virgo is spiritual perfection, work as a sacred act, an expression of Divine Love in action.

Some Personality and Soul Centered expressions of VIRGO

Personality:	Soul:
Helpful	Divine Feminine
Analytical	Divine Mother and Child
Methodical	Grounding Divine Love in practical ways
Efficient	All Work is Love-In-Action
Critical	Recognition of Divine Vocation
Perfectionist	Realising Perfection in one's Soul

Libra

At the Soul level Libra is about Divine harmony and balance. The highest vibration of Libra is Divine Law, Ultimate Truth, Harmony, and peace on Earth.

Some Personality and Soul Centered expressions of LIBRA

Personality:	Soul:
Relationship-oriented	Balancing Universal Systems
Fair	Right Relationship
Gracious	The Process of Harmonising
Manipulative	Mastery of Harmonics
Indecisive	Mastery of Ethics as a Spiritual Path
Co-operative	Oneness: Divine Union of All That Is

Scorpio

At Soul level Scorpio is about the transformation of darkness into light. The highest vibration of Scorpio is to embody Divine Love.

Some Personality and Soul Centered expressions of SCORPIO	
Personality:	**Soul:**
Insightful	Embodying Divine Love
Powerful	Personal Transformation
Passionate	Healing with Energy and Light
Penetrating	Transforming Darkness into Light
Jealous	Mastery of Energy (Alchemy and Tantra)
Secretive	The Power of Love

Sagittarius

At Soul level Sagittarius is about truth, freedom and wisdom. The highest vibration of Sagittarius is ultimate freedom through the true liberation of mind.

Some Personality and Soul Centered expressions of SAGITTARIUS	
Personality:	**Soul:**
Optimistic	Clear Intuition
Enthusiastic	Clear-light Wisdom
Freedom-loving	Uplifting Humanity
Dogmatic	Revelatory
Gregarious	Ultimate Truth
Freedom-loving	True Liberation of Mind

Capricorn

At Soul level Capricorn is about sacred geometry and the deepest mysteries of engineering structures of light. The highest vibration of Capricorn is living heaven on earth through the integration of light or rainbow body.

Some Personality and Soul Centered expressions of CAPRICORN	
Personality:	**Soul:**
Organised	Path of the Disciple
Ambitious	Path of the Initiate
Strategic	Spiritual Mastery
Controlling	Right Use of Resources
Ruthless	Engineering of Light
Disciplined	Spiritual Ambition

Aquarius

At Soul level Aquarius is about channeling and specifically directing the vital life force energies of love and life for the upliftment of humanity and the evolution of human consciousness. The highest vibration of Aquarius is the accumulation and dedication of personal spiritual energy for the benefit of the collective.

Some Personality and Soul Centered expressions of AQUARIUS	
Personality:	**Soul:**
Independent	Collective Consciousness of Humanity
Rational	Evolution of Human Consciousness
Unconventional	Dedicating personal energy for the collective
Inflexible	Mastery of directing Spiritual Energy
Superior	Flowing Love and Life for thirsty Humanity
Humanitarian	Path of bodhisattva

Pisces

At Soul level Pisces is about emanating radiant, unconditional Divine Love for the benefit of all. The highest vibration of Pisces is the expression of Christ Consciousness.

Some Personality and Soul Centered expressions of PISCES	
Personality:	**Soul:**
Sensitive	Universal Love
Psychic	Universal Compassion
Imaginative	Activating the Sacred Heart of Humanity
Sentimental	Path of the World Savior
Escapism / Addictions	Path of The Sacred Heart
Passive	Oceanic (Universal) Consciousness

This is a very brief overview of the signs. It can take a lifetime of self-observation through deep meditative practice before you fully recognize and understand your personality and Soul Signs as deep energetic patterns within you that you have come to heal and transcend in this lifetime.

In *Esoteric Astrology* The Tibetan describes how we are each on a path of personality-Soul fusion. There is more to this deep process than we are able to cover in this chapter (you can read more in chapter two), but basically you are here to shift from the lower personality expressions of your signs to the higher Soul-Centered expressions, through a process of self awareness.

> *"There are no levels of Reality,
> only levels of experience for the individual."*
>
> - Ramana Maharshi

Whether you are able to complete this process in one lifetime, and live as a fully integrated Soul-Centered individual, depends upon your capacity for self-perception, in other words your ability to perceive your own energy field.

Suggested Fieldwork

- Deeper Self-observation. Take out your own horoscope (natal chart) and in your Soul Astrology journal make a note of your Rising Sign and in what signs you have personal planets. Especially your Sun and Moon (the personal planets are The Sun, Moon, Mercury, Venus and Mars).

- Attune to the Zodiac Signs. If you didn't do so already, begin your daily meditation practice. In your meditation begin attuning to the energy of each sign. Take your time, you have the rest of your life for this! If you don't feel anything at first, contemplate the descriptions above and allow your imagination to take you into the imaginal realms. From there open your heart and mind and allow the subtle energies to guide you. Take as long as you need to, to build a strong connection. Write your experiences in your journal.

- Further Reading: In your copy of *Soul Astrology* study and meditate on chapters two, three, and four.

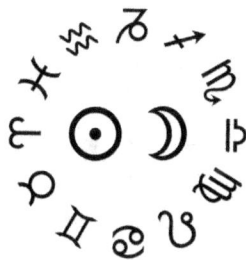

8. Houses: Mansions of The Soul

Mansions Of The Soul

So far in this book we have discussed how your horoscope shows *what* your prevailing energy is by way of the planets, and *how* this energy is expressed by way of the zodiac signs.

To determine *where* in your life experience these energetic dynamics are being played out, astrology divides your horoscope into 'slices' (like a pizza) with a system of 'houses'.

There are many different house systems with most (in Western Astrology) creating twelve divisions or 'houses' in your chart. For example, I personally use the placidus house system and sometimes the equal house system, but there are many, many others.

House systems vary greatly and, depending on which one you use, your planets can end up in different houses! For example in my own chart Uranus is in the third house using the placidus system and 'moves' to the second house in the equal house system.

However, house meanings do overlap, and flow into one another, so if you have a planet near the cusp of two houses you will probably have the experiences of both houses in your life, so it is worth studying the meaning of them both.

Astrological Houses Chart

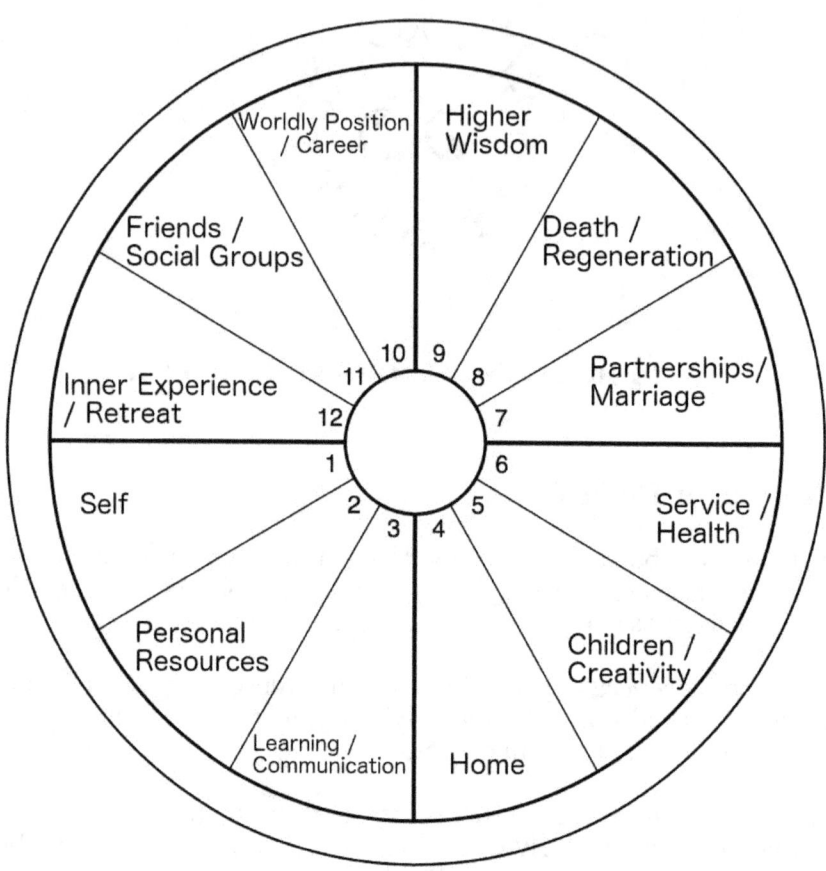

If you have had your chart drawn up by an astrologer, they will have already chosen a house system in preparing your chart, so you don't need to worry about different systems- just familiarize yourself with the meaning of each house below.

So we can see that, while the houses represent our earthly experience, they are also a more fluid, less clear-cut, facet of astrology. When interpreting horoscopes it is important that you develop a strong intuitive relationship with one house system, and keep that as your main system because in situations where the meaning is less obvious, it is your own intuition that will bring you the deepest meaning.

The houses can be one of the more challenging areas of astrology to understand, because you are not only looking at your energy field as a stand alone, but also you are bringing in an added layer of complexity by looking in what areas of life experience your energy is being expressed, how it might relate to and interact with other people, society, the environment, and the world around you, and what life experiences that will bring you, for your Soul's growth.

"[Houses represent] The Spectrum of Individual Experience"

- Dane Rudhyar

Mundane and Soul-Centered Meanings

In chapter two we explored how we are all on a journey of spiritual awakening which The Tibetan described as personality-soul fusion. We will each have different experiences of the houses depending upon our progress in this process of personality-soul fusion, and our level of consciousness. In *Esoteric Astrology* The Tibetan also described three levels of consciousness, which he termed the mutable, fixed, and cardinal *crosses*.

> *"The Mutable Cross is where the majority of humanity is at this present time. This is where the individual is totally personality identified and personality driven. There is little or no personal experience of a spiritual life. Although the person may believe in a Soul, they have not yet experienced it for themselves.*
>
> *The Fixed Cross is where the individual is becoming aware of, and aligned with, the Soul life. They are aware of personality and Soul, but the two are still seen as separate and so there is duality. It seems that a significant growing minority of people on the planet at this time are currently experiencing this Soul awakening.*
>
> *Finally the Cardinal Cross describes individuals where personality and Soul are fully integrated. The illusion of personality has dissolved and the individual leads a Soul-centered life."*

- Chapter one, *Soul Astrology*[37]

---

[37] Hadikin, R. (2016) Soul Astrology: How Your Rising Sign Reveals Your Soul Path and Life Purpose. Ruth Hadikin Associates. Order online at https://soulastrologybook.com

If you are on the *mutable cross* in terms of your spiritual awakening, you may relate more to the mundane meaning of the houses, if you are on the *fixed cross* you may relate to both, and if you are on the *cardinal cross* the Soul-centered interpretations may be more meaningful to you.

On a mundane (worldly) level the houses will show in which areas of life experience your energy is focused and/or drawn to. For example if you have a lack of planets in a house, rather than your own energy being focused there, sometimes you can find yourself drawing those experiences to you.

Yet also, at the same time, the houses will indicate those life experiences that are opportunities for you to step into a higher awareness of your spiritual nature.

For example on a mundane level, the house where Saturn is placed will indicate which life experiences are calling for you to be more responsible, authoritative, and/or bound by a sense of limitation. On a Soul level Saturn brings a spiritual 'reality check', so at the same time those very life experiences are pointing to higher truth, prompting you to ask, "what is really, REALLY, real?"

The journey to your Soul involves clearing, purifying and healing your personality. You could think of your personality as your individualized pathway to your Soul. With this in mind the houses then can indicate life experiences that bring you 'tests' or challenges along the way, that will support you in maturing and growing into your Soul alignment.

Psychological astrologer Dane Rudhyar described the Houses as Twelve 'Tests' or 'experiences of existence'[38]. Rather than 'tests' (which implies someone or something outside of ourselves is judging us) I prefer to think of the houses as *fields of experience* that we are unconsciously contributing to, and which therefore provide the causes and conditions for our spiritual awakening.

Having said that, Rudhyar's keywords for the twelve houses are still very helpful in understanding the specific psychological and spiritual experiences each house offers:

---

[38] Rudhyar, D. (1978) *An Astrological Triptych: Gifts of the Spirit, The Way Through, and The Illumined Road.* Aurora Press.

1. Isolation
2. Ownership
3. Thought
4. Stability (emotions)
5. Purity (of motive… being 'total' uncontaminated by 'ego-self')
6. Suffering
7. Mutuality
8. Responsibility
9. Significance
10. Position
11. Discontent
12. Cloture

The Twelve Houses

Next we have a brief overview of the twelve houses, showing what life experiences they represent, both from a mundane (or worldly) perspective and also what area of Soul awakening they may be prompting:

First House

Mundane: Personality; Self; Your physical body.

Soul awakening: Your core identity, your essential Self. The First House cusp is your Ascendant/Rising Sign or, from the Soul Astrology perspective: your Soul Sign. So the First House says a lot about the embodiment of your Soul and the purpose or motive for this specific incarnation. Your body as a vehicle for spiritual awakening.

Second House

Mundane: What you have that is yours. Finances, income, possessions.

Soul awakening: Discovering your true inner value as a being. Your inner treasure. Your sense of self-worth. Your inner resources and how you value yourself. Your prana, or spiritual energy.

Third House

Mundane: School, learning, communication, short-distance travel, siblings.

Soul awakening: Discovering Higher Mind. Awakening to the realization of the "Rainbow Bridge" between lower and Higher Mind. The development of higher mental capacities such as telepathy. Developing your capacity for clarity and awareness.

Fourth House

Mundane: house, home, mother, family of origin, current family.

Soul awakening: Your spiritual foundation. Where you can put down roots that will serve as a solid foundation for your spiritual path. Your ancestral connection to the Divine Mother. Your personal experiences can awaken you to the presence of Divine Motherly Love, which serves as the foundation for realizing that the Greatest Compassion lies within you.

Fifth House

Mundane: Creativity, gambling, luck, romance, children.

Soul awakening: Realizing the presence of Divine Will and the power and purpose of individuation. Merging Divine Will and personal will. Expressing Divine Will through individual creativity.

Sixth House

Mundane: Duty, service, work, pets, dependants.

Soul awakening: Realizing the distinction between service and servitude. Opportunities to be of service. The cultivation of skill-sets, "skilful means", in other words, the development of techniques that inspire, awaken, and enhance spiritual development in yourself and others.

Seventh House

Mundane: Overt relations with other, partnerships, marriage, projection, litigation.

Soul awakening: Recognition and deeper understanding of right relationship. This doesn't just mean human relations but includes your relationship with Mother Earth and all her creatures.

Experiences here can lead to the realization of Divine Union, or Oneness.

Eighth House

Mundane: Covert relations with others: Sex, joint finances, other people's money, debt, taxes, death.

Soul awakening: Personal transformation, healing and regeneration. Experiences here can lead to a recognition of what you need to let go of in your life, in order to heal, transform, and let your spirit soar.

Ninth House

Mundane: Higher education, religion, long-distance travel, foreigners and foreign lands.

Soul awakening: Higher wisdom. Where you seek (and find) higher knowledge. The higher wisdom teachings that are pure and free from dogma. Cosmic wisdom.

Tenth House

Mundane: Career, accomplishment, achievement, father, status, worldly position, authority figures.

Soul awakening: The nature of spiritual aspiration. The path and the result of your spiritual journey. The disciple and the path. The house of the Masters. Your spiritual lineage.

Eleventh House

Mundane: Friends, groups, community, society, ideology and shared goals.

Soul awakening: Higher group consciousness. The higher collective consciousness of humanity. Your role within the brotherhood/sisterhood of humanity. Your greater contribution to the evolution of human consciousness.

Twelfth House

Mundane: retreat or escape, institutions: hospitals, prisons, monasteries, movie-theatres, self-undoing.

Soul awakening: Your inner Self. There may be a remembering of past lives. Universal Love. Completion. The Tao; The Great Perfection. The realization that all is one and Love is All. Experiences here offer an opportunity to awaken completely, and either step off the wheel of death and rebirth forever, or to 'fall' into greater illusion - beginning another cycle of reincarnation.

Remember, when interpreting horoscopes it is important that you develop a strong intuitive relationship with one house system, and keep that as your main system (although there may be circumstances when you use other systems) because in situations where the meaning is less obvious, it is your own intuition that will bring you the deepest meaning.

It can also be helpful to meditate on the meaning of each house, so that deeper insights can come to you.

Suggested Fieldwork

- Deeper Self-observation. Take out your own horoscope (natal chart) and in your Soul Astrology journal -make a note of which houses in your chart are 'populated' by planets, and which are 'empty' houses.

- Attune to the Houses. Develop a strong intuitive relationship with one house system, and keep that as your main system (although there may be circumstances when you use other systems) because in situations where the meaning is ambiguous, it is your own intuition that will bring you the deepest meaning. Meditate on the meaning of each house, so that deeper insights can come to you. Take as long as you need to, to build a strong connection. Write your experiences in your journal.

- Further Reading: In your copy of *Soul Astrology* study and meditate on chapter one. Book recommendations: *The Houses of The Horoscope: An Introduction*, by Alan Oken; *The Astrological Houses: The Spectrum of Individual Experience*, by Dane Rudhyar; *An Astrological Triptych: Gifts of The Spirit, The Way Through and The Illumined Road*, by Dane Rudhyar.

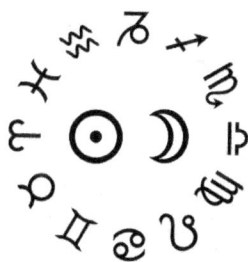

9. Navigating The Depths of Karma

Karma in Soul Astrology

In chapter eight we looked at the houses of the horoscope to see how the energetic dynamics of your signs and planets, play out as the circumstances and experiences of your life (indicated by the houses). One word that covers the totality of both your inborn energy dynamics, AND the circumstances and experiences through which they play out, is karma.

Whenever you're looking at anything other than your Soul Sign (Rising Sign) in your horoscope, you're basically dealing with karma in the sense that you're dealing with repeating energetic dynamics that have been established in past lifetimes. (Indeed even the energy of your Soul Sign will be part of your karma until you have a certain capacity for conscious awareness).

Yet the whole concept of karma is possibly one of the most misunderstood, by our modern Western society. It is essential that we have at least a basic understanding of what The Tibetan would have meant by karma, and what we mean by karma in terms of Soul Astrology, if we are to fully comprehend our horoscope from a Soul-Centered perspective.

Fortunately for us, as a result of the dedicated work of authentic translators[39], in the West we now have direct access to the highest ancient teachings and practices of Tibetan Buddhism that the Tibetan himself would have studied and been familiar with. At the time of writing *Esoteric Astrology* Alice Bailey, as his amanuensis, would have had limited (if any) access to these ancient scriptures.

This affords us a precious opportunity to go even deeper in trying to understand the principles that the Tibetan was trying to convey through *Esoteric Astrology*. I believe it is impossible to understand Soul Astrology, in the deepest sense of which the Tibetan spoke, without deeply understanding reincarnation and karma.

What is Karma?

As we mentioned above, karma is possibly one of the most misunderstood concepts here in the West. It is an Eastern term that we have adopted with little or no understanding of its original meaning. When we say "oh it must be karma" we speak of karma as though it is a fate, destiny, punishment or even a curse that has been imposed on us by something outside of us, but it's not quite like that.

In Buddhist traditions it is said that karma is one of the most complicated of phenomena to understand and can only truly be understood by buddhas (enlightened beings) themselves! So we can forgive ourselves if we don't fully get it, and by the same token neither can we assume that we fully know what it really is.

> *"The word karma means action ...*
> *karma may be cause or may be effect."*
>
> - Thich Nhat Hahn

From my studies of *Esoteric Astrology* and different spiritual traditions, I have a little understanding of karma which I'll share here, just bear in mind this is also very likely to be incomplete (since I'm neither a buddha nor an enlightened being)!

Karma is said to be both cause and effect. I have listened to different

---

[39] Authentic translators are buddhist practitioners who understand the essence of the work, and not just the literal meaning of the words. Some outstanding examples include Christopher Wilkinson (http://levekunst.com/interview-with-christopher-wilkinson/), Keith Dowman (https://en.wikipedia.org/wiki/Keith_Dowman) and Tony Duff (http://padmakarpotranslationcommittee.org/).

teachers and some say that karma is the action, some say it is the result, and some say it is both since you cannot separate the action from the result[40]! A bit like the well-known chicken and egg scenario: which came first? Without eggs there are no chickens, without chickens there are no eggs. In a sense that's karma, the chicken and the egg, continuing the endless cycle of death and rebirth.

So karma refers both to our actions and the effects of our actions on ourselves, others, and the world around us. For example we, our children and our grandchildren, are reaping the karmic rewards from our unconscious and unbridled use of plastic, in the form of toxic plastics polluting our oceans.

Yet karma also relates to our behavior on a day to day basis. In addition to our genetic predisposition (whether we are plant, animal, mineral or human) we also have our behavioral conditioning, based on the family and the society that we were born into. So we experience karma on different levels.

We each have our own individual karma, which are our behavioral tendencies carried over from past lives. If you were a Beethoven or a Mozart in a past life, there will be energetic traces in your energy field, so you will know what to do immediately the first time you sit in front of a piano.

We also have shared 'family' karma in the sense that our individual energetic patterns are in some way intertwined with the family we are born into, and then there is the collective 'karma' of society at all levels: our school or work, village, town, city, nation and ultimately the collective consciousness of humanity. All of these influence our actions, and therefore the results we experience. So it all affects our 'karma'.

In Soul Astrology, our Soul Sign (Rising Sign) indicates the light of our Soul that is wanting to shine through. Everything else in the chart is indicating some kind of karma, whether it be at individual, social or collective level.

Even our Soul Sign can become a source of more karmic conditioning if we are not yet spiritually awake, and fully aware of our actions, underlying motivations, and the effects of our actions.

---

[40] Why Do People Have Different Karma? Thich Nhat Hanh. YouTube Video at https://www.youtube.com/watch?v=B7I4jP9s8bQ

Seeds of Karma

Most of our behavior is learned behavior. Western sociologists and psychologists debate on just exactly how much of human behavior is learned from our environment (our family, friends, the society we live in) and how much is genetic (inherited from our parents)[41]. When we introduce the idea of reincarnation it swings the debate strongly in favor of everything being learned.

When it comes to explaining our behavioral traits many eastern traditions include the concept of 'karma'. This is a difficult concept but it might be helpful for the purpose of understanding Soul Astrology to simply think of karma as everything you have ever learned in this and past lives. In the Tibetan Buddhist tradition they use the analogy of 'seeds': as though everything you ever learned (positive and negative) is lying dormant as a 'seed' in your 'mindstream' (your energy field).

Basically these 'karmic seeds' are impressions formed in your energy field by both your own past actions and actions you are exposed to from those around you and, these days, also through exposure to media, including movies and video games. Under the right circumstances, the right 'conditions' (your environment and your mental and emotional state) these seeds can ripen as your own present action.

An example would be a young child who is not from a musical family and has never been taught how to play, but when he picks up a flute he just knows what to do and plays a tune. The 'seed' of a memory from a past life was already in his mindstream, and the circumstance of feeling the flute in his hand and putting it to his lips caused the seed to 'ripen' and he recalled how to play.

Or a young adult from a tee-total family who walks past a bar and finds the smell and taste of beer irresistible, only later to discover they are an alcoholic. According to the Tibetan tradition the 'seeds' for strong attraction (addictions) and/or strong aversion, are set out through associations that you made in past lives. This is your Karma.

Why does one person have a predisposition for high blood pressure, while another is predisposed to low blood pressure? These are all

---

[41] *Nature vs. Nurture.* Online document at https://courses.lumenlearning.com/atd-hostos-childdevelopment/chapter/nature-vs-nurture/

said to be karmic 'seeds' or traits that are present in your energy field, which can 'ripen' in specific circumstances. Western medicine might call it an inherited genetic trait, in other words these "seeds of potential in your energy field" are your karma and certain branches of astrology such as Vedic Astrology and Medical Astrology specialize in reading the predispositions and potentials of your energy field.

This is why astrology can never tell you what will happen, only what may happen, because actions always depend upon conditions for those seeds to ripen, and one of those conditions is your own conscious awareness.

Individual and Collective Karma

As we said above, you will have your own individual karma, family karma and group karma based on the society that you were born into. Your group karma is behavior that is based on the culture and traditions of the society you were born into, that varies from country to country. The normal 'codes of behavior' if you like. Within that you will have 'familial' karma that is based on the 'codes of behavior' or habits of the family you were born into, and then within that you will have your own unique experience, and the 'seeds' you are carrying from past lives and will therefore have your own behavior based on your individual karma.

Karma in Your Horoscope

Your *individual karma* is indicated in the energetic dynamics and conditions of your *personal planets*, by sign and house. These are *The Sun, Moon, Mercury, Venus and Mars*.

Your *social and familial karma* is indicated in the energetic dynamics and conditions of the *social planets*. These are *Jupiter and Saturn*.

Your role in the *collective karma* of the society you were born into, and the world we live in, is indicated by the energetic dynamics and conditions of the *transpersonal planets, Uranus, Neptune and Pluto*. The condition of the *Lunar Nodal Axis* by sign and house will also tell you much about your relationship to the society that you were born into, and what that society expects from you[42].

---

[42] See chapter twelve, *The Moon's Nodes*.

"Karma means action"

- Thich Nhat Hahn

Understanding Your Actions

One of the fundamental principles of Buddhist practice is to watch body, speech and mind. Checking your motivation in this way, is a basic practice in mindfulness.

Once you start to look at your underlying motivations, you begin to see how you flow your energy: what moves you into action? What kinds of actions do you take? and why? What are your predispositions? tendencies? and habits? What shape or form do your habitual thoughts take?

By observing your own body, speech and mind very closely, you will see the seeds of your own karma in your own energy field. Do your actions arise from a compassionate heart? or are your actions simply the reactions of negative emotions?

You can then use the knowledge you have learned so far from Soul Astrology to relate your thoughts, actions and predispositions to your horoscope.

Do You Create Your Own Reality?

Your horoscope is a representation of YOUR energy field. It is showing you all YOUR habits and traits from this and past lives. You are the one who created your karma, and you are the only one who can change it, so in this very broad sense then yes, you have created your reality. However, it is not as simple as some people would have you believe.

For most people, karmic conditioning is not a conscious choice but rather the result of unconscious habits and reacting, combined with exposure to impressions in your environment that take root in your mindstream[43].

You didn't create your karma overnight and you cannot change it overnight. You cannot change what you can't see. First you have to

---

[43] See the section entitled *Social Conditioning and Karma* in chapter one of *Soul Astrology*.

become aware of your unconscious habits and reactions, which is why closely observing your body, speech and mind is an important beginning. Once you begin to see negative patterns, then you can take steps to change those patterns, which will change your karma in future.

Ultimately you are responsible and, while this might seem overwhelming, it also means you have the power to change. Such change often involves a lifetime of dedicated mindfulness, and changing behavior a little at a time.

"any karma, whether it is individual or collective, affects the whole"

- Thich Nhat Hahn

Karma and Magnetic Fields

In *Esoteric Astrology* the Tibetan emphasizes the importance of the *science of triangles*. In astrology when we start looking at *aspect patterns*[44] in our charts we see different kinds of triangles. Each configuration carries a different energetic signature. They are 'karmic' in the sense that these are energetic traces that we carry from this and past-life conditioning. They form part of your personality, your conditioning.

How can this conditioning carry over from one lifetime to another? Magnetic fields can be very powerful and can bind groups and individuals together. British scientist Rupert Sheldrake has written much on the subject of 'morphic memory' and 'morphogenetic fields'[45]. It's the inherent memory in nature, embedded in our DNA, that during embryonic development tells one group of cells to develop into an eye, while another group of cells 'knows' how to become a brain, or a heart etc. Sheldrake extends this theory to include how 'birds of a feather flock together'. Ant colonies know how to group together, so do bees, geese, fish etc. And humans...

It's as though there is a kind of 'magnetic field' that holds us together as a group, and this group bond is possibly created in past lives.

---

[44] See chapter thirteen for more about aspects and aspect patterns.

[45] Sheldrake, R. *Morphic Resonance and Morphic Fields - An Introduction*. Online document at https://www.sheldrake.org/research/morphic-resonance/introduction Accessed December 7th 2019.

When we meet someone with whom we have shared a very close bond in a past life, there is still a magnetic trace. There is still a resonance, and we feel it. Sheldrake uses the concept of morphogenetic fields to explain how animals (and humans) know when one is missing from the group. He says these fields can 'stretch' over long distances but never break. If one group member is missing, the whole group feels it, until they return.

Morphogenetic fields are generated by mental and emotional energy and as such, they are a result of karmic conditioning. The science of morphogenetic fields helps us to understand what the Tibetan means by the 'science of triangles'. It can also be thought of as the science of karma!

How You Flow Your Energy

The best way to understand your individual karma is to check your underlying motivation in every moment of every day, to reveal your underlying drives, intentions, habits, tendencies etc. In other words, why are you thinking, saying or doing whatever you are, right now? Your deepest observation will reveal how and why, you flow your energy in every situation.

As you continue your journey of self-observation, getting more familiar with how you flow your energy in different situations, and noticing how you react and respond to different people, and how that relates to the elements, you might begin to notice associations: "Whenever this happens I notice I always feel this, or say that, or do something else".

When your self-observation reaches that point, you are beginning to see your own conditioning. In other words you are beginning to see how your body and mind has been conditioned in this and past lifetimes to react or respond in specific ways to specific events.

At first you might not be thinking about Karma, but that is what you are observing: your own 'karmic mind'. In the Tibetan tradition karmic mind is described as your ordinary, everyday mind, as opposed to the 'clear awareness' of your mind's expansive true nature. Because of their fundamental connection to the true nature of reality, the elements also play a role in the formation of karma.

It is very important to observe your own energy field from the inside: in other words, meditation. It is only through cultivating the skill of deep observation that you will become aware of the most subtle energies. It is therefore highly recommended that you set aside time each day to meditate, whether sitting or active, to observe your energy field and to develop the habit of observing yourself. then as you become more experienced, continue your meditation throughout your day, until your whole life, waking and sleeping, becomes an observation of you.

"there is no self ... there is only a continuation"

- Thich Nhat Hahn

The Importance of Knowing Your True Nature

Knowing that most of who you think you are is a result of past conditioning is an important step in the path of discovering who you really are: your true nature. There are many people these days who would have us believe that anger, hatred and violence for example, are just a part of human nature, yet every spiritual teacher who has reached enlightenment tells us this is not so. Every spiritual tradition tells us that we are loving kindness and compassion, at our core.

Love IS who you are. If that is not your everyday reality, then you need to understand what is getting in the way of you experiencing yourself as love. That which is in your way, is your karmic conditioning. Layer upon layer of conditioning, obscures the clear truth of who you are, at your core. If you examine your motivations deeply, and discover that you are not flowing compassion in every moment, then you need to understand why.

Once you see your own conditioning, it is only a matter of peeling the layers, one by one, through your deep awareness reveal the real treasure that is the heart of YOU.

Suggested Fieldwork

- Deeper Self-observation. Take out your own horoscope (natal chart) and in your reflective journal - make a list of some repeating actions and habits you have observed in yourself. Make a note of how they might relate to your personal planets: Sun, Moon, Mercury, Venus and Mars. Meditate on what karmic conditioning you have observed in your own life.

- Further Reading: In your copy of *Soul Astrology* study and meditate on chapter one. Book recommendations: *The Crystal and The Way of Light*, by Chögyal Namkhai Norbu; *Becoming Supernatural*, by Dr Joe Dispenza

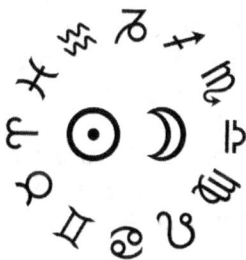

10. The Sun

It isn't possible to overestimate the importance of the Sun. We live in a Solar System, and it is the Sun's life-giving force that provides life-force energy (chi/ prana) for all things within that system, including us.

At the Soul level the Sun is the major 'spaceholder' for life to exist. The Sun is prana: the very life force that animates and breathes 'life' into physical forms. As a living being, the Sun itself has it's own consciousness. The activities of the Sun not only sustain life on Earth, but also the entire planetary system to which we belong. The heart of the Sun creates and sustains the conditions for the development of our heart and Soul, and the consciousness of the Sun permeates our own consciousness, through the action and activities of prana.

No accident then that when many people talk about their horoscopes, often all they really know is their Sun sign and, given they know little else about their horoscope, they can recognize themselves based on this one factor alone. The Sun is that important in influencing our sense of self and identity.

In astrology the Sun and Moon are known as the two 'luminaries' because they are (or appear to be) 'luminous', in other words they give light. So already we can see that the Sun brings us light, and life. The Sun therefore has the potential to bring the light of awareness to whatever area of the natal chart it is placed.

The Sun as Identity or Ego

The Sun can also represent our ego, or that which we identify with the most. This is due to an egoic 'trick of the mind' whereby as soon as we become aware of something, the intellect claims the credit for it! So rather than attributing the light of awareness to a higher power, when we are operating at the level of the personality with our small minds, the ego thinks "I did that" and we attribute that power to ourselves! This happens as we are passing through the "intellect" stage of the evolution of consciousness.[46]

> *"Egoism, the limiting sense of 'I',*
> *results from the individual intellect's*
> *attributing the power of consciousness to itself"*
>
> — Patanjali

So here we have the reason behind both the personality-based and the Soul-centered experience of the Sun in the natal chart:

- *At the level of the personality*, the position of the Sun is where we will find the greatest sense of self-identification: our ego-personality, the greater part of our "story of me" (although all the planets play a role the Sun and Moon are the major contributors to our egoic personality patterns). In Western psychological astrology the Sun is therefore associated with our identity. However, it is important to remember that our identity is not 'who we are', but is rather a collection of characteristics and behavioral traits resulting from karmic conditioning. It is because we currently identify with them that they form part of our ego-personality[47].

- *At the level of the Soul* the position of the Sun is where we can bring the light of awareness, consciousness itself, to illuminate our life and that of others. At this level we can see from experience that there is no separation and that both the conscious light of awareness, and the life-giving energy of chi, or prana, are one and the same. Life is awareness, and awareness is life.

The Sun in your chart says a lot about your energy levels and your vitality. It shows you how and where you use and flow your 'prana'

---

[46] See *The Evolution of Consciousness* in chapter six.

[47] See the previous chapter, *Navigating the Depths of Karma*.

or 'life-force' energy. Ask yourself:

- What are my main activities throughout the day?
- What do I find myself 'doing' most of the time?

The activities that come as an answer to those questions relate to how you flow your prana or life-force energy, and will be reflected in the placement and condition of the Sun in your natal chart.

There is a radiant quality to the Sun's energy, which at first may be more easily perceived through the actions you are doing. However, with observation and experience, it can also be perceived as a subtle radiance emanating continuously from your being, even during quiet periods of meditation when you aren't 'doing' anything!

As 'prana' is also the energy of creation, the Sun in your chart can also indicate where (which house) and how (which sign) you like to express your creativity. Although the Sun is a large part of your personality make-up, because it indicates how you generally flow your energy on a day to day basis, it's energy can also be offset, enhanced and/or diminished by other astrological factors in your chart. (This is why some people don't relate to the descriptions of their Sun sign).

Because the Sun brings vitality and life-force energy, whatever sign the Sun is in shows how you may manifest your Soul's Purpose once you have the consciousness to transcend the karmic conditioning of your ego. Once you have recognized and aligned with the energy of your Soul Sign (Ascendant) and de-personalized the habits of your ego, your Soul-Light can be expressed into the world, and your Soul's ultimate purpose be fulfilled, mainly through the activities of your Sun sign.

The Hero's Journey

Astrologer Liz Greene calls the Sun our individual 'Hero's Journey'. It can be thought of as the 'main plot' of how your Soul is wanting to express its purpose in this lifetime, but before that can happen there are challenges to overcome.

> *"A hero ventures forth from the world of common day
> into a region of supernatural wonder:
> fabulous forces are there encountered
> and a decisive victory is won:*

> *the hero comes back from this mysterious adventure*
> *with the power to bestow boons on his fellow man"*

- Joseph Campbell

Psychological Astrology vs. Soul Astrology

Before we go further it is important to acknowledge an important distinction between psychological astrology and Soul Astrology, based on the work of The Tibetan. First, there are a number of key distinctions between Western Psychology and Tibetan Buddhist Psychology.

All 'psychology' is about the study of mind however, Western Psychology usually approaches mind as a system of mental processes and cognitive (thoughts) patterns that influence our behavior. In Western psychology there is thought to be a 'person' at our core who experiences these behaviors and patterns.

> *"It is the Sun in us which senses*
> *that there is a quest to be pursued,*
> *a journey toward an unknown future,*
> *a profound mystery at the core of 'me'"*

- Liz Greene, *The Luminaries*

In Tibetan Buddhist psychology, 'mind' refers to the totality of being: your entire energy field, to include thoughts, emotions, actions and your underlying motives. With regard to the person, the higher Buddhist teachings of *dzogchen*[48] and *mahamudra*[49] tell us that no such person exists in reality, and that we can discover this truth for ourselves by deep investigative meditation.

No matter how deeply we look, no 'I' can be found. The sense of 'me'

---

[48] *"The practice of Dzogchen is the most ancient and direct stream of wisdom within the Buddhist tradition of Tibet. Sogyal Rinpoche describes it as "the heart-essence of all spiritual paths and the summit of an individual's spiritual evolution". As a way in which to realize the innermost nature of mind—that which we really are—Dzogchen is the clearest, most effective, and most relevant to the modern world."* - From https://www.rigpawiki.org/index.php?title=Dzogchen

[49] *"Mahāmudrā literally means "great seal" or "great imprint" and refers to the fact that "all phenomena inevitably are stamped by the fact of wisdom and emptiness inseparable"."* - From https://en.wikipedia.org/wiki/Mahamudra

or 'I' that we experience is not in fact a person, but rather it is an illusion created by repeating thought patterns. In other words, no 'me' actually exists outside of thoughts about 'me'.

These are important distinctions to keep in mind especially when interpreting the placement of the Sun in your chart, because it explains why some astrologers will say the Sun IS who you are - whereas Soul Astrology says the Sun *contributes to the illusion of a separate self that is part of your karmic conditioning.* It indicates a set of habitual thoughts and actions that you are identified with, and which are to be released as you continue your spiritual journey.

The behavior patterns indicated by the Sun are not who you really are, rather they are the challenges and obstacles to be overcome on your 'hero's journey' to discovering the real treasure: your own true nature. The Sun has it's own Divine consciousness, which is more mysterious than we can imagine. The Sun does indeed call us up to a quest, to our own hero's journey toward the unknown, but the profound mystery to which it leads, lies way beyond any sense of 'me'.

> *"The Sun is not really concerned with the concrete world*
> *as it's final destination ...*
> *Solar goals are inner,*
> *and are concerned with self-realization*
> *and experiencing one's life*
> *as special and meaningful."*
>
> - Liz Greene[50]

The Path to Self-Realization

As spiritual beings we innately sense the 'specialness' of our true nature, but everything in the mundane world tries to negate this and define us as 'ordinary'. At the ego level the Sun in our chart demands that our 'specialness' be recognized, but for all the wrong reasons - namely egoic pride. Egoic pride is based on this false sense of self derived from man-made designations, for example the society labels you as a prince or a pauper. None of these labels bears any relation, or relevance, to who you really are as a spiritual being. So the path of the Sun is to light your way: to illuminate your own hero's

---

[50] Greene, L; Sasportas, H, (1992) *The Luminaries: The Psychology of the Sun and Moon in the Horoscope (Seminars in Psychological Astrology).* Red Wheel.

journey: the path to self-realization.

At the personality level the Sun will therefore indicate your everyday activities: those activities, possibly even habitual ones, that you engage in on a frequent (if not a daily) basis that will continue to contribute to your karmic conditioning until you are consciously aware of your currently unconscious motives. The good news about the Sun is that it is the light, so even though we may be aware of repeating patterns and tendencies (for example with the Sun in Gemini we might have a talent for communication) we can become more conscious of them with relative ease (in contrast to the Moon where our habitual reacting can be unconscious).

As long as you are identified with those activities, thinking or feeling that "this is me", they remain part of your ego-personality. So we can see at the personality level that the Sun is contributing to the formation of ego, and therefore our karmic conditioning. For example with Sun in Gemini we might spend a lot of time communicating and this becomes part of our identity. We might even think, "I am a good communicator". When this happens, the great expanded consciousness that is your true nature contracts into a small, limited, sense of "I".

When we look deeply in meditation, we can see that when communication happened, rather than just letting it be, the mind added an extra layer of thought in "I did that". This is how ego works. When we don't challenge this thought, the belief in our ego-personality (me) goes unchallenged. When we look closer we can see that communication simply happened, and there never was a 'me' involved. When you realize this, your consciousness relaxes and expands once again into the vastness that is your true nature.

The Sun signs are therefore showing us twelve ego-personalities that are to be transcended on the path to realizing our true nature. So for those of us on a committed spiritual path, our true 'hero's journey' is one of transcending the habit of identification with body, speech and mind. The Sun illuminates this path by showing us the specific experiences of body, speech and mind that we are identified with.

Twelve Ego-Personalities: The Sun Through The Zodiac Signs

Within the context of Soul Astrology the Sun in each of the twelve Zodiac signs can be thought of as twelve *egoic states* to be transcended.

Transcending the "I" is an advanced spiritual realization that we are working towards. At this stage in our development it is enough to entertain it as simply an idea. The 'spiritual challenge' given below for each sign is for deeper contemplation: for example with Aries, what would it be like to simply bask in pure existence, with a quiet mind and no 'story of me' running in the background?

While reading please remember that the formation of a healthy ego is a vital stage of human psychological development. In contemplating the transcended "I" this is not an invitation to by-pass your ego development. You would not wish to be stuck in a pre-egoic state, and denial of one's ego is actually an obstacle to healthy psychological and emotional growth. Ideally what you should strive for is a healthy formation of ego that becomes your foundation for self-awareness and eventually self-realization, whereby you go beyond ego to further your spiritual development.

Sun in Aries – transcending "I AM"

Self-assertion is energizing and self-affirming

The Sun in Aries is *exalted*[51], meaning that it's energy is at it's strongest and most creative. In Aries individuals it is associated with the primary formation of ego, which can result in a 'me first' attitude as the individual's attention is focused on developing their sense of self. There can be an almost unbridled urge towards self-projection and self-expression, as the individual projects himself outside of himself, in order to know himself.

It is the job of the Sun in Aries to express the 'self' out into the world. For this reason Aries individuals are associated with boldness, courage, impulsiveness, spontaneity and directness. Unless the Sun is otherwise *afflicted*[52] they appear to have boundless energy, which can exhaust others around them. They are pioneers who naturally take the lead and intuitively know the best course of action to take. The flip side is that others may experience them as being rash, impatient, domineering and/or arrogant. When afflicted over-confidence can be a problem.

---

[51] A Planet is said to be exalted when in a sign where it's energy is strong and most actively creative.

[52] Planets are said to be *afflicted* when they have many or all negative aspects eg. squares, and few positive ones eg. trines, and/ or when they are in the sign of their own detriment or fall. See chapter 13 for more on aspects.

If you have Sun in Aries it's likely that your life's energy flows primarily through spontaneous, inspired, intuitive action. Aries is the energy of Creation in its purest form and Sun in Aries creates the space for existence. Esoterically it is the spark of Divine Will that initiates all Life. Through your life experiences you are learning how to use your inner knowing to consciously lead others. Your Soul's Purpose is vitalized, activated and energized through innovative, inspired ideas and actions.

The spiritual challenge with the Sun in Aries is to release identification with your own existence. You are here to literally "get over yourself' (I mean that in the best possible way)! Yes, you exist. Yes, it is miraculous. Yes, you are amazing. Now, move beyond that - there are vast universes waiting for you. When you transcend the Aries ego, existence remains as a sense of being, pure awareness, without an added story of "I" or "Me" as 'The One who exists'.

Sun in Taurus – transcending "I HAVE"

Abundance is energizing and self-affirming

With the Sun in the Taurus the main focus is on anchoring the sense of self (ego) into the world. The individual's attention and energy is directed to those activities that will establish financial and material security in life. For this reason Taureans are renowned for their hard work and 'staying power'. Steadfast, practical and grounded, they are content to continue steadily plodding, while slowly and surely watching their wealth (bank balance, home and/or possessions) grow. The ego seeks to establish itself through material security, so they are cautious and want to keep what they have acquired. They will not make a move until they have carefully considered the pros and cons, and then they are more likely to take tried and tested routes, rather than high-risk options. The flip side is that others may perceive them as slow and/or stubborn. When afflicted possessiveness can be a problem.

If you have Sun in Taurus it's likely that your life's energy flows primarily in very considered practical ways. You resonate to beauty, which is harmony expressed in physical form, and your energy may be focused on creating beautiful environments where you can be at peace. You may also have an artistic streak, a beautiful voice, or at least a love and appreciation of music, because you understand harmonics through your physical senses. Through your life experiences you are learning to understand how light manifests in physical forms through harmony and beauty. Your Soul's Purpose is vitalized, activated and energized through building a beautiful, practical and solid personal foundation.

The spiritual challenge with the Sun in Taurus is to release identification with your possessions and/or financial status (or lack of them). You are here to release attachment to form so you may know the true beauty of the formless. When you transcend the Taurus ego, your money and possessions will still be there, but without an "I" or "Me" that is the 'owner' of these things.

Sun in Gemini – transcending "I THINK"

Intellectual pursuits are energizing and self-affirming

With the Sun in Gemini the focus is on expressing the sense of self (ego) in the world through intellectual growth. The individual's attention and life-force energy is attracted to a myriad of experiences for learning and growing their mind. Quick-witted and intelligent, Gemini individuals are able to think, learn, and talk, really fast. In order to experience a variety of opportunities for learning they may flit from one topic to the next like a butterfly, rarely settling for long on one subject. Indeed if they are forced to focus on one thing for too long they can feel frustrated and their vitality can soon fade. Gemini is associated with communication and speech so they can be very eloquent orators. The flip side is that others may perceive them as fickle, unreliable and superficial. When afflicted gossip can be a problem.

If you have Sun in Gemini it's likely that your life's energy flows primarily through communication. Gemini is the energy of the threads of life and you may focus much of your time on 'pulling threads together'. This can be threads of information: 'connecting the dots' in your mind and communicating them through speaking, or writing, and/or you may equally find yourself connecting people through social networks. Through your life experiences you are learning about the interplay of light. Your Soul's Purpose is vitalized, activated and energized through speaking, writing, sharing information and communicating.

The spiritual challenge with the Sun in Gemini is to release identification with thought. Your mind is not your true nature. Your thoughts are not who you are. Your being has the potential to bask in pure awareness, way beyond thought. When you transcend the Gemini ego you still experience thought, but without the additional story of an "I" or "Me" that is 'The Thinker'.

Sun in Cancer – transcending "I FEEL"

Emotional intelligence is energizing and self-affirming

When the Sun is in Cancer the focus is on making the sense of self (ego) feel safe in the world. The individual's attention and energy is directed toward activities that establish emotional safety and security. As a result the sign of Cancer is the one most associated with home, family, motherly love, nourishment and nurturing - all of the things we normally associate with feeling safe and secure in our world.

Cancer individuals are concerned mainly with how they and others feel, which makes them excellent at reading and sensing other's emotions.

High in empathy they are able to sense what others are feeling and are able to accurately respond to another's needs - often before the other person even realized the needed it!

Like their namesake the crab, they are tenacious and are able to hold on to other people and situations - sometimes long after it is healthy or wise to do so. The flip side is that others can perceive them as moody, needy or clingy. When afflicted over-protectiveness can be a problem

If you have Sun in Cancer it's likely that your life's energy flows primarily in ways that are nurturing. You may be highly empathic and able to sense what other people are feeling.

Cancer is the sign most closely associated with mass consciousness which means you may have an ability to send your Cancerian radar deep into the mass consciousness, take a measurement, and sense what is needed next for the benefit of all.

Through your life experiences you are learning the art and skills of emotional intelligence. Your Soul's Purpose is vitalized, activated and energized through compassionate nurturing of self and others with emotional intelligence.

The spiritual challenge with the Sun in Cancer is to release identification with feelings. When you transcend the Cancer ego feelings still arise, but without a sense of "I" or "Me" as "The One who experiences feelings".

Sun in Leo – transcending "I WILL"

Creative self-expression is energizing and self-affirming

The Sun is in *dignity*[53] in it's own sign of Leo, which means it's energy is expressed most freely and uninhibited. The individual's attention and energy is focused on the development of a healthy sense of self (ego) through constant and consistent self-expression and the creative use of personal will. There is usually a need to keep friends and family close to continuously reflect one's self-image back to oneself.

As a result it is not surprising then, that the sign of Leo is the one most associated with ego. Ego arises with the thought of "me". More than any other sign, Leo is liable to get caught in the roles he or she plays by identifying with them: "I am an actor", "I am a CEO", "I am..." and so on and so forth.

Warm hearted, playful and highly creative, Leo (like the Sun) brings dignity, warmth and light to any role he or she plays. The flip side is that others may experience them as pompous, bombastic, and overly egotistical. When afflicted narcissism can be a problem.

If you have Sun in Leo it's likely that your life's energy flows primarily through creative action. Creative self-expression is the key to Leo because you are learning about your own creative power through the correct use of will. Any role that you can play (the more the merrier) allows you to explore the true nature of yourself.

Leo is a sign of the heart and through your various life experiences you are really learning the power of your heart. Your Soul's Purpose is vitalized, activated and energized through heart-centered leadership, play, and creativity.

The spiritual challenge with the Sun in Leo is to release identification with actions and the roles you play. The show must go on. There will always be players. When you transcend the Leo ego actions still happen, but without the additional idea of an "I" or "Me" who is "The Actor".

---

[53] A Planet is said to be in dignity when in a sign where it's energy is most free and uninhibited. It is considered to be in it's own sign and this is the sign of the planets rulership. For example the Sun is the planetary ruler for Leo.

> *"All the world's a stage,*
> *And all the men and women merely players;*
> *They have their exits and their entrances,*
> *And one man in his time plays many parts"*
>
> *- William Shakespeare*

Sun in Virgo – transcending "I ANALYSE"

Service is energizing and self-affirming

When the Sun is in Virgo the focus is on opportunities to reinforce one's sense of self through service or by being needed. For this reason Virgoans are drawn towards orderliness, perfection and techniques for healing and self-development. Imagine the well organized herbalist who can put his hand on exactly what you need, precisely when you need it. Or the homeopath who knows the subtle distinctions between conditions with very similar symptoms. In Virgo the sense of self is reinforced by feeling needed, which is a result of having the discernment, precision and techniques to deliver to others what they need. The Virgo mind is analytical, often running through a myriad of options and dissecting each one before choosing a path forward. As a result there can be a tendency to worry. The flip side is that others may see Virgoans as intrusive, nosy and/or interfering. When afflicted there can be a tendency to foster dependency in others.

If you have Sun in Virgo it's likely that your life's energy flows primarily through service. You have an exquisite sense of discernment and a fine eye for detail which means you could be very good at analysis, and you want to make sure that whatever you are giving your attention to, has some beneficial, practical, application in the real world.

Through your constant striving for perfection and 'that which is good', you are learning to flow love into the world by being of service in practical ways. Your Soul's Purpose is vitalized, activated and energized when you approaching your work as an act of loving service. Work is 'love in action'.

The spiritual challenge with the Sun in Virgo is to release identification with critical thinking and analysis. When you transcend the Virgo ego analysis still happens, but without the additional thought that there is an "I" or "Me" who is 'The Analyst'.

Sun in Libra – transcending "I BALANCE"

Relating is energizing and self-affirming

The Sun is in *fall*[54] in Libra, which means that it's energy is restricted and it's responses are limited. The result is there can be an inhibition of self-expression. The individual's attention and energy can be too much on other, at the expense of self, and much effort may needed to bring the relationship back into harmonious balance.

Balancing therefore becomes a life theme and Librans have an innate sense of harmonizing, since balance only truly happens when opposites can be harmonized. Self and 'other' need to be honored equally.

Librans often excel in areas where balance and harmony are required, such as law, ethics, ecology, diplomacy and relating. The flip side of this is that others often find Librans to be manipulative, and/or evasive as they may dodge and swerve to avoid confronting issues head on. When afflicted the Libra Sun may see the world only through rose-tinted glasses and form a 'Pollyanna' type personality.

If you have Sun in Libra it's likely that your life's energy flows primarily through relating. You have an innate sense of harmony, balance, poise and grace and you resonate highly to beauty in all its aspects. Libra is the sign of the diplomat and you can be most charming when you set your mind to it. Indeed you gravitate towards grace and anything vulgar repulses you.

You have a deep sense of ethics and care that the decisions you make are for the right reasons. Through your life experiences you are learning the art of right relationship. Your Soul's Purpose is vitalized, activated and energized through balance, harmony and right relationship.

The spiritual challenge with the Sun in Libra is to release identification with balancing. When you transcend the Libra ego balance happens naturally, without the additional idea of an "I" or "Me" as "one who is balancing".

---

[54] A Planet is said to be in fall when in a sign where it's energy is most restricted. One's responses to it become limited, and If one's ruling planet is in fall it can inhibit self-expression.

Sun in Scorpio – transcending "I DESIRE"

Seduction is energizing and self-affirming

When the Sun is in Scorpio the focus is on the use of energy for self-transformation. The sense of self arises from awareness of, use of, and identification with, inner power. At the personality level Scorpio prefers to use other people's energy rather than risk losing themselves by losing their own power.

Scorpio is a feminine, magnetic sign that attracts energy towards it (in contrast to masculine signs which radiate energy out). Scorpio's therefore become very adept at drawing other people to them, to get their needs met. Think of the Spider that seduces the fly into it's web. The power of seduction, and confidence in their power to attract (or not) form part of the Scorpio identity.

When Scorpio releases the fear of losing power, by rising above their lower personality drives, they discover great healing, transformative and regenerative power within, which can be of immense benefit to themselves and others.

The flip side of this is that others can experience them as probing, invasive, domineering, and controlling. When the Sun is well placed they make excellent depth psychologists and healers. When afflicted there can be covetousness, jealousy, and a need to exert control and power over others.

If you have Sun in Scorpio it's likely that your life's energy flows primarily through intense feeling and passion. You may experience life deeply and passionately through your feelings. Your life force energy may be very potent and you might sometimes feel that you are behind the wheel of a powerful racing car that you are learning how to handle!

Through your life experiences you are learning to transform energy through the right use of power. Your Soul's Purpose is vitalized, activated and energized through your own journey of personal transformation and healing.

The spiritual challenge with the Sun in Scorpio is to release identification with your desires. You do not die when you don't get what you want, rather, you are transformed. When you transcend the Scorpio ego, desire still arises but without the additional complication of an "I" or "Me" who is experiencing the desire.

Sun in Sagittarius – transcending "I SEEK"

Adventure is energizing and self-affirming

When the Sun is in Sagittarius the focus is on seeking activities that will expand the sense of self through the acquisition of wisdom. The sense of self is derived from systems of thought or understanding: this could be a wisdom school, a philosophy or a religion. They believe there is an ideal path or 'way of being' and are dedicated to the search for that path. A sense of identity may form around being the one who has discovered "the right path" or "the truth". There is a need for constant growth and expansion so freedom is one of their highest priorities, which they often combine with a sense of adventure since they love testing their limits and boundaries (and other people's) to see how far they can go. Since they have so much life experience to share, Sagittarians often find themselves teaching, either formally or informally. The flip side is that others may find them pedantic and/ or opinionated. When afflicted dogmatism can be a problem.

If you have Sun in Sagittarius it's likely that your life's energy flows primarily through wisdom-in-action. Sagittarius is the sign of great sages, philosophers, spiritual seekers and teachers, but the key word for you is philosophy. This means that thinking, for you, is important because of how it guides your actions. Through your life experiences you are learning about ultimate spiritual truth and higher wisdom. Your Soul's Purpose is vitalized, activated and energized through seeking higher goals, higher truth and higher freedom.

The spiritual challenge with the Sun in Sagittarius is to release identification with seeking wisdom. No thought system leads to truth. Truth itself lies beyond thought. When you transcend the Sagittarius ego wisdom still arises, but without the additional idea of an "I" or "Me" who is 'the wise one'.

Sun in Capricorn – transcending "I USE"

Prestige is energizing and self-affirming

When the Sun is in Capricorn the focus is on those activities that will provide ongoing self-advancement. In Capricorn the fully developed self (ego-personality) is establishing its position in the world. The sense of self is derived from one's status, and one's ability to structure one's life and manage one's resources to maintain and advance that position. Whether it be the school janitor or CEO of a multinational company, Capricorn never wants to take a step back. As an exquisite manager of resources, nothing will ever be done to threaten one's current position and wherever possible all the chess pieces will be masterfully slid into position (with expert timing) to increase the possibility for further advancement. Like it's symbol the mountain goat the direction is always up, one step at a time. Capricorn's precise, methodical approach makes excellent engineers and accountants. The downside of this is that others may experience them as uncaring and insensitive in their determination to reach their goals. When afflicted there can be ruthlessness and even cruelty.

If you have Sun in Capricorn it's likely that your life's energy flows primarily through practical initiatives. You have an eye for detail, precision and a great ability to stay focused until you have achieved your desired result. You are an excellent resource and project manager, because you think in terms of what is needed to get things done. Through your life experiences you are learning how to anchor spiritual energy into the Earth in practical ways that benefit humanity. Your Soul's Purpose is vitalized, activated and energized through building structures that support enlightened civilization.

The spiritual challenge with the Sun in Capricorn is to release identification as the manager of resources. When you transcend the Capricorn ego resources are still utilized, but without the additional idea of an "I" or "Me" who is 'using' them.

Sun in Aquarius – transcending "I KNOW"

Humanitarianism is energizing and self-affirming

The Sun is in *detriment*[55] in its opposite sign Aquarius, which means its energy is repressed, weakened, and unable to find harmonious release. As a result the individual may feel as though he never really quite knows him or herself, and is often looking outside of himself for himself. Their attention and energy may be focused on experimenting with unconventional lifestyles, and on the improvement of humanity at large, envisioning idealistic utopian societies.

Aquarians often excel in medical research where they can remain objective while working on projects that will benefit humanity at

---

[55] A Planet is said to be in detriment when in a sign where it's energy is most repressed, weakened, and unable to find harmonious release.

large. There may be an interest in psychology, for the purpose of understanding the structure of the self, but this would be approached from an objective, detached, standpoint, as though the individual himself was never really involved.

As the individual gathers knowledge, a sense of identity can form around what he or she knows. The flip side of this is that others may find them aloof, imperious, shallow and/or dismissive. When afflicted the individual may be eccentric to a fault and/or may be attracted to cults as a way to seek identity from a group identity.

If you have Sun in Aquarius it's likely that your life's energy flows primarily through structured thinking. Thinking in a structured way, while organizing information into categories, helps you to understand your world. With this capacity for structured thinking you have the mind of a scientist, yet you may also have a great entrepreneur streak.

Through your life experiences you are learning how to flow love and life into the world in ways that unite the collective consciousness of humanity. Your Soul's Purpose is vitalized and energized through humanitarian ideals and endeavors.

The spiritual challenge with the Sun in Aquarius is to release identification with knowledge. When you transcend the Aquarius ego, pure knowing spontaneously arises from clear light mind. There is no need to collect 'information' and mentally construct an idea of an "I" or "Me" who is 'The One Who Knows'.

Sun in Pisces – transcending "I BELIEVE"

Faith is energizing and self-affirming

When the Sun is in Pisces the focus is on those activities that will provide opportunities to alleviate suffering. Being deeply sensitive, Pisceans are acutely aware of the suffering in the world and have tremendous compassion. Because of this their sense of identity often stems from a belief system or religious doctrine that they have held since childhood, wherein loving kindness and compassion are attributes to be cultivated within oneself in order to benefit others.

As a result Pisceans are sometimes attracted to caring professions such as nursing however, due to their brilliant imaginations and dream-like nature they often excel in areas such as photography or the movie industry. The flip side of this is that others may see them as passive, vague, and/or airheaded. Because of their tendency toward escapism, when afflicted addictions can be a problem.

If you have Sun in Pisces it's likely that your life's energy flows primarily through sensitive feeling. You have a sensitive, empathic, nature, which allows you to sense accurately what others are feeling – sometimes even before they know it themselves!

Through your life experiences you are ultimately learning how to transform suffering into Universal Love. Your Soul's Purpose is vitalized, activated and energized through the transformation of suffering into compassion by the power of your heart.

The spiritual challenge with the Sun in Pisces is to release identification with beliefs. When you transcend the Pisces ego you realize that Divine Presence is real, and it exists without the added 'fantasy' of an "I" or "Me" to believe in it.

The Sun Through the Houses

*"Where the Sun is placed by house
is where the ability to make
a significant contribution to life lies."*

- Isabel M. Hickey[56]

The house position[57] of the Sun is showing which area of life experience gets most of your attention.

It is where you invest most of your time and energy (or want to) and where you will most likely express yourself.

Once you are no longer driven by the demands of the ego, this is the area of life experience where you are most likely to manifest your Soul's Purpose.

---

[56] Hickey, I.M. (1992) *Astrology A Cosmic Science: The Classic Work on Spiritual Astrology.* CRCS Publications.

[57] Read more about houses in chapter eight.

First House: To Be[58]

With your Sun in the First House of self you probably invest much of your 'prana' or life-force energy into your personal journey of self-awareness and self-realization. Throughout your life you may find yourself examining and questioning everything beginning with 'self': self-image, self-identity, self-esteem, self-awareness, etc. Everything that others tell you are, or are not, comes under close scrutiny as you realize your own true nature for yourself, and question externally imposed ideas about who you are. When the Sun is in this position your spiritual journey becomes the quest for your real Self, and you may often find yourself at times in your life, re-visiting the question 'who am I?' Care must be taken not to become ego-centric - overly identified with your ego.

On a Soul level this is a great placement for developing awareness of your Soul and for recognizing and manifesting your Soul Purpose.

Second House: To Possess

With your Sun in the second house of personal resources and values you may find that you invest much of your prana, or life-force energy, into building your resources and/or those things that you value and appreciate. This can include your personal income and many people with this placement tend to be self-employed.

On Soul level this is an excellent placement for recognizing your innate value and self-worth as a spiritual being. In meditation you may recognize your innate spiritual nature, which encompasses the higher qualities of love, peace, joy, clear wisdom and inner light. Once you recognize that these inner treasures are an inherent part of you, which no-one can ever take away from you, then you will have discovered your real spiritual 'treasure' and will be able to share it with others.

Third House: To Know

With your Sun in the third house of mental processes and communication, you probably invest much of your life force energy into your thought processes, learning and/ or communication. You may enjoy learning and 'collecting' information and when you

---

[58] Keywords for the Sun through the houses from "*Astrology A Cosmic Science*" by Isabel Hickey

choose to share your thoughts with others you may have a flair for teaching.

On a Soul level this is a great placement for developing conscious awareness of the 'substance' of mental energy (manas) and how it transforms as thought manifests into matter. It is a good placement for the development of the *Rainbow Bridge*[59] between lower and higher mind, and for the cultivation of Higher Mind capacities such as telepathy.

Fourth House: To Establish

With your Sun in the Fourth House of home and family you may find you invest much of your prana or life-force energy on your family and/or on creating a home base for yourself. This also includes your psychological roots and ancestry so you may invest time and energy in your ancestry in some way either by researching your family tree, and/or collecting photographs of your ancestors.

On a Soul level you may be aware of the patterns of societal and family conditioning that have helped to shape your own ego-personality, and what you can release within your psyche to experience the freedom of your Soul.

Fifth House: To Express

With your Sun in the Fifth House of children and creative self-expression you probably invest much of your life-force energy in your 'creations'. This could be your children (if you have any) or it could be any projects that you are creating.

You probably love to express yourself through your creativity, whatever form that takes. You may also have a natural flair for children and have a playful side to your nature that is also very child-like. Children are likely to have fun with you and enjoy being (and playing) with you.

On a Soul level this is a great placement for expressing Divine Will through your creative self expression. This is good for recognizing Higher Self as distinct from ego, for expressing spiritual will rather than personal will, and for expressing will in the form of love.

---

[59] The Rainbow Bridge is explained in chapter fifteen, *Mercury's Sacred Path to The Rainbow Bridge*

Sixth House: To Improve

With your Sun in the Sixth House of service you probably flow much of your life force energy into creating opportunities to be of service in general, and in particular to be of service to those who depend on you - perhaps by using your creativity to develop tools, techniques and technologies for improving and/or restoring health and well being or through techniques for personal growth and development.

On a Soul level this is a great placement for consciously building the antahkarana, or rainbow bridge, between lower and higher mind, through conscious service to humanity.

Seventh House: To Relate

With your Sun in the Seventh House of partnerships and relating you may find yourself investing much of your prana or life force energy in relationship of all kinds: whether they be close family, friends, co-workers, professional or business associates. Much of your life-force energy may be invested in supporting others through relationship.

On a Soul level this is a great placement for choosing relationship as a spiritual path. The eternal dance of self and other, balancing one's own needs within the context of relationship, while loving one's partner as one loves oneself: all are sources for deeper spiritual

connection and insight. The skills that one must develop in order to remain balanced in relationship, lead to greater self-awareness and spiritual growth.

Eighth House: To Transform

With your Sun in the Eighth House of personal power and transformation you may find that you invest much of your prana or life-force energy in situations that bring personal power into your awareness. This may be situations where you have power over others, or others have held power over you, causing you to question and transform the balance of power. Self-empowerment through personal healing and transformation is likely to be a major theme in your life.

On a Soul level this is a great placement for becoming more conscious of the relationship between the healing process and how you flow your personal energy, and the transformational healing power of love when it is consciously directed by your attention.

Ninth House: To Understand

With your Sun in the Ninth House you probably invest much of your life-force energy into higher wisdom and your search for deeper meaning in life. This could take the form of simply seeking higher education, or it can take the form of a committed ongoing spiritual path. From a Soul Astrology perspective this also means connecting with the higher wisdom of your own inner knowing, your inner spiritual path.

On a Soul level this is a great placement for recognizing that all paths lead to one Universal Truth. It is an opportunity to recognize one's own Higher Mind, Higher Wisdom, and to tap into Universal and Cosmic Truth.

Tenth House: To Achieve

With your Sun in the Tenth House of career and ambition, much of your prana or life force energy is likely to be channeled largely into your career, and/or your position in the world. You possibly seek higher knowledge and teach others higher wisdom as part of your

worldly role. Esoterically the Tenth House is the domain of the Masters, so you may also have awareness of your connection with your ancient lineage of wisdom teachers, or at least be aware of the vast storehouse of ancient wisdom-knowledge that you have brought into this life from previous lifetimes.

On a Soul level this is a great placement for expressing Divine Will as your life purpose, for cultivating spiritual ambition, aligning your will with the will and purpose of Spiritual Masters, and for expressing and channeling your life-force energy into a field of service.

Eleventh House: To Transfigure

With the Sun in your Eleventh House of social groups and collective consciousness, you may find that you invest much of your prana or life-force energy in friendship, social networks and/or groups, especially those that have a strong humanitarian goal or focus.

On personality level this is often about aligning with people who share and support your individual values so they can be applied to society in constructive ways. From a Soul level it becomes more about how you can be of service to humanity, to support the evolution of human consciousness, and what people you are drawing to you to support you in that collective goal.

Twelfth House: To Transcend

With your Sun in the Twelfth House of privacy and hidden talents, you may find that your pranic or life-force energy gets re-charged by periods of solitude. You may find that you need to retreat into your 'cave' now and then to re-charge your batteries.

You may enjoy meditation and/or activities where you can engage your imagination, and enjoy spending time in your inner world. You may have hidden skills and talents that you are unaware of until later in life.

On a Soul level this is a great placement for meditation, cultivating conscious awareness of your inner being, and developing awareness of your true nature as a spiritual being.

The Sun: Lighting Your Path

The placement and condition of the Sun by sign, house and aspect (whether afflicted or not) will tell you so much about your own hero's journey in terms of what, how, and where you will be able to illuminate your individual 'story of me' in order to release it, in addition to the nature of any help and/or challenges you will encounter along the way.

In short the Sun is showing you:

- your *vitality* (how you use and flow your life force energy)
- your *identity* that is transcended as you awaken spiritually

The Sun illuminates the path to your own deeper spiritual truth, which is an inner journey through your heart to your spiritual core.

Once you awaken to the connection between your heart and the heart of the Sun your daily activities no longer become a source of karma, but rather become a means of spiritual service.

Suggested Fieldwork

•   Deeper Self-observation. Take out your own horoscope (natal chart) and in your reflective journal - make a note of which sign and house the Sun occupies in your chart. Read the descriptions above and meditate often on the energy of the Sun. Record your impressions and insights in your reflective journal.

•   Further Reading: In your copy of *Soul Astrology* study and meditate on chapter five: *The Planetary Spaceholders*.

Book recommendations: *Soul Centered Astrology: A Key to Your Expanding Self,* by Alan Oken; *Astrology A Cosmic Science*, by Isabel Hickey; *The Luminaries: The Psychology of The Sun and Moon in The Horoscope*, by Liz Greene and Howard Sasportas

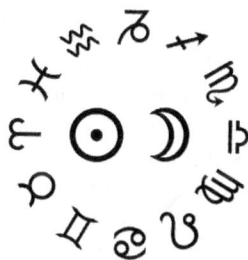

11. The Moon

For our current level of consciousness, the Moon is probably the most important planet in our horoscope because it symbolizes the unconscious karmic conditioning from past lives that we are carrying forward (and acting out) in this life.

Many astrologers believe that the Moon indicates our most recent past life. Indeed we can often see our Moon patterns in our early childhood behavior, as though we 'woke up' in this lifetime carrying the momentum of energetic and character traits from our previous incarnation. In this sense the patterns of our Moon sign can be thought of as a 'karmic hangover'!

Probably the most important thing you can do in this lifetime is to heal the energy dynamics of your Moon sign before your next reincarnation. This will not only purify your own energy field, so you will not be carrying karmic traces over to your next life, but it will benefit humanity greatly by cleansing the polluted ocean of collective consciousness.

Although we think we have free will, most of us (until we have fully spiritually awakened) are driven predominantly by desire and avoidance. When we move into action it is usually to strive for something we want or to avoid something we don't want. The desire to obtain what we want can include food, sustenance, material possessions, emotional security, safety, relationships, warmth, love, acceptance, wealth, power, authority, knowledge, status, good health etc. (the list is endless). The desire to avoid that which we don't want can include pain, infirmity, poverty, homelessness, rejection, ostracization, isolation, loneliness, sickness etc. (this list is also endless).

Although human beings are considered to be 'higher order' intelligent mammals (and there's no denying our lives are immeasurably complex), at the mundane level all of our behavior can really be boiled down to these two simple drives: to gravitate towards pleasure (the wish for happiness) and avoid pain (the wish to avoid suffering). This means that, in spite of all our complexity, until we awaken to our spiritual nature we are no different from any other sentient being. Even a simple amoeba will gravitate towards pleasure and withdraw from pain. In spite of our social complexity, this simple animal drive still resides within each of us, (attachment) (aversion) and astrologically, the specific form it will take in our life is indicated by the Moon. We are lunar creatures indeed.

The Dark of The Moon - Unconscious Reacting

It is always challenging to work with our lunar patterns precisely because they are largely unconscious until we start doing some personal development work to cultivate self-awareness around our own habits of acting and reacting and begin to awaken to our spiritual nature.

For most people the unconscious reactions of their Moon sign will be a mystery to them their whole lives, known only by their family, friends and co-workers, as the unconscious behavior that 'slips out' when they are under pressure (and which they may vehemently deny when anyone tries to point it out).

If we take a review of our lives, we might notice a pattern where our personality is more in the nature of our Moon sign when we are children. As we grow older we blossom more into our Sun Sign, and then in mid-life (35 to 40) we 'grow' more into our Rising Sign. Maybe its because we awaken to the call of our Soul Sign as we get older, but that's a conversation for another day!

Of the two sides of our personality, the yin and yang, the Sun is in the light (yang), that which we are conscious of, while the Moon is in the shade (yin), that which we are unconscious of. It is through our interactions with others that our Moon Sign qualities 'come to light', and not through a conscious, considered, response on our part, but more often through our unconscious reacting.

The reactive patterns of the Moon are thought to originate from our last lives. In a sense the Moon is a repository of past-life energy that we are ready to release. The physical Moon itself is a symbol of this. The Moon itself has no life-force energy of it's own. It does not emanate light, but reflects the light of the Sun. So it can be considered to symbolize a 'dead weight' that we are carrying around in our energy field. But it has a powerful effect. Just like the physical Moon affects the earth's tides and weather, so our astrological Moon indicates our instinctive tides and emotional weather.

Even though it is 'dead' (relating to the past) The Moon is creating ripples in your energy field that you have to deal with on a daily basis. Just like a dead rock in the middle of a river will cause the river, the fish and all life associated with the river to flow around it, so your Moon sign dynamics will create a tidal pull on your life, and be a constant drain on your energy field, until you make those dynamics conscious (by cultivating self-awareness), and move towards healing and integration.

Your Enemies Are Your Best Teachers

For those on a committed spiritual path it is often said that your enemies are your best teachers. That is because the people who bring out the worst in you, are giving you an opportunity to see what karmic traces you are carrying, so that you can change them. You can't change what you can't see, and it is only when other people bring your reactions out into the open that you have a precious opportunity for self-awareness.

Your Moon Sign will indicate your conditioned emotional reflexes and show you how you unconsciously react when you feel hurt. Do you lash out (verbally or physically)? Do you brood and sulk? Do you withdraw, plot revenge, and/or lick your wounds? Part of your journey of becoming conscious is to bring loving awareness to these unconscious reactions. Understanding the characteristics of your Moon sign can be helpful because you can start to watch out for them.

When you are in the grip of a full-blown emotional meltdown is not the best time or place to get to know and understand your Moon sign attributes! Often when you have been in the grip of a strong emotion you aren't always able to remember what you said or did. A better way is to observe yourself as you go through the rhythms of the day. Who are you in the morning? Then around lunchtime? At dinner? In the evening? And especially who are you late at night? Or if you are awake at night, who are you then? We are often very different at 3am than we are at 3pm in the afternoon. Spend some time this month observing the different versions of 'you', and see if you can notice when your Moon creeps in!

Who You Become Under Stress

It is important to know that when you feel hurt, it doesn't mean anybody intended to hurt you! It can be part of your conditioned reaction to the world around you. Also the way you react to a perceived threat, can be a clue to deeper emotional healing that you can work towards. For example, the dramatic emotional reaction of someone with Moon in Leo can indicate a deeper need for acknowledgement and/or being valued. When you work on meeting this need for yourself you are doing your own deeper emotional healing.

The Sun and Moon are the basic 'drivers' in our life. Everything else in the chart can be thought of as a modifier to the Sun and Moon. If we were talking about a car the Sun and Moon would tell us the basic make and model, while the other planets, aspects etc. would tell us additional features and details: the color, the upholstery, the engine size, whether there is air conditioning or not etc.! So to begin with keep it simple and start by going deeper in your understanding of your own Sun and Moon sign.

Next, practice mindfulness. Be present in any and every moment. Notice your speech, your reactions, your responses. Notice your emotions. Watch yourself with great attentiveness as you go through your day. Notice how you react and/or respond to others. Notice what motivates you. Notice how you think and feel. What catches your interest and what turns you off? Especially notice what pushes your buttons and what those buttons are!

As we saw in the previous chapter, your vitality will be connected to your Sun sign. Watch for that. Can you see where and if that is true for you? Then, your emotional responses, instinctive needs, and who you become in relationship will be indicated by your Moon sign. Look at how you react and respond to others, and when under stress. Your Moon sign can indicate both your positive and so-called 'negative' emotional responses to others.

When stressed you may default to the instinctive reactions of your Moon sign. Observe yourself closely without judgment and see if you can see the dynamics playing out in your life. Remember the energy dynamics are already there, astrology is simply a way of putting language to your experience. Don't worry if you don't seem to be a 'pure' example of your Sun or Moon sign. No-one is a pure type in any psychological system because each of us is a unique blend of the energies involved.

On a day to day basis it will be the personality expressions of your Sun and Moon signs that you notice first. Your Soul Sign (Ascendant or Rising Sign) will show up as an essence, more of a 'perfume' that permeates your personality expression. Your Soul's Purpose is carried out through the activities of your Sun and Moon Signs but to keep it simple at first it's better to only focus on the energy dynamics of your Sun and Moon signs until you become familiar with them.

Rather than looking for yourself in one sign, begin looking where the energy of the signs shows up in different areas of your life, and how they interact with each other. Using astrological language, you will be able to recognize energetic patterns more quickly and take action to change where needed. Then you have a practical tool that can support your ongoing spiritual development.

Emotional Intelligence, Instinct and Feelings

In an earlier chapter we discussed how the evolution of human consciousness AND your individual path of spiritual awakening are one and the same, and that (from our current perspective) there appear to be 'stages' on the path, as follows:

> instinct > intellect > intuition > illumination > emptiness[60]

The Moon in your chart symbolizes the energy of your emotional world and is very much associated with he first of these 'stages', instinct. It can show how you react and respond to others and what you need in order to feel emotionally safe and secure.

---

[60] These stages will be repeated frequently throughout the book because they are fundamental to our understanding of the evolution of human consciousness, and its application to Soul Astrology.

The Moon is associated with the past and it is possible that the reactive patterns of our Moon sign were created in past lives. We therefore need to be gentle and compassionate with ourselves, if we are take an honest look at the energy of how we react to others. If we are courageous, and willing to walk the path of our Moon sign, there is a treasure of healing, deep wisdom, and compassion to be gained.

The Moon probably has more influence over us on a day to day basis than even the Sun. In astrology she represents our instincts, feelings, and emotions. We all know that the Moon affects the ocean and influences the tides, and modern science is coming to understand that the Moon might be so much more important than we ever realized.

Karmic Conditioning: The Magnetic Pull of The Moon

If the Rising Sign (Ascendant) indicates our Soul, and the Sun indicates our prana or life-force energy, the Moon represents our karmic conditioning, both individually and collectively. Like the pull of the Moon on the Earth's tides, conditioning probably has the most power over us until we start to awaken to our spiritual nature and soul purpose. The whole of humanity is driven by conditioning, and therefore falls under the magnetic 'pull of the Moon'.

So what do we mean by conditioning? Simply put it is learned behavior. Yet, most of what we think and do, most of our behavior, including our identity is actually conditioning. It has been given to you by the society into which you were born. Conditioning is what we learn from those around us, and then we identify with it and it becomes habit. The name you were given, the language you speak, the food you eat, and even your sense of 'right' and 'wrong'. This is all conditioning. Even if it seems innate, like someone has a natural talent for computers while another is a born athlete, this has likely been 'conditioned' in a past life.

To really understand the power of conditioning think about a time when you had to go against the majority. If you have ever experienced what is known as 'peer-pressure'[61], that is when you would have felt the pull of the Moon at it's strongest. It is the pressure we feel to conform to the group, the tribe, the community, the club, the gang, the mob and/or the family. The Moon represents the consciousness of the masses because it is the energy of emotional

---

[61] Read more about Peer Pressure at https://en.wikipedia.org/wiki/Peer_pressure

attachment. When we are 'swept away' on a tide of emotion, and/or when we feel pressure to conform that is the influence of the Moon.

We all like to think we could and would act independently from the group but time and again studies, (such as the classic Asch[62] and Milgram[63] psychology experiments) show how the majority of people succumb to the power of peer-pressure and/or authority. In other words we conform to what is expected of us by the group or society. This magnetic pull to conform to mass consciousness is lunar in nature and is part of what we learn to release and transcend as we evolve in consciousness[64]. This is why the process of individuation is so important for the evolution of human consciousness. Individuation leads to awakening.

The Full Moon and Dreaming

Why do we dream more vividly at the Full Moon? While we are asleep our psyche is processing our unconscious or 'karmic' mind. The Full Moon therefore represents an important time for karmic clearing and becoming more aware of our Moon Sign dynamics.

Often around the time of a Full Moon we notice our dreams. Either someone who doesn't usually dream much will have a significant dream, or someone who dreams often will have a clearer dream, or a more meaningful dream. Whatever the case it seems that around the time of the Full Moon, our dreams can get our attention.

In the Tibetan Buddhist tradition dreams are divided into three categories:

- karmic dreams
- clear light dreams
- lucid dreams

Karmic dreams are 'ordinary' dreams. The kind that western

---

[62] Learn more about the Asch Conformity Experiment at https://www.simplypsychology.org/asch-conformity.html

[63] Learn more about the Milgram experiment at https://explorable.com/stanley-milgram-experiment

[64] You can read more about karma and conditioning in Chapter one of *Soul Astrology*: Your Healing Journey: Duality, Polarity, and Wholeness.

psychologists and dream researchers speak of when they say our mind is processing the events of the day, or of our everyday lives. We might dream about our family, or a problem, what we saw on TV, a celebrity, or memories and people from our past. These are all 'karmic' because they pertain to our 'karma', in other words they arise out of our present condition and circumstances, and the conditioning of our everyday mind. These dreams can be very 'foggy' - we may not remember much about them yet we can be left with a 'hangover' where we either feel dull when we awaken, or we are experience an emotional 'charge' that begins in the dream and remains with us when we awake.

Clear light dreams can be prophetic in nature. As the name suggests they are characterized by a quality of light and clarity that supersedes our everyday existence. In these dreams we may experience visions, premonitions, meet our teachers and guides, and receive teaching and instruction. When we awake we invariably feel at peace, joyful, loving and we usually have a very clear sense that we just experienced something special.

Lucid dreaming is where we are aware within the dream state, that we are dreaming. In the Tibetan tradition of dream yoga lucid dreaming is cultivated so that one's spiritual practice can continue through the night as the dream state is used to further one's spiritual development.

"Dreams are a reservoir of knowledge and experience, yet they are often overlooked as a vehicle for exploring reality"

- Tarthang Tulku

Love/Hate Relationship

Have you ever noticed that you have a love-hate relationship with your Moon sign? It's an interesting dynamic to watch in your life. To understand this more deeply, it can't be emphasized enough, how important it is to observe your own dynamics when you are relating with others. This means watch yourself, take your attention off what the other person is saying and doing, and notice your own thoughts, words and reactions to them. In particular notice how you are with people who have the Sun in the same sign as your Moon. They are openly living out your Moon sign qualities, bringing them into the light for all to see (how dare they when maybe you've spent a whole lifetime trying not to be like that)!

The Moon

People whose Sun is in the same sign as your Moon may be challenging for you at some times, while at others, you may adore them. Especially if you don't yet recognize those qualities in yourself. When they are displaying the highest octave, love-based, so-called positive qualities of that sign, you may admire them greatly and wish you could be like that. When they display the fear-based, so-called negative, qualities of that sign you may think "I would NEVER be like that". Whereas the truth is, you really are like that in the sense that you are carrying the same energy, although it expresses itself differently through the Moon (sometimes, but not always, more sensitively and low-key than the Sun's expression).

The Moon is associated with our instincts and emotions. When we feel hurt, and/or when others 'push our buttons' we are likely to react in a manner according to the qualities and temperament of our Moon sign. For example you could be a gentle, sensitive, kind and compassionate Sun in Pisces yet you have Moon in Sagittarius. When hurt you may be scathing in your sarcasm, leaving your shocked and stunned friends wondering where that came from because "It's not like you".

The qualities of your Sun sign are in the light, easily recognized (usually), and you can often relate to them. When it comes to your Moon sign, you may be either unaware of those qualities, don't recognize them in yourself or you've spent a lifetime trying 'not to be like that'! Our example of a Pisces friend (with Sagittarius Moon) may be thinking "I try not to be like that but when people push my buttons it just comes out".

With your Sun sign, you can usually embrace both the positive and so-called negative qualities more easily. So you may be able to openly say to a friend with Sun in Sagittarius, "You know I admire your honesty, and the fact you speak your mind, but you can be tactless at times", and they may well shrug their shoulders and say "I know I can be like that sometimes, I'm working on it". They are more likely to already be aware of it and to embrace the characteristic objectively, without too much of an emotional charge. That would be the Sun.

Not so with the Moon. Try saying that to our Pisces friend with Moon in Sagittarius! If they don't break down in tears saying "I don't know what you're talking about", or get sarcastic with you and not realize they're doing it, they may get defensive and accuse you of being mean. In other words there is likely to be unconscious reacting and/or an emotional charge. That would be the Moon.

The reason is that the Moon is a very sensitive point for all of us. As we continue our own journey of self-exploration through Soul Astrology, we need to approach the dynamics of our Moon sign very gently, with loving awareness and great compassion for ourselves. If we have reacted to someone in an unconscious, reactive way, that is a great opportunity for healing and awakening for us both. If we look at what happened, and what got triggered in us, we can see where we need to do some healing work.

When you can embrace people whose Sun is in the same sign as your Moon, and think "I am that, and that am I" then you will be well on your way to healing your Moon sign. Remember what you really want is to be flowing the clear light of your Soul Sign into the world, but before you can do that you need to 'clean' the lens of your personality signs (which is what focuses your Soul's light into the world). Healing your Moon-sign is one of the ways your clear your lens and let your Soul-light shine!

Most likely the dynamics of your Moon sign were created in a past life, and then something happened in this life during your early childhood to re-awaken that pain and reinforce your impulse to hide it away. So whenever you look at healing the dynamics of your Moon sign (and you usually don't even want to look), you are doing important inner child work.

The reason it is such a sensitive area for you, is that when it comes to your Moon sign work you are dealing with a vulnerable, hurt, and very young inner child that needs your loving attention.

The Catch 22 of The Moon: The Tidal Push-Pull of Fear vs. Need

As we have seen The Moon in your chart can tell you so much about your inner world. It indicates your fears, vulnerabilities, insecurities, instincts, irrational reactions and your emotional world. Much of this is as a result of past life wounding.

Our Moon can be very helpful in pointing to where we have important personal needs, and it can also be indicating the ways in which we can get them met, but there is often fear around the Moon too. So although we may be able to recognize where we have a personal need, and we might also be able to see various ways that we can get it met, at the same time we may experience an irrational fear that we can't quite put our finger on!

First let's get clear on what personal needs actually are. We all have needs, which humanistic psychologist Abraham Maslow described in terms of his famous *Hierarchy of Human Need*[65]. At the bottom of the hierarchy we have those basic needs that are common to all our human family, for example warmth, food, shelter, love etc. It is important to note that needs differ from 'wants' in that they are essential for our health, well-being and continued growth. We won't die if we don't get what we want, but we can 'die' or live a compromised/ impoverished life, if we don't get our needs met.

Our own journey of personal growth moves us up the hierarchy towards self-actualization, and our needs then become more unique to us, as individuals. They then become more personal (hence the term *personal* needs).

There are a wide variety of personal needs, which can include a need for creative expression, a need for nature, a need for solitude, a need to express our truth, a need for community, a need for artistic expression, a need for beauty, a need for financial security, a need for independence etc. (This list is also endless). These are also common throughout humanity but for individuals some will take priority over others.

So now let's look at an example of how personal needs can be indicated by your Moon sign, and what I mean by this 'Catch 22' that often comes with the Moon. For example if you have Moon in Leo you might have identified a need for appreciation (which is just one expression of a need for love) that wasn't met in childhood.

You might even know how you can go about getting your need for appreciation met for yourself (perhaps through self-appreciation, or by being involved in groups where others verbalize their appreciation for you and your work), *but* there may also be this niggling doubt/ fear accompanying it. As though if you really did just go for it, something 'bad' might happen. This is what I mean by the 'catch 22' of the Moon: even when things are going well there always seems to be a 'but' involved!

To understand this more deeply let's look at the difference between the Sun and Moon in the same sign. Sun in Leo might get their needs for appreciation met by performing on stage, in the spotlight, and

---

[65] https://en.wikipedia.org/wiki/Maslow%27s_hierarchy_of_needs

then without reservation basking in accolades and curtain-calls from an appreciative audience. Their need is getting met cleanly, without any undercurrent of fear, because it forms part of their identity. That would be The Sun.

When the Moon is in Leo, you might still perform well on stage. You might also see how this could get your need for appreciation met, but you somehow have a niggling feeling that something might go wrong, something bad could happen, or that you shouldn't be 'showing off' in this way. There will be some undercurrent in your psyche that is making you feel wrong for needing attention, or light. This is the hidden side - the dark of the Moon.

Inner Child Healing with The Mother of Compassion

When we work with the energy of our Moon sign, we begin healing our wounded inner child. This is very delicate work, because we may be dealing with emotional blocks and traumas that were created when we were very young. When we move into the 'unconscious reacting' that we spoke of earlier, we are actually acting out a former version of ourselves, with the emotional age of that time.

For example I once worked with a Chief Surgeon who, when he didn't get his own way, would have a tantrum worthy of any three-year old and throw his instruments all over the operating theatre. Most people passed this off as stress, but not all surgeons react this way to stress! What was happening for him is that his stress was landing on prior childhood trauma, and when triggered he was reverting at least emotionally (if not mentally) to that age.

We all have a similar wounded 'inner child' - an emotional age at which some childhood event marked our emotional development in such a way that it became our default way of reacting to stress. Our emotional age may be 5 or 15 but either way, we will see the dynamics in the horoscope, indicated by the condition of the Moon.

For most of us our first experiences of compassion and nurturing, start with our Mother. How we were nurtured (or not) and how we will develop the nurturing (Mother) principle in ourselves (or not) will be indicated in our horoscope by the placement and condition of the Moon by sign, house and aspect.

If we are to develop compassion for self, for our own inner child, for the one that hurts, for our own vulnerability, for the terrified animal instinct that we all have inside, we need to access and cultivate the higher qualities of The Moon in ourselves.

On a personality level the Moon rules Cancer: associated with Mothering, birth, breastfeeding and nourishment. On a Soul level the Moon is the Ruler of Virgo: the Divine Mother and sacred feminine. Just as necessity is the mother of invention, then the circumstances of our own Moon Sign, our particular Moon challenges, and the path to our own inner child healing, becomes the Mother of Compassion in our own lives. As we heal our Moon Sign challenges we become more empathic and compassionate towards ourselves, and others.

If we ignore the call of the Moon we are ignoring our own inner child's cries for healing. By fully embracing and acknowledging the needs of our Moon sign, we set course on our own path to integration and healing. We shift from worldly mother to Sacred Mother and the Divine Feminine. We embody compassion and, just like Mother Mary, Quan Yin, and Avelokiteshvara we may become a manifestation of the bodhisattva of compassion.

The Moon as Destiny

So far The Moon dynamics have sounded a bit deterministic: as though we are trapped in destiny, controlled by the movements of the Moon, and powerless to exercise free will or break out of the clutches of this 'evil Moon'. In fact this is how the Moon, and indeed all the planets, were thought of in earlier periods throughout the history of astrology. In medieval times for example it was thought that everything was predetermined, destiny or 'the fates' dealt their hand and we were pretty much powerless to intervene. They were very suspicious, and fearful, of the Moon. There is still a residue of this belief in our modern culture, as many people still believe that most of life is predetermined and we don't really have much choice or free will.

However this belief is very limiting and disempowering. It denies your own power. The reality is that while we cannot always exercise control over external circumstances, we do have total control over how we react or respond to them, once we develop more conscious awareness. When we are unconscious we allow ourselves to be driven by our instincts, urges, desires and compulsions and fail to recognize our own power. We are motivated not by choice and free will, but more from unconscious reacting and conditioned reflexes. This can be our experience of the Moon at personality level and, as long as we continue reacting impulsively, and not exercising our free will, our lives may as well be predetermined. The Moon at this level doesn't seem to be our friend!

Once we begin our spiritual journey of awakening, the Moon becomes our best friend and ally. On the path of awakening, the Moon illuminates: bringing to our conscious awareness, those previously unconscious compulsions, desires, habits and reactions that would keep us stuck in lower consciousness. The Moon illuminates our emotional attachments and, through our relationship with others, shows us where much of our spiritual healing is to be done. On our spiritual journey, the Moon becomes our best friend.

Ways To Study The Moon in Your Horoscope

There are many ways to study The Moon in your horoscope, including:

- Your Moon's Sign
- The House placement of your Moon
- Aspects to The Moon[66]
- The Lunation Cycle
- The Nodal Axis

The Moon Through The Signs

Below are some very brief ideas of how to interpret each Moon sign, bear in mind there is so much more to your Moon sign than we have space for here!

Start with the brief description below and then make a note of your observations about how you experience your own Moon sign energy. If you have never done this before you might need to take some time in observation and reflection, before you can really see how you react and respond to others. Contemplating the element might also be helpful in attuning to the energy of the sign, but remember where the Moon is involved there is always an emotional component.

---

[66] See chapter thirteen, *Aspects*.

When your Moon is in:

Aries (Fire) you may respond to others intuitively and with enthusiasm. When you feel hurt your temper may flare and have an impulsive, possibly explosive quality to it, but it burns out just as quickly. Your key to healing is through recognizing that YOU exist, and because you exist, you matter. Start by listening to your intuition and trusting your own inner guidance.

Taurus (Earth) you may respond to others quietly and considerately. When you feel hurt you may tend to 'dig your heels in' and become stubborn. You like to arrive at decisions in your own time and not feel pushed. Your key to healing is through recognizing your inherent value, and trusting your own inner resources.

Gemini (Air) you may respond to others communicatively with a desire to share information. When you feel hurt you may change the subject, side step the issue and/or use your skill with words to avoid a direct confrontation. Your key to healing is through letting go of mental 'stories' and connecting with the deeper wisdom of your heart.

Cancer (Water) you may respond to others in ways that are caring and nurturing. When you feel hurt, you may feel it more than you show. You may withdraw into your shell completely although sometimes the 'crab's claws' can be upfront and you can give another person a sharp 'nip' as a warning! Your key to healing is through overcoming fear by compassionate nurturing of yourself and recognizing your innate emotional intelligence.

Leo (Fire) you may respond to others with warmth and generosity. When you feel hurt you may be prone to sulking or brooding, but you may also over-react very dramatically to make your point if you feel you are not being paid enough attention! Your key to healing is honoring your creativity, your individuality, and by having the courage to follow your unique heart's passion.

Virgo (Earth) you may respond to others in ways that are generally helpful and dependable. When you feel hurt you may be prone to anxiety and worry, as you try to find practical ways out of your predicament. Your key to healing is through cultivating somatic (body) awareness and then recognizing how you flow love tangibly into your world.

Libra (Air) you respond to others in ways that are congenial and companionable. When you feel hurt you may try to manipulate the situation to keep the peace and avoid confrontation. Your key to healing is through finely balancing your own needs and those of others in all your relationships. Each is as important as the other.

Scorpio (Water) you may respond to others with an air of mysticism as you keep your private life to yourself. When you feel hurt you may tend to brood and withdraw into a private world of silence, however, if pushed you may equally face a perceived 'enemy' head-on, with claws and 'sting' at the ready. Others may know the 'sting' in the Scorpion's tail if they don't back off! Your key to healing is through allowing yourself to feel your own feelings and express them in ways that feel safe for you. Only by allowing your emotional energy to move and flow, will your personal healing journey begin.

Sagittarius (Fire) you may respond to others in a friendly gregarious manner. When you feel hurt you may have a tendency to sarcasm, and/or shoot out a barrage of 'arrows' in the form of 'facts' or 'evidence' that you have gathered to support your 'case'. Your key to healing is through quieting your mind and resting in inner silence where you will access your own higher truth, spiritual power and the deepest wisdom that is beyond words.

Capricorn (Earth) you may respond to others in practical and responsible ways. When you feel hurt you may withdraw emotionally, becoming cold, and /or you may withdraw physical resources and/or practical support. Your key to healing is through recognizing your inherent connection to the Divine, accessing your deepest inner resources and shining your light in the world.

Aquarius (Air) you may respond to others with intelligence yet in impersonal and objective ways. When you feel hurt you may distance yourself from others, cutting them off completely. Your key to healing is through releasing mental ideals and accepting this present reality just as it is. Then you will start recognizing a real, tangible, flow of Divine love through your own heart-center.

Pisces (Water) you may respond to others with sensitivity and imagination. When you feel hurt you may tend to withdraw from the world completely, and may feel a deep sense of hurt and sadness. Your key to healing is through recognizing and cultivating the power of your own heart's radiant energy to transform suffering in both yourself, and others.

The Moon Through The Houses

First House

With your Moon in the First House of self you probably feel most emotionally safe and secure when you can anchor yourself deeply in your own path of self awareness. Having the space in your life for self discovery and self exploration is more than just a pastime for you, it fulfils a deep emotional need. The more time you can spend in your own rich self discovery, where you can honor and acknowledge your own experience and intuition, the more emotionally nurtured and nourished you will feel.

Second House

With your Moon in the second house of personal resources and values you may get a great deal of emotional satisfaction from those activities that increase your sense of self-value of self-worth. You may find that generating your own income, or being self-employed, brings you a great deal of emotional safety and a feeling of security.

Third House

With your Moon in the third house of communication, language and learning, you may get a great deal of emotional satisfaction in situations where you are able to communicate your feelings. You may have a gift for talking about feelings and emotions, and feel nurtured and nourished when you are able to do so. You may also be a passionate speaker and be able to convey the power of emotions through your speech. Since the third house also involves teaching and learning you may also have a talent for emotional intelligence and/or teaching others how to talk about emotions.

Fourth House

With your Moon in the Fourth House of home, family, and ancestry you may get a great deal of emotional satisfaction from your home and family. This may be your family of origin or it could be through building and creating a sense of family for yourself in your current situation. You may feel emotionally nurtured and nourished when you feel a sense of family around you.

Fifth House

With your Moon in the Fifth House of children and creative self-expression you probably get a great deal of emotional satisfaction from your children (if you have any) or from any projects that you are creating. You may find that you feel emotionally nourished and nurtured by your own creative self-expression. Even if you are a male, children may see you as quite a 'motherly', nurturing figure.

Sixth House

With your Moon in the Sixth House of service you possibly have an emotional need or urge to be of service, and feel most emotionally secure (as though all is well in your world) when you have opportunities to be of service in general, and in particular to be of service to those who depend on you - perhaps by using your creativity to develop tools, techniques and technologies for improving/ restoring health, well being and personal development in some way.

Seventh House

With your Moon in the Seventh House of relationships and partnerships, all your relationships whether they be close family, friends, co-workers, professional or business associates, are very important to you. You feel nurtured and nourished by good relationships and you also love to nurture and nourish others through high quality connections.

Eighth House

With your Moon in the Eighth House of transformation you probably experience your emotions very deeply, and feel a great deal of emotional safety and security when you are able to create time and space to fully experience and process your feelings in private. With the Moon in this position your personal journey of healing and transformation is experienced through your emotional world, whereby you are learning about how to navigate through different emotional frequencies, and how the power of your own self-awareness can transform fear-based emotions into higher spiritual energies such as love.

Ninth House

With your Moon in the Ninth House of higher wisdom, you probably feel a great deal of emotional satisfaction when you are pursuing your own search for higher knowledge and deeper meaning. Understanding the meaning of life is more than a mere intellectual pursuit for you, when you connect to higher wisdom you actually feel nurtured and nourished by it. It touches and feeds your Soul, bringing you a sense of emotional safety and security.

Tenth House

With your Moon in the Tenth House of career and ambition, much of your emotional energy is likely to be invested in your 'place in the world'. Achieving a certain position or status could bring you a deep sense of emotional satisfaction and security. This could mean through a conventional career, but from a soul-centered perspective it also means the 'work you came to do in the world'. Esoterically the Tenth House is the domain of the Masters, so you may also sense or feel an emotional connection with your ancient lineage of wisdom teachers, and/or sense the vast storehouse of ancient wisdom-knowledge that you have and can bring forth into this life from previous lifetimes.

Eleventh House

With your Moon in the Eleventh House of social groups and collective consciousness, you may find that you get a great deal of emotional satisfaction from group activity and social networks. You may find that you feel emotionally nurtured and nourished in your friendships, and you may find that working in groups, especially towards humanitarian goals, brings you emotional satisfaction and security.

Twelfth House

With your Moon in the Twelfth House of privacy, hidden talents, and your inner world, you may find that you get a great deal of emotional satisfaction from periods of solitude. You may feel emotionally nurtured and nourished in silence or by spending long periods just 'being' in your own awareness. You may have quite a psychic connection, and sometimes this can bring irrational fear. The solution is to remain very self-aware - be aware that you are not the fear, but rather YOU are the observing consciousness that is aware of the fear.

The Lunation Cycle

Another important way that we look at the Moon in your chart is through the lunation cycle: whether the Moon is waxing, waning and in which phase of the Moon's cycle you were born in (crescent

Moon, Full Moon etc.). Generally speaking, waxing Moon types are said to be more subjective in their experience, while waning Moon types are said to be more objective, nevertheless the Lunation Cycle is telling us something about how we as individuals relate to the world around us, and how we make an impact, or not, on our environment. Master astrologer Dane Rudhyar considered the Lunation Cycle[67] to be an extremely important tool for revealing aspects of our psyche of which we may be unaware.

Although some astrologers divide the lunar cycle into four phases, Rudhyar divided the lunar cycle into eight. I have found Rudhyar's eight lunation types to be quite accurate in describing an individual's character, but before we get into the specifics, let's take a look at the basic symbolism of a lunar cycle and what that means for us.

A lunar cycle tells us something about cycles of life. Rudhyar believed the lunar cycle to be one of the most basic 'cycles of relationship' simply because it is one that we can all understand and relate to. He said similar 'cycles of relationship' can be found throughout all life and if we understand something of the lunar cycle, we will understand a principle that holds true for all such relationships.

What did he mean by a cycle of relationship? Well when we talk about a lunar cycle, we are really talking about the Moon's relationship with the Sun. To understand this we need to know a little bit about what the lunar cycle is. The lunar cycle begins with what we refer to as a 'New Moon'. A *New Moon* is when the Sun and Moon *occupy the same point* in the sky so the Moon is not visible to us, because of the brightness of the Sun.

In contrast a *Full Moon* happens when the Moon is *directly opposite* the Sun. We can see it clearly because it is lit up by the light from the Sun. So as we continue, and describe the *phases of the Moon*, we begin to realize that the Moon itself has no actual *phases* as such, but they are *apparent* phases created by the Moon's *relationship to the Sun*.

When we talk about the relationship between the Sun and Moon we are beginning to explore the deepest yoga: the union of Sun and Moon, yang and yin, light and dark, outer and inner, exoteric and

---

[67] Rudhyar, D. (1967) *The Lunation Cycle: A Key To The Understanding of Personality.* Servire; distributed by Llewellyn Publications, St. Paul, Minn.

esoteric. We are beginning to move away from separation towards the ultimate union: oneness. No matter how wise or educated we become, we cannot claim to be in oneness, or enlightenment, while our Moon sign dynamics are still keeping us in the dark.

Rudhyar's Eight Moon Phases

Basically we know the Moon is either waxing, as the energy builds up to a Full Moon, or waning as the energy 'dies down' and dissolves into the next New Moon. However within the waxing and waning process Rudhyar also saw distinct phases. To calculate your own Moon Phase check below to see where the Moon is in relation to the Sun in your natal chart:

Waxing

New Moon (0 - 45° ahead of the Sun). The New Moon is a time of new beginnings. Something is emerging and people born around this time can be impulsive initiators. They are carrying the 'seed' of something and like to begin things.

Crescent (45 - 90° ahead of the Sun): People born at this time may have a pioneering spirit but also have a sense of being 'held back' by the past. May need to work to assert and establish themselves.

First Quarter (90 – 135° ahead of the Sun): People born at this time can be strong-willed adventurous, exploring, types.

Gibbous (135 – 180° ahead of the Sun): People born at this time may have a sense of being on a mission, or quest, which can include your personal search for meaning.

Waning

Full Moon (180 – 135° behind the Sun): People born at this time may be visionaries with a clear sense of purpose and an ability to 'fertilize' a situation and bear fruit.

Disseminating (135 – 90° behind the Sun): People born at this time can be passionate crusaders, with a powerful desire to share what they have learned.

Last Quarter (90 – 45° behind the Sun): People born at this time may be more reflective and philosophical. There may even be a sense of 'dying on the vine' as energy is withdrawn back into the cycle. They may have an urge to share what they have learned yet may also be discarding what has not worked, and be perceiving the inklings of a new future yet to come.

Balsamic (Waning Crescent. 45 – 0° behind the Sun): This is the closing of the cycle. Ending. People born at this time may have a need for space and solitude. There may be a sense of something gestating that is about to be birthed.

We may find in the lunar cycle a deeper understanding of some of those irrational feelings that we sometimes experience, that don't seem related to current events in our lives.

Astrologer Demetra George[68] goes one step further and relates the lunation cycle to our Soul's evolution:

> *"The phase signifies the kind of energy that flows between our solar consciousness and lunar instinctive awareness, and indicates the quality of interactive energy that we can best use to express (Sun) and actualize (Moon) our life purpose. Our lunation phase also points to the current stage of our soul's development within a larger cyclic process."*

- Demetra George

Other ways to study the Moon's influence in your chart include the *Nodal Axis* and *Aspects*, which we will cover in the next two chapters. For now it is enough to say that there are many ways to look at the Moon but whichever way we look at it, once we commit ourselves to our spiritual journey the Moon becomes a friend, ally, and powerful guide along the way.

Whichever approach you take it is most important to practice being compassionate with yourself. When you are dealing with your Moon you are dealing with your unconscious. You cannot imagine the circumstances of your past lives, where these behaviors were created to protect you, so that you would survive. In their day, they had a purpose and served you well, and they are to be respected for that.

In this lifetime it is simply time to become aware, and release that which is no longer serving you on your spiritual path.

---

[68] https://demetra-george.com/

Suggested Fieldwork

• Deeper Self-observation. Take out your own horoscope (natal chart) and in your reflective journal - make a note of which sign and house the Moon occupies in your chart. Read the descriptions above and meditate on the qualities of the Moon. Record your impressions and insights in your reflective journal.

• Set a conscious intention to become fully aware of your Moon sign dynamics so that you can heal them in this lifetime.

• In your journal, reflect on what you have read, and list three new things you have learned about the Moon and how they apply to your own life.

• Further Reading: In your copy of *Soul Astrology* study and meditate on chapter five: *The Planetary Spaceholders*. Book recommendations: *Soul Centered Astrology: A Key to Your Expanding Self*, by Alan Oken; *The Luminaries: The Psychology of The Sun and Moon in The Horoscope*, by Liz Greene and Howard Sasportas; *The Lunation Cycle: A Key To The Understanding of Personality*, by Dane Rudhyar; *Finding Our way Through The Dark*, by Demetra George.

• Video: *Do We Need The Moon?* BBC (58:54 minutes) This documentary is long but well worth it for a clearer understanding of the Moon's energy and her impact on Earth. *The Asch Conformity Experiment* [69](5:47); *The Milgram Experiment* [70] (10:47)

---

[69] YouTube video at https://www.youtube.com/watch?v=NyDDyT1IDhA Accessed December 7th 2019.

[70] YouTube video at https://www.youtube.com/watch?v=y6GxIuIjT3w Accessed December 7th 2019.

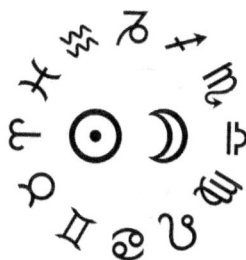

12. The Moon's Nodes

In the previous chapter we took an in-depth look at The Moon in our Soul Astrology. Another way we can see the Moon's influence in our life is to look to the Lunar Nodal Axis. The Lunar Nodal Axis doesn't refer to the Moon itself but rather the Moon's passage through the sky and it's relationship to the Sun, most importantly the two points where the Moon's path intersects the ecliptic (the path of the Sun). This is the point in the sky where two paths cross (the path of the Sun and the path of the Moon).

The Moon's Nodes and Our Soul Path

When interpreting the Moon's Nodes in our Soul Astrology we need to be very clear which astrological system we are using because Indian or Vedic astrology ascribes a different meaning than Western Astrology. Even within Western Astrology, when we are studying Soul Astrology based on the teachings of The Tibetan in *Esoteric Astrology* it is important to clarify the role of the Moon's Nodes. Some Western astrological schools teach the Nodal Axis as an indicator of the Soul's Path[71], whereas in Soul Astrology we use the Ascendant to indicate the Soul's path and purpose[72]. So therefore, in Soul Astrology, what significance do we ascribe to the Moon's Nodes?

---

[71] See "*Evolutionary Astrology: How Our Nodal Axis Defines the Soul's Path*" online at https://llewellyn.com/journal/article/2365

[72] See chapter four.

Before looking at the significance of the Moon's nodes, let's be clear what we are talking about. The Moon doesn't have 'nodes' as such, meaning they aren't physical, tangible, things! The lunar nodes are astrological points: points in space where the Moon's path crosses the path of the ecliptic (the apparent path of the Sun across the sky) so for me there is the first clue to how we should approach their interpretation (we are talking about an energetic path or direction, rather than an embodiment of energy). They can be regarded as "trail markers" pointing to a well-worn path. The second clue is they intersect the path of the Sun, meaning they want our attention.

The Moon's Nodes are a "heads up" for our spiritual journey, because they are showing us where we have recurring patterns that can potentially limit our experience to the mundane (worldly affairs) and keep our attention stuck at the personality level. The South Node is associated with the past, while the North Node is associated with the future. So depending upon whether we are talking about the South Node (SN) of the North Node (NN) we could be talking about either a well-worn path (SN) or a new direction (NN).

In short, the Lunar Nodes *symbolize our choice between growth and stagnation - evolution or entropy*.

Revision: Personality vs. Soul

Since Soul Astrology is all about the process of personality-Soul fusion[73] as described by the Tibetan in *Esoteric Astrology*, before studying the Lunar Nodal Axis, it is worth grounding back in with two fundamental questions so that we may understand if, and how, studying the Moon's Nodes can support us in that process. So before going further into the Moon's Nodes we need to stop and check in with ourselves:

Where do you now stand, in your understanding of these two questions:

- What is personality?
- What is Soul?

Make some notes in your journal, about your current understanding of personality and Soul. Revise chapters one and two in *Soul*

---

[73] See chapter two.

The Moon's Nodes

Astrology[74]. Read more about personality, Soul and the process of personality-Soul fusion in chapter two.

The answers to these questions will become important as you continue studying the Moon's Nodes from a broader perspective, taking into account other astrologer's interpretations (as we discuss below). The clearer you are on the distinctions between personality and Soul, the clearer you will be in your understanding of the Lunar Nodal axis from a Soul Astrology perspective.

Differences in Interpretation

If you search the internet there is probably more contradiction about the meaning of the lunar nodes than any other astrological significator, which makes it quite difficult for people who are learning astrology themselves using search engines as their main source of information. The reason we are mentioning this here is because, in your studies, you will read articles and books from valid and respected sources suggesting that the Lunar Nodes indicate your Soul's Path, whereas in Soul Astrology we use the Ascendant to determine the Soul's Path.

First of all it is important to know which astrological system you are using, because not all schools of astrology agree with one another in terms of interpretation, and different cosmologies often don't mix. Until relatively recently, the lunar nodes didn't feature too highly in Western Astrology, although they had been used for many years in Vedic Astrology[75] as *Rahu* and *Ketu*, the dragon's head and tail. In Vedic Astrology they have a specific meaning, and it is unwise to take an interpretation out of context from one astrological system and try to transplant it into another, where it is likely to become distorted.

In Soul Astrology we need to be very clear about how we are interpreting the lunar nodes, relative to our Soul's journey. The different interpretations of the Lunar Nodal axis could be potentially confusing, which is why it is important whenever possible to

---

[74] Hadikin, R. (2016) *Soul Astrology: How Your Rising Sign Reveals Your Soul Path and Life Purpose*. Ruth Hadikin Associates. Order online at https://soulastrologybook.com

[75] See Hindu Astrology on Wikipedia at https://en.wikipedia.org/wiki/Hindu_astrology

approach your Soul Astrology from the place known by the Tibetans as *clear light mind*[76]. This reinforces the importance of meditation to still the 'monkey mind' and access Higher Mind (clear light)! Once you have access to clear light mind, your intuition will be your guiding light.

From our current level of consciousness it is not possible to fully perceive the Soul, and we all have a tendency to project our ego onto the Soul, thinking of it as an extension of our personality. In chapter nine we discussed how, in the Tibetan system a distinction is made between *clear light mind* and *karmic mind. Clear light mind would be the level of Soul, while karmic mind is our ego-personality.*

In discussing the Moon's Nodes, some contemporary astrologers have noted that they are indicators of karmic patterns and conclude that because of this they must therefore be pointing to our Soul Path. For clarification, from a Soul Astrology perspective based on the Tibetan tradition and the teachings of the Tibetan through Alice Bailey, we could perhaps agree that the lunar nodes are significant indicators of our karmic patterns, but karmic patterns are not our Soul's true nature because they are not of the nature of clear light.

Indeed, if the Moon's Nodes are indicators of our karmic conditioning then (from a Tibetan viewpoint) they would be revealing aspects of our ego-personality. They are therefore revealing the obstacles that prevent us from directly perceiving our Soul's true nature! So from a Soul Astrology perspective it might be better to say that the Moon's Nodes indicate past-life patterns that we are here to heal and release so our pure Soul light can shine through.

Western astrologers are currently doing some very important work in clarifying the meaning of the lunar nodes and once we are clear about the distinction between our true nature (Ascendant), and karmic patterns (Moon's Nodes), we may then use this growing body of knowledge about the Lunar Nodes to bring us deeper understanding of our karmic conditioning, relative to the society we were born into.

The Nodal Axis and Collective Consciousness

The Nodal Axis takes about 18.6 years to complete a cycle, which

---

[76] See the Tibetan Buddhist definition of "clear light' at http://www.rigpawiki.org/index.php?title=Clear_light

means that the Moon's nodes remain in the same sign for roughly seventeen to eighteen months (the Moon's cycle is erratic so the nodal axis doesn't remain in a sign for an exact period of time). This means that a great number of people born within that timeframe will all have their North and South nodes in the same signs. This suggests that the meaning is somewhat collective in nature. A group of Souls born with the same Nodal signs will have different individual Soul paths (Ascendants) however they will have some shared karma on a collective level, indicated by their nodal axis.

North Node - Indicator of Dharma

According to Soul Astrologer Alan Oken[77] the Nodal Axis always represents a person's relationship to the collective consciousness and, as such, it tells us something about our role in the society to which we were born.

How the society sees us, and what the society expects from us, can be determined by the sign and house positions of the nodal axis. The nodal axis itself is saying something about our relationship with the society into which we were born, while the North Node is specifically indicating how we may be of service to humanity, and something about our *dharma*[78] or spiritual purpose in this lifetime.

The Moon's Nodes and Karma Yoga

The nodal axis therefore seems to be what the society is asking from us: what the society is calling forth from us, in a sense what roles we are required to play. In some spiritual traditions this aligns with the principle of *karma yoga*[79] - the spiritual practice of consciously meeting our karma head on, so that we become aware of what we need to purify and heal in this lifetime, so that we may advance spiritually.

In terms of our Soul Astrology this can also be seen as a kind of spiritual prescription that helps us to break free from old patterns of familial and societal conditioning.

---

[77] https://alanoken.com

[78] See the definition of dharma in chapter one.

[79] See definition of karma yoga on Wikipedia at https://en.wikipedia.org/wiki/Karma_yoga

The South Node - Your Familiar Comfort Zone

The South Node is often seen as the familiar old path. Old patterns and roles that you have become very comfortable with, even skilled and proficient. If you continue to follow that path you may still make a valid and valuable contribution to the world, but would you grow? Because it indicates an area of life that you are somewhat complete with, it is thought that there are few lessons left for you to learn. So following the path of the South Node could keep you stuck in your own past, like a virtuoso violinist who just keeps playing the same old familiar piece - so he or she is not pushing his own growth edge.

The South Node is sometimes called the path of least resistance. This is the familiar and well-worn path that you may have walked for many lifetimes.

The North Node - Your Spiritual Prescription

In contrast the path of the North Node is often called the path of resistance. If you choose this path it won't be easy, simply because it is unfamiliar territory and you don't yet have the necessary skills. Yet it may also be exactly where your Soul wants you to go. It is thought that if you do choose this path, if you do accept the challenge of your North Node, then you will be sent teachers and guides to show you the way.

If you choose this path, this is the path that could bring you new experiences, deep insights, and awareness that awaken you even more to your Soul's presence. As such, the North Node is like a spiritual 'prescription' indicating the 'best medicine' to support your healing, growth, and Soul Awareness.

Example: South Node in Virgo - North Node in Pisces

For example if you have your lunar south Node in Virgo, you may be very comfortable being hands-on and practical in your spiritual journey: flowing love into the world by running the soup kitchen and giving practical support to others, because you have played a similar role in society so often in many of your past lives. Nothing wrong in that, but you need to be careful that in this lifetime it isn't distracting you from what you need to do to progress, in terms of your current spiritual development and growth.

In this example the North Node in Pisces is calling you to walk a less familiar path by lifting your head up, and seeing the big picture: to have some real transcendental experiences of "spiritual awakening" through meditation or devotional practices, so that you experience Divinity for yourself, and realize your own true nature as a spiritually awake and aware being. Running the soup kitchen is very commendable, but will not in itself, lead you to true spiritual awakening.

Where is Your Life Calling You?

Now take a look at your own natal chart and see, by sign and house, where the nodal axis lies in your chart. Some charts show only the North Node, which looks like a horseshoe (see the picture above). The South Node is always exactly 180° opposite, so if your North Node is at 10° Gemini your South Node is 10° Sagittarius. Make some notes in your journal about how you experience your South Node (note the qualities and characteristics of the sign, and the life activities of the house). Now take a look at your North Node by sign and house. Jot down some ideas of where it may be calling you.

What might your life look like if you followed your own spiritual prescription: the path of your North Node?

When the Lunar Nodal Axis Shifts, Humanity Shifts.

The Lunar Nodes tell us about our spiritual journey. On a personal level they indicate a well worn path, patterns of behavior that we need to change if we are to set ourselves free of karmic conditioning, and move towards spiritual liberation and enlightenment. On a collective level, they can tell us about the current values and priorities in the collective consciousness of humanity. When the Lunar Nodal Axis shifts, this can be reflected in a deep shift in values on a collective level.

Example: from Austerity in Virgo to Individual Rights in Leo

From November 2015 to April 2017, the lunar North Node had been in 'frugal' Virgo. During this time in the UK the governing Conservative Party forged ahead with a policy of 'austerity' (where there was tight control and limits placed on public spending) designed to boost the British economy. On May 9th 2017, the lunar nodes shifted from the Virgo-Pisces axis, to the Leo-Aquarius axis (where they remained until November 7th 2018).

On June 8th 2017, the lunar North Node had been in 'individualistic' Leo for just under one month (Leo always stands up for the individual, asking 'what about me?'). Theresa May, the UK Prime Minister at that time, called an election to demonstrate that she had public support for her Government's policies. Her strategy backfired. Not only did her government lose their majority (indicating a lack of public support) but the following 18-month period saw mounting public outcry and protests at the impact of austerity on individual health, rights and freedoms (Leo). In October 2018 UK Prime Minister Theresa May declared an end to austerity: one month before the North Node was set to shift again, this time from 'individualistic' Leo into 'nurturing' Cancer.

Collectively the Moon's Nodes are like a barometer, indicating the current condition of humanity on a collective level, and what we are working on balancing in our society so that we collectively shift to the next level, the next turn on the evolutionary spiral.

Our nodal axis is therefore also a reminder that, although we can act independently, we cannot act in isolation - our actions have a ripple effect throughout the consciousness of humanity.

What happens when the North Node and Ascendant are in the same sign?[80]

In this case, there is increased potential for the individual concerned to transcend the personality vibration of the sign and shift into alignment, spiritual awakening and personality-Soul fusion. For this to happen, the individual still has to choose the path that is presented to them, shift their attention inwards, and be open to developing their senses and perceptual capacity. Again, just like a prescription, in this case it might have a faster effect, but only if you take all the medicine!

Once you choose a spiritual path or practice, as indicated by your North Node, this maximizes the potential for you to not only hear your Soul's calling, but to transcend the personality attachments of the sign and give full expression to the Soul vibration of the sign. The North node in this position indicates that of all the possible

---

[80] This question was originally posed by Pat Paquette of RealAstrologers.com You can read my original response on her website at
https://realastrologers.com/2011/01/22/the-lunar-north-node-and-your-spiritual-journey/

spiritual paths and teachers available, one that invites the individual to develop these qualities would be most effective. However, our focus must always be one of going within, if we are to make spiritual progress.

For example, let's say the North Node and Ascendant are both in Gemini. The personality ruler of Gemini is Mercury, but the Soul ruler is Venus. Both planets are said to have a lower and higher vibration. Well, to be more accurate, it's the same energy but is perceived differently, depending upon the individual's level of consciousness and perception. Depending upon your own degree of spiritual progress, you would be more influenced by the personality ruler or the Soul ruler of that sign.

So through undertaking typical Gemini activities of writing, speaking, and communicating, a spiritually inclined individual could gradually experience a spiritual opening. There is the potential to experience a shift in their perception from the purely rational mind, with its lower Mercurial qualities of merely "passing along information," to a place where they integrate their higher, intuitive mind and the higher purpose of Mercury: opening themselves more fully to intuition and creating a bridge to higher mind. As a result they will develop an ability to perceive, receive and convey the higher Venusian vibrations of transpersonal, unconditional, Love and right relations.

Our spiritual journey is one of exploring our inner world, opening our heart and mind to higher possibilities and recognizing Divinity, within ourselves. The very word *esoteric* derives from the Greek root *eso*, which means *within*[81].

Soul Astrology and Esoteric Astrology describe the Astrology of our inner world, our spiritual journey. Given that our personality is a mask we wear to interact with the outside world, when we begin to move deeply inwards on our Soul Journey, it stands to reason that our Natal Chart takes on a deeper significance.

"I hope that you understand what the word "spiritual" really means. It means to search for, to investigate, the true nature of the mind. There's nothing spiritual outside.

---

[81] In contrast, *exoteric* astrology is derived from the Greek root *oxo*, which means *inclined outwards*.

> *My rosary isn't spiritual; my robes aren't spiritual.*
> *Spiritual means the mind,*
> *and spiritual people are those who seek its nature."*
>
> - Lama Thubten Yeshe

In an earlier chapter we mentioned how, in terms of our spiritual development, The Tibetan taught that each of us is either on the *Mutable Cross*, the *Fixed Cross* or the *Cardinal Cross*[82]. The Mutable Cross means we are wholly personality-driven, with no experience of our Soul. The Fixed Cross means we are awakening, and although we are still largely personality-driven, we're beginning to awaken and have some Soul Awareness. Those on the Cardinal Cross are fully awakened in that they have completed the process of Soul Integration; the fusion of Soul and personality is complete, and they are Soul-Centered Beings.

Few people on the planet are on the Cardinal Cross, and those that are, are highly enlightened spiritual teachers. However, many of us are beginning the journey from the Mutable Cross to the Fixed Cross as we go deeper into our spiritual journey and seek to experience for ourselves the truth of our Soul.

There is no way for an Astrologer to tell just by looking at a chart whether a Soul is on the Mutable, Fixed or Cardinal Cross. This can only be deduced by learning about the character of the person and through the use of intuition. For example we might deduce that someone like the Dalai Lama would be on the Cardinal Cross, because of his highly developed spiritual realizations, but in reality only he would know.

The purpose of our spiritual journey is to progress from the externally-focused Mutable Cross, with its emphasis solely on personality, to the internally-focused Cardinal Cross, in which we have full fusion of personality and Soul. It is a very gradual, inner journey, and the lunar North Node is acting as a pointer to steer us away from repeating habits that could keep us attached to personality and stuck on the Mutable Cross for longer than we need to be.

It is time to wake up and evolve. It is a challenge, and there are no guarantees. We can still get it wrong if we undertake North Node

---

[82] Also read about the three crosses in chapter eight.

activity in a very externally-focused and personality driven way, with our attention "inclined outwards!" Your North Node is pointing the way to avoid repeating past habits, and this will be most effective if you also shift your focus and "incline inwards." To benefit fully, you need to keep turning your attention inwards and familiarize yourself with your inner world.

The Moon's Nodes Through The Signs and Houses

In looking at the Moon's Nodes through the signs and houses remember that the signs are indicators of behavior patterns while the house positions show in which areas of your life these patterns will manifest. The south node shows repeating past-life patterns or tendencies that you are ready to leave behind, and the north node shows a path, antidote, or 'prescription' to help you break free from habitual patterns so you can grow and evolve. I have intentionally taken a more spiritual approach to the path of the North Node, that will hopefully support you in your journey of spiritual awakening.

As with everything to do with the Moon, you are invited to be gentle and compassionate with yourself when exploring these patterns. They were formed in past lives when your circumstances may have been a great deal harsher than they are now. You may be dealing with past life trauma and wounding that requires your gentle loving kindness to facilitate your healing journey.

The Moon's Nodes Through The Signs

Aries North Node

With an Aries North Node you would benefit from spiritual paths and practices that support you in cultivating your independence. You are here to create your own spiritual pathway – to learn to trust your own intuition and follow your heart. This is extremely important so that you understand the deeper significance of individuality, within the Divine Order of Nature.

Libra South Node

In past lives you may have become overly dependent on others by avoiding difficult choices and letting others make decisions for you. In this life you're beginning to see how this habit can lead to dependency, and are learning to make choices that lead you to greater independence.

Taurus North Node

With a Taurus North Node you will benefit from spiritual paths and practices that encourage you to let go of desire, including 'spiritual seeking' and invite you to recognize spiritual truth right here and now, in your everyday life. An important part of this path is to cultivate your own resources so that you have a solid foundation and aren't overly dependent on the resources of others.

Scorpio South Node

Past life patterns may include covetousness, lust and seduction, misusing one's personal magnetism to bend others to one's will. In this life you're releasing this 'grasping' energy as you realize the truth that everything you need is already within you and that, in terms of your spiritual nature, it is not possible for others to have something that you do not.

Gemini North Node

With a Gemini North Node you would benefit from studying a broad range of wisdom traditions, knowledge systems and going deeper with spiritual and/or psychological methods that give you experience of resolving dualities and polarities. Practices such as Zen which use the practice of riddles and koans, to confound the mind are beneficial because they loosen fixed ideas, reduce any tendency toward fixed opinions or mental arrogance, and open us up to experiences of going beyond mind.

Sagittarius South Node

Past life patterns may include mental arrogance, dogma and blind pursuit of religious ideals. In this life you're learning to question your beliefs and to understand higher truth by having diversity in your activities and life experiences.

Cancer North Node

With the Lunar North Node in Cancer this indicates that you would benefit greatly from spiritual paths and practices that expand your perception, increase your capacity for 'sensing' your spiritual energies and your Soul, build up your reserves of spiritual energy and bring you into deeper experience of your own spiritual nature.

Capricorn South Node

Past life patterns may include the ruthless pursuit of one's own ambitions with little regard for others, and an attitude of dominating or stepping on others in order to reach your goals. In this life you are learning the importance of developing compassion for others you meet on your journey.

Leo North Node

With a Leo North Node you would benefit from spiritual and/or psychological methods that encourage you to seek your true self and find your own way. Ramana Maharshi sat in meditation for many years simply asking of himself this one question: "Who Am I?"

Aquarius South Node

Past life patterns may include self-absorption, entitlement and distancing oneself from others due to feelings of, and a mistaken belief in, one's own superiority. In this life you are realizing the innate value of every individual as a spiritual being.

Virgo North Node

With a lunar North Node in Virgo this indicates that you would benefit from spiritual and/or psychological methods that have a practical, methodical or ritualistic component to them that supports you in becoming more aware of how you flow your energy. This will help you to keep your focus on flowing spiritual energy into the world in practical yet loving ways.

Pisces South Node

Past life patterns may include victimhood whereby one blames others rather than taking personal responsibility. There can be feelings of entrapment and strong tendencies towards all form of escapism, through alcohol, drugs, movies, games and/or other fantasy pursuits. In this life you are learning to take personal responsibility by developing awareness of your own needs and cultivating the skills to get them met.

Libra North Node

With a Libra North Node you would benefit from spiritual and/or psychological paths that invite you to explore relationship, as a spiritual path. The essence of Libra is right relationship, and artful use of harmonics.

Aries South Node

Past life patterns may include extreme self-assertion to the point of selfishness and/ or aggression. In this life you are learning to take other's needs into account to break past-life patterns of self-absorption and self-centeredness.

Scorpio North Node

With a Scorpio North Node you would benefit from releasing attachment to material wealth and power, and following a spiritual path that encourages you to deepen your Quest for Self knowledge.

Indeed it is the very nature of your mind, the nature of Self and the true nature of your Soul that you would gain most benefit from understanding.

Taurus South Node

Past life patterns may include an over-emphasis on materialism, attachment to possessions and to securing one's position through material wealth. In this lifetime you are learning that you won't die if you release your grip on material 'things', and that your true wealth is within.

Sagittarius North Node

With your Lunar North Node in Sagittarius you would benefit from choosing one spiritual practice or method and going deep, staying with it to the end of the line. This position indicates that in past lives you have studied with many different teachers, and explored many different paths.

Gemini South Node

Past life patterns may include dissipating your energy through a lack of focus, and engaging in too many diverse projects at a superficial level. In this life you are learning to focus on one project at a time in order to stabilize the energy and build up your power.

Capricorn North Node

When the North Node is Capricorn you would benefit from following a specific path, methodically, and studying Ancient Wisdom in depth. Patience, discipline, and single-pointed focus are your allies as you slowly and surely progress up the mountain to spiritual enlightenment.

Cancer South Node

Past life patterns may include acquisitiveness, clinginess and an emotionally needy self-centeredness. In this life you are developing emotional resilience, and learning the inner strength that comes from the deep understanding that other people cannot meet your emotional needs.

Aquarius North Node

When the Lunar North Node is in Aquarius you will benefit from spiritual and/or psychological methods that invite you to dedicate your personal energies for the benefit of humanity, without draining yourself.

Leo South Node

Past life patterns may include misuse of power, pomposity, ego-centricity and self-aggrandizement. In this life you are learning deep lessons of interdependence so that you understand how your greatest power is really the power of the collective, that comes from the brotherhood and sisterhood of humanity.

Pisces North Node

With a lunar North Node in Pisces, you would benefit greatly from methods that introduce you to personal experience of oneness and deep connection with Divinity. This might mean first using visualization and meditative techniques that bring you to an understanding of the power of your imagination to change your feeling state, and thereby your perception of reality. This allows you to connect with the real tangible essence of life that flows through everything.

Virgo South Node

Past life patterns may include perfectionism, overwork and excessive judgment and/or criticism. In this life you are learning to accept life in all its imperfection, and realizing the deep spiritual truth of what is known in the Tibetan tradition as *The Great Perfection*[83]: that all really is already perfect, just as it is.

House Axis Themes

When we speak of a nodal axis, we are speaking about a pair of opposites. Just as the 12 Zodiac Signs are arranged in six pairs of opposite signs, so the houses are also arranged into six dynamic pairs. So for example the First House is directly opposite the seventh, the second house is opposite the eighth and so on.

As with all opposites, we are always dealing with the same energy, just at different ends of the spectrum. Each pair on a house axis is therefore dealing with a specific theme, and the individual house will tell us where we stand in relation to that theme.

For example, with the second-eighth house axis the theme is resources. If my focus is on the second house, my attention is on my resources, whereas if my focus is on the eighth house it is on other people's resources. Same theme, different perspective.

A foundational concept in Soul Astrology is *the integration of polarities*, or opposites, as part of our journey to wholeness through personality-Soul fusion.

When we start to study the Lunar Nodal Axis in our horoscope, in addition to considering the meaning and significance of the North and South lunar nodes individually, we should never lose sight of the fact that we are always dealing with a polarity that is ready to be healed and integrated, as part of our ongoing journey of spiritual awakening[84].

---

[83] *"The Great Perfection (in Tibetan sDzogs chen), is a philosophical and meditative teaching in Tibetan Buddhism. Its parallel in Chinese Buddhism isCh'an, and Zen in the Japanese Buddhist tradition".* Karmay, S. G. (2007) *Dzogchen: A Philosophical and Meditative Teaching of Tibetan Buddhism.* Brill, Leiden, Boston.

[84] Read more about the integration of polarities in *Soul Astrology,* chapter four: *The Integration Process.*

The Moon's Nodes

The house axis where your Lunar Nodal Axis falls, is therefore indicating a major karmic theme that you are working on healing in this lifetime.

Table of House Axis Themes

Houses 1-7 = identity

Houses 2-8 = resources

Houses 3-9 = intellect

Houses 4-10 = security

Houses 5-11 = expression

Houses 6-12 = service

The Moon's Nodes Through The Houses

North Node in the 1st: South Node in the 7th

Life's circumstances will create the conditions for you to release past-life patterns of dependence on others, so you can discover and cultivate independence.

North Node in the 2nd: South Node in the 8th

Life's circumstances will create the conditions for you to release past-life patterns of relying on other people's money and resources, so you can develop your own powers of attraction.

North Node in the 3rd: South Node in the 9th

Life's circumstances will create the conditions for you to release past-life patterns of dogmatic belief, dreaming, and blind faith, so you can cultivate logic, reason and a realistic attitude to analyzing your immediate surroundings and problems.

North Node in the 4th: South Node in the 10th

Life's circumstances will create the conditions for you to release past-life patterns of outwardly seeking achievement, ambition and public recognition, so you can go deeper in your spiritual journey and quietly find your sense of contentment and inner peace at home, within yourself.

North Node in the 5th: South Node in the 11th

Life's circumstances will create the conditions for you to release past-life patterns of dependence on others, so you can discover your own willpower and find fulfillment in your own creative self-expression.

North Node in the 6th: South Node in the 12th

Life's circumstances will create the conditions for you to release past-life patterns of isolation and separation, so you may discover the deep insights and understanding that only come through authentic self-less service to others.

North Node in the 7th: South Node in the 1st

Life's circumstances will create the conditions for you to release past-life patterns of excessive independence by providing opportunities for balance through partnerships, collaboration, and co-operation with others.

North Node in the 8th: South Node in the 2nd

Life's circumstances will create the conditions for you to release subconscious past-life patterns of excessively acquiring personal wealth and resources (as a form of self-protection) by providing opportunities for you to support others in developing their own resources.

North Node in the 9th: South Node in the 3rd

Life's circumstances will create the conditions for you to release past-life patterns of narrow-mindedness and attachment to the lower intellect through familial conditioning, by providing opportunities for you to experience higher mind and higher consciousness through travel and exposure to people from vastly different cultures than your own.

North Node in the 10th: South Node in the 4th

Life's circumstances will create the conditions for you to release past-life patterns of lifetimes spent in spiritual retreat, so you may bring your mastery and spiritual wisdom out into the world for the benefit of others.

North Node in the 11th: South Node in the 5th

Life's circumstances will create the conditions for you to release past-life patterns of hedonism and avoiding responsibility, by providing opportunities for you to work with groups where you may experience the sense of satisfaction and community that comes from pursuing shared goals and humanitarian ideals with like-minded people.

North Node in the 12th: South Node in the 6th

Life's circumstances will create the conditions for you to release past-life patterns of disease due to worry and obsessive thinking, by providing opportunities for you to clear the subconscious karmic patterns within your own psyche that are the root cause of such disease. You may then be of service and reduce the suffering of others by teaching them how to do the same.

Are You Approaching Through Personality or Clear Light Mind?

When it comes to your personal journey of spiritual awakening, you cannot measure your progress by astrology alone. This is why I keep emphasizing how important it is to make meditation and mindfulness an integral part of your life. Your deepest insights will come from within, which is what esoteric (inner) astrology is all about.

I mention this important point here because, as with everything else in astrology, if you approach the subject of the Moon's Nodes purely from the perspective of the personality, it will not advance you in your spiritual journey one bit.

For example, if you do have South Node in Pisces, and North Node in Virgo, as we discussed above, your past lives may have been dominated by Piscean themes: slavery, addiction, victimhood, and escapism. The key to breaking the habits of the past, are to move towards the Virgo North Node, but if you do this mindlessly, purely from the materialistic view of the personality, you could just become distracted by Virgo themes: striving for perfectionism, excessive criticism, overwork, bogged down in minutiae etc.

There is nothing inherent in a Virgo personality that will catapult you into spiritual enlightenment, in fact you can just as easily be distracted from your spiritual path by Pisces OR Virgo activities. Simply replacing a Pisces personality with a Virgo personality is not spiritual! Remember that the Lunar Nodal Axis is another polarity, to be integrated on your journey to personality-Soul fusion. So you don't want to find yourself stuck at either extreme, but rather by integrating the pair you can shift to the highest expression of both signs.

In moving toward the path of your North Node then, the best way to prevent it from becoming another distraction from your path, is to consciously choose to take a spiritual approach (which is why I described the North Node descriptions above within a spiritual perspective). Thanks to the internet, we now have open access to information more than any other previous generation. This means you can thoroughly investigate all the various spiritual paths and traditions. You are in a position to be able to consciously choose spiritual paths and practices that will support you in shifting to the highest octave of your North Node.

In making choices, the best way is to access your intuition by connecting with what the Tibetans call the "mind of Clear Light". This clear light mind is your true nature. It is the pure awareness that is beyond thought. It is not something you have to go and get from somewhere, or something you have to work hard at creating. It is already there within you, but mostly we don't notice it because we are busy following our thoughts. The more we meditate and allow the thinking mind to settle, the more the clear light mind becomes apparent. It is the part of you that is always aware. The part of you that is aware that you are reading this.

Spending some time each day, accessing clear light mind and simply resting in that pure awareness, will greatly enhance and accelerate your understanding of your Soul Astrology. It is from there that you should approach your studies of the North Nodes, then your own inner light will illuminate your path through the confusion.

Suggested Fieldwork

• Deeper Self-observation. Take out your own horoscope (natal chart) and in your reflective journal - make a note of which signs and houses the Lunar Nodes occupy in your chart. Read the descriptions above and meditate on the qualities of the Moon's Nodes. Record your impressions and insights in your reflective journal.

• Further Reading: continue your studies of The Moon from the previous chapter.

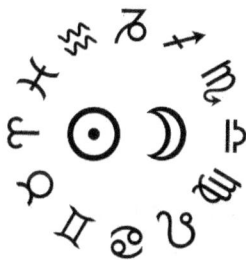

13. Aspects

The Geometry of Aspects

Aspects are the 'geometry' of your chart. They are the relationships between planets and points in your chart based on their geometric angle. So, for example, two planets at a 60° angle to one another are said to be 'sextile'. 'Sext' is the Latin numeral prefix for the number six. Within a circle there are six points at 60° angles to each other and if we drew a line between them we would get a six-sided shape: a hexagon (see picture above).

The term aspect refers to an angle between two planets, points (like your Rising Sign or MC) or a planet and a point. Where more than two planets or points are involved they can form an aspect pattern. In *Esoteric Astrology* The Tibetan places huge emphasis on the science of triangles. Triangles are indeed one of the patterns formed by aspects, and aspects can also form other shapes. It is quite rare but if we found six sextiles in a chart it is possible they could form a hexagon shape. In astrology this is called a Grand Sextile (they are also known by other names such as the Star of David).

But now we're getting ahead of ourselves! Aspect patterns are quite complex and getting to know the meaning of the major aspect patterns in your chart can take many years of study and self-observation, but you can begin by knowing what the major aspects are, and what they mean.

How You Flow Your Energy

Aspects indicate how light and energy flows. In terms of your own Soul Astrology, aspects are an important factor showing how your energy flows into the world. We can understand a lot about aspects if we know how water flows (or not).

Flowing Like Water

Nature always takes the path of least resistance. So as water flows down a mountainside on its journey back to the ocean, it will form tiny streams that eventually become raging rivers and open meandering plains. The journey of water takes many shapes because water simply flows around things. Water always gravitates to the lowest point, and just flows around any obstacles in its way.

In addition to thinking about physical energy flowing like water, it is also important when considering aspects, to have some understanding of how light behaves and how angles affect light. For example a prism is an object with polished sides that changes the angle of the light passing through by a process known as *refraction*[85]. Some prisms are also able to *disperse*[86] light, which means they can separate visible white light into its component colored rays.

Bouncing Light

Photographers among you may be familiar with the technique of *bouncing light*[87], whereby light is 'bounced' of an object to illuminate the subject. We do not need to go too much into the mathematics of these processes, but it is simply enough to understand how different conditions will affect how light flows and is received. When considering aspects it is important to remember that we are dealing with light and energy, and to remember the various ways light and energy will react and respond in different environments. Aspects in astrology create an environment that affects how light and energy

---

[85] See explanation of refraction at https://en.wikipedia.org/wiki/Refraction

[86] See how prisms disperse light at https://www.physicsclassroom.com/class/refrn/Lesson-4/Dispersion-of-Light-by-Prisms

[87] Learn more about the photographic technique of bouncing light at https://www.lightstalking.com/12-simple-ways-to-bounce-light-and-capture-better-portraits/

flows. When you become familiar with your aspects, you'll know how light 'bounces' around in your life (or not)!

If we look at a birth chart we can see how some angles would be more conducive to the flow of energy and light, while others would make it more difficult for the energy to flow easily. There are many possible angles in a 360° circle but for astrological purposes some are considered more important than others. Therefore aspects are divided into 'major' and 'minor' aspects - the 'major' aspects being those that are considered to be of most significance.

Allowed Orbs

Before going further you might also hear astrologers talking about an 'allowed orb'. This is where we look at how close an aspect can be before it is really considered valid or not, in terms of it's ability to influence the energy. So with a sextile for example we can usually allow about 4° and still consider it valid. With oppositions and squares we might allow 8° or more and they can still be valid in terms of their effects on the individual's life experience.

Major Aspects

Now let's look at the major aspects that you might find in your birth chart and see whether they are considered 'easy' or 'difficult' in terms of the energy flowing between them:

Conjunction (0-8°): This is where two planets or points are so close that their energies blend and merge. This can be positive or negative effects depending on the nature of the planets involved.

Opposition (180°): This is where the two objects are directly opposite each other in the chart. The energy can swing between the two like a pendulum. It is considered challenging for the personality because the task ahead for the individual is to integrate the energies involved. Although from a Soul-Centered perspective this can be a very positive experience, because one learns to address and integrate polarities!

Square (90°): This is considered a challenging aspect. On a personality level we may experience obstacles, setbacks, feeling stuck, or like Murphy's Law[88] things just don't turn out the way we

---

[88] Murphy's Law suggests that anything that can go wrong, will go wrong! See https://en.wikipedia.org/wiki/Murphy's_law

would want. From a Soul-Centered perspective, rising to the challenge of our squares can be an amazing catalyst for our Soul's growth.

Trine (120°): This is considered an easy aspect where the energies flow easily. This is considered easy for the personality because we can find that things turn out as expected or people show up that support us and we can make easy progress in the areas concerned. From a Soul-Centered perspective this can be a good thing if we stay focused and determined, but it can also lead to a lack of Soul growth. If things always come to us easily we may never be challenged to develop new skills, seek new horizons or use our creativity!

Sextile (60°): This is also considered an easy aspect where the two planets or points work harmoniously together. A keyword for sextiles is harmony and the two objects concerned will find it relatively easy to harmonize.

In interpreting aspects we also have to take into account the sign and house positions of the two planets (or points) involved, and whether they have a natural affinity.

For example Venus and Jupiter naturally go well together and are both generally beneficial so even if you have a very challenging aspect such as a tight square, the worst that could happen is too much of a good thing, so you may get an exaggeration of their traits resulting in self-indulgence, or an over-inflated ego.

When the two planets don't naturally align with one another it's a different story. For example, Mars square Saturn. Mars is the planet of individual self-assertion, Saturn is the planet of limitation and responsibility. Mars says go, Saturn says no. A square is one of the most challenging aspects, so a Mars-Saturn square has been described as trying to drive with the brakes on.

The specific signs and houses would tell you more about the energy involved and in what area of life the challenge is experienced, but the feeling is always going to be a sense of trying to move forward while at the same time being held back.

There are thousands of potential combinations of aspects so we couldn't possibly cover them all here. In learning your own aspects, it is better to start with the most common aspects listed above, and (at least to begin with) look only at the aspects to your Sun, Moon and Rising Sign.

The Science of Triangles

In *Esoteric Astrology* The Tibetan emphasizes the importance for astrologers of the future to understand what he refers to as the *science of triangles*. What might he mean by this?

When we study 'aspects' we're simply looking at the relationship between planets and points[89] in your birth chart, based on the degree of the angle between them. We only need *two planets or points in relationship to one another* in this way to form an aspect.

Aspect Patterns

Where *three or more planets or points* are involved, aspects can also form patterns, and the most basic pattern of all is a triangle. Aspect patterns can also be considered harmonious or challenging, some examples you may have heard of are Grand Trines and T-squares. Understanding and interpreting aspects and aspect patterns forms a large part of the astrologer's art. I remember thinking the first time I saw the aspects and patterns on my chart, how it just looked like a ball of string that a cat has been playing with and tangled around the furniture!

It takes time and experience to begin to see the meaning of aspects and aspect patterns in your chart, and I believe The Tibetan is also referring to something much more than just interpreting two-dimensional patterns on a chart. As with everything else in *Esoteric Astrology*, he is talking about *energy and energy dynamics*. Remember, your two-dimensional birth chart is only a symbol of your energy field. So when we start looking at aspects and patterns in your chart, how does that relate to your energy field?

Imagine two pegs in the ground with a piece of string tied between the two of them: two points connected by a single line of energy. This is what an aspect is like. If we add a third peg, and run a string around all three, we have created a *field of energy*. We have the line of energy and the area contained within. This is what an *aspect pattern* is like. When studying aspect patterns we not only look at the energy running between the points, but we must also consider what kind of energy field is being created.

---

[89] Points are factors in your chart that, even though they aren't planets, they are still important such as your Rising Sign, midheaven etc.

When we have an aspect in our chart, we have an energy that is running between two planets or points in the chart. The harmonious or challenging nature of the aspect will tell us more about how we are running that energy in our lives. When we have an aspect pattern in our chart, we not only have the energy running between three or more planets or points but we also have the energetic field contained within their boundary. Understanding the nature of aspect patterns begins to make more sense when we can understand the nature of energy as a field or container.

Animation For Contemplation

For an intuitive sense of how energy flows within aspect patterns, it may be helpful to simply gaze at this fascinating video[90]. Don't try and analyze or figure it out. Just relax, allow yourself to become familiar with the flow of energy, and notice how different it feels when flowing within a triangle, square, hexagon etc. Allow yourself to receive impressions, and feelings.

Aspect Patterns as Karma

All aspect patterns are karmic[91] in the sense that they are pointing towards an energy field that pre-existed in you at the time that you were born. When I say karma I mean in its simplest sense of cause and effect. For example the 'cause' of an apple tree is an apple *seed*, and it is the 'karma' of an apple seed to become an apple tree. In this way aspect patterns are indicating a pre-existing energetic field that you were born with[92].

I think the Tibetan's emphasis on understanding the science of triangles is an invitation for us to consider how these energetic patterns are formed in the first place. Esoterically it is said that all forms manifest initially from thought. Energy follows thought, but not necessarily conscious thought as we know it. In Buddhist traditions there is a saying that if you want to know your past life, look at your present conditions and if you want to know your future life look at your present actions.

---

[90] Polygons, by Magic PI animations. Video online at https://www.facebook.com/magicpi2/videos/1000224170157690/

[91] Read more about karma in chapter nine.

[92] Also read *Karma and Magnetic Fields* in chapter nine.

Once you have some understanding of the aspect patterns in your chart, it is important to begin observing how they are showing up in your everyday life. Do you experience them as supportive or obstructive? Even though they may be karmic in nature, they are also 'sacred' in the sense that they are indicating deep energetic factors at work in your psyche that may be catalysts for your Soul's growth. Remember they are not a sentence that has been 'imposed' on you by anything outside of you. It is your own energy field, and you have the power to dissolve old patterns that no longer serve your Soul's growth, and replace them with more supportive patterns. This is done through clear intention and action.

Through observation and self-awareness you can become aware of, and heal, your own karmic patterns, by understanding and meditating upon the aspects and aspect patterns in your own chart!

Suggested Fieldwork

- Deeper Self-observation. Take out your own horoscope (natal chart) and in your reflective journal - make a list of the major aspects to your Sun and/or Moon. Choose just one that grabs your attention. Note which signs, houses and planets are involved. Then read the descriptions above and write some notes on how the energy may be affected. Meditate on how this aspect might be showing up in your life. Record your impressions and insights in your reflective journal.

- Further Reading: Refer to the appropriate sections of these books for more information on how to interpret aspects, *Chart Interpretation Handbook*, by Stephen Arroyo; Alan *Oken's Complete Astrology*, by Alan Oken; *Soul Centered Astrology: A Key to Your Expanding Self*, by Alan Oken; Astrology*: A Cosmic Science*, by Isabel Hickey.

- Video: It is interesting to contemplate this animation (published on Facebook by Magic Pi): https://www.facebook.com/magicpi2/videos/1000224170157690/

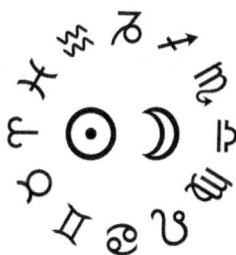

14. Esoteric Astrology

Upon reading *Esoteric Astrology*[93] it soon becomes apparent that there are references to certain topics that do not feature in other schools of astrology, including[94]:

• The Seven Rays
• Sacred and Non-Sacred Planets
• The Earth, and
• Vulcan

Before we go further I just want to re-iterate that the study of Esoteric Astrology is by no means a 'compulsory' part of our journey of spiritual awakening. Remember the Buddha became enlightened without studying Esoteric Astrology!

That said, because these topics were intentionally introduced into *Esoteric Astrology* by The Tibetan, I feel it is important to discuss them, to perhaps discern what their deeper meaning may be, and how they might be helpful to those of us who are committed to a sincere spiritual journey.

---

[93] Bailey, A.A. (1951) *Esoteric Astrology: Volume III, A Treatise on The Seven Rays*. Lucis Publishing Company, New York. Lucis Press Ltd, London.

[94] There are others, such as hierarchical rulerships but they would be considered too advanced for this foundational study of Soul Astrology. Interested readers can go deeper by reading *Esoteric Astrology*.

In reading *Esoteric Astrology*, I always ask myself what does it mean? To the best of my ability I try and understand the deeper essence of what The Tibetan is trying to convey: is it helpful? relevant to spiritual practice? and in what way(s) is it meaningful to those of us on a committed journey of spiritual awakening?

So with those questions in mind, let's begin this chapter by first looking at who the Tibetan was.

Who Was The Tibetan?

In order to understand who the Tibetan was it might be helpful to consider some background to give our discussion relevant context. In the Tibetan tradition, yogis, lamas and spiritual masters are often said to have special 'powers', which are a natural result of their great clarity. In other words as a result of going 'beyond' the conditioned, karmic mind (which we often refer to as brain wiring) and abiding in the clear light beyond, extraordinary abilities become possible.

These abilities include telepathy, teleportation (the ability to transport oneself from one location to another), the ability to make impressions in solid rock with one's hands and/or feet, the ability to run and cover vast distances at unimaginable speed, levitation, and even the power of flight!

Although we might think such events are myth, or only happened in ancient times, there are modern day accounts of yogis and high lamas who are still able to demonstrate these extraordinary abilities. We don't have the space here to go into many examples of these but one recent verified first-hand account from a living master is described in the documentary *"Yogis of Tibet*[95]*"* where Choje Togden Rinpoche describes his own feet making an impression in solid rock. This was witnessed by the monks and nuns who were with him at the time.

In the Tibetan tradition these special abilities are known as the "Five Ngönshes" or the five higher forms of awareness, the third of which is the knowledge of the minds of others, which we might call telepathy. You can read more about the Five Ngönshes and real-life

---

[95] *Yogis of Tibet* is a rare documentary on the few remaining Tibetan yogis that voluntarily decided to show and explain their secret and exclusive practices. Read more at https://tibetspirit.com/the-yogis-of-tibet-dvd/

examples in Chögyal Namkhai Norbu Rinpoche's book *"The Crystal and The Way of Light"*. Of the five higher forms of awareness, telepathy is not the ultimate capacity. The fifth (and highest) capacity is known as real knowledge of miracles.

As far-fetched as some of these abilities might seem to Westerners, it is important to realize that such capacities are an accepted part of the Tibetan tradition among yogis, lamas and spiritual masters of high capacity. The knowledge of how to attain these high spiritual capacities, up to and including the *Rainbow Body*[96], was handed down verbally from master to disciple and recorded in precious ancient texts, which were stored in the great libraries of Tibet's monasteries.

The early 20th century was a volatile time in Tibet with many monasteries being destroyed, together with the precious ancient sacred and esoteric texts contained therein (some were thousands of years old). It was a matter of extreme urgency that the precious wisdom be saved. It makes sense then, that someone with a capacity for telepathy would use it to 'transmit' the ancient wisdom so it could be received, recorded, and preserved for future generations.

The Tibetan transmitted his teachings through a Western woman, Alice A. Bailey who once said,

> *"I have been strictly his amanuensis and secretary ...
> I do not change what he has said in any way."*[97]

In a statement first published in 1934 The Tibetan described himself as *"a Tibetan disciple of a certain degree"*. He said he lived in a physical body, on the borders of Tibet, and at times presided over a large group of Tibetan lamas[98]. He is also known by the name Djwal Khul. It is believed that his name first appeared in H.P. Blavatsky's *"The Secret Doctrine"*[99] It is variously spelled *Djwhal Khul* and

---

[96] *"Rainbow Body 101: Everything You Didn't Know"* online document at https://www.gaia.com/article/rainbow-body-101-everything-you-didnt-know

[97] *"The Unfinished Autobiography"* by Alice A. Bailey, (1951) Lucis Press

[98] The statement by the Tibetan appears at the beginning of *"Esoteric Psychology Vol I"* by Alice A. Bailey, (1936) Lucis Press

[99] *"The Secret Doctrine: The Synthesis of Science, Religion and Philosophy"* by H.P. Blavatsky, (1888) Theosophical University Press.

Djwal Kul. Alice Bailey once referred to a friend of hers who traveled to *Shigatse* in Tibet and met the Tibetan in person. In Shigatse there is one large well-known monastery, and that is *Tashi Lhunpo*[100].

And so it seems, that the master whom we know as The Tibetan, or Master DK (Djwal Khul), was actually a Tibetan lama, based at or near Tashi Lhunpo monastery in Tibet, with a capacity for telepathy (not an uncommon ability among high lamas).

In my newsletter I have often mentioned the great *Kalachakra Masters*, whose capacity for clear light mind enabled them to perceive the movement of the Universe *directly*. The Kalachakra Tantra is still practiced in some schools of Tibetan Buddhism (in fact the Dalai Lama himself has offered Kalachakra initiations[101] to large groups of people) and it is certainly possible that The Tibetan was a Kalachakra Master himself.

During volatile and troubled times in Tibet, it appears that he found a way to transmit some of that precious wisdom so that it could still be received and applied for the advancement of human consciousness.

The Seven Rays

The volume *Esoteric Astrology* is part of a series known as *A Treatise on The Seven Rays*, which was transmitted by The Tibetan to Alice Bailey. The concept of The Seven Rays was first introduced in H.P. Blavatsky's book *The Secret Doctrine* in relation to seven Divine Buddhas[102] (Dhyani Buddhas). The Seven Rays were later expounded upon in the five volumes that make up Alice Bailey's *A Treatise On The Seven Rays*.

> "We shall find, as we study, that words will greatly handicap our expression of the realities involved, and we must endeavor to

---

[100] Tashi Lhunpo monastery is still in Shigatse, the second largest city in Tibet. See https://en.wikipedia.org/wiki/Tashi_Lhunpo_Monastery

[101] *Introduction to The Kalachakra* online document at https://www.dalailama.com/teachings/kalachakra-initiations

[102] *Our Seven Divine Parents*, online document at https://blavatskytheosophy.com/our-seven-divine-parents/

penetrate beneath the surface meaning to the esoteric structure of truth. These rays are in constant movement and circulation, and demonstrate an activity which is progressive and cyclic and evidences increasing momentum.

They are dominant at one time and quiescent at another, and according to the particular ray which is making its presence felt at any particular time, so will be the quality of the civilisation, the type of forms which will make their appearance in the kingdoms of nature, and the consequent stage of awareness (the state of consciousness) of the human beings who are carried into form life in that particular era."

- The Tibetan, *Esoteric Psychology*[103]

The Seven Rays are rays of conscious light (Divine Impulses and/or Intelligences) and, just like the different colors of the rainbow, each Ray has a special quality that makes it distinct from the other rays. We may think of them as fields of awareness, each holding a specific pure intention for the spiritual advancement of our Solar System[104].

As we become more advanced in our consciousness (beyond the intellect and the realm of language) we will become increasingly able to discern subtle qualities of energy, light and, eventually, the Seven Rays. With practice, as we become more attuned to *clear light mind*[105], we will be able to perceive the consciousness of the seven Divine Buddhas, in other words, the *Seven Rays*.

One of the highest teachings in the Tibetan tradition is that of Dzogchen[106] where the true nature of reality has been simply described as *the richness of dancing activities*[107]. In Dzogchen and

---

[103] *Esoteric Psychology: Volume I A Treatise on The Seven Rays.* Bailey, Alice A. (1936) Lucis Publishing Company.

[104] See *Seven Creative Forces* in *Soul Astrology*, chapter six.

[105] In Tibetan Buddhism mind is said to be of the nature of clear light. Read more at https://www.rigpawiki.org/index.php?title=Clear_light

[106] See the definition of dzogchen in the footnotes for chapter ten.

[107] *Heart Drops of Dharmakaya: Dzogchen Practice of the Bön Tradition.* Gyaltsen, Shardza Tashi with commentary by Lopon Tenzin Namdak. (1993) Snow Lion Publications.

other spiritual traditions, there are practices that involve *sky-gazing*[108] or even *sun-gazing*, to attune one's attention to increasingly subtle qualities of light. In the Tibetan Bön tradition there are spiritual practices that involve raising awareness by focusing on the *five lights* (these are associated with the five Ngönshes that we mentioned above). So we can see that attuning to 'light' is considered an important practice in many of the different schools within the Tibetan tradition. As we progress in our own journey of spiritual awakening our experience becomes less attached to the mental realm of words and language, and more attuned to the subtler qualities of light.

> "*I cannot too strongly reiterate the constant necessity for you to think in terms of energies and forces, of lines of force, and energy relationships...*
>
> *The whole story of astrology is, in reality, one of magnetic and magical interplay for the production or externalization of the inner reality...*"
>
> - The Tibetan, *Esoteric Astrology*

Characteristics of The Seven Rays

Ray 1. The Ray of Power or Will

Ray 2. The Ray of Love-Wisdom

Ray 3. The Ray of Active Intelligence.

Ray 4. The Ray of Harmony, Beauty and Art.

Ray 5. The Ray of Concrete Knowledge and Science.

Ray 6. The Ray of Devotion end Idealism.

Ray 7. The Ray of Ceremonial Order or Magic.

---

[108] *The Incredible Mind Altering Meditation of Sky Gazing and How To Do It*, online document at https://www.thewayofmeditation.com.au/the-incredible-mind-altering-meditation-of-sky-gazing

Of the Seven Rays the Tibetan pointed out that not all of them are in manifestation at this current time:

- *Ray 1* - Not in manifestation.
- *Ray 2* - In manifestation since 1575 A.D.
- *Ray 3* - In manifestation since 1425 A.D.
- *Ray 4* - To come slowly into manifestation after 2025 A.D.
- *Ray 5* - In manifestation since 1775 A.D.
- *Ray 6* - Passing rapidly out of manifestation. It began to pass out in 1625 A.D.
- *Ray 7* - In manifestation since 1675 A.D.

> *"You must remember that only a few of the planets are the bodies of expression of the Lords of the rays. There are ten "planets of expression" (to use the term employed by the ancient Rishis), and only seven ray Lives are regarded as the Builders of the system.*
>
> *The great mystery, which is finally revealed in the higher initiations, is the relation of a ray to a planet. Therefore seek not full information at this time."*
>
> - The Tibetan, *Esoteric Psychology*

There are also associations of the Seven Rays to planets and zodiac signs that we don't have the space to discuss here. Interested readers may contemplate further by studying *Esoteric Astrology* and the remaining four volumes of *A Treatise on The Seven Rays*.

We do not yet have the spiritual capacity to perceive these rays directly and, until we do, our attempts to understand them intellectually can lead us further into confusion.

The Centipede's Dilemma

A centipede was happy – quite!
Until a toad in fun
Said, "Pray, which leg comes after which?"
Which threw her mind in such a pitch,
She laid distracted in a ditch
Considering how to run.

- Anon. attributed to Katherine Craster

It is always important to remember that the evolution of consciousness passes through the following stages:

    instinct > intellect > intuition > illumination > emptiness

We cannot possibly grasp the nature of the Seven Rays from the level of intellect. We may get some hint of understanding through intuition, but we will really only know the Seven Rays fully when we reach the highest wisdom of emptiness. The Tibetan emphasized the importance of experiential awareness over hearsay or even theoretical knowledge:

"I deal not basically with theory but with that which may be known, provided there is growth and intelligent application of truth. I deal with possibility and with that which is capable of achievement.

Many these days like to talk and think in terms of that One Life, but it remains but speech and thought, whilst the true awareness of that essential Unity remains a dream and an imagining. Whenever this reality is put into words duality is emphasized..."

                                                  - The Tibetan, *Esoteric Psychology*

It is to be noted in *Esoteric Astrology* how often the Tibetan prefers the term 'disciple' (as in one who practices a discipline) to student. This indicates the importance of personal practice and experiential learning over theoretical knowledge. Remember, reading a book about driving doesn't equip you to drive a car!

The Seven Rays themselves are to be known and understood in experience as energetic realities, once we have the capacity to perceive them, not merely imagined as abstract intellectual concepts from the lower mind (intellect).

In introducing the topic of the Seven Rays The Tibetan himself was aware that he was introducing a level of complexity but felt this was acceptable as a temporary measure to lead the student to a deeper level of insight, through spiritual practice and personal experience:

"I am aware, therefore, that in giving out this relatively new teaching upon the rays I may, in my endeavor to shed fresh light, temporarily increase the complexity of the subject. But as experiment is made, as people are studied in the laboratories of the

psychologists and the psychoanalysts in connection with their ray indications, and as the newer sciences come into wise use and their proper sphere, we shall gain much and the teaching will find corroboration.

We shall see emerging a new approach to the ancient truths, and a new mode of investigating humanity. In the meantime let us concentrate upon the clear enunciation of the truth anent the rays, and seek to tabulate, outline and indicate their nature, purpose and effects."

- The Tibetan, *Esoteric Psychology*

In approaching the study of the Seven Rays it is therefore important to remember that it is experiential knowing that will bring us the highest wisdom. We need an intellectual framework to begin with, hence the Tibetan introducing the subject, but we must then work diligently to ensure theory is always integrated into our spiritual practice. It would also be wise to receive transmissions / initiations from living high lamas wherever possible, to deepen our capacity for integrating wisdom beyond the intellect.

By itself, a highly developed intellect can actually be an obstacle to spiritual awakening, so we must at all times be mindful that we are not getting caught in analysis, and that our actual meditative and spiritual practice balances and grounds any intellectual study of the subject.

Sacred and Non-Sacred Planets

In *Esoteric Astrology* there is also the concept of sacred planets and non-sacred planets. According to *Esoteric Astrology*, not all planets are considered equal! The sacred planets carry the power to transmit higher energy and elevate consciousness.

According to the Tibetan non-sacred planets primarily affect life in our everyday world (we might associate them more with karmic conditioning), while sacred planets:

"aid in the processes of affecting the fusion of soul and body, of consciousness and form; it will also produce the quickening of the intuition"

- The Tibetan, *Esoteric Astrology*

We can think of the non-sacred planets as denser and more likely to perpetuate our karmic conditioning (unless we become extremely mindful). We can think of the sacred planets as purer, lighter, and as providing conditions and circumstances that are more conducive to our spiritual development.

> *"The Logos of a sacred planet ... is occupied with the task of synthesizing into one unit of conscious response and activity, the higher divine aspect ... the will aspect.*
>
> *When this is accomplished, will, love and intelligence are blended and spirit, soul and body are at-one.*
>
> *Then the quality of divine expression will be divine purpose, impulsed by will, motivated by love and carried forward with intelligence."*
>
> - The Tibetan, *Esoteric Astrology*

The Five Non-Sacred Planets

1. The Sun
2. The Moon
3. The Earth
4. Mars
5. Pluto

The Seven Sacred Planets

1. Vulcan
2. Mercury
3. Venus
4. Jupiter
5. Saturn
6. Uranus
7. Neptune

The Earth

One of the many things that distinguishes Esoteric Astrology from other branches of astrology, is the placement and consideration of the Earth. In conventional Western Astrology the Earth isn't normally factored in, but in Esoteric Astrology it is taken into consideration because it shows the conditions that are present to support your Soul's growth and development.

Your Rising Sign indicates the spiritual energy that is wanting to flow into the world through you; your Sun and Moon signs tell us how this will play out in the 'theatre' of your life; and the Earth tells us the condition of the stage upon which the play of your life gets acted out. The Earth is the stage, the scenery, and all the other actors. They provide the causes and conditions for your Soul's highest expression.

> *"There is one aspect of energy for which the modern astrologer makes very little allowance, and yet it is of paramount importance. This is the energy which emanates from or radiates from the Earth itself.*
>
> *Living as all human beings do upon the surface of the Earth and being, therefore, projected into the etheric body of the planet (for the reason that "man stands erect") man's body is at all times bathed in the emanations and the radiations of our Earth and in the integral quality of our planetary Logos as He sends forth and transmits energy within His planetary environment.*
>
> *Astrologers have always emphasized the incoming influences and energies as they beat upon and play through our little planet, but they have omitted to take into adequate consideration the emanating qualities and forces which are the contribution of our Earth's etheric body to the larger whole."*
>
> — The Tibetan, *Esoteric Astrology*

If we think in terms of the stages of evolution of consciousness (mentioned above) we can see how important our time spent incarnated on Earth is, which affords us the conditions and experiences to pass through the stages of instinct and intellect and on to intuition. The Earth in your chart will therefore tell you much about your own 'path' in life in terms of both the experiences that you will be presented with that provide opportunities for you to develop skills and refine your talents, while at the same time using those same skills and talents to be of service.

According to Esoteric Astrologer Alan Oken, the position of the Earth is symbolic of our 'journey' both in terms of the external 'path' that we walk through this life and the simultaneous inner journey that we experience along the way. In this way he suggests that The Earth in a horoscope can also be an important indicator of one's karma and 'dharma' (sacred path) for this incarnation:

> *"The polarization and the eventual synthesis of the animal nature and the Presence of the Soul, the battle and the fusion, takes place on the Earth. The position of our planet in the natal chart thus reveals two things: the area of one's life where Active Intelligence [Ray 3] anchors into the form of our daily existence; and the place where the work of the present incarnation has to be expressed, via our physical presence and influence on others."*

— Alan Oken, Soul Centered Astrology

Locating The Earth in Your Chart

It's easy to find the Earth in your chart because it is exactly 180° opposite the Sun, so if you have Sun at 12° Cancer for example, the Earth will be at 12° Capricorn in your chart. You may then find that you attract Capricorn people, places and situations into your life to broaden your experience and 'set the stage' for your ongoing development.

> *" All I seek to do is to point the way towards a new science and towards those esoteric combinations of energies which will, when recognized, enable humanity to make more rapid progress ... and transform our Earth ... into a sacred planet."*

— The Tibetan, *Esoteric Astrology*

The Earth Through The Twelve Signs

Remember the Earth is the 'stage' upon which the play of your life is being acted out. So what does that mean? It indicates the way through which you may best anchor your soul-light into the Earth. It is often reflected back to you through the people and circumstances that surround you, and those conditions that you experience that become catalysts for your growth.

For example if you have Earth in Aries you may find that Arians in your life have in some way inspired, supported, motivated, and/or even provoked you!

If you are not fully embodying your Soul's essence you may find that people, places and situations akin to your Earth sign will show up outside of you to provoke and catalyze you into awakening to your highest power. You may then find a way to be of service to the Earth and all sentient beings through this path.

If your Earth is in:

ARIES you may best anchor your soul-light by inspiring others with your intuition and Divine ideas.

TAURUS you may best anchor your soul-light by dispelling illusions and revealing the light within the form.

GEMINI you may best anchor your soul-light by teaching right human relations.

CANCER you may best anchor your soul-light through emotional intelligence and compassion

LEO you may best anchor your soul-light through creative self-expression.

VIRGO you may best anchor your soul-light by flowing Divine Love through your work.

LIBRA you may best anchor your soul-light through right relationship and harmony.

SCORPIO you may best anchor your soul-light through personal healing and transformation.

SAGITTARIUS you may best anchor your soul-light through the revelation of truth and wisdom.

CAPRICORN you may best anchor your soul-light through right use of your spiritual energy.

AQUARIUS you may best anchor your soul-light by dedicating your personal energy to humanitarian endeavors.

PISCES you may best anchor your soul-light by flowing Universal Love through your heart.

Because your Earth sign is the opposite of your Sun Sign, you can see how balancing the energy of these two signs by expressing the highest 'octaves' of both, will bring you in closer alignment with your Soul's path and purpose, indicated by your Rising Sign[109].

It is through your Earth sign that your Soul's essence (Rising Sign) is connected to your vitality/ life force energy (Sun Sign). So if you are feeling unmotivated, listless and disconnected from your deeper sense of purpose connect with your Earth sign energy to hook yourself up again!

The Earth through The Houses:

First House. Your journey in this life is rooted in self-understanding through personal experience. Your life experiences will guide you towards self-awareness and ultimately self-realization, through which you may then be of service.

Second House. Your journey in this life is rooted in your own personal resources. Your life experiences will center around the development of a firm foundation of both material and inner resources, through which you may be of service by offering support to others.

Third House. Your journey in this life is rooted in learning and communication. Your life experiences will bring you learning experiences and language to be of service through communication with others.

Fourth House. Your journey in this life is rooted in your sense of home, family, ancestry and personal history (including your psychological roots). Your life experiences may bring you opportunities to be of service in some way through your home and family.

This could be either by providing a secure psychological base for the nurturing and growth of others and/or by transforming traditional concepts of 'family' to include our wider human family.

---

[109] Also see chapter four in *Soul Astrology, The Integration Process.*

Fifth House. Your journey in this life is rooted in your own creative self-expression, through which you may then be of service to humanity.

Sixth House. Your journey in this life is rooted in your approach to your vocation or daily work as 'love-in-action', which is how you may be of service.

Seventh House. Your journey in this life is rooted in right-relationship as a spiritual path. Your life experiences will guide you towards the art of right relationship, through which you may then be of service to others by bringing greater balance and harmony to all our relating.

Eighth House. Your journey in this life is rooted in the path of power and re-balancing power dynamics through personal transformation. Your life experiences here will bring you greater awareness of potential uses and abuses of power, through which you may be of service by modeling the power of self-transformation.

Ninth House. Your journey in this life is rooted in the search for meaning and higher wisdom. Your life experiences will guide you towards seeking the highest wisdom, through which you may then be of service by teaching others.

Tenth House. Your journey in this life is rooted in your worldly position. Your life experiences will guide you towards achievement, career or worldly status, through which you may then be of service by using your position to influence better outcomes for all.

Eleventh House. Your journey in this life is rooted in group work and social connections. Your life experiences will guide you towards working with groups of like-minded people, through which you may then be of service through the power of networking and organizing collectively towards a shared goal.

Twelfth House. Your journey in this life is rooted in your inner world. Your life experiences will guide you towards greater insights, perhaps through transcendental meditative experiences, through which you may then be of service by sharing your experiential knowledge of your true spiritual nature.

Vulcan: Master of Transformation

Another unique feature of *Esoteric Astrology* is the use of the planet Vulcan. In the 19th Century French Mathematician Urbain le Verrier was given the task of explaining Mercury's erratic orbit around the Sun. Verrier had successfully predicted the existence of Neptune by applying Newton's laws of motion and gravitation to calculate that a planet must be distorting the orbital path of Uranus. He applied the same laws to suggest that a small planet, which he named "Vulcan", would account for the anomalies in Mercury's orbit.

The Discovery of Vulcan - Now You See Me, Now You Don't

On 26 March 1859 French physician and amateur astronomer Edmond Modeste Lescarbault described a small black dot on the face of the Sun, which he thought at first was a sunspot. However, as time went by he realized that it was moving. Because he had experience of observing planetary transits he thought that is what he was seeing. Le Verrier was satisfied that Lescarbault had seen the transit of an unknown planet. On 2 January 1860 he announced the discovery of Vulcan to a meeting of the Académie des Sciences in Paris. However, another astronomer who was observing the Sun from Brazil at that time, failed to see anything that could be a transiting planet. So the 'discovery' was unconfirmed.

Eighteen years later, during the total solar eclipse of July 29, 1878, two experienced astronomers, Professor James Craig Watson and Lewis Swift both claimed to have seen a Vulcan-type planet close to the Sun. Unfortunately the measurements from both astronomers did not match, so again it could not be confirmed.

Despite many searches, to date no-one has ever confirmed a definitive Vulcan-type planet. In 1915 Albert Einstein explained the motion of Mercury with his theory of relativity, and people dropped the idea of Vulcan. However, it still has not been established what it was exactly that the previous astronomers were observing, and as recently as the 1970's astronomers were still looking for asteroids or planetoids that could lie between Mercury and The Sun.

Observing Transits across the face of the Sun was, and still is, an important astronomical technique for gathering information about the Universe, and it can be hundreds of years before such transits repeat. For example, transits of Venus occur every 243 years, with pairs of transits eight years apart separated by long gaps of 121.5 years and 105.5 years.

These days, with sophisticated telescopes, minor planets are numerous and are discovered with great frequency. According to the International Astronomical Union (IAU) Minor Planet Center[110], at the time of writing 323 Minor Planets had been discovered *in the past seventeen days*, and as recently as 2017 astronomers had observed an unknown object[111] passing the Sun.

Vulcan may be a small asteroid that occasionally transits the Sun. The issue is one of definition. Le Verrier's proposed Vulcan would have been a planet that orbited entirely within Mercury's orbit, which is unlikely in the light of current scientific data. Asteroids, on the other hand, like 2007 EB26[112] do orbit the Sun and at times are closer to the Sun than Mercury, but since their orbit is not entirely within Mercury's orbit they are not considered to be Vulcan.

However, as we shall see, perhaps it is not so much the physical embodiment of Vulcan that is of the greatest significance in Esoteric (Inner) Astrology, but rather the symbology, and whether that is meaningful and helpful for you or not, in your ongoing journey of spiritual awakening.

The Tibetan on Vulcan

What follows are some pertinent quotes from The Tibetan that may be helpful for you to contemplate, to see whether Vulcan resonates for you or not, in your own journey of self-exploration.

> *"At present the mechanism of the majority of the human family is not tuned to the reception of the rays from Vulcan ... Vulcan is never an exoteric ruler and only comes into real activity when a man is on the [spiritual] Path"*
>
> - The Tibetan, *Esoteric Astrology*

---

[110] https://minorplanetcenter.net//

[111] *Mysterious object seen speeding past sun could be 'visitor from another star system'*. The Guardian 27 Oct 2017. Online article at https://www.theguardian.com/science/2017/oct/27/mysterious-object-detected-speeding-past-the-sun-could-be-from-another-solar-system-a2017-111 Accessed December 2nd 2019

[112] https://en.wikipedia.org/wiki/2007_EB26

"Vulcan [is] the forger of metals, the one who works in the densest, most concrete expression of the natural world (from the human angle). He is the one who goes down into the depths to find the material upon which to expend his innate art and to fashion that which is beautiful and useful.

Vulcan is, therefore, that which stands for the soul, the individual, inner, spiritual man; in his activity we find the key to the soul's task upon the eternal round of the wheel of life. You will remember how Hercules upon the Fixed Cross had to fashion his own weapons before he succeeded in the struggle.

This is in reality a reference to the art of Vulcan who rules the inner man and guides his fashioning."

— The Tibetan, *Esoteric Astrology*

"Vulcan controls the anvil-like processes of time and strikes the blow which shapes the metal into that which is desired ... he will be destructive because "bull-headed" and because the hammer aspect of Vulcan will be dominant."

— The Tibetan, *Esoteric Astrology*

"the energy which streams from Vulcan is fundamentally the strength and potency which sets the world evolutionary process in motion; it embodies also the energy of the first ray, that force which initiates or begins and that which also destroys, bringing about the death of the form in order that the soul may be set free"

— The Tibetan, *Esoteric Astrology*

"Vulcan stands for the glorification, through purification and detachment, of matter ... in order through form experience to achieve release and the "uplift of matter" in Vulcan."

— The Tibetan, *Esoteric Astrology*

"the success which is incident to proved discipleship and consequent readiness for initiation, [which is] the seeing of the vision with which Jupiter rewards the disciple, and the experience which Vulcan confers."

— The Tibetan, *Esoteric Astrology*

In contemplating Vulcan we see a strong connection to the earth in general, and more specifically to the mineral kingdom: molten rock, lava, volcanic eruption from deep underground. There is also an association with direct experience (see above where the Tibetan refers to 'experience' conferred by Vulcan).

We can imagine a baby as it first begins exploring the world, learning by touch, taste and experience: "what does this do ... ouch"! So we are coming to 'know' the nature of our existence initially by touch with our hands, feet and mouths, and eventually through the entirety of our physical existence.

It is through the influence of Vulcan that we begin to experience our own creative power as we shape, forge and thus 'materialize' that which we desire, and by so doing we get to reap what we sow.

We get to experience the results of our desire: that which is beautiful or useful, and that which is helpful or harmful. Either way, we learn from our experience.

> *"It is the stimulating Energy of Vulcan which creates the need to penetrate through our material existence – indeed, through the use of matter and form– in order to detach ourselves from identification with the form life."*
>
> - Alan Oken, Soul-Centered Astrology

At the personality level Vulcan's influence has led to the exploitation of minerals (metals) to forge weapons of war. For the majority of people who are still spiritually 'sleeping' the planet Vulcan will act on a subconscious level as a powerfully destructive undercurrent, like a volcano ready to 'blow'. It will bring challenges to the ego-personality (crises, losses and troubles that appear to come from outside oneself) to 'wake up' the individual to the presence of Soul.

Once you begin to awaken, you first enter what Esoteric Astrologer Alan Oken calls a 'transition period' (see below) and these 'Vulcanic' challenges appear to get worse before they get better! Just like you can't build a peaceful home and sleep easily on an active volcano, neither will you be able to remain complacent and spiritually 'asleep' once you have experienced the activity of Vulcan in an area of your life.

As Vulcan is a catalyst for our detachment from form (possessions and people) we can experience a great sense of isolation and loss which, in turn, becomes a catalyst for our search for 'something more'. Our 'desire' itself is transformed from desire for people and things, to desire to be reconnected with our own true nature as we reunite in wholeness with all that is.

Vulcan's main function is to release humanity from the attachment to physical form. The main message of Vulcan is therefore: you are not your body. You are not your possessions. Raise your anchor and set sail to find your true spiritual nature.

Vulcan in our horoscope will therefore be showing us, through personal and practical experience, where we need to release attachment to the form of something so it can change (trans-form), go beyond form, and support us in recognizing ourselves as being of the nature of light.

> *"Awakened heart comes from being willing to face your state of mind"*
>
> - Chogyam Trungpa Rinpoche

Calculating the Position of Vulcan in Your Chart

Vulcan is always located within eight degrees and twenty minutes (8° 20') of the Sun. Due to its largely esoteric nature, very few astrology software programs will calculate the position of Vulcan[113].

As with any planet the effects of Vulcan are contingent upon other chart factors especially aspects to Vulcan itself, The Sun, your chart ruler, and the angles of your chart. Because Vulcan is always conjunct the Sun, for most people the effects of Vulcan will not be felt because they are synonymous with the activity of the Sun. This is what The Tibetan means by the Sun 'veiling' Vulcan.

Once we begin our journey of spiritual awakening, it seems as

---

[113] Astrological software programs that calculate the position of Vulcan include *SolarFire* for Windows and *Kairon* for Mac. In terms of free online charts, Astrodienst will calculate the position of Vulcan however the process is not straightforward: you must first choose the *Extended Chart Selection* - then enter your details (or log in) - scroll down to Additional Objects > and under 'manual entry' enter h55 (the code for Vulcan) > then click 'show the chart'.

though Vulcan's role is to prevent us from falling back asleep by constantly agitating our ego, until we eventually awaken to the truth of our own being, and finally release the illusion of our ego once and for all.

> *"from the ego's point of view spiritual progress is 'one insult after another'"*
>
> - Chogyam Trungpa Rinpoche

Very few astrologers have studied Vulcan to any great degree. Vulcan is not included in Western Astrology in general, and even in *Esoteric Astrology* The Tibetan speaks about the activities of Vulcan only in general terms, with the exception of a small number of signs such as Taurus for whom Vulcan has particular significance. He does not give meaning specific to all twelve signs and houses. That is up to us to determine, as we awaken more fully into our intuition enough to be able to discern the effects of Vulcan.

What follows then, are some thoughts as to how we might begin to interpret Vulcan in our chart.

Vulcan Through The Signs

Soul-Centered astrologer Alan Oken describes Vulcan in terms of the three crosses[114] that symbolize three defined stages in the evolution of human consciousness.

He suggests that, because we are unaware of Vulcan while we are solely personality-driven, we only become aware of his influence when we enter a transitional stage, as we become ready to 'mount' the fixed cross of spiritual awakening.

Below are some of Alan Oken's thoughts on interpreting Vulcan through the *signs*[115]. In addition are some of my own thoughts on how

---

[114] For a reminder about the role of the three crosses in human evolution and spiritual awakening see chapter eight. For a more detailed explanation you can also read *Personality-Soul Fusion and The Three Crosses*, in chapter one of *Soul Astrology*.

[115] These are short excerpts from Alan Oken's descriptions of Vulcan through the signs. For a deeper understanding you would be well served by reading the full descriptions in his book, *Soul Centered Astrology: A Key to Your Expanding Self*.

we might begin to consider Vulcan through the *houses*. This is clearly not conclusive, and is intended only as a springboard for the insights you may receive from your own study, contemplation, intuition and meditation upon the effects of Vulcan in your life.

Aries

> "When in the transitional state, this position of Vulcan often indicates a person with a very strong but highly self-righteous mind. Once the transition to the Fixed Cross is accomplished, the mind of the individual is then focused on service to humanity ... [and] can help to break down other people's resistance to higher consciousness."
>
> - Alan Oken, Soul-Centered Astrology

Taurus (Soul Ruler)

> "In the transitional phase, the individual is presented with main, often painful, tests of detachment. This may manifest as loss of either objects of people. Once the Fixed Cross is mounted, the Soul-centered individual then becomes a vehicle for the 'redemption' of matter, so that it (as well as the individual) may serve some larger, impersonal function."
>
> - Alan Oken, Soul-Centered Astrology

Gemini

> "In its initial phase, Vulcan in this position gives rise to a very critical mind, yet once a person secures them self on the Fixed Cross, this would lead them to create those interventions and scientific discoveries that evoke the hidden Light contained within matter."
>
> - Alan Oken, Soul-Centered Astrology

Cancer

> "Vulcan's placement in this sign points to those tests of release from past patterns of attachment, especially relative to the expressions of the emotions and the astral body. ...

When on the Fixed Cross, this position would tend to stimulate the creation of those mental and physical channels and structures that would be most appropriate to the unfolding of the [Divine] Plan."

- Alan Oken, Soul-Centered Astrology

Leo

*"Vulcan in Leo indicates those tests which serve to free the individual from a self-centered attachment to the creative potentials of the lower self. Egocentricity now must yield to a focus of group consciousness. ...
Once Vulcan is externalizing through the Fixed Cross, all the potency of the Will and the Concrete Mind ... can be utilized as expressions of group consciousness and channels for the Second Ray energy of the Sun."*

- Alan Oken, Soul-Centered Astrology

Virgo

"This placement of Vulcan creates a great conflict, because the attachment to the nurturing process is quite intense ... The individual would have to allow the healing and cohesive life force of the Universal Mother to sustain the objects of her caring. ... When the Fixed Cross has been mounted, the individual with Vulcan in Virgo is aligned with the Mother, and can then be a conscious vehicle, co-creating the force for any necessary healing."

- Alan Oken, Soul-Centered Astrology

Libra

"During the transition from the Mutable to the Fixed Cross, a person with Vulcan in Libra is apt to experience a deep change in the scope of his personal relationships ...

once the individual has made the necessary transition to life on the Fixed Cross ... Uranus then overshadows Vulcan, and group will and purpose emerge."

- Alan Oken, Soul-Centered Astrology

Scorpio

"*One could say that in Scorpio, those situations necessary to bring forth the required results for mounting the Fixed Cross are intensified. The First and Fourth Rays are brought into play through Scorpio, Pluto, Vulcan and Taurus, while Mars and the Sixth Ray lead to the cultivation of the one-pointedness required for maintaining one's focus of soul orientation (Discipleship) on the Fixed Cross.*"

- Alan Oken, Soul-Centered Astrology

Sagittarius

"*Vulcan in this position breaks those attachments to the personal mental body, allowing the Third Ray influence of Sagittarius's ruler, the Earth ... to function from the level of the Higher Self.*

... in the present incarnation, the individual may encounter some crisis of disillusionment with his previous belief systems. This leads to the acceptance of those higher concepts and broader ideas that can be communicated to others for the benefit of all."

- Alan Oken, Soul-Centered Astrology

Capricorn

"*Non-regenerative thought processes are challenged and broken down as the lesser self finds that it can no longer maintain its place or status in the outer world. ... Such a transition requires a person to restructure their will and broaden their awareness so that new mental patterns are created. These structures are aligned to the needs of the collective, and serve to anchor the evolutionary Plan for humanity.*"

- Alan Oken, Soul-Centered Astrology

Aquarius

"*The function of Vulcan in Aquarius is to shatter all human attachments that do not serve the purpose of the Higher Self, and hence the needs of the collective.*

In initial phases, the individual with this placement may find that there is a crisis in the life brought about by gradual detachment from friends and associations. ...

When the Fixed Cross has been mounted, the motivation for relationships becomes increasingly centered in the urge for World Service."

- Alan Oken, Soul-Centered Astrology

Pisces

"An individual with this placement would experience a crisis of releasing any blocks to the power of Love as it seeks to express in the outer world.

Personal prejudices would thus ... be replaced by a gradual expansion of loving devotion to the [Divine] Plan, and ... the urge to be of service to the expansion of Love/Wisdom in the world of humanity."

- Alan Oken, Soul-Centered Astrology

Vulcan Through The Houses

Because Vulcan is always conjunct the Sun, once Vulcan becomes active in your life there is always a sense of *releasing attachment to your identity* (The Sun), and eventually *completely releasing the habit of self-identification* through attachment to your life experiences and activities (Sun in the Houses).

First House. The detaching, de-constructing, power of Vulcan may be experienced here as the destruction of concepts and illusions that form the egoic sense of self, while allowing the formation of an authentic expression of Higher Self in alignment with Divine Will and Soul Purpose.

Second House. The detaching, de-constructing, power of Vulcan may be experienced here as the release of attachment to personal wealth and possessions allowing the awareness and development of one's inner resources.

Third House. The detaching, de-constructing, power of Vulcan may be experienced here as the destruction of mental concepts and release of all forms of familial and societal conditioning that do nor reflect the truth of who you are as a spiritual being. Allowing the construction of thought forms that lead to mental clarity and the development of the rainbow bridge to Higher Mind.

Fourth House. The detaching, de-constructing, power of Vulcan may be experienced here as the release of attachment to your home and family of origin, including the transformation of your psychological roots and belief systems, to allow for centering of your being in your true 'home' - your intuitive awakened heart.

Fifth House. The detaching, de-constructing, power of Vulcan may be experienced here as the release of attachment to 'your creations' (including your children) and the re-forming of creativity as a dancing expression of Divine Will. The transformation of egoic will into the expression of Divine Will.

Sixth House. The detaching, de-constructing, power of Vulcan may be experienced here as the release of attachment to work as a form of simply supporting yourself (your ego needs) and a transition to your daily activities being a form of service to others.

Seventh House. The detaching, de-constructing, power of Vulcan may be experienced here as the release of attachment to relationship (partnerships, marriage) as a form of obligation or contract, and a transition to freedom, liberty and harmony in unconditionally relating to our wider human family, without strings attached.

Eighth House. The detaching, de-constructing, power of Vulcan may be experienced here as the release of attachment to external power (money, other people's resources) and/or power over others, and a transition to using one's inner power for the purpose of self-transformation.

Ninth House. The detaching, de-constructing, power of Vulcan may be experienced here as the release of attachment to external forms of higher knowledge and a transition to following the path of deeper meaning and inner wisdom.

Tenth House. The detaching, de-constructing, power of Vulcan may be experienced here as the release of attachment to one's worldly position as a source of authority and status, and a transition to spiritual ambition and/or discipleship, through the recognition of one's inner authority derived from one's spiritual lineage.

Eleventh House. The detaching, de-constructing, power of Vulcan may be experienced here as the release of attachment to group or peer conformity, and the transition to shared experience and humanitarian intentions through the higher collective consciousness of humanity.

Twelfth House. The detaching, de-constructing, power of Vulcan may be experienced here as the release of attachment to one's inner fears, addictions, dreams and fantasies, and a transition to experiencing the reality of illumination through an awakened heart and the mind of clear light.

In closing our brief exploration of Vulcan, what seems most apparent, is that Vulcan brings us experiences of changing form, that may result in a transformation of consciousness. Vulcan therefore ignites our transition to the next stage in the evolution of human consciousness.

And so this also concludes our brief tour of some of the distinguishing features of *Esoteric Astrology* namely:

- The Seven Rays
- Sacred and Non-Sacred Planets
- The Earth, and
- Vulcan

I trust that this discussion has been helpful and meaningful to you on your journey and, if not, just let it go. Remember, you are the custodian of your mind on this journey of spiritual awakening.

It is always much more beneficial for your spiritual growth to spend five minutes resting in clear light mind, than to agitate your mind trying to grapple with intellectual complexities that could keep you stuck at the 'intellect' stage in the evolution of human consciousness.

Your intuition will always be your best guide!

Suggested Fieldwork

•   Deeper Self-observation. Take out your own horoscope (natal chart) and make a note in your journal of the signs and house positions of both The Earth and Vulcan. Then read the descriptions above and make a note of any ideas and insights that come to you. Meditate on how The Earth and Vulcan might be showing up in your life. Record your impressions and insights in your reflective journal.

•   Further Reading: *Soul Centered Astrology: A Key to Your Expanding Self*, by Alan Oken, refer to the appropriate sections for more information on The Seven Rays, The Earth, and Vulcan. Read about The Earth and Vulcan as the Soul Rulers for Sagittarius and Taurus in chapters four and five of *Soul Astrology* and read more about The Seven Rays in chapter six.

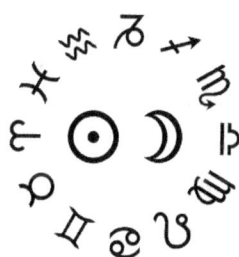

15. Mercury's Sacred Path to The Rainbow Bridge

Mercury in Astrology

Mercury is the personality ruler of Gemini and Virgo, and the Soul Ruler of Aries. According to *Esoteric Astrology* Mercury is a sacred planet, because Mercury creates the conditions for the development of mind, mental processing, and communication appropriate to our group and species. At the physiological level Mercury governs the nervous system and cellular communication. All mammals have some kind of communication or 'language'. Whether you are born into a gorilla troop, a herd of elephants, or a whale or dolphin pod, Mercury creates the conditions for you to learn the rules of connection and communication within your group.

This is why Mercury is exalted in Aquarius because it creates the conditions for the development of primary (primitive) awareness of group (in our case human) consciousness and how we connect within our group. As such, the activities of Mercury then are what allow us to develop a link between lower and higher mind and therefore become increasingly aware, or conscious, on our path of spiritual awakening. This is why is said that, esoterically, Mercury creates the *Antahkarana*[116] or *Rainbow Bridge* between lower and higher mind.

---

[116] Meader, W. (2005) *Antahkarana: The Bridge to the Sacred.* Online document at https://meader.org/articles/antahkarana-the-bridge-to-the-sacred/ Accessed December 8th 2019.

Mercury is associated with our mind and mental processing and as such governs all 'mental activity', in particular communications, commerce, sales, technology (especially digital commerce) and short journeys. Anything to do with movement, the movement of mind, the movement of thoughts is associated with Mercury and therefore is inextricably linked to our spiritual journey. In mythology Mercury was the 'messenger of the Gods' because, as we shall see, it is precisely this changeable activity of Mercury that can set us on (and keep us on) our spiritual path.

Mercury Retrograde

Before we go further, let's take a moment to look at Mercury retrograde. Even people who haven't studied astrology to any degree, have heard of 'Mercury retrograde' so it is worth taking a moment to explore this idea. With the exception of the Sun and Moon, all the planets in your horoscope can, at times, have what is known as 'retrograde motion'. In astrology a retrograde period is where the planets appear to go backwards. Of course planets don't really go backwards but due to the relative position of planets to earth, from our perspective here on earth they can seem to[117].

During a retrograde period we can experience the effects of a planet for longer periods of time as it passes over, back, and over again, certain areas of our charts in a wave-like motion. Not only do we experience the effects for longer but retrograde motion also changes the quality of the energy, so in effect there is an intensification of a more introspective, reflective, form of that planet's energy.

Because Mercury 'rules' sales, commerce, short-distance travel, communication, exchanging information (like backing up computer information!), sales, commerce, our speech, learning, mind and mental processing, we can expect all of these areas to take on a quieter, less frenetic, more reflective tone during a Mercury retrograde period.

Rather than being a time when we can forge ahead with our plans, a retrograde period is often more of a time of inner reflection. When Mercury is retrograde, rather than enhanced communication, we often notice miscommunication. There can be misunderstandings and breakdowns in communication. There can be technical hitches

---

[117] Short video demonstrating retrograde motion at https://www.youtube.com/watch?v=72FrZz_zJFU

and glitches, and minor disruptions in commerce and/or short distance travel. It might not be the best time to launch your next sales and marketing initiative, but it can be a time for consolidating previous efforts, doing your background research, taking stock, evaluating your progress, and contemplating your next move.

The Deeper Meaning of Mercury Retrograde

During a Mercury retrograde period, as our everyday thoughts are interrupted, we have an opportunity to sneak a peek at the gap between thoughts and catch a glimpse of the innate clear light mind that lies beyond.

It is always wise to work with a Mercury Retrograde period by planning ahead, making sure you are not engaging in commerce or travel if you can avoid it, and using the time wisely for periods of deep inner reflection. They are excellent times for spiritual retreat, for example. During these periods the messenger of the Gods is letting you know that your attention is needed elsewhere, not on the outside world.

These are not periods for increasing external output and action, but rather they are times for quiet meditation and contemplation. Even if great ideas and inspiration come to you during a Mercury retrograde period, better to take note and wait until Mercury turns direct again before you execute your plans. It is natural during periods of Mercury retrograde that we want to withdraw some of our energy from these outgoing activities and place more of our energy and attention on our inner journey.

This is where we can really harness the sacred power of a Mercury retrograde period and tap into the benefits to support our own inner journey. Mercury also rules the nervous system, our neural networks, our mind, thoughts and mental processes. To be more specific, according to Soul Astrologer Alan Oken, Mercury rules the 'movement' of mind (whereas Saturn rules the 'structure of mind' and Uranus rules 'Higher Mind') and this might be a key to understanding how Mercury is able to bridge the worlds between lower and Higher Mind.

During this time if we consciously concentrate on our inner journey we can use the sacred energy of a Mercury Retrograde to deepen our meditation and cultivate more awareness of our inner world. The more we place our attention on the inner flow of energy in our body, the more calm we will feel. The more often you do this, the more the chattering 'monkey mind' settles down, like when the wind suddenly drops and you are in stillness. The more often you do this, and enter your clear, calm, oasis of peace within, the quicker you will be able to do it at will. This is because, under the influence of Mercury, your nervous system has the capacity to 'rewire' itself by laying down new nerve pathways to replace the old ones.

This is much more important than it sounds. Everything we experience is largely due to our nervous system sending signals from our sense organs up to our brain. Depending upon how those nerve pathways are set up we will experience pain or pleasure, fear or love, anxiety or calm. Our nerve pathways are created by conditioning: basically our behavior becomes habitual because the more often we repeat something, the more nerve pathways get created and strengthened to support that behavior.

When we experience something new there is a tiny glimmer, and electrical spark in our nervous system. If we repeat the new behavior, the body starts building a nerve pathway so that we can 'learn': in other words, through experience, we can get better and faster at something. So the more frequently we can go within and enter our Higher Mind, the quicker and better we will be able to do it, because we will have literally created the pathways in our mind! At the same time old pathways that are no longer used begin to shrivel up and eventually disappear. So we can also permanently let go of states of mind that no longer support us.

Rather than looking to each Mercury Retrograde period with dread and foreboding, we can welcome it as a truly sacred time when it is possible to deepen our 'communion': our ability to connect with our Higher Power. We can also release old habit patterns, and obstacles to our path, that no longer support the highest of who we are.

If we fully align ourselves with it we have a great opportunity at this time to make progress on our spiritual path: crossing that bridge to Higher Mind once and for all. As Mercury lays down new neural pathways for accessing Higher Mind more easily on a regular basis, eventually, Higher Mind becomes our permanent state of being!

During a retrograde period, the energy is naturally more introverted and contemplative. Instead of trying to push the river, use a Mercury retrograde period to your advantage by setting aside more time for quiet contemplation and meditation. Be clear in your intentions, and set your sights on experiencing the clear light mind that lies beyond words and your normal everyday activity.

It is also important to remember that nothing happens in isolation. Each Mercury retrograde period differs from the one before - not only because Mercury is in different signs, but because the aspects to Mercury are different too.

There is much to learn about the inner workings of your mind, and your unique spiritual journey, if you remain still, awake, and aware during each Mercury retrograde period.

Mercury in Our Inner World

When our Mercurial energy moves out into the world we have the 'outer' activities of Mercury, communication, learning, sales, commerce, the exchange of information, ideas, goods, money etc. When we turn our Mercurial energy inwards something very sacred and beautiful happens: we have the ability to be aware of ourselves. We have the ability to observe and learn about our own minds and mental processes. We have the ability to self-reflect, observe ourselves, practice mindfulness, and become self-aware. It is the activity of Mercury in our inner world, that makes our spiritual journey possible, and when Mercury is retrograde we have an increased opportunity to go deeper into self-exploration and self-awareness.

No accident that in mythology Mercury's Greek predecessor Hermes was a messenger of the Gods who was also responsible for guiding Souls to the underworld. Of all the power and awe of the Olympians, Hermes (Mercury) was the only one with this ability to travel freely between the ordinary world and Hades (the underworld and word of Souls). It is when Mercury is retrograde that we have an increased ability to listen to our own inner guidance, and truly receive 'the messenger of the Gods'.

A Mercury retrograde period needn't be a cause of anxiety. Yes there can be some disruption to the outer activity of Mercury, as our energy changes direction and moves inwards. The tide has turned and, just like when we work late at night under artificial light we feel off-balance because going against nature disrupts our circadian rhythms, so we will be most challenged by Mercury retrograde if we insist on going against the tide.

During a Mercury retrograde period it is more natural for us to be quieter and reflective. It is a perfect time to plan spiritual retreats and anything that is more contemplative and designed to open us up to our inner world. Mercury retrograde is a natural period of much-needed downtime when our inner world, and Higher Mind, can really open up to us if we go with it, rather than push against it.

According to Soul Astrologer Alan Oken, Mercury rules the movement of mind. This might be what we first experience when we try to meditate. At the personality level Mercury is responsible for the 'monkey-mind' the apparently constant activity of mind jumping from one though to the next, but it is precisely Mercury's capacity for change that allows us the possibility of liberating our mind, because it gives us the power to shift our awareness from lower, unhelpful, states of mind. Mercury gives us the opportunity to break free from fixed states of mind so that we can move to higher states of awareness.

This is especially important when it comes to disturbing emotions. By nature, emotions are fleeting states of mind. We can see this in children as they play in nursery, laughing one minute, crying the next and then laughing again. As we grow older we develop the capacity to fixate on our thoughts, which allows us to 'hold' things in our mind. This ability is what allows us to learn and retain knowledge, but it also allows us to remember past wrongs, pain, and to brood and fixate. When we repeat certain thoughts over and over, our fleeting emotion can become a mood, and if it remains unchecked that mood can become habitual and become a temperament, and if it still remains unchecked it then becomes our character, forming part of our personality.

Yet with the light of conscious awareness, we can change these habitual thinking-feeling patterns and set ourselves free. It is the condition of Mercury in our chart that brings us the power to change these habits. If it were not for Mercury's capacity for change, we could remain stuck in a 'depressed' state of mind for days, weeks, months or even years (and some people do).

Navigating the Emotional Scale

It is precisely our mind's great capacity for change, indicated by Mercury, that can set us on (and keep us on) our spiritual path. Every day is a new beginning.

No matter how far 'gone' you think you might be, you can always change your mind. It is Mercury that gives you the power to choose where to place your attention.

In his book *Power Versus Force*[118] Dr. David Hawkins describes a spectrum of emotions similar to a musical scale. Much like a kind of 'emotional scale'. Similar ideas have been described by other authors, however in his book he calls it a 'map of consciousness' and relates emotional states such as despair, anxiety, trust and optimism, to increasingly higher vibrational states of consciousness.

Due to the actions of Mercury, we have the capacity to 'navigate' this scale: to consciously lift our state of mind out of blame and despair, into states such as serenity and bliss. It isn't easy, it takes focus, method and perseverance, but it is possible, and it is our capacity for change that makes it possible.

Mercury and The Rainbow Bridge

With awareness, as we consciously choose spiritual practices such as meditation to support our spiritual awakening, we can work with the natural movement of mind (thank you Mercury) to shift gears into higher states of consciousness.

If we have a well-placed Mercury we will find it somewhat easier to focus on increasingly higher states of consciousness, much like climbing our own stairway to heaven. This is how Mercury enables us to build our inner *Rainbow Bridge* to higher mind.

If Mercury is afflicted we may be challenged to shift our awareness, and find that we have sticking points, where it is more difficult to shift our consciousness, but it is important to remember that we are never powerless to change. Even if we have a chart packed with planets in fixed signs, that will bring us a capacity for stability and discipline that we can then use to engineer our path to enlightenment.

Spiritual Awakening and The Mind

First, what do we mean by spiritual awakening? According to consciousness researcher Steve Taylor[119], our current everyday state of consciousness (where we think of being 'awake' as the opposite of being 'asleep') is in fact a kind of sleep!

---

[118] *Power vs. Force: The Hidden Determinants of Human Behavior.* Hawkins, David. R. (2014) Hay House.

[119] Taylor, S (2010) *Waking from Sleep: Why Awakening Experiences Occur and How to Make them Permanent.* Hay House.

He compares this to higher states of consciousness and peak experiences where people have a kind of 'spiritual awakening' and experience a more vivid and expanded perception of reality, which they often describe as being more 'real'. Often these higher states of consciousness, or awareness, last for a few days or possibly even months before the individual eventually returns to a more mundane level of consciousness. In rare cases it becomes a permanent state of being, in which case the individual is then said to be 'awake' or 'enlightened'.

"I hope that you understand what the word "spiritual" really means. It means to search for, to investigate, the true nature of the mind. There's nothing spiritual outside. My rosary isn't spiritual; my robes aren't spiritual. Spiritual means the mind, and spiritual people are those who seek its nature."

- Lama Thubten Yeshe

Now let's look at this journey from lower mind, to spiritual awakening. In Astrology there are three planets which are specifically associated with our mind, and the workings of our mind. These are Mercury, Saturn and Uranus. For simplicity, we'll use the analogy of 'lower mind' and 'higher mind'. It isn't really like that because that would be an either/or, black/white polarity and when we really 'awaken' into higher consciousness we are beyond such duality, but before it gets too confusing, let's stick to our simple metaphor of lower and higher mind!

We can think of Mercury and Saturn as both being associated with lower mind. According to Soul Astrologer Alan Oken, Saturn rules the structure of mind (your ability to think methodically, plan and organize your thoughts, your brain wiring, neural pathways, and how Saturn plays a role in building your belief system), while Mercury rules the movement of mind (the thoughts themselves and the repeating cycles and patterns of those thoughts). He uses the analogy of a bee hive where Saturn is the structure (the structure of the hive and the honeycombs) and Mercury is the movement of the bees themselves going about their daily business!

Saturn rules our established brain wiring, the neural networks through which our thoughts are created and experienced, but when it comes to re-wiring our brain (changing our neural networks so something can be experienced differently) then Mercury and Saturn work together. Esoterically Mercury is said to be responsible for creating the antahkarana or rainbow bridge between lower and higher mind. One thing we know about mind is that it is changeable. If it weren't we could never learn and grow and this changeability, this capacity to learn, comes under Mercury's domain.

Much of our mind works by association. If you have been watching your mind closely you will see this. On a daily basis we associate certain experiences people, thoughts, feelings and memories, like movies and popcorn or even having sugar and cream in our coffee. Neuroscientist Dr. Joe Dispenza explains that "nerve cells that fire together, wire together"[120]. This means that associated thoughts eventually hook up and become our brain wiring. It's like that game where one person says a word and you say the first thing that comes into your mind. The first thought that comes is likely to be one that is currently 'wired' to the other word, for example 'coffee' and 'cream'.

On a daily basis we tend to unconsciously follow the habitual patterns of our brain wiring. In the past I have said this is the result of our following the movement of Mercury and the 'monkey-mind', but we can also see that Saturn is just as involved here, because Saturn is holding the neural network in place. All that needs to happen for that to change, is for us to stop following our thoughts. Once we no longer energize the neural networks with our thoughts, they actually shrivel up and die, and our thoughts seek out new neural pathways. Mercury will seek out alternative pathways (change and learning) and then Saturn will create neural networks so we can easily remember and take our new path.

Mercury is able to create the Rainbow Bridge from lower to Higher Mind because Mercury can help us to change habit patterns that have us stuck, and allow us to step into new ways of being. However, we also need consciousness otherwise we can simply substitute one habit for another, which keeps us equally stuck. This is where Uranus comes into the picture.

Uranus is the planet of intuition and is associated with Higher Mind. Uranus is also associated with electricity, lightening, and flashes of insight. It used to be thought that our nervous system was one continuous, unbroken, network like a railway track upon which our thoughts run like trains (a train of thought)! However, modern science and high-powered electron microscopes tell a different story.

---

[120] *Breaking The Habit of Being Yourself: How to Lose Your Mind and Create a New One.* Dispenza, J. (2012) Hay House

Our nervous system is a network of individual nerve cells that appear to be connected but if we look closely there is a gap between each one called a synapse. As thoughts pass through our nervous system, they actually leap across this synaptic gap in the form of an electrical charge. If you could see your brain at microscopic level while you are thinking, it looks like a lightening storm. So if the gap between our thoughts is electrical in nature (like lightening), then it comes under the rulership of Uranus!

If Saturn rules the structure of mind (our neural network) and Mercury rules the movement of mind (the thoughts themselves) then Uranus rules the gap between our thoughts, and that is the domain of intuition. It is in the space between our thoughts that we are able to access higher perception and discern a higher reality beyond the normal limitations of our senses and our brain wiring. So what is intuition?

Alan Oken describes intuition as:

> *"The ability to perceive that quality of energy—the true essence of meaning—within any form of expression"*

Mercury governs the bridge between lower and higher mind because our thoughts are a vehicle for our consciousness. When we follow our thoughts, we are actually giving our attention to them. We are allowing our consciousness to follow the thoughts. But it is when an individual thought leaps into the gap that, for the very briefest of moments, we have an opportunity to drop the thought, get off the train, release the vehicle, and experience pure perception: pure consciousness itself, uncontaminated by thoughts, ideas and concepts. It is in that moment that we can 'wake up' and directly perceive our true nature as spiritual beings.

> *"There may come to you an awakening of the intuition which will translate modern astrology into something of real moment and significance to the world"*
>
> - The Tibetan, *Esoteric Astrology*

It is this ability to directly perceive reality, without any thoughts or concepts clouding our perception, that we call intuition. While our awareness is in that gap between thoughts (the synapse) we are free. We have access to the entire Universe through Universal Mind, free from the conditioning of our brain wiring. It is from here that we are truly 'awake' and all can be known. This is why meditation is so important. It is through some form of meditative practice (basically observing ourselves and how our mind works) that we are able to cultivate the ability to remain in the gap between our thoughts for longer and longer periods.

It is though direct perception that the ancient Kalachakra Masters were able to practice astrology without telescopes, tables, or ephemerides. In other words, they were able to directly perceive the entire workings of the Universe through their intuition. You have this potential, the key is to jump into the gap between your thoughts and stay in clear light mind for as long as you can. Then you too may discover that the Universe lies in the gap between your thoughts!

Mercury Through The Signs

In short, the essence of Mercury then, is movement of mind: in it's most tangible form this is thinking, learning, communication. Movement of mind, in the form of all kinds of thoughts and ideas.

The sign Mercury occupies in your horoscope will therefore tell you much about the type of movement: is it slow and steady, is it graceful and flowing, is it fast and erratic, darting here and there?

Mercury through each of the twelve zodiac signs, describes twelve very distinct different kinds of mind.

Mercury in Aries - Esoteric or Soul-Centered Ruler of Aries

This kind of mind is enthusiastic, intuitive and impulsive. There can be a tendency to blurt out, and/or act impulsively on, one's thoughts without considering the impact on others. Impatience, and/ or a quick temper, can be a problem if one experiences interruptions or blocks to one's thinking process.

Mercury is the Soul ruler of Aries so this is an excellent position for reducing attachment to one's own thoughts, developing one's intuitive capacity to greater depths, being more aware in the present moment and directly accessing the mind of clear light.

Mercury in Taurus

This kind of mind is steady, cautious, and deliberate. The individual will favor practical, kinesthetic and experiential learning over textbook study. This is a mind well-suited to a steady, graduated path to enlightenment (such as the Lamrim[121]) but not from the perspective of laborious intellectual study. Learning is best approached through practice, which brings understanding through the senses and is integrated through one's personal experience. At the personality level stubbornness can be a problem, and great care must be taken not to become dogmatic in one's thinking, which can hinder one's progress and spiritual development.

At a Soul level Taurus is associated with illumination. According to Buddhist astrologer Jhampa Shaneman the historical Buddha had six planets in Taurus[122], one of which was Mercury. If stubbornness and rigid patterns of thinking can be overcome, the steadiness of this type of mind is a great asset to developing stability in clear light, once the clear light mind has been recognized.

Mercury in Gemini - Dignity

This kind of mind is quick, versatile and intelligent. Mercury is the personality ruler of Gemini and, unless otherwise afflicted, often brings a skill with words, language and/or communication (In conventional astrology Mercury is said to be in 'dignity' or in the sign of it's own rulership). The individual may learn quickly, gathering and distributing information at the speed of light, however there could be a problem retaining and/or integrating what has been learned, as knowledge may be 'dropped' in favor of the next novelty to come along. Restlessness can be a problem and if afflicted this can be the epitome of the 'monkey-mind': a constant chattering mind (even when the lips are silent) that hops like a frenzied grasshopper from one thought to the next. There can be an over-stimulation of mental activity, which can lead to mental exhaustion and fatigue.

On a Soul Level this can be a challenging mind to 'tame' for the purposes of spiritual advancement. The benefit of such changeability is the speed at which the individual can, with some practice, shift gears out of lower emotional states of mind and into higher levels of

---

[121] The lamrim ("graduated path") is a textual tradition that organizes Shakyamuni Buddha's teachings into a complete step-by-step path to enlightenment. See *Lamrim* online document at https://fpmt.org/education/teachings/texts/lam-rim/ Accessed December 16th 2019.

[122] See Jhampa Shaneman's chart for The Buddha online at https://tinyurl.com/y4425sqs

awareness. The challenge will be to remain in higher states of consciousness and not be distracted by the next passing thought that comes along. Active meditations may be of benefit until the individual has developed the capacity to 'observe' thoughts passing like a river, without jumping in and following along! One advantage is that this kind of mind often has great powers of observation, so if curiosity can be kept at bay, this individual would benefit from remaining in 'observation' mode, to develop deeper awareness in meditation.

Mercury in Cancer

This kind of mind is fluid, receptive, and reflective. Thoughts are 'felt' and feelings are 'thought'. If the Sun is also in Cancer, and especially if conjoined, there can be difficulty separating thoughts from feelings. Intelligence takes the form of emotional intelligence, and developing one's emotional language, including one's vocabulary of 'feeling' words is very important. There can be a facility for communicating emotions with ease. Learning takes the form of absorption rather than textbook study. Similar to Mercury in Taurus, experiential learning is important but with Mercury in Cancer instead of the learning happening as a direct result of one's own experience, knowledge is often absorbed like a sponge through a field of sense impressions, empathic feeling and awareness of other people's emotions. Learning also happens by 'sensing' other people's experiences.

On a Soul level the challenge is to rise above the level of emotions so that the mind of clear light can be perceived. If there is too much focus on emotions the individual may become mired in their emotions and unable to navigate to higher states of awareness. With practice the individual can learn to use their great sensing capacity to recognize ever-widening circles of awareness within their field of consciousness. This placement has great potential for recognizing and abiding in the level of bliss, which is a precursor to the mind of clear light. Care must be taken not to remain 'stuck' at any point (including bliss) but to keep expanding one's capacity for awareness.

Mercury in Leo - Full

This kind of mind is creative and self-expressive. There can be a facility for acting and/or speaking. Mercury is said to be in 'fall' in

Leo, which means its energy is restricted. Because of the strong orientation to self that is the path of Leo, there can be a tendency to 'personalize' thoughts, ideas and communication too much, so that it becomes difficult to be objective. Thoughts become 'my' thoughts, ideas become 'my ideas' and so forth. At the personality level facts can become confused with opinions, and knowledge can be used to serve a pedantic egocentricity.

On a Soul level, Leo is a sign of the heart and intuition is the language of the heart. If the tendency for the ego to hijack the mind can be overcome, so that the mind of clear light can be accessed, this can be a beautiful placement for expressing a warm, passionate creativity, that arises from clear, intuitive thought processes.

Mercury in Virgo - Dignity

This kind of mind is orderly, meticulous, precise, analytical and detail-oriented. When well-placed there can be a facility for math and/or statistical analysis. Mercury is the personality ruler of Virgo, and it is important that Mercury's energy is consciously grounded in this earth sign otherwise there can be stress to the nervous system (In conventional astrology Mercury is said to be in 'dignity' or in the sign of it's own rulership). Care should be taken not to take analysis and evaluation to the extreme in a never-ending cycle causing burnout and fatigue. On the personality level thoughts can be overly idealistic causing one to strive for a non-existent 'idea' of perfection that can never be attained.

On a Soul level this is a great placement for cultivating somatic awareness and body intelligence. Practical methodologies that calm the mind while developing body awareness, such as yoga, will allow the thought-train to slow down long enough for this individual to catch a glimpse of the calm, clear light mind beyond.

Mercury in Libra

This kind of mind is intelligent, objective, and strives for balance, harmony and good judgment. There can be a natural tendency toward 'ethical' thinking, understanding the process of how we make decisions and/or how we decide and choose 'right' from 'wrong'. When afflicted there can be a tendency to 'sit on the fence' for too long and vacillation can be a problem. There can be a predilection for relationships, yet there can sometimes be an over-emphasis on objectivity at the expense of a deeper emotional connection.

On a Soul level this is a good placement for cultivating a balanced, calm and harmonious mind, which can serve as a foundation for stable meditation leading to deeper spiritual realizations, such as the potential to rest with stability in clear light mind for long periods.

Mercury in Scorpio

This kind of mind is highly intelligent, sharp, intense, probing, strategic and secretive. There can be a talent for depth psychology and/or any deep kind of investigative work where their innate probing capacity can uncover that which was previously hidden. There is often an innate understanding of human behavior. Depth in one subject is the preferred learning style, rather than covering many topics at a surface level. They would be well-suited to spiritual or psychological study that can further develop their understanding of human nature.

On a Soul level this placement is perfect for attaining deep spiritual realizations. There can be a tendency to brooding or obsession, which can be an obstacle if the mind is held in lower emotional states of consciousness. Once the individual has learned to navigate through emotional states, to higher states of awareness there is a capacity to hold higher states of consciousness until great spiritual realizations are achieved and integrated.

Mercury in Sagittarius - Detriment

This kind of mind is enthusiastic, honest, idealistic, adaptable and independent. There can be a capacity for speaking and communicating ideas clearly and articulately. There may be a facility for teaching. At the personality level there can be a tendency to exaggerate one's own opinions at the expense of others, and/or to present personal opinions as though they were facts or established 'philosophies'. When afflicted there can be attachment to one's ideas and opinions, to the point of dogma. Speech can be direct to a fault, sometimes even blunt, with little or no consideration of the impact on others. Mercury is in detriment in Sagittarius so its energy is ineffective. Thoughts can be disconnected and lacking a basis in practical reality.

On a Soul level this placement brings vision and an innate interest in all things 'spiritual'. Sagittarius is the sign of the spiritual seeker and it is said that liberation of the mind is possible in Sagittarius. Care needs to be taken not to be distracted by spiritual ideas, at the expense of spiritual experience, which leads to actual insight, true wisdom, and true spiritual realization.

Mercury in Capricorn

This kind of mind is practical, serious, strategic, ambitious, calculating and disciplined. There is a capacity for structuring thought processes for practical purposes. There may be a flair for engineering, accounting, or resource management. This can be a 'heavy mind, and excessive seriousness and/or sense of duty could lead to a lack of humor and joy in one's life. At the personality level care must be taken to avoid being too stern and controlling where others are concerned, and empathy may need to be consciously cultivated.

On a Soul level this placement can bring spiritual 'ambition' with the power of focus and discipline which, when applied to one's spiritual path with determination can accelerate one's spiritual development, leading to amazing breakthroughs. The danger here would be of being excessively controlling, which would become a mental block and prevent deeper insights into the clear light mind beyond. Balancing one's *shamatha*[123] (concentration) meditation with *vipassana*[124] (open) meditation is extremely important when Mercury is in Capricorn, so that one's mind remains free, flexible, and open to new experiences and higher perspectives.

Mercury in Aquarius - Exaltation

This kind of mind is original, independent, intuitive, communicative and inventive. Mercury is said to be exalted in Aquarius, which means its energy is most active and able to flow freely. There is a capacity for original, unorthodox and/or unconventional thinking, which is often combined with a flair for speaking. The individual is often group-oriented and can contribute much when collaborating

---

[123] https://www.rigpawiki.org/index.php?title=Shamatha

[124] https://www.rigpawiki.org/index.php?title=Vipashyana

with like-minded individuals, especially on collective and/or humanitarian issues. There can be mental stubbornness and care must be taken not to be too opinionated and attached to one's own ideas.

On a Soul level this placement can be excellent for opening higher increments of intuition and experiencing higher states of consciousness. The challenge would be stubbornness and attachment to one's own ideas and mental constructs, which can become obstacles to higher states of awareness. Similar to Capricorn (above) balancing one's shamatha (concentration) meditation with vipassana (open) meditation is extremely important, so that one releases attachment to fixed mental concepts and keeps one's mind free, flexible, and open to transcendent experiences.

Mercury in Pisces - Fall

This kind of mind is fluid, sensitive, impressionable and psychic. Mercury is said to 'fall' in Pisces since it's energy is somewhat restricted. There is often a sensitive, artistic nature with a capacity for poetry. In some cases psychic and/or mediumistic abilities are present. Due to the fluid nature of Pisces there can be a lack of clear-thinking and a vagueness to one's thoughts. Thinking takes the form of sense-impressions rather than clear-cut thoughts and objectivity can be challenging.

On a Soul level this is an excellent position for following a spiritual path to awakening through compassionate actions and transcendent experiences. There can be a strong leaning towards transcendental states, while altruistic states such as compassion and unconditional love may come with relative ease. The challenge lies in not becoming 'lost' swimming around in vague, blissful, states of mind, which cloud one's path and become a distraction. It is important to remain clear and focused in one's meditation and remember the 'goal' is the clear light mind that lies even beyond states of bliss. For you, balancing your vipassana (open) meditation with strong shamatha(concentration / focused) meditation would be important so you don't lose your way.

Mercury In The Houses

The house position occupied by Mercury, tells you which life area stimulates (and is stimulated by) your entire thought processes, which include thinking, learning, and communicating (language, writing and speaking).

Mercury in the First House draws the mind/mental energy into the area of all things Self. There can be great energy and vitality. Self-concern needs to be consciously transformed into Self-realization through self-awareness if the individual is to advance spiritually and not become caught in self-absorbed egocentricity.

Mercury in the Second House draws the mind/mental energy into the area of one's inner and outer resources: including material possessions, income, finances and one's inner values and talents. Income may come through communication such as writing, speaking, sales and or education.

Mercury in the Third House draws the mind/mental energy into the area of the processes of communication and learning. There can be great curiosity and a love of study and research. May enjoy learning just for it's own sake and may be a gifted teacher. If spiritual progress is important to the individual, then care must be taken to choose study topics that will further advance one spiritually, so one's time and energy isn't wasted studying non-productive areas.

Mercury in the Fourth House draws the mind/mental energy into the area of home and family. There is a need for personal safety and security and care must be taken that excessive concern over one's home and family doesn't become obsessive worry and/or anxiety. There can be a restlessness with Mercury in the 4th that may lead to frequent alterations to, or changes of, residence. This position can be good for someone who wants run a home-based business.

Mercury in the Fifth House draws the mind/mental energy into the area of self-expression and creativity. There is often an ability to connect well with children, although care must be taken not to worry excessively about ones own children or any of one's 'creations'! There can be great creativity with possibly a flair for writing, speaking, or acting.

Mercury in the Sixth House draws the mind/mental energy into the area of one's work and responsibilities. There can be a tendency to focus too much on tasks and care must be taken to avoid being excessively busy and overworked to the point where it is impossible to complete all one's duties. There is always a busy-ness when people have Mercury in the 6th so it is important to be discerning about which tasks you take on board, and which ones you can delegate. You would be well served, and serve those you are responsible for, if you support others more by teaching them, rather than by doing things for them that they can (and should) do for themselves.

Mercury in the Seventh House draws the mind/mental energy into the area of one's partnerships and relationships. Communication and intellectual stimulation may be a hallmark of all such relationships. If afflicted there could be disputes or arguments that involve court judgements.

Mercury in the Eighth House draws the mind/mental energy into the area of personal transformation and healing. There can be an intense, probing, quality to the mind, which may also have the capacity to be a catalyst for healing and transformation in others. There may be an interest in the deep undercurrents of life, such as the processes of death, dying, karma and reincarnation, and metaphysical phenomena. There could be inheritance through the death of relative's and/ or an interest in tax, insurance or financial investments.

Mercury in the Ninth House draws the mind/mental energy into the area of higher learning, higher education and religion, and the deeper search for meaning. Advanced learning through travel to foreign countries or through contact with people from different cultures is likely. One's dreams and visions may be too far-out to be practical and concentrated focus may need to be cultivated to ground one's visions into practical reality.

Mercury in the Tenth House draws the mind/mental energy into the area of one's achievements, career, public standing or worldly position. Ambitions are a priority, and may be achieved through some form of communication writing and/ or speaking. At the least, one's career or profession may involve communication, writing, and/or public speaking. There may also be involvement with politics or public office in some form.

Mercury in the Eleventh House draws the mind/mental energy into the area of groups, societies, friends, and shared goals. One may be drawn to become actively involved in groups and societies working towards humanitarian causes. Friendships are likely to be based on intellectual connections rather than deeper emotional bonds.

Mercury in the Twelfth House draws the mind/mental energy into the area of one's inner world. Silence may be preferred and one might find it easier to think clearly in quiet environments. There can be a tendency to seek solitude and to 'withdraw' into one's inner world and thoughts. This can be excellent if used wisely in meditation, but care must be taken not to become a prisoner of one's own mind.

Mercury's greatest gift is *the power to change our mind*. There is a story that Buddha was once asked how to meditate and he said that our mind should be like a guitar string: neither too tight, nor too loose. It is Mercury that gives us the power to change and find that perfect sweet spot: if our thinking is too rigid, Mercury brings us the power to be more flexible; if we are too distracted, Mercury brings us the power to choose where we place our attention to develop more focus. In this way, it is Mercury that brings us the power
to navigate our own path to spiritual awakening.

Suggested Fieldwork

• Deeper Self-observation. Take out your own horoscope (natal chart) and make a note in your journal of the sign and house position of Mercury. Then read the descriptions above and make a note of any ideas and insights that come to you. Meditate on how Mercury might be showing up in your life. Record your impressions and insights in your reflective journal.

• Further Reading: *Soul Centered Astrology: A Key to Your Expanding Self*, by Alan Oken, refer to the appropriate section for more information on Mercury. Read about Mercury in chapter five of *Soul Astrology*.

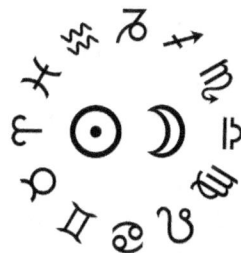

16. Venus and The Law of Attraction

In Western Astrology Venus is associated with love, beauty, our esthetic sense, our appreciation of art and music, and... personal magnetic attraction. In other words, Venus in your chart will show you where the law of attraction is at work (or not) in your life.

The Law of Attraction

The Law of Attraction, as we shall see, is one of the most basic, fundamental, and necessary natural laws yet it is not passive like water simple meandering downhill. The attracting power of Venus is an active magnetism. There is an active pulling in of that which she desires, such as when two attracting poles of a magnet pull each other in. It takes great force to pry them apart. Wherever Venus is found in your chart, she brings the power to attract benefit, to a greater or lesser degree, depending upon her condition by sign, house and aspect, and taking into account other chart factors which may be enhancing or diminishing her power of attraction.

Known in traditional astrology as the Lesser Benefic (Jupiter would be the greater) Venus is said to bestow benefits in life. The type of 'benefit' would be indicated by the sign she is in, and the area of life affected is indicated by the house placement in which she is found. Where Venus is concerned there is always benefit of some kind, however when afflicted, it can be in the nature of 'too much' of a good thing, laziness, vanity, and/or excessive self-indulgence.

Following the initial idea of 'me' that arises under the influence of Mercury, the next stage on our developmental journey is to find a mate. We temporarily leave our fascination with 'me' and enter into curiosity about 'other'. Are others like me? How do 'I' relate to them, and 'them' to 'me'? and (most importantly in our search for a mate) am I attractive? and Are they attractive? The whole field of relating, attraction, and vanity, opens up under the influence of Venus.

Venus awakens our senses. She is our muse. Sooner or later, in one way or another, she tempts us onto the path of love. At the personality level, Venus stimulates our desire nature, and awakens in us a sense of beauty, taste, esthetics. All our senses awaken under her influence and we become aware of our sensual nature. It isn't long however before we also discover the pain and suffering that comes from attachment to sense pleasures. When we step through Venus' door, from the perspective of lower consciousness, it would seem that we become prone to a myriad potentials for addiction - through our senses.

> *"A goddess on a mountain top*
> *Was burning like a silver flame*
> *The summit of beauty and love*
> *And Venus was her name"*
>
> - "Venus" by Shocking Blue, 1969.

Venus may be known in Greek myth and popular culture as the "Goddess of Love", but in esoteric terms she does not resonate to Ray 2, *love-wisdom*, but rather Ray 5, *concrete knowledge*.[125] Esoterically then, Venus is opening the door to a path of knowledge, not the path of love-wisdom (which is the domain of The Sun and Jupiter). This might then help you to understand why we experience the initial high followed by the pain of romantic love, and 'broken' hearts. The love of which we speak, with regard to Venus, is not Divine love. Not yet. It is a more earthly kind of romantic love.

Where Mars would be associated with sex, Venus would be associated with romance and eros, that which is erotic. Remember, on our evolutionary journey, we are still at the level of 'instinct' having only just ventured forth from the mental domain of Mercury. So when love is experienced as romantic and/or erotic, there is very

---

[125] Read more about *The Seven Rays* in chapter 14.

much a mental element of conceptualizing, fantasizing and projection involved. It has little to do with the other person, and everything to do with what is going on inside our own head.

To understand the 'love' of Venus, and how it relates to the path of knowledge, we need to make clear distinctions between romantic love, eroticism, and Divine love. Ultimately, our experiences of romantic love have the potential to open our hearts and minds to Universal Divine Love and compassion, which is why Venus is said to be exalted in Pisces, but at the level of romance and sexual attraction Divine Love is still very much only a potential.

Venus in Esoteric Astrology

Conventionally Venus is associated with love, beauty, art and esthetics. She is thought to enliven and awaken our senses, and how sensuous we are (or not) can often be directly related to the condition of Venus in our chart. This makes sense for a sacred planet, because our whole process of spiritual awakening is experienced very personally and directly, through our five senses (sight, sound, touch, taste, smell).

In *Esoteric Astrology*, Venus is said to be a sacred planet and a 'companion' planet to Earth. As we saw earlier, according to The Tibetan non-sacred planets primarily affect life in our everyday world, while sacred planets:

> "*aid in the processes of affecting*
> *the fusion of soul and body,*
> *of consciousness and form;*
> *it will also produce*
> *the quickening of the intuition*"

> "*The Logos*[126] *of a sacred planet ... is occupied with the task of synthesizing into one unit of conscious response and activity, the higher divine aspect ... the will aspect.*
>
> *When this is accomplished, will, love and intelligence are blended and spirit, soul and body are at-one.*

---

[126] Logos: the Greek word logos meant "word, speech, discourse or reason" and by the 16th century had come to mean "the Divine Word". In Esoteric Astrology the term Logos refers to a Higher Mind, reason or purpose, so for example there is a Solar Logos and a Planetary Logos.

> *Then the quality of divine expression will be divine purpose,*
> *impulsed by will, motivated by love*
> *and carried forward with intelligence."*
>
> - The Tibetan, *Esoteric Astrology*

The Evolution of Human Consciousness

In earlier chapters we explored the evolution of human consciousness and your individual path of spiritual awakening. It is worth remembering here, that the planets are creating conditions for you that support distinct stages of your evolutionary development:

- Instinct: Sun, Moon, Mercury, Venus, Mars.
- Intellect: Jupiter, Saturn.
- Intuition: Uranus
- Illumination: Neptune
- Emptiness: Pluto

These stages are not rigid, but serve as a general guide[127].

We can see from the list above that The Sun, Moon, Mercury, Venus and Mars contribute to the conditions that allow for the arising and unfolding of the *instinctive* stage of our evolution.

As we evolve through the levels of instinct > intellect > intuition > illumination and emptiness (clear light mind), it is important to remember that each stage is necessary. It's not that we 'lose' our instincts as we move into intellect, but rather that each stage is a vital foundation for what comes next. So by the time we reach the level of the wisdom realizing emptiness, we also realize that we are all of it. We are everything that has gone before. We don't 'transcend' instinct by 'getting rid of it' but rather it becomes integrated into our whole being.

Instinct is our basic animal sense: the primal force that gives us the drive to exist, protect, survive, and reproduce. It is also Mother Nature operating at her finest, keeping all the subconscious physiological systems working that are beyond your conscious

---

[127] Read more about these stages in chapter six.

control - from your beating heart to the neural networks that allow a thought to cross your mind at the speed of light.

At the instinctive level of our development, attraction is a vital force in the continuation of life on Earth. Without attraction the species would not survive. This is true for every species on the planet, from a tiny bug to an elephant. Even in the plant kingdom: many plants, when they are ready to multiply, give off perfume to attract insects as pollinators to propagate the species. At some level, in some way, the power of Venus and the law of attraction is at work throughout nature.

Venus creates the conditions for us to recognize and attract what is needed for the continued survival of the species. Through Venus we recognize beauty, harmony, and cultivate personal magnetism. Physiologically Venus rules the 'harmonizing' and 'balancing' factors in the body and so governs hormonal activity, including the chemistry of love and attraction. Through the activities of Venus we will attract our mate and be able to fulfill our function within our group. Venus is exalted in Pisces the sign of Universal Love, and we can see that the presence of love, as magnetic attraction, is indeed universal throughout the animal kingdom.

Venus and Your Soul's Journey

According to *Esoteric Astrology* Venus has 'rulership', or custodianship, over four signs: she is the personality ruler of both Taurus and Libra ; the Soul ruler of Gemini ; and the hierarchical ruler of Capricorn. (It is beyond the scope of this foundational volume to discuss the meaning of hierarchical rulerships, however if you are interested you can read more in *Esoteric Astrology*[128]).

The Five Bodies

Patanjali, one of the founders of modern Yoga, described five 'bodies' that we can experience on our spiritual journey of awakening. He related these to the five elements of earth, fire, water, air and ether. He called them the physical or 'earth' body (annamay kosh), the energy 'fire' body (pranamay kosh – also known as the 'vital' body in other traditions), the mental 'water' body (manomay kosh), intuitive 'air' body (vigyanamay kosh), and the bliss 'ether'

---

[128] Bailey, A.A. (1951) *Esoteric Astrology: Volume III, A Treatise on The Seven Rays.* Lucis Publishing Company, New York. Lucis Press Ltd, London.

body (anandmay kosh). Our spiritual journey is one of awareness and movement through each of these inner 'bodies'. Once all five have been transcended, we attain 'Universal Mind'. Venus plays a vital role in awakening us to these bodies.

Venus and Taurus

We become aware of those different states of consciousness, which Patanjali referred to as 'bodies', initially through our senses. Venus plays an important role in our spiritual journey by first awakening our senses in Taurus, igniting within us the desire to explore our senses more fully. In Taurus the loving energy of Venus works initially through the physical senses to awaken awareness of the physical body.

As Venus works through desire in Taurus, she awakens our sense perception through the physical senses of sight, sound, taste, touch and smell. This has the potential to open us to sense pleasures, and develops our somatic awareness (felt sense) through the physical body.

As we grasp at more external 'objects' to feed the sensual experience: clinging to possessions of beauty, beautiful people, music, a beautiful body, we form attachments and a materialistic facet to our ego-personality begins to take shape. This is why the spiritual path of Taurus is one of practicing non-attachment, to transcend this aspect of ego.

When we begin our journey of spiritual awakening, we 'unlearn' all the attachments we have accumulated. We can practice by being fully present to our experience, enjoying it (so we still get to experience sense-pleasure) but without becoming attached to the experience itself. For example we can still enjoy ice-cream without it becoming an 'addiction' and a cause for grasping and craving. Without attachment we are free: ice-cream becomes a non-issue, we can enjoy it if we have it, and we can still feel happy if we don't.

Venus and Libra

In Libra Venus endows her subjects with a harmonizing aspect that manifests through the mind: in terms of conceptualizing or idealizing ideas of ethics, beauty, attractiveness and justice. Her work in Libra is more closely linked to harmony in the mental body.

Venus brings the energy of magnetic attraction. Initially this is animal magnetism, and at the personality level she awakens desire and passion within the individual, which lays the foundation for experiences of Love.

In Libra we can conceive of Higher Love and harmony at the personality level and express this into the outer world through right relationship between Self and other.

Venus and Gemini

Gemini is ruled by Venus at Soul level. Once the activity of Gemini's personality ruler Mercury has expanded our perception, we are open to the activity of Venus through the heart center. The journey of Gemini is about resolving 'duality' and one of the major themes for anyone with Sun, Moon or Gemini Rising is the 'marriage' of the head and the heart.

> *"Attraction and repulsion are therefore conditioning factors in our solar life, and this conditioning reaches us through Gemini. It is the effect of a cosmic energy at present unknown to humanity."*
>
> - The Tibetan, *Esoteric Astrology*

The experience in Gemini, once the personality has been transcended, is the shift from the intellect to intuition; from the head to the heart; from separation and duality, to non-duality (oneness). Venus opens us up to the senses and, through the experience of sexual attraction, awakens in us desire for, and love of, 'other'. In doing so, Venus awakens us to our sense of polarity: self and other. In the pursuit of this desire, with conscious awareness, we then have an opportunity to return home: by raising our consciousness from the lower chakras to the higher chakras: the heart and above.

Esoterically, Gemini is a sign of communion and connection. It is said to be the only sign that touches the remaining 11 zodiac signs. No other sign is able to go where Gemini can go. The experience of Venus in Gemini therefore brings a spiritual awakening in the form of a deep sense of communion and connectedness with all sentient beings. There is an awareness of Love, not as an idea, but as a living energy that permeates and radiates throughout all life. This shift in perception brings us to the realization of our interrelatedness with one another and all living things.

> *"In the last analysis, we come back to the eternal dualities, leading as they ever do to the interplay of the polar opposites, to the cyclic ebb and flow of the inner life and the outer periphery of expression, and to that attraction and repulsion which leads to a steady shift of the attracting force to an ever higher and wider appeal."*
>
> - The Tibetan, *Esoteric Astrology*

We can see how the harmonizing influence of Venus is expressed as sensuality at personality level in Taurus, as right relationship at personality level in Libra, and as a pathway through Higher Mind to Higher Love at Soul level in Gemini. All for the purpose of supporting spiritual awakening at different stages of your Soul's journey.

Venus as Personality and Soul Ruler

As you read on, take note if you have Taurus or Libra Rising. If so Venus is your Personality Ruler[129] and the condition of Venus by sign, house and aspect will be playing a particularly significant role in your life, by bringing you people and circumstances that have the potential to bring your karmic conditioning into your awareness, for healing, transformation, and release.

As we mentioned above, Venus is the Soul Ruler of Gemini. So if you have Gemini Rising, Venus will also be playing a significant theme in your life by bringing you people and circumstances that are catalysts for your Soul's Awakening.

Venus Through The Signs

Venus draws magnetically towards her, that which she is attracted to. So the condition of Venus in our personal horoscope, by sign and house, describes our capacity for magnetism or attraction, and our aesthetic sense: whether we resonate to beauty and harmony, or not; whether we have an artistic nature, or not, and even our capacity to attract benefits that can support us in terms of financial and material wealth, personal value and/or a valuable partner.

---

[129] Read more about the personality and Soul rulers of the signs in chapter four.

Venus in Aries - detriment

When Venus is in Aries our power of attraction can be 'hi-jacked' by impetuous desire. Venus is said to be in detriment in Aries, meaning her energy is weakened and her power is minimized. Therefore the romantic, harmonizing, and beautifying capacity of Venus can be lost in an impulsive drive to satisfy one's desire. When afflicted, love can be self-centered and may give way to 'lust'.

On a Soul level there is an opportunity to develop awareness of the power of desire, and to gain deeper understanding of our underlying motivations and energies. It may be difficult however, to cultivate the required objectivity to develop such self-awareness. A regular open (vipassana) meditation where one's energetic drives can be observed, without being acted out, may prove very beneficial for this individual

Venus in Taurus - dignity

When Venus is in Taurus our power of attraction can be strong. Venus is said to be indignity in this sign meaning her energy flows well and she is most free and uninhibited in her effects. There can be a very strong sense of beauty, harmony and esthetics. The individual may have a strong artistic streak and possibly a beautiful voice. The senses can be strong and the individual may be sensually oriented - enjoying all the pleasures of their senses. When afflicted there can be excessive attachment and possessiveness toward the 'object' of one's desires.

On a Soul level this can be a challenge to spiritual awakening because of too much attachment to the sense pleasures and the material realm. The challenge is to release personal attachment so one can ultimately enjoy sense pleasures without attachment, but this can be difficult. In the first instance, practicing abstinence may be helpful to break long-held patterns of attachment.

Venus in Gemini

Venus in Gemini is light, airy, and versatile. This Venus loves to flirt. Relationships can be playful, easy, and changeable. Love may be experienced through the intellect rather than the heart, unless a deeper emotional connection is indicated elsewhere in the chart. There can be more than one love interest as this social butterfly enjoys experiencing variety through multiple relationships, though not necessarily at the same time.

On a Soul level the challenge for Gemini is to 'marry' the head and the heart. Venus in this sign challenges the individual to go deeper in their relating, long enough to experience a true heart opening. A catalyst for higher love. Multiple relationships become a playground for learning right human relations.

Venus in Cancer

Venus in Cancer is homely, loyal, and cares about family, siblings and parents. Emotional depth and security are the priority, so Venus in this sign is not given to passionate flights of fancy, although Cancer is a cardinal sign, so someone with this placement may be the first to make the move in relationship, once they have identified a prospective partner whom they feel 'safe' with. When afflicted there can be too much attachment, possessiveness, clinginess and dependency on their partner.

On a Soul level Venus in Cancer is excellent for opening up to higher states of consciousness through love: with awareness and non-attachment, one understands how romantic love, when properly nurtured, becomes the highest form of love: true compassion.

Venus in Leo

Friendly, outgoing, and with a touch of the dramatic, Venus in Leo makes a warm, passionate and loyal partner. May find self-expression through the arts, or theatre. When afflicted there can be a tendency to dominate and/or view one's partner as an extension of oneself.

With Venus in the sign of self-realization, on a Soul level Venus in Leo brings opportunities for self-awareness through one's love relationships. The path becomes one of self-realization: awakening into one's own true nature, through love. This is especially true if one has Libra or Taurus Rising, whereby Venus in Leo becomes one's chart ruler.

Venus in Virgo - fall

Venus in Virgo is quite practical and responsible in relationships. Although there can be sensuality (Virgo is an earth sign) these are not people who will throw caution to the wind and fall headlong into a whirlwind romance! Venus is said to 'fall' in Virgo, which means her energy is somewhat repressed and unable to flow freely. Venus in Virgo can be so caught up in details, or an unrealistically high expectation of 'perfection', that they simply 'miss' the moment. Social relationships are usually formed for practical reasons and/or their perceived 'usefulness'. When afflicted there can be too much emphasis on 'getting it right' to allow for artistic expression, and there can be coldness and excessive criticism towards friends, family and lovers.

On a Soul level there is the potential to experience self-awareness, and explore the true nature of self as love, through somatic awareness. If the senses can be developed, through grounding practices such as yoga, Venus in Virgo can bring a deep, experiential, understanding of the practical, tangible, reality of love as a living awareness in the body, rather than a romantic fancy.

Venus in Libra - dignity

Venus in Libra is romantic, with a natural inclination to establish harmony and beauty through relationships. Like Taurus, Venus is also considered in dignity in Libra, meaning her energy flows well and is most free and uninhibited, but whereas Taurus is an earth sign (so Venus expresses sensuality) Libra is an air sign, so her mode of expression is more intellectual: through charm, tact and diplomacy, Venus in Libra ensures harmony through social relationships. When afflicted her social strategizing can become excessively manipulative and self-indulgent.

On a Soul level, unless otherwise afflicted, Venus in Libra bestows a graceful, dispassionate, quality that can be very helpful in developing the state of 'equanimity' or 'evenness', in one's meditation, and then carrying that over into one's everyday thoughts, words and actions. This is a state of consciousness that paves the way for liberation and enlightenment, by allowing the practitioner to experience a calm state that is less prone to disturbing emotions and agitated states of mind.

Venus in Scorpio - detriment

Venus in Scorpio can be intense and passionate. Venus is said to be in detriment in this sign, meaning her energy is weakened and her power is minimized. Therefore the individual cannot access the lighter, harmonizing influence of Venus, which is lost to the intensity of passion. Relationships can be seen as a means for self-advancement and may be approached strategically, with an ulterior motive. The individual may seek to control the relationship, being the one to initiate a relationship and then also to destroy the relationship once it no longer serves them. When afflicted there can be obsession, possessiveness, jealousy and even cruelty.

On a Soul level Venus in Scorpio presents a great challenge, but with the promise of great opportunity if the individual can rise to that challenge. Their intense passion needs to be channeled into a warrior-like energy and unselfishly dedicated to spiritual advancement, if their highest spiritual potential is to be fully realized. The advantage is that Venus in Scorpio brings a great capacity for strategic focus and when their attention is placed unwaveringly on the spiritual path, there is the potential to transform the energy of one's desires into great spiritual power. Here is the potential for personal spiritual mastery.

Venus in Sagittarius

Venus in Sagittarius is friendly, outgoing and sociable. There can be a wide circle of friends and a love of socializing, but the individual may avoid relationships that could potentially place limitations on their freedom. The grace and tact that we normally expect from Venus may be lacking since The Archer likes to be direct and can be honest to the point of bluntness, however they are usually very likeable and can be the life and soul of the party. When afflicted there may be a tendency to throw caution to the wind. Extravagance and gambling could be a problem.

On a Soul level Venus in Sagittarius can be helpful in seeking higher truth and the deeper meaning of life, by opening one's senses to explore higher states of consciousness. The challenge will be to keep one's attention focused on the inner adventure, since Venus in Sagittarius has a great love of life and can easily keep him or herself occupied (distracted) with life's many outer adventures!

Venus in Capricorn

Venus in Capricorn approaches relationships and social situations with seriousness and caution. There can be a conscious or unconscious sense of insecurity and the individual may feel more comfortable in formal social situations where they have a degree of control. Desire for status and prestige may be enhanced. When afflicted there may be disappointment in love relationships and the individual may choose aloneness rather than risk being hurt. There is the potential to heal and experience steady love, if bitterness and resentment can be released in favor of love.

On a Soul level Venus in Capricorn can enhance one's sense of sacred geometry and Divine harmonics. There is the potential for spiritual advancement through diligent study and the application of ancient wisdom.

Venus in Aquarius

Venus in Aquarius is happier in friendships, groups and social situations than intimate personal relationships. Somewhat cool and aloof, relationships that demand a deeper emotional connection may be avoided. However these individuals are considered friendly and loyal, and may have many acquaintances in their network. Indeed they make avid networkers and can also be excellent fundraisers for a shared humanitarian cause. When afflicted they may be too cold, lacking in empathy and understanding of others.

On a Soul level Venus in Aquarius initially presents a challenge to the cultivation of compassion. If an individual is spiritually oriented they would need to make a conscious effort to cultivate empathy and compassion, through acts of unconditional loving-kindness and generosity to others. Once compassion has become second nature, this opens the door to experience the highest vibration of Aquarius: the bodhisattva path whereby one's individual spiritual energy is generated, accumulated, and dedicated to the collective.

Venus in Pisces - exalted

Venus in Pisces is compassionate and sensitive. In Pisces Venus is said to be exalted, which means its energy is most active and able to flow freely. Love is transformed from romantic love to Universal Love. Artistic expression may take the form of poetry and/ or music. The individual may need to learn discrimination in relationships if people are not to take advantage of them. When afflicted there can be a lack of boundaries and/or withdrawal from relationships and/or social engagements to avoid being hurt.

On a Soul Level this is an excellent placement for the flowering of compassion and experiencing the higher transcendent states of Oneness and Universal Love.

Venus in The Houses

Venus in the First House bestows magnetic attraction, benefits, love, grace, and beauty upon the sense of self. The individual is often attractive either through physical beauty, or through one's grace and charm enhancing the personality. There may be an artistic and/or balanced nature. When afflicted there can be excessive self-indulgence, conceit and/or narcissism.

Venus in the Second House bestows magnetic attraction, benefits, love, grace, and beauty upon the area of one's inner and outer resources: including material possessions, income, finances and one's inner values and talents. The individual with this placement may attract financial and material benefits with ease, enjoying and sharing the benefits freely and generously. When afflicted this could manifest as miserly, grasping and/or ungenerous.

Venus in the Third House bestows magnetic attraction, benefits, love, grace, and beauty upon the processes of communication and learning. The individual may have a balanced, harmonious, mind and be able to bring harmony through communication. There may be an artistic nature, and a dislike of arguments. When afflicted there may be intellectual laziness and possible disputes with neighbors and/or siblings.

Venus in the Fourth House bestows magnetic attraction, benefits, love, grace, and beauty upon the area of home and family. There may be a desire to own one's own home, and at least to make one's 'home' beautiful, peaceful and harmonious. The individual may have come from a wealthy background and may also be blessed with a comfortable environment in later life. When afflicted there can be issues with, or estrangement from, one's parents and/ or family of origin.

Venus in the Fifth House bestows magnetic attraction, benefits, love, grace, and beauty upon the area of self-expression and creativity. The individual may be talented in creative expression through art or music. Their warm, generous, nature may give them a natural affinity with children and they may have successful romantic relationships and/or love affairs. There could also be success with financial speculation. When afflicted, there could be problems with love affairs and/ or children and/or financial loss through poor speculative deals.

Venus in the Sixth House bestows magnetic attraction, benefits, love, grace, and beauty upon the area of one's work, health, and responsibilities. The individual prefers balance and harmony in the workplace, both with their co-workers and in terms of their working conditions. They would want equal pay and to receive fair and appropriate remuneration in relation to their investment of time, skill and energy. They could be talented in the area of conflict resolution, but would not want to remain in disharmonious environments for long. Venus in this house usually blesses the individual with good health. When afflicted there can be ill health due to self-indulgence, and/or ongoing problems/ disputes in the working environment, which have a detrimental impact on health.

Venus in the Seventh House bestows magnetic attraction, benefits, love, grace, and beauty upon the area of one's partnerships and relationships. The individual is usually friendly, outgoing, and attracts love (unless other chat factors negate this). There may be success in marriage, partnerships and/or legal contracts. When afflicted there can be difficulty finding the 'right' partner, a string of unsuitable partners, and/or loss or failure through divorce, legal proceedings and/or legal contracts.

Venus in the Eighth House bestows magnetic attraction, benefits, love, grace, and beauty upon the area of other people's money, personal transformation and healing. There can be the potential for personal transformation through close relationships, and/or the power to have a transforming role within the relationship. Venus in the eighth house often indicates an inheritance, possibly through one's partner or their relatives. When afflicted there can be problems through intimate relationships: loss of money, sexually transmitted disease, jealousy, obsessions, and/or excessive possessiveness.

Venus in the Ninth House bestows magnetic attraction, benefits, love, grace, and beauty upon the area of higher learning, higher education and religion, and the deeper search for meaning. The individual may have an idealistic, philosophical outlook with an appreciation for fine art through higher learning. There could be an appreciation for travel and a love relationship with someone from foreign lands is a possibility. There may even be benefits through one's in-laws or, when afflicted there could possibly be problems with one's in-laws.

Venus in the Tenth House bestows magnetic attraction, benefits, love, grace, and beauty upon the area of one's achievements, career, public standing or worldly position. The individual may attract beneficial contacts and circumstances in their career, professional or business sphere and/or their worldly status. They are likely to succeed in their chosen field, and may be popular, because of their loving, amicable, worldview. Unless negated by other chart factors, they probably enjoy public performing and/or speaking and may be quite successful at it. When afflicted there can be difficulties with authority or parental figures and/or there may be a tendency to use contacts solely to advance their own personal ambition.

Venus in the Eleventh House bestows magnetic attraction, benefits, love, grace, and beauty upon the area of groups, societies, friends, community, and shared goals. There may be a strong interest in social values, in joining groups associated with shared social values and working with friends and groups of friends towards shared goals in the humanitarian field. Personal benefits may come through friends and one's network of social contacts. With Venus in this position friends can become lovers, and lovers can become friends. When afflicted there can be anti-social behavior and/or a lack of discrimination in choosing one's friends, leading to associations with friends or groups (gangs) that could be detrimental to oneself.

Venus in the Twelfth House bestows magnetic attraction, benefits, love, grace, and beauty upon the area of one's inner world. The individual may get greater pleasure from spiritual pursuits than worldly success. There may be a desire for solitude, although they are not necessarily lonely. There can be great compassion and a desire to be of service, maybe with a talent for helping the disadvantaged or disabled in some way. They may have a secret romance, or at least be very private about their romantic interests. When afflicted there can be a lack of discrimination in romance, and this individual may become 'imprisoned' in a relationship in some way.

Venus' greatest power lies in her ability to awaken the stirrings of human love which, when properly directed, become the beginning of a journey of awakening that culminates in Universal Divine Love and the realization of our true nature as spiritual beings.

Suggested Fieldwork

- Deeper Self-observation. Take out your own horoscope (natal chart) and make a note in your journal of the sign and house position of Venus. Then read the descriptions above and make a note of any ideas and insights that come to you. Meditate on how Venus might be showing up in your life. Record your impressions and insights in your reflective journal.

- Further Reading: *Soul Centered Astrology: A Key to Your Expanding Self*, by Alan Oken, refer to the appropriate section for more information on Venus. Read about Venus in chapter five of *Soul Astrology*.

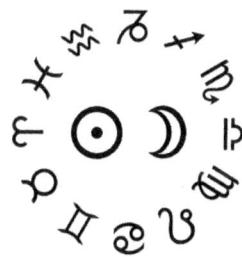

17. Mars, The Pulse of Life

In contrast to Venus' power of attraction (to secure a mate and ensure the ongoing propagation of the species), Mars is the power of propulsion. Mars takes your vitality, the life-force energy given by The Sun, and pulses it into your life activities...

As the God of War it is Mars' job to protect by 'repelling' enemies, potential invaders and other such harmful entities that would be a threat to the continued survival of the species. As such Mars also rules the immune system in the body.

Whereas the energy of Venus is magnetic, Mars' energy is electric. As Venus pulls in, Mars pushes out. Where Venus seductively pulls towards her that which she desires, Mars organizes a war party and goes out and takes it (by force if necessary)! With the two ends of a magnet: Venus would be the attracting pole, Mars would be the repelling pole. So let's explore the purpose of this propelling, repelling, expelling energy of Mars for ongoing spiritual journey.

We are continuing to follow the evolution of human consciousness (and our spiritual development) through the planets. Remember we are evolving through instinct> intellect> intuition> illumination> emptiness (clear light).

To revisit this point see chapter six and, as we proceed with our exploration of Mars, keep in mind that we are still talking at the level of *instinct*.

Mars is the energy of asserting ourselves. If we look to nature, after we have found our mate through the activities of Venus, we may well have a 'nest' and young to protect and provide for. That's where Mars comes into the picture. Mars would be both the energy of 'going out' to find food and resources, and the energy of repelling our foes, protecting our mate, our young, and defending our territory.

So we can see that we are still talking about very primal, instinctive, levels of behavior. It is important to remember how important this level is. In our exploration of Soul Astrology it is tempting to fast-forward to the higher realms and ignore the level of base animal instinct, but if we ignore our foundations, our ivory tower will crumble and fall.

> *"If Venus alone governed the actions of individuals there would be no enterprise, no initiative, no strength to battle with the lower sides of the nature. We would not have the energy to meet the tests of life successfully. We call Mars a malefic, but is it?*
>
> *... What we need is to have the right proportion of every energy operating in our magnetic fields. If you have Mars in a poor sign or afflicted to other energies, study it well. You have the power to change the pattern."*
>
> - Isabel M. Hickey, Astrology: A Cosmic Science

The instinctive level of human behavior is our foundation and as such, deserves great respect. When we ignore our basic needs and drives we run the risk of spiritual bypass[130] and self-delusion. In a culture where we are striving for peace and the realization of our most altruistic self, it can be tempting to step over the fighter, the aggressive, and sometimes violent, facet of our nature. But we would be foolish to do so. The energy represented by Mars plays a very important role in self-assertion and the development of a healthy ego, which serves as a firm foundation for healthy spiritual development.

Just as Venus is the archetype for feminine energy Mars is the archetype of male energy. A positive Mars represents the healthy

---

[130] *Spiritual Bypassing: Avoidance In Holy Drag.* Masters, R. Online document at https://robertmasters.com/2013/04/29/spiritual-bypassing/ Accessed Dec 2nd 2019.

warrior: like the monks of Shaolin[131], with the physical energy, stamina, energy, endurance and ability to complete a project, and all put to good use. The key to healthy and balanced spiritual development is to understand our Mars, rather than rejecting or denying him. When we know our warrior within, understand his energy, and his objectives, we may wield our weapons wisely and appropriately to serve our highest purpose.

Mars the Maleficent

While Venus is considered beneficial because of her capacity to bestow graces and benefits, so in ancient astrology Mars was considered *malefic* because of his capacity to bring trouble and strife. However, as astrology itself has evolved to incorporate psychological astrology, modern astrologers are less inclined to use the term 'malefic' and rather to acknowledge certain challenges which, when addressed, strengthen the individual by providing valuable opportunities for developing qualities such as patience and self-awareness; and for learning important skills such as how to be assertive rather than aggressive, thereby contributing to our healthy self-development.

Mars the Protector God

In mythology Mars was the Roman God of war and while he is often likened to Ares, the Greek God of war, there are significant and important differences. Mars as the God of war is (like Ares) strongly associated with the energies, emotions and worldviews of a warrior: assertion, aggression, strength, energy, activity, fighting, violence, anger, sectarianism, zealotry, tribalism, nationalism; and the tools, processes and activities of war: metal, mechanics, weapons, knives, guns, engineering, military activity.

However it is also important to recognize the other 'face' of Mars. Where the Roman Mars differed from Ares, is that he was not only associated with war but was also a protector, a guardian, a father figure, the epitome of male 'goodness' with the strength and willingness to protect the weak:

"Although Ares was viewed primarily as a destructive and destabilizing force,

---

[131] https://en.wikipedia.org/wiki/Shaolin_Monastery

Mars represented military power as a way to secure peace, and was a father (pater) of the Roman people."[132]

Mars and Aries

On it's journey through all twelve Zodiac signs the Soul begins in Aries as *"a point of light in the mind of God"*. Through the activity if Mars, Aries therefore carries the initial spark of inspiration: the first impulse to exist.

> *"Mars is definitely the planet which rules and controls the physical vehicle. Mars appears first of all as the orthodox ruler in Aries, the sign in which the first move is made towards bringing about objective manifestation, or physical incarnation."*
>
> - The Tibetan, *Esoteric Astrology*

The Soul in Aries is carrying the blueprint and the potential. While we might have a map, and guides to help us keep to it, the success of our grand expedition also depends upon our own efforts and the conditions we meet along the way. At the personality level Mars is the primary energy providing the motivating, driving force. Mars is related to the 'vital body' and brings life-force energy into physical existence. It provides the motivation, power, and movement, that causes the tender shoot to break out of the dark womb-like seed, to strive against the earth and stones, against all odds, to reach the light.

Mars brings drive, motive and motivation. It is the driving force that pushes life-force energy into the physical world. It is the energy of creation, conception and new life (think sperm)! It enlivens and 'vitalizes', brings life and vitality, and is closely related to Patanjali's 'energy' body (see *The Five Bodies* in the previous chapter). The driving force of Mars motivates us into action. This universal force is present throughout Nature.

While it's true that Mars moves us into action, ultimately it is up to us to choose the action we take: conscious action or unconscious reaction. The outcome of our actions depends on our own motivation. It is important for anyone with planets in Aries, especially Mars, to continuously check their motives: are your actions motivated by your ego or your heart and Soul?

---

[132] Mars Mythology on Wikipedia at https://en.wikipedia.org/wiki/Mars_(mythology)

Mars rules the lower octave of Aries, the personality, empowering Aries with motive – the need to move the Self forward into life and light. For the Soul-centered individual, who has fully integrated personality and Soul, the ruler of Aries is Mercury.

Mars and Scorpio

> *"God's idea in Aries becomes the concrete plan in Capricorn whether that objective is the full flower of the planetary life in all its forms, the ambition of a personality working out its own ideas and ambitious worldly projects, or the spiritual aspiration (worldly ambition transmuted into its higher aspect) of the initiate who seeks to work out God's plans and make them his own; in every case, Mars leads to the battle ground of Scorpio."*
>
> - The Tibetan, *Esoteric Astrology*

Following the journey of the Soul through the twelve signs of the Zodiac, after the point of balance between body and Soul has been reached in Libra, the final struggle takes place in Scorpio, the last of the four signs of crisis[133]. This is a kind of birthing and, just like the contractions in physical childbirth, this spiritual rebirth happens in waves.

As the personality gradually comes under the command of the Soul, there are waves of 'depression' where the personality feels as though it is being 'squashed', followed by waves of rebellion where it fights back. The personality doesn't give up easily without a fight! The personality isn't being squashed however, it is being gradually assimilated, as more spiritual energy is able to enter into the being. The end result of this struggle is total fusion of Soul and personality, body and Soul. The personality is the 'interface', the meeting place between the body, with all its animal urges and instinctive impulses, and the finer energies and ethereal vibrations of the Soul: or as The Tibetan described it above, the battle ground in Scorpio.

Three planetary rulers, or space-holders, are the midwives of this birthing process in Scorpio, which is vital for the evolution of humanity from an animalistic being into a fully awakened Soul-centered being. Both Mars and Pluto are guardians of this process at personality level, while Mars is the guardian at Soul level. In

---

[133] See *Signs of Preparation, Crisis and Service* in chapter four.

Esoteric Astrology Mars is considered a greatly beneficial planet. It is through the necessary activity of Mars that this final struggle between personality and Soul is fought and won, with the fully integrated Soul emerging victorious.

Triumph and victory are keywords with Scorpio and it is important to remember this especially when the going gets tough. Mercury is the planetary ruler at Hierarchical level which we won't explore here except to notice that this again hints at the vital importance of Scorpio for the spiritual evolution of humanity.

Mars as Personality and Soul Ruler

As you read on, take note if you have Aries or Scorpio Rising. If so Mars is your Personality Ruler[134] and the condition of Mars by sign, house and aspect will be playing a particularly significant role in your life, by bringing you people and circumstances that have the potential to bring your karmic conditioning into your awareness, for healing, transformation, and release.

If you do have Scorpio Rising know that Mars is also your chart ruler at a Soul level, so the condition of Mars in your chart deserves some deep, ongoing, study and contemplation to develop deeper understandings of your Soul's journey and the unfolding process of personality-Soul fusion[135].

Your Personal Power Indicator

Just like the battery/power indicator on your phone tells you how much energy you have, so you can instantly look to the condition of Mars in your chart to tell you:
- *how much* natural physical power/ energy you have (element),
- *the way it is expressed* (sign) and
- *where* it shows up in your life (house).

For example whether you are someone who invests their energy in sports and physical pursuits (Mars in Aries or Scorpio) or whether you invest more of your energy in conversation (Mars in Gemini).

---

[134] See personality and Soul rulers of the signs in chapter four.

[135] For more about the process of personality-Soul fusion see chapter two.

That said, it is also important to take into account other factors in your chart that influence how you flow your energy. Your Soul Sign (Ascendant) for example will say much about your motivation in life, how you move into new situations, and can even reflect your physical build, your gait and physical movement.

The Sun in your chart also has a great influence on your vitality, or the amount of life-force energy directly available to you at any given time. So you may have a well-placed Mars in a strong sign, but if you have a weak Sun, possibly in the Twelfth House, you would not have as much free energy to draw upon as your Mars would like, in order to drive home your goals.

So in considering Mars, you might think of your Sun more in terms of your overall vitality, and Mars as your personal will, willpower or drive, to get things done.

Mars in the Elements

Unless mitigated by other chart factors Mars in a fire sign will usually have an abundance of energy, stamina and endurance. These are the "Duracell Bunnies" of the zodiac due to their seemingly boundless energy and ability to just keep on going!

Mars in earth and water is slowed down. There is more of a steady flow of energy, or it may even trickle and dry up so there is an apparent lack of energy.

Mars in an air sign can activate and agitate mental activity. This can bring an erratic quality, excessive mental activity, and potentially nervous exhaustion. It is important to focus and ground this mental activity to avoid burnout.

Mars Through The Signs

Martian energy emanates outwardly to protect, defend, or acquire that which he owns, needs, or desires. The condition of Mars in our personal horoscope, by sign and house, describes our will, drive, warrior-like energy and personal power. The sign in which Mars is placed describes what kind of 'inner warrior' we have. The sign will indicate how we express our personal drive or will: how energetic we are (or not), how we express or assert our will (or not), our capacity to protect and defend ourselves and our own, the nature of our personal 'inner warrior', and the nature of our sexual drive.
The house will indicate where in your life this energy is directed.

Mars in Aries - dignity

When Mars is in Aries the individual usually has a great deal of energy. They can be energetic, enthusiastic, courageous, driven, passionate and assertive. Mars is said to be indignity in this sign meaning his energy flows well and he is most free and uninhibited in his effects. Depending upon aspects to other planets Mars here can also be combative and aggressive. This is the archetype of the warrior. If well placed this brings someone with great endurance, drive, and much energy to drive projects forward. If poorly aspected this can be someone who constantly drives themselves (and others) to the point of exhaustion. There could also be constant conflict and/or violence. Their sexual nature can be direct and passionate but may often lack consideration for their partner.

On a Soul level this placement can be a challenge due to the constant activity it brings. These individuals are people who like to keep themselves busy, whether with mental or physical activity depends upon other chart factors but nonetheless it is all too easy to keep oneself distracted from spiritual goals. When this passion is directed into spiritual activity and practice, it can be a powerful force for accelerating one's progress on the spiritual path.

Mars in Taurus - detriment

When Mars is in Taurus the individual usually asserts their energy with patience and determination towards tangible material outcomes. Mars is said to be in detriment in Taurus, meaning his energy is weakened and his power is minimized. Therefore there can also be an inertia or lack of drive to assert oneself toward one's goals. Individuals with Mars in Taurus like to see tangible results and a good 'return on investment' for 'spending' their energy. They can therefore be motivated into action by some kind of material or financial reward. When they do move into action they can be very patient and persistent in their approach. When afflicted there can be excessive possessiveness, acquisitiveness and miserliness. Their sexual nature is likely to be very sensual.

On a Soul level this placement could initially present an obstacle to spiritual development if it keeps the individual's energy engaged in the material world and the acquisition of material wealth and worldly success.

If the individual has an interest in spiritual growth, and channels their energy into a dedicated spiritual practice, this placement can then become an asset, bringing the necessary patience, persistence and determination to stay with their chosen path until higher realizations are attained.

Mars in Gemini

Individuals with Mars in Gemini often direct their energy toward many varied and different goals. They have great versatility and can often handle many projects at once. There may however be a tendency to dissipate one's energies due to too many projects. Lack of follow through and/or completion can be a problem as a result. There can be many ideas, but procrastination can exist as ideas may be more often talked about, rather than acted upon. Other chart factors would indicate whether there is a capacity to bring projects through to completion. Mars in Gemini tends to talk rather than fight, so individuals with this placement are often fervent communicators however their speech can be combative, especially if the third house is involved. When afflicted words can be used as a weapon, so there can be sarcasm and/ or gossip. The sexual nature seeks versatility and is stimulated by ideas and communication.

On a Soul level Mars in Gemini can bring challenges through the scattering of one's energy to the winds. This placement is good for studying many different religions and/or spiritual paths, and developing an eclectic, non-denominational, non-sectarian, approach to spirituality with a healthy respect for the many different traditions. However, for the purpose of their own spiritual growth, the individual will also need to learn to concentrate and focus their energy into one spiritual path or religion, to go deeper with that, so that intellectual understanding can be translated into actual spiritual experience through practice.

Mars in Cancer - fall

Individuals with Mars in Cancer often approach goals and projects covertly and/or in a roundabout way. Mars is said to 'fall' in Cancer, which means his energy is somewhat repressed and unable to flow freely. This means the individual's energy tends to circle around a goal, project, or conflict, rather than approaching it head on. Mars in Cancer is more the protector than the warrior. There can be a lack of drive, energy and/or motivation unless home and/or family are involved, in which case the individual will direct their energy into securing their home base and ensuring their family's needs are met. Safety and security are their priorities. There can be an emotional sensitivity that is not outwardly expressed but can lead to inner brooding. The sexual nature can be lazy so the partner may have to work hard at keeping their sexual relationship alive. Can be excessively possessive and jealous when afflicted.

On a Soul level this can be a good placement for someone who chooses to become consciously celibate and re-direct their sexual energy inwardly, to ensure spiritual progress. Enthusiastic energy may need to be consciously developed, and care taken to ensure one is on a valid spiritual path with a qualified teacher to prevent self-delusion, but with those parameters in place there is potential to make steady progress in terms of one's spiritual development.

Mars in Leo

Individuals with Mars in Leo have great passion, enthusiasm and vitality. Unless mitigated by other factors in the chart, they also often have a great capacity for inspiring others which, combined with their own boundless energy and enthusiasm, means they are capable of achieving seemingly impossible tasks, projects and goals. Mars in Leo is the energy of getting things done, however there can also be a great need for acknowledgement of, and appreciation for, one's achievements. Can be argumentative and jealous if afflicted. The sexual nature is passionate.

On a Soul level Leo is the path of self-realization. Mars in Leo brings a great deal of courage, energy and enthusiasm to activate one's path to deeply understanding your own true nature. The challenge will be in releasing your need for attention, feedback, or approval from others, so that you can walk your own path clearly, without distraction, keeping your own attention on you.

Mars in Virgo

Individuals with Mars in Virgo are diligent, often with a great capacity for hard work and a desire to be of service. Energy is often filtered through mental activity: so there can be self-doubt, too much over thinking of projects, and energy can be wasted by spending too much energy analyzing minor details. When afflicted, Mars in Virgo can be unproductive and may appear lazy, as goals are thwarted by procrastination and over-analysis. The sexual nature can be erratic: one may be sensual at times, but over thinking can quickly pour cold water on one's passion. Sometimes there is an overly moralistic or prudish approach to sexuality.

On a Soul level Mars in Virgo can be good for steady progress in terms of one's spiritual development. If over thinking can be redirected into study and contemplation, and combined with a devotional approach to spiritual practice, there is the potential for great spiritual realizations through personal experience.

Mars in Libra - detriment

Individuals with Mars in Libra are most enthusiastic and energetic in relationships and partnerships. Like Taurus Mars is also said to be in detriment in Libra, meaning his energy is weakened and his power is minimized. Therefore there can be a lack of personal willpower or drive and a reluctance to assert oneself. One's personal energy is most active and 'enlivened' when engaging in interactions with others: relating, relationship and partnerships. When afflicted however, there can be a tendency to be argumentative. The sexual nature can be lazy with an over-reliance on the partner making all the moves.

On a Soul level Mars in Libra can present distractions from one's own spiritual development by keeping the individual engaged in interactions, arguments and verbal conflicts, with others. If one can release attachment to others and re-direct this energy into a healthy relating with oneself, there is potential for a deeper understanding of self and higher mind.

Mars in Scorpio - dignity

Individuals with Mars in Scorpio have formidable strength and power. They are focused, intense, strong-willed and persistent, ensuring they get what they want. Like Aries, Mars is also said to be in dignity in this sign meaning his energy flows well and he is most free and uninhibited in his effects. There can be a great drive for power and dominance but such a powerful energy needs to be handled wisely. Having Mars in Scorpio is like being gifted with a powerful racing car that you need to learn how to drive. When afflicted there can be stubbornness, jealousy and cruelty and much energy can be wasted by brooding and plotting revenge against perceived 'enemies'.

Care must be taken not to waste one's vital life force energy in constant sparring or feuding. The sexual nature is often intense and passionate. When Mars is in Scorpio there is an orientation toward sex, and unless mitigated by other chart factors, an active sex life is to be expected. However when afflicted, there can also be control, dominance and manipulation of one's partner to serve one's own purposes. When well placed there can be powerful healing ability.

On a Soul level the focused, transformational, power of Mars in Scorpio brings great potential for the development of spiritual energy and realizations. It is a powerful placement to support personal transformation and healing. Care must be taken not to misdirect this energy, so time spent choosing one's spiritual teacher, to ensure one is on a valid spiritual path and not deluded by one's own ego, will be time well spent.

Mars in Sagittarius

Individuals with Mars in Sagittarius are often energetic, enthusiastic and inspiring. There can be a restless quality as Mars in Sagittarius seeks the next 'adventure' to inspire him. Mars here is more the adventurer and explorer, than the warrior. Depending upon other chart factors this can be actual physical adventures or adventures of the mind, as he broadens his horizons and formulates his 'philosophies'. When afflicted he can be bombastic and overly opinionated. Sagittarius is symbolized by the centaur: half man and half horse, so the sexual nature depends upon which aspect is dominant in any individual. Depending upon other factors in the chart, there could either be a free-spirited, possibly lustful or even animalistic quality to the sexual nature, or there could be a more philosophical approach where the sexual nature is restrained or suppressed by idealistic moral or religious beliefs.

On a Soul level Mars in Sagittarius is an excellent placement for channeling one's energies into self-exploration and the adventure of one's own spiritual journey. Because of an idealistic outlook there is a danger of attachment to belief systems, getting caught up in cults or following false teachers, so working with a qualified teacher or guide is imperative to ensure one is aligning with authentic spiritual practices that will lead to the desired results of true liberation and enlightenment. Esoterically Sagittarius is associated with liberation of the mind, so it is important that our Archer doesn't settle too easily, but always keeps re-aligning his sights on the highest possible goal.

Mars in Capricorn - exaltation

Individuals with Mars in Capricorn are ambitious, conservative, strategic, responsible and determined in the pursuit of their personal goals. In Capricorn Mars is said to be exalted, which means his energy is most active and able to flow freely. The drive, endurance, energy and stamina of Mars, combined with the focus and disciplined approach of Capricorn, is a powerful force for achieving one's objectives and driving projects through to completion. When well placed there is great potential to channel this energy through positions of power and responsibility to do great good in the world. When afflicted there can be ruthless, even cruel, ambition as the individual does whatever it takes to get themselves to the top and undermine their competitors. Depending upon other chart factors the sexual nature can be either controlled and restricted, or self-indulgent and controlling.

On a Soul level Mars in Capricorn has great potential. Here is the archetype of the "warrior monk", like the world-renowned kung-fu monastics of the Shaolin temple in China. The challenge is to set aside worldly power and ambition and re-direct one's warrior energy into one's spiritual practice. If this can be done successfully, spiritual ambition replaces worldly ambition, spiritual goals replace worldly goals, and there is the potential to become a great spiritual master through the correct application of enthusiastic energy, wisdom, patience and discipline.

Mars in Aquarius

Individuals with Mars in Aquarius can be unorthodox both in the types of goals they pursue, and in their efforts to pursue those goals. They may choose idealistic and/or bizarre goals, often involving a humanitarian element. They may pick up the ball and run with it one minute, and drop it the next, as they pursue a new goal or direction. They can swing between periods of inactivity and periods of activity. When Mars is afflicted they can be antagonistic and argumentative. Their energy is often best channeled through social or group activity. The sexual nature can be unpredictable and/or unconventional.

On a Soul level Mars in Aquarius presents the challenge of the bodhisattva[136]: how to dedicate one's personal will, actions, and energy to the collective, for the highest good of all, without depleting or diminishing one's energy in the process? To reach this high level of spiritual capacity involves the right use of personal energy. The challenge for Mars in Aquarius is to apply oneself consistently enough to be able to reach this level of spiritual mastery. In some Buddhist traditions they teach about the 'generation' stage and the 'completion' stage. This refers to one's capacity to generate

---

[136] *"Bodhisattva — someone who has aroused bodhichitta, the compassionate wish to attain enlightenment for the benefit of all beings and also wishes to bring them to that state."* From https://www.rigpawiki.org/index.php?title=Bodhisattva

spiritual energy and then to direct it and use it wisely and appropriately. This is the highest path of Aquarius that becomes available once one's personal energy (Mars) has been tamed and directed appropriately.

Mars in Pisces

Individuals with Mars in Pisces can be inconsistent and indiscriminate in their choice of goals and their approach. There can be a failure to achieve one's goals due to a lack of strength or drive to push them through. Depending upon other chart factors there can sometimes be a strengthening of inner will, and an increased inner determination, as if to compensate for perceived weakness however, this is rarely expressed outwardly. Where Mars in Pisces does experience success, unless other chart factors mitigate, it is likely to be from controlling situations behind the scenes, away from public view. The sexual nature is sensitive and emotional.

On a Soul level Mars in Pisces is a good placement for directing one's energies inwards and pursuing inner goals. There is a transcendent quality to Pisces that allows for the transformation and transmutation of physical, Martian, energy into real spiritual energy. However, due to the indiscriminate nature of Pisces it is also all too easy to be misguided and misdirect one's energy: getting 'lost' in self-delusion, following false teachers or wasting time and energy in wrongly-applied practices. It is therefore extremely important to triple-check that one is on a valid spiritual path with an authentic spiritual teacher.

Mars in The Houses

Mars in the First House directs one's will, drive, warrior-like energy and personal power to the sense of self. The individual may see themselves as a 'warrior' someone who stands and fights for their cause (what they have and/or what they believe in). Unless other chart factors mitigate they are likely to have great energy, drive, enthusiasm, and can be fearless, confident, assertive and even aggressive when confronting an issue.

Mars in the Second House directs one's will, drive, warrior-like energy and personal power to the area of one's inner and outer resources: including material possessions, income, finances and one's inner values and talents. Individuals with this placement may generate income from Mars-type pursuits such as engineering, mechanics, sports or the military. (Mars rules metals so professions that use metal knives or weapons also fall into this category such as surgeons and even butchers)! When afflicted there can be loss of income, finances, possessions and/or property due to conflict.

Mars in the Third House directs one's will, drive, warrior-like energy and personal power to the processes of communication, thinking and learning. The individual may have an over-active mind, which is not necessarily conducive to learning. There can be an agitation, restlessness, and an impatience with the learning process, which the individual may also find confining: either they dislike being confined to one subject, or to a particular environment, as they prefer to keep moving both mentally and physically. If afflicted there can be nervousness and/ or arguments with siblings and/ or neighbors. These individuals may find it helpful to apply their mental energy to some kind of research or investigative work where their constant mental activity can be put to good use.

Mars in the Fourth House directs one's will, drive, warrior-like energy and personal power to the area of home and family. The fourth house is also said to be the area representing our psychological roots because according to Western Psychology and Psychological Astrology, much of our own psychology and unconscious behavior has its roots in our early childhood experiences in the home. Soul Astrology would simply add that there are also past life influences that we carry forward in our own psyche. Mars here activates the home environment. This could be the family that keeps busy and engages in activities together, such as sports and the individual may be very active in and around their home. There may have been restlessness, agitation, domestic troubles or violence in the early childhood environment. When afflicted this individual may have difficulty finding peace in their home, which could be blighted by conflict and arguments.

Mars in the Fifth House directs one's will, drive, warrior-like energy and personal power to the area of self-expression and creativity. Individuals with this placement may throw themselves into life's pleasures with gusto. They may have a love of children and/or a playful approach to life. Love of sports, gambling and high-risk activities are likely. There can be a strong tendency to indulge the passions, and these individuals are likely to enjoy the pursuit of romance, rather than the long-term subtleties of romantic relationships. When afflicted there can be break ups in romantic relationships due to conflict.

Mars in the Sixth House directs one's will, drive, warrior-like energy and personal power to the area of one's work, health, and responsibilities. Individuals with this placement will throw themselves into their work, which may include a talent for mechanics. Care must be taken to avoid challenges to health due to excessive work activity and too little focus on self-care. When afflicted there can be conflicts with employees and/ or co-workers.

Mars in the Seventh House directs one's will, drive, warrior-like energy and personal power to the area of one's partnerships and relationships. Much of the individual's energy is invested in relationships and/or partnerships. They can be very inspiring partners and bring a great deal of enthusiasm and energy to the partnership. Sometimes relationships and partnerships may be entered into impulsively with too little planning. This can lead to conflicts and break ups further down the road due to incompatibilities. When afflicted there can be conflict, aggressiveness, divorce or other legal battles.

Mars in the Eighth House directs one's will, drive, warrior-like energy and personal power to the area of other people's money, personal transformation and healing. Individuals with this placement have a great deal of energy and, unless mitigated by other chart factors, they will have a strong sex drive. Their involvement with other people's money and resources can take the form of supporting others in re-arranging, transforming or regenerating their resources or, if afflicted, the individual may become dependent upon the other person's resources to meet their own needs. When well placed by sign and aspect this can be a powerful position to support regeneration and healing of oneself and others.

Mars in the Ninth House directs one's will, drive, warrior-like energy and personal power to the area of higher learning, higher education and religion, and the deeper search for meaning. Individuals with this placement often have a great enthusiasm for higher learning, education, long-distance travel and/or the search for the meaning of life. They are usually independent thinkers actively engaged in the constant expansion of their own minds. However, when afflicted, their natural zeal and enthusiasm may turn into fanaticism and conflict can result from being too attached to one's own opinions and/or belief systems. There can be great restlessness and an inability to settle down, due to constant activity and either frequent long-distance travel, or a constant longing for travel and excitement that takes them away from the present moment.

Mars in the Tenth House directs one's will, drive, warrior-like energy and personal power to the area of one's achievements, career, public standing or worldly position. Individuals with this placement usually direct their energy and activities toward their career and/or worldly status. Unless offset by other chart factors, they may desire a formal public position, status, award, validation or some form of public recognition, for they like their efforts and achievements to be noticed and acknowledged. There can be a talent for promotion, which is usually self-promotion. They can sometimes be excellent promoters of others, provided they receive formal acknowledgement that recognizes and elevates their own status. When afflicted there can be estrangement from the father and/or conflict with authority figures.

Mars in the Eleventh House directs one's will, drive, warrior-like energy and personal power to the area of groups, societies, friends, community and shared goals. The individual is likely to invest a lot of energy and enthusiasm into goals and objectives, especially those that are working towards a shared goal. Much of their energy can also be directed into friendships however, when afflicted, the individual may have difficulty sustaining friendships, tend to use friends to achieve their own objectives, and/or friends may become enemies. These are people who are likely to initiate, activate, and energize group activities and they may take the lead very quickly in any groups, communities, and societies that they belong to. When afflicted there can be a tendency to dominate group and/or social activities.

Mars in the Twelfth House directs one's will, drive, warrior-like energy and personal power to the area of one's inner world. Individuals with this placement may have an air of secrecy about their actions and activities. This can be because of a conscious choice on their part to keep their actions secret but it can also be because the type of activity they are engaged in are not openly seen by others. There can be an interest in matters of the occult, the psyche and/or the unconscious mind, and/or the individual may work with others who are involved in some form of confinement: prisons, monasteries or institutions. When afflicted there can be hidden enemies who may attempt to undermine one's actions and/or there can be a backfiring of one's actions that leads to self-destruction.

Mars creates the conditions for us to assert ourselves as an individual and to move forward into the world to get what we need. Physiologically Mars rules the blood, sexual activity and our body's inflammatory responses. At the instinct level of human development and evolution Mars is all about protect and survive. Through the conditioning of Mars we seek out what is needed to provide for ourselves and our mate, protect ourselves, our family and our tribe from adversaries, fight off the competition (so we get to keep our chosen mate), and engage in the necessary sexual activity for the reproduction and ongoing survival of our group and species. Mars is exalted in Capricorn, the sign of the resource manager and esoterically the sign for right use of resources. It is the conditioning of Mars that ensures that all of earth's creatures have access to the resources we need to survive.

This concludes our exploration of the *instinct* level of evolution by exploring how, throughout the animal kingdom, the conditions for the instinctive existence and survival of a species are held in place by the activities of the personal planets, The Sun, Moon, Mercury, Venus and Mars: the planetary spaceholders for the instinct level of our development.

In the following chapters we will explore the social planets and their role in the evolutionary development of human intellect.

Suggested Fieldwork

• Deeper Self-observation. Take out your own horoscope (natal chart) and make a note in your journal of the sign and house position of Mars. Then read the descriptions above and make a note of any ideas and insights that come to you. Meditate on how Mars might be showing up in your life. Record your impressions and insights in your reflective journal.

• Further Reading: *Soul Centered Astrology: A Key to Your Expanding Self,* by Alan Oken, refer to the appropriate section for more information on Mars. Read about Mars in chapter five of *Soul Astrology*.

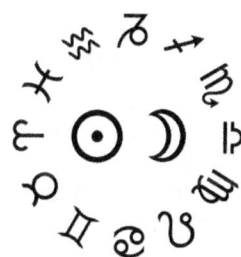

18. Jupiter and The Emergence of God Consciousness

Jupiter is the personality ruler of Sagittarius and Pisces and the Soul Ruler of Aquarius. According to *Esoteric Astrology* Jupiter is a sacred planet because Jupiter creates the conditions for the expansion of learning and wisdom. When we think of wisdom we think of the fine-tuning of the intellect and, as we continue our evolutionary journey from instinct to intellect[137], Jupiter does indeed create the conditions for our first expansion of intellect beyond our instinctive nature. However, esoterically Jupiter is associated with Ray 2[138] - the path of Love-Wisdom, and the higher wisdom of Jupiter has the potential to propel us way beyond intellect into higher states of awareness.

Jupiter is the energy of growth and expansion. We can see that once we have established ourselves as individuals, with a home and family, the next part of our human journey, both personally and collectively, is to expand our horizons: to see beyond our immediate family; to take steps to connect with, build, create and contribute to, a sense of community. Who is our tribe? and what do we stand for? It is the energy of Jupiter that creates the conditions for us to expand our personal experience, and therefore our mind, wisdom and belief systems, beyond the conditioning of our immediate family.

---

[137] See chapter six: The Planets.

[138] Read more about the Seven Rays in chapter one4.

Jupiter, Saturn, and The Evolution of Intellect

As we evolve through the levels of instinct > intellect > intuition > illumination and emptiness, it is important to remember that each stage is necessary. It's not that we 'lose' our instincts as we move into intellect, but rather that each stage is a vital foundation for what comes next. So by the time we reach the level of the wisdom realizing emptiness, we also realize that we are also all of it. We are everything that has gone before. We don't 'transcend' instinct by 'getting rid of it' but rather it becomes integrated into our whole being.

Intellect is where we use our thinking mind as a tool. We are able to think, and to use our thinking for personal and collective advancement. It is important to distinguish intellect from intelligence, as the two are often confused. All animals have innate intelligence. The instinct that we have been discussing so far in this book is also a form of intelligence, and when we get to the next stage of intuition that too, is a form of intelligence. Intelligence is our capacity to be aware. Intellect is our capacity to think.

In astrology, the Sun, Moon, Mercury, Venus and Mars, are known as the personal planets because their influence is more about us, directly, as individuals. Next we come to the social planets, Jupiter and Saturn. Although they do have a powerful effect on us individually, they are also the interface where we, as individuals, meet and mingle with the wider society beyond our immediate family.

Jupiter creates the conditions for us to expand our minds beyond our immediate self-consciousness. Through Jupiter we expand our learning, give and receive education, and distribute knowledge. We are able to cultivate a 'philosophy' by thinking, what is the 'best' way to do, or be? Or, what is good? Jupiter is known as the 'greater benefic', bringing all that is beneficial.

As humankind began to move out of our immediate family and organize ourselves into larger communities, we were able to share wisdom and knowledge so that we could learn from each other, spread knowledge and share resources, and our groups could evolve faster together than we could alone.

No surprise then that Jupiter is exalted in the sign of Cancer, the sign of nurturing, empathy, emotional intelligence, and human connection.

Jupiter and Civilization

If we stop to think about evolution for a moment, evolutionary theory tells us that way, way back, when humans first appeared on earth, we initially just lived together in large families. Much like we can imagine other primates do today: gorillas, orangutans and chimpanzees organize themselves loosely in large extended families. Some groups (especially chimpanzees) can grow pretty large but we wouldn't say they organized themselves into a 'tribe', at least not in the way that humans would think of a tribe.

The development of intellect, under the influence of Jupiter, allowed us to organize ourselves into increasingly larger societies: initially by tribe, then by village, town, city, and eventually by nation. As our experience expanded so did our sense of identity (we often think of ourselves as belonging to groups of various sizes from our family to our nation and everything in-between), and our 'philosophy'.

Jupiter and Philosophy

Jupiter is the planet most associated with philosophy and religion, indeed belief systems of all kinds. Following the expansion of knowledge and learning, through the expansion of intellect, the next logical step is to apply what we have learned systematically to support the organization and smooth running of the society. Jupiter also rules logic, and reason.

Although the literal translation of philosophy is *love of wisdom* (from the ancient Greek *philos* = love and *sophia* = wisdom) the conventional meaning is *the study of general and fundamental questions about existence, knowledge, values, reason, mind, and language*[139]. As societies became civilizations, by bringing the intellectual capacity to develop logic and reason, Jupiter played a huge role in the formation of *culture* (the behavioral 'norms' of any group, society or nation).

As human group sizes also grew exponentially, we needed more advanced ways to communicate and, as we shall see, it was about much more than just sharing information...

---

[139] *"Philosophy is the study of general and fundamental questions about existence, knowledge, values, reason, mind, and language."* Online document at https://en.wikipedia.org/wiki/Philosophy Accessed Dec 2nd 2019.

Grooming, Gossip and the Evolution of Language: the deeper meaning of social networking

A fascinating hypothesis is posed in one of my all-time favorite books, *Grooming, Gossip and the Evolution of Language*[140] by Dr. Robin Dunbar. Basically the idea is that language evolved as a way for humans to 'groom' larger groups of allies.

Amongst primates, daily grooming is vital for bonding in the formation of essential group loyalty ties. When a fight breaks out in the group, this is how chimpanzees will know in a split second who to side with, and who has their back. When all hell breaks loose, it is loyal and favorite grooming partners who will side with each other.

It might be an idealist concept to think that we shouldn't be prejudiced or have favorites, but this denies the actual reality of how primate groups (including us) have always operated since beginningless time!

In primitive groups, meaning groups where behavior is largely determined by instinct such as a gang, loyalty bonding is an essential process. Hanging out is not just purposeless socializing, it is a matter of life and death. Chimpanzees without adequate *alliances* in the group have been known to be beaten to death[141]. We can see it is not so very different in human gangs.

Clearly, you can only get around to physically grooming so many people in a day! Dunbar's theory is that, as human groups grew in size, we evolved language as a way to 'groom' larger groups of people and thereby cement those all-important loyalty bonds. He proposes that this is why the ideal military unit is no larger than 150, because that is about the limit of our capacity to feel a sense of loyalty and reciprocal protectiveness.

While Mercury has a role to play in the actions of communication itself, Jupiter plays a role in the forging of beneficial alliances, and in determining who are the beneficial influencers in your network. Basically, Jupiter influences who's got your back!

---

[140] Dunbar, R. (2004) *Grooming, Gossip and the Evolution of Language.* Faber and Faber.

[141] Moss, S; Attenborough, D. (2018) *Dynasties: The Rise and Fall of Animal Families.* BBC Books.

Jupiter - The Greater Benefic

In conventional astrology two planets are considered generally beneficial: Venus and Jupiter. We discussed in a previous chapter how Venus was considered the lesser benefic, and now we have Jupiter: The Greater Benefic. Wherever he is placed in your chart Jupiter is said to bring all good things: health, wealth, wisdom and abundance. However, this is not always the case and, as we shall see, some of the excesses of Jupiter can also bring health challenges and other obstacles to our spiritual growth.

Jupiter in Excess - Too Much of A God Thing

Jupiter connects us with (and expands) the faculty of intellect, however this expansion does not come with a commensurate measure of spiritual truth, realization or experience. So there can be an expansion of belief systems, opinions and philosophies that are pure mental constructions with no basis in spiritual reality afflicted, the exaggerating tendencies of Jupiter can have deleterious effects on the personality, bringing delusions of grandeur, a "God-like" demeanor, self-indulgence, and sometimes a tendency to weight gain through over-indulgence.

In our ego-centric society, where individuality is not only acknowledged but actively encouraged, some of the more grandiose and materialistic facets of Jupiter can actually present huge obstacles on our spiritual path. Often what the ego-personality thinks of as a good thing: comfort, leisure, material gain, wealth, can be a 'bad' thing in terms of our spiritual development. We can develop what Herman Hesse (in his classic book *Siddhartha*) referred to as the "Soul-sickness of the rich", meaning we simply become too comfortable where we are. Hanging out in the 'god-realms', enjoying our sense pleasures, and having a good old time, can create strong attachment to the illusion of a separate self, and this will carry us farther away from spiritual progress and the realization of our true nature.

It is important to remember that what often seems like a 'bad' thing to the ego, can actually be excellent from the Soul's perspective! For example, in my own chart Jupiter in serious Capricorn doesn't seem like much fun from the personality's point of view. Yet this is precisely what enables me to explore deeper wisdom (Jupiter) from various spiritual paths (Capricorn), and then be of service (Sixth House) by sharing insights with others.

Look to Jupiter by sign, house, and aspect, in your own chart to see where Jupiter may be enhancing your wisdom, exaggerating your self-delusion, or both.

Jupiter and Generosity

Jupiter is considered a planet of benevolence and generosity. Wherever Jupiter appears in your chart, unless mitigated by other chart factors, he is said to bestow a spirit of generosity.

According to some Buddhist schools of thought, the practice of generosity is considered an important spiritual practice because it is considered an antidote to the powerful energy of ego-grasping that keeps us stuck in *samsara*[142] (the suffering cycle of death and rebirth). It is therefore considered an important practice on the path to enlightenment (liberation from samsara).

So in his role as bringer of generosity, we are already beginning to see a glimpse of Jupiter's vital role in our path to spiritual awakening.

Jupiter - The Sky God

In mythology, Jupiter was the Roman God of the Sky. He is often considered to be the Roman equivalent of the Greek God Zeus, and is also known as Jove. Like Zeus he was also considered to be the King of the Gods, and was the chief deity in the Roman pantheon. He is identified by his thunderbolt and his sacred animal is the Eagle.

The Romans where not the only ones to identify the Sky and the Eagle with the supreme Divinity. In the Tibetan tradition the most important state of consciousness that we can reach, the ultimate enlightenment of 'clear light mind' is often described as being 'like the sky'.

---

[142] *"Samsara, (Sanskrit: "flowing around") in Indian philosophy, the central conception of metempsychosis: the soul, finding itself awash in the "sea of samsara," strives to find release (moksha) from the bonds of its own past deeds (karma), which form part of the general web of which samsara is made. Buddhism, which does not assume the existence of a permanent soul, accepts a semipermanent personality core that goes through the process of samsara."* - definition of Samsara from *Encyclopoedia Britannica*. Online document at https://www.britannica.com/topic/samsara Accessed December 10th 2019.

"Everything is like the sky - this is what I have to realize"

- Shantideva

There is also great significance of the Thunderbolt or Dorje (Vajra in Sanskrit) in the Tibetan tradition as a ritual object used to symbolize both the properties of a diamond (indestructibility) and a thunderbolt (irresistible force). In Tibetan Buddhism 'diamond-like' mind is often used as a metaphor for clear light mind, our innermost awareness that is said to be clear and indestructible like a diamond.

In some Native American traditions the eagle is also a symbol of Great Spirit, the ultimate Divinity, Supreme Being, or universal nature that permeates all.

Jupiter in Esoteric Astrology

In *Esoteric Astrology* Jupiter is associated with Ray 2[143], Love-Wisdom, also known as *The Path of Love*. The Earth is considered a Ray 2 planet, and the path of love is considered to be the path which humanity is to follow, if earth is to become a sacred planet like her sister Venus.

> *"Jupiter and its influences indicate that the way of incarnation is the "beneficent" method of evolutionary unfoldment and that the way of love-wisdom (second ray) is the way for humanity to go."*

- The Tibetan, *Esoteric Astrology*

Jupiter therefore has an important role to play in the process of Personality-Soul Fusion, and during the early stages of spiritual awakening this happens by creating conditions that awaken us to our Soul's presence.

For those who are on the mutable cross in terms of their spiritual development Jupiter can bring those initial early awakening experiences, that first 'quickening' that perhaps there is more to this being human than meets the eye, and therefore begin the process of awakening onto the fixed cross and the awareness of one's spiritual nature.

---

[143] Read more about the Seven Rays in chapter fourteen.

> *"Jupiter gives an inherent tendency to fusion which nothing can arrest. The achievement of ultimate synthesis is inevitable, and this Jupiter promotes"*
>
> - The Tibetan, *Esoteric Astrology*

It is through the effects of Jupiter, namely the development of intellect and our ability to conceptualize, that we are first able to wonder: where did we come from? Who created us? and ... Who, or what, is God. It is through this aspect of Jupiter that we develop primary God-consciousness in the sense that we are first able to conceptualize, or have an idea, that one god, many gods, or a Creator exists.

Jupiter Crossing Your Ascendant

When transiting Jupiter crosses your Rising Sign (Ascendant/AC) there are often challenges for the personality that are also great opportunities for Soul activation and awakening. For example, if you have Cancer Rising, transiting Jupiter (which is exalted in Cancer) crossing your AC may lead to over-indulgence and an expansion of the waistline! However, from a spiritual perspective it is an opportunity for you to identify where you can let go of attachment; change limiting habit patterns; and look to where you have a deeper need for spiritual nourishment.

Jupiter and Sagittarius

Jupiter is the personality ruler of Sagittarius. As a planet of expansiveness and higher mind, Jupiter's role in conditioning us at personality level is one of expanding awareness and consciousness. It is through the influence of Jupiter, that one realizes there is something 'higher' to aim for: a bigger, larger, grander picture of ourselves beyond our small, limited, mind.

Jupiter invites us to expand our vision, our awareness and our experience of our self. Initially the earliest inkling of self-awareness shows up as self-consciousness in Leo. Jupiter's expansive influence in Sagittarius then invites us to expand our experience on all levels, so we can expand our awareness.

Taken to extremes at personality level this expansive tendency can lead to self-indulgence and leave our Sagittarian friends with an expanding waistline! However it is important to note that although Jupiter is the largest planet in the solar system, it is largely comprised of gas. The symbology here implies expansion beyond the density of physical matter. Jupiter encourages us to expand our minds.

Jupiter's role is to create the conditions to guide us from small mind to higher mind. When we are in small mind we are limited by mental concepts and ideals. We impose limitation on ourselves by creating mental concepts and then adhering to them as though they were truth.

When we know the difference between small mind (personality level) and higher mind (Soul level), we see a distinction between religion and spirituality and begin to understand why both are associated with Sagittarius.

When we follow a religious path, at first we adhere closely to a creed or code of conduct. Although religious traditions are mental constructs, they have been created for the ultimate purpose of taking us beyond religion itself to experience higher spiritual truth. It is a path that someone created. The danger lies in mistaking the path itself for spiritual reality, and this is one of the pitfalls of Sagittarius.

Under the guardianship of Jupiter, Sagittarius resonates with the highest truth of our spiritual nature but before this is realized, the Sagittarian personality has to let go of all mental conceptions that are mistaken as truth. Sooner or later the Sagittarian personality realizes that his beloved mental concepts actually obscure his perception of truth.

"The weighing of opinions only prevents the perception of truth"

- Jiddu Krishnamurti

Jupiter and Pisces

Jupiter is co-ruler of Pisces with Neptune at the personality level. Jupiter's role here is transcendental: to expand the sense of self beyond the individual. Ultimately Pisces is the sign of Universal Mind (the Soul Ruler of Pisces is Pluto), so Jupiter's role at the personality level is to bring to the individual those experiences that expand one's awareness beyond the personality: beyond the sense of an individual mind, beyond conventional concepts of individuality and mind, to experience the boundless, oceanic, universal mind beyond, where we may be receptive to the blissful transcendent experiences of Neptune.

Jupiter and Aquarius

Jupiter is the Soul ruler of Aquarius. The heightened intuition of Aquarius' personality ruler Uranus, combined with the expansiveness of Jupiter, serve to expand the fullness of experience towards Universal Mind by supporting the fusion of mind energy (intuition) and heart energy (bliss). Jupiter then plays a major role in the fusion of head and heart, so that the 'dual waters' in the Aquarius Soul combine to form one steady stream that we may call 'heart-mind'.

Jupiter as Personality and Soul Ruler

As you read on, take note if you have Sagittarius or Pisces Rising. If so Jupiter is your Personality Ruler and the condition of Jupiter by sign, house and aspect will be playing a particularly significant role in your life, by bringing you people and circumstances that have the potential to bring your karmic conditioning into your awareness, for healing, transformation, and release.

If you have Aquarius Rising know that Jupiter is your chart ruler at a Soul level, so the condition of Jupiter in your chart deserves some deep, ongoing, study and contemplation to develop deeper understandings of your Soul's journey and the unfolding process of personality-Soul fusion.

Jupiter Through The Signs

Jupiter's energy is unbounded in his infinite expansion of your horizons. The condition of Jupiter in your personal horoscope, by sign and house, describes your capacity for wealth, abundance and generosity, in addition to the acquisition of knowledge and wisdom. The sign in which Jupiter is placed describes what kind of 'inner benefactor' you have. The sign will indicate how you express your wisdom and generosity (or not), and how you approach wisdom, higher learning and even religion. The house will indicate where in your life this energy is directed.

Jupiter in Aries

Individuals with Jupiter in Aries tend to expand their general wisdom and knowledge through personal growth and self-development. They learn about life by learning about themselves, and because of their high intuition can often accurately extrapolate personal learning to higher wisdom. They may pursue travel and higher education that allows them to expand their wisdom-base through experiential learning.

On a Soul Level this can be an excellent placement for developing expanded awareness of higher mind, and experiencing higher states of consciousness, provided one can resist any tendency for ego to stake a claim in any growth and knowledge insights that may arise!

Jupiter in Taurus

Individuals with Jupiter in Taurus often have an ability to attract wealth and material benefit. Unless ameliorated by other chart factors their urge for expansion is often focused more in the area of material growth than intellectual or spiritual. If poorly aspected there can be a tendency for over-indulgence in good food and fine wine with a commensurate tendency for weight gain.

On a Soul level this placement of Jupiter can present an obstacle to spiritual development, simply from the fact that spiritual experiences are not where this individual's attention naturally wants to go. Having said that, if such an individual were to determinedly pursue a spiritual path this can be an excellent placement for using one's senses to experience the reality of an expanded sense of being and to experientially feel the truth of one's spiritual nature as love-wisdom.

Jupiter in Gemini - detriment

Individuals with Jupiter in Gemini tend towards self-expansion through the intellect. Jupiter is said to be in detriment in Gemini, meaning his energy is weakened and his power is minimized. This means that the expansive urge of Jupiter is not effectively used but rather the energy can be fragmented and dissipated. This can lead to a tendency to simply collect an inordinate amount of facts that, unless otherwise supported in the horoscope, may lack grounding in any deeper knowledge or wisdom.

On a Soul level this presents a challenge to spiritual development because the individual may lack the concentration needed to cultivate deeper levels of study, meditation and insight. A helpful technique for such individuals is to identify themselves (at least at first) with the witnessing mind. If you can learn to observe the monkey mind in action, rather than pursuing every monkey thought, this will help to create a stable base for further spiritual development.

Jupiter in Cancer - exaltation

Individuals with Jupiter in Cancer tend towards self-expansion through caring and a compassionate understanding of the human condition. In Cancer Jupiter is said to be exalted, which means his energy is most active and able to flow freely. Personal growth and development can be easily assimilated into higher wisdom, through deep understanding and experiential learning. If well-placed can attract material and financial gain. If afflicted (and especially if associated with the Sixth House) there may be overindulgence leading to weight gain and related health issues.

On a Soul level, unless other chart factors present distractions, this is an excellent placement for deep meditation leading to wisdom insights from higher states of consciousness, an expansion of love-wisdom, and the realization of compassion.

Jupiter in Leo

Individuals with Jupiter in Leo tend towards self-expansion through their creative self-expression whether it be through art, drama or some kind of executive or leadership role. They are often generous, friendly, big-hearted, and playful. They often love (and are loved by) children. Usually larger than life, they bring much enthusiasm to whatever they turn their attention to and can make excellent teachers: turning their own study and learning into wisdom to share with others. When afflicted there can be too much ego and a domineering personality.

On a Soul level this is an excellent placement for deeper wisdom insights through self-realization. Exploring the question 'who am I' and really diving deep until one realizes one's own true nature. Care must be taken to avoid ego-inflation and self-delusion so it is always wise to consult a qualified spiritual teacher to ensure you are not straying from your path.

Jupiter in Virgo - detriment

Unless mitigated by other chart factors, individuals with Jupiter in Virgo often put limitations on their own self-expansion through a tendency to be overly analytical. Jupiter is said to be in detriment in Virgo, meaning his energy is weakened and his power is minimized. There is often a talent for discrimination, scrutiny and analysis, which is an asset in work that calls for thorough research with attention to detail. If afflicted they can be overly critical and tend to get bogged down in minutiae, missing the big picture.

On a Soul level it can be difficult for these individuals to experience their spiritual nature. There can be too much criticism, analysis and dissecting of spiritual or religious theory (from the personality), without giving it a chance to be proven in practice. It would serve them well to experiment: to use their great talent for discrimination to choose a qualified and respected spiritual teacher, and then to take a pragmatic approach by putting the theory into practice, so that they experience spiritual progress for themselves. Personal experience in spiritual and/or meditation practice is essential for them, because they need to see tangible results for their efforts, rather than be expected to proceed on blind faith alone.

Jupiter in Libra

Individuals with Jupiter in Libra tend towards self-expansion through all their relations with others: companions and partnerships on all levels (marriage and business) and their social circles. Jupiter in this sign can bring an increased sense of justice, especially social justice. Care must be taken that the expansion of social rules, expectations and obligations doesn't become burdensome (especially if Saturn or Capricorn is involved). There is usually a natural co-operative spirit and a willingness to share what one has learned.

On a Soul level Jupiter in Libra can have similar challenges to Jupiter in Gemini. There tends to be a predilection for expansion of the intellect, and there may be a talent for practicing law, all of which can become a distraction from the spiritual path keeping the individual 'trapped' in the 'intellect' stage of development. Having a regular spiritual practice such as meditation as an integral part of one's day that one keeps sacrosanct, is essential for maintaining balance between intellectual and spiritual growth.

Jupiter in Scorpio

Individuals with Jupiter in Scorpio tend towards self-expansion through intense experience of their passions and emotions. There is often a capacity to gain wisdom by probing the deeper meaning beneath spiritual and religious teachings, and there may be an innate understanding of nature. When afflicted there can be manipulation and an excessive desire to gain power over and control others.

On a Soul level this is an excellent position for developing deep spiritual insights through a dedicated exploration of one's own mind and the search for one's own true nature. There can be healing potential with this placement, once a certain degree of spiritual awareness has been reached. It would be wise to seek guidance from a qualified teacher, or guide, to ensure one's spiritual path is true and has not become distorted by egoic desires and self-delusion.

Jupiter in Sagittarius - dignity

Individuals with Jupiter in Sagittarius tend towards self-expansion through travel and higher education. Jupiter is said to be in dignity in Sagittarius meaning his energy flows well and he is most free and uninhibited in his effects. There can be a love of nature, personal freedom and (unless otherwise indicated) foreign travel or at least a love of outdoor pursuits, for these individuals are expanding their minds by wholeheartedly engaging in life. If afflicted there can be a lack of patience, recklessness and excessive risk-taking.

On a Soul level this is an excellent placement for the expansion of consciousness, connecting to and experiencing, higher states of consciousness. There can be a tendency towards dogma and mistaking belief systems for higher truth. It is therefore always wise to follow qualified teachers and ensure there are appropriate checks and balances in place to guard against self-delusion.

Jupiter in Capricorn - fall

Unless mitigated by other chart factors individuals with Jupiter can limit their self-expansion through excessive caution and too much emphasis on methodologies. Jupiter is said to 'fall' in Capricorn, which means his energy is somewhat repressed and unable to flow freely. Jupiter can still bring benefit, but often there must first be an expansion of hard work and diligently applied methodology on the part of the native. Jupiter in this position earns his wisdom and abundance.

On a Soul level this can be an excellent placement for steady, focused spiritual progress. Similar to Virgo, individuals with this placement usually like to see tangible results for their efforts and may not be naturally inclined toward a spiritual path. However if one is so inclined, a structured spiritual path (such as the lam-rim approach) can yield the tangible results that will inspire these individuals to go deeper. Esoterically, Capricorn is the sign of the disciple, and this sure and steady climb up the spiritual mountain can bring great benefit and deep spiritual wisdom.

Jupiter in Aquarius

Individuals with Jupiter in Aquarius tend toward self-expansion through unconventional means with a sense of idealism. They are usually very quick to take on new ideas and derive their knowledge and wisdom from participating in and sharing with groups and communities of like-minded individuals. When afflicted there can be a dogmatic attitude and a stubborn attachment to 'being right'.

On a Soul level this can be an excellent placement for resolving the duality between the head and the heart through higher love. Esoterically Jupiter is associated with Ray 2 (love-wisdom), while the Soul Purpose of Aquarius is to generate and dedicate spiritual energy to the collective (similar to the bodhisattva path).

This only happens through an authentic personal experience of non-duality, where head and heart, wisdom and compassion, are one. Individuals with this placement would do well to cultivate compassion, and find qualified spiritual teachers in a non-dual tradition such as Advaita, Zen or Dzogchen.

Jupiter in Pisces - dignity

Individuals with Jupiter in Pisces tend toward self-expansion through a deep spiritual connection, faith, universal love and compassion. Like Sagittarius, Jupiter is also said to be in dignity in Pisces, meaning his energy flows well and he is most free and uninhibited in his effects. There can be an innate sense of spiritual reality and care must be taken to anchor this in personal experience so that it does not turn into blind faith or religious dogma. If afflicted there can be a tendency to drift through life and using sensual experiences, addictive substances, as a form of escapism.

On a Soul level this is an excellent placement for developing higher wisdom and deep spiritual insight through transcendental states of consciousness. Care must be taken not to become addicted to expanded blissful states[144], without the added wisdom of higher awareness such as clear light mind. A qualified teacher or guide is essential to ensure one is safely navigating higher states of consciousness.

---

[144] See chapter sixteen for a discussion of Patanjali's *Five Bodies* and why the 'bliss' body is not the end of our journey.

Jupiter in The Houses

Jupiter in the First House brings self-expansion and abundance to the sense of self. Individuals with this placement generally tend to have an optimistic, generous, buoyant spirit that others often find uplifting.

When afflicted there can be pomposity, excessive self-indulgence and extreme self-centeredness. There can be a fondness for adventure and travel.

Jupiter in the Second House brings self-expansion and abundance, to the area of one's inner and outer resources: including material possessions, income, finances and one's inner values and talents. Individuals with this placement may have an ability to attract wealth and abundance easily, and/or they may be very generous with their resources.

When afflicted there can be loss through excessive extravagance and/ or taking risks with one's resources.

Jupiter in the Third House brings self-expansion and abundance to the processes of communication, thinking and learning. Individuals with this often enjoy learning through the school of life experience. They may have a talent for communication through higher education or learning.

When afflicted there can be restlessness, exaggeration, and educational progress may be impeded by an unfocused, disorganized, approach as too many interests compete for one's attention.

Jupiter in the Fourth House brings self-expansion and abundance to the area of home and family. Individuals with this placement may have an ability to attract a good home. They may experience a happy home life in early childhood, and their chosen homes may be large, spacious, comfortable and/or opulent.

When afflicted there can be challenges obtaining a home, or there can be losses through overspending and/or upside down mortgages.

Jupiter in the Fifth House brings self-expansion and abundance to the area of self-expression and creativity. Jupiter here can bring gain through investments and may be 'lucky' in gambling. Much joy and happiness can come through children and creativity, and individuals with this placement are likely to be extremely generous with their time, money, and energy, towards children.

When afflicted there can be financial loss or personal injury through excessive risk-taking.

Jupiter in the Sixth House brings self-expansion and abundance to the area of one's work, health, and responsibilities. Individuals with this placement tend to demonstrate a very generous spirit when it comes to being of service to others, and have much wisdom to share for the benefit to those they serve. They may also benefit from experiential learning in their approach to being of service.

When afflicted there can be personal health issues through over-indulgence and/or excessive care-taking with a lack of self-care.

Jupiter in the Seventh House brings self-expansion and abundance to the area of one's partnerships and relationships. Individuals with this placement are often able to benefit, either financially, socially and/or educationally, through partnerships. There can be an abundance of potential partners and may be more than one marriage.

When afflicted there can be a tendency to marry for personal gain, and/or to be demanding and attention-seeking, and/or to undervalue one's partner.

Jupiter in the Eighth House brings self-expansion and abundance to the area of other people's money, personal transformation and healing. Individuals with this placement may benefit from inheritance, and they could be successful in stock-market investments, both for themselves and others. They may have a strong sex-drive, and sexuality can play a major theme in their life. There may be an interest in esoteric and metaphysical teachings and, if well-placed, there could be great potential to be a catalyst for great transformation and healing in others.

When afflicted there can be wastefulness, heavy debt, and the potential to exploit other people's resources for one's own gain.

Jupiter in the Ninth House brings self-expansion and abundance to the area of higher learning, higher education and religion, and the deeper search for meaning. Individuals with this placement often have a great love for higher learning, philosophy, religious and/or metaphysical study, and due to their innate spiritual nature are often seekers of the deeper meaning of life. They often enjoy and benefit greatly from travel, possibly to foreign countries. When afflicted there can be distorted opinions, faulty belief systems, delusion, exaggeration and/or much confusion about one's religion, philosophy or spiritual path.

Jupiter in the Tenth House brings self-expansion and abundance to the area of one's achievements, career, public standing or worldly position. Individuals with this placement tend to be successful and prosperous in their chosen career, profession, and/or whatever they desire to achieve. They may attract beneficial public status, and/or benefits from people in positions of power.

When afflicted this can indicate someone who is catapulted to a senior or public position for which they are under-qualified and ill-equipped to deal with.

Jupiter in the Eleventh House brings self-expansion and abundance to the area of groups, societies, friends, community, and shared goals. Individuals with this placement tend to have an abundance of friends and associates who support them in achieving their goals. They derive great benefit in terms of self-growth and advancement through their contacts and networks.

When afflicted there can be a dissipation of energy through excessive socializing and/or associating with the wrong type of friends can have a negative effect on the individual.

Jupiter in the Twelfth House brings self-expansion and abundance to the area of one's inner world. Individuals with this placement have the potential to achieve greatness simply by being vast and unbounded in their thinking. There is no limit to their imagination and they often attract help from hidden sources. They have great compassion and may be able to use their inner strength and resources to benefit others.

When afflicted there can be self-deception and/or loss through poor judgment.

Through the conditioning influence of Jupiter we are able to reach out to our fellow human brothers and sisters and connect with them, not as adversaries, but as our larger human family.

It is through Jupiter, and our capacity to think, that we can begin to ask ourselves the higher questions: Who am I? Why am I here? What is the meaning of life?

It is also through Jupiter, and altruistic thinking, that we are able to ask, who or what is God? We are able to seek our spiritual nature, and to form belief systems, and religions, for the purpose of 'formalizing' and expressing our spiritual beliefs. It is through the conditioning of Jupiter that we are able to go beyond our instincts and expand ourselves, into and through the development of intellect.

Suggested Fieldwork

• Deeper Self-observation. Take out your own horoscope (natal chart) and make a note in your journal of the sign and house position of Jupiter. Then read the descriptions above and make a note of any ideas and insights that come to you. Meditate on how Jupiter might be showing up in your life. Record your impressions and insights in your reflective journal.

• Further Reading: *Soul Centered Astrology: A Key to Your Expanding Self*, by Alan Oken, refer to the appropriate section for more information on Jupiter. Read about Jupiter in chapter five of *Soul Astrology*.

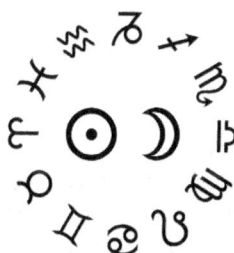

19. Saturn, Catalyst for Self-Mastery

Saturn is the personality ruler of Capricorn and Aquarius and is the Soul Ruler of Capricorn. Saturn is considered to be exalted in Libra for reasons that will become clearer as we continue our exploration (Esoterically Saturn is also the hierarchical ruler of Libra but it is beyond the scope of this volume to discuss hierarchical rulerships).

In *Esoteric Astrology* Saturn is considered a sacred planet because Saturn creates the conditions for us to develop Self-Mastery, which allows us to go beyond our limitations. Esoterically Saturn is associated with Ray 3[145], the path of intelligent action. The highest vibration of Ray 3 would be what we might call *compassionate action*.

Saturn brings the ultimate reality check. Through the natural limitation that Saturn places on our greed and ego-conflation, we are forced to confront reality as it is. When we truly, deeply, understand our true nature then our actions become born out of a deep, humble, compassion, for ourselves and our human family.

Jupiter, Saturn, and The Evolution of Intellect

Remember, as we evolve through the levels of instinct > intellect > intuition > illumination and emptiness, it is important to understand that each stage is necessary. It's not that we 'lose' our instincts as we

---

[145] See *The Seven Rays* in chapter fourteen.

move into intellect, but rather that each stage is a vital foundation for what comes next. So by the time we reach the level of the wisdom realizing emptiness, we also realize that we are also all of it. We are everything that has gone before. We don't 'transcend' instinct by 'getting rid of it' but rather it becomes integrated into our whole being.

Saturn creates the conditions for us to build structure and organize systems. As we become part of larger groups and societies, some kind of structure and organization becomes a necessity if we are to succeed. Through the influence of Saturn we are able to formalize and structure our systemic thinking so we are better able to manage finite resources and live in harmony together. Saturn brings a sense of limitation to the expansion of Jupiter.

Human communities cannot just infinitely expand without there being harmful consequences on ourselves, the environment and the creatures who share our Mother earth with us. There have to be checks and balances on our extravagance and self-indulgence, so that we can live in harmony with our planet, and each other. An example would be rampant and widespread logging that has decimated the Amazonian rainforests in South America[146].

Through the conditioning influence of Saturn, we realize that life simply does not expand continuously, and that in our evolution we also need to embrace limitation and death. Saturn rules the structure of mind, and it is through the conditioning influence of Saturn that we develop structures and systems in our societies to distribute finite resources fairly among one another. Saturn brings us a sense of justice, consequences, and boundaries. Under the influence of Saturn we learn to curb our excesses and to put formal systems in place to regulate our communities and societies. No accident that Saturn is exalted in Libra, the sign of harmony, but also the sign of justice, balance, and legal systems.

Through the conditioning of Saturn we use our intellect to develop systems of law for managing ourselves, our society, and our resources on a scale that goes way beyond our immediate family. We use our intellect to formalize these structures in the form of laws, government, banks and corporations. Once we have our systems of

---

[146] *Tropical Rainforest Destruction: Reasons and Consequences.* Online document at https://www.rainforestmaker.org/tropical-rainforest-destruction-reasons-and-consequences.html Accessed December 2nd 2019.

justice in place we also need to regulate and police those systems, so Saturn brings us structure, balance, justice, government, regulation, authority and policing as our societies grow into larger civilizations.

So we can see that throughout humanity, the conditions for human advancement into larger, organized, groups and societies are held in place by the activities of Jupiter and Saturn: the spaceholders for the development of intellect.

However with Saturn we also begin to feel the squeeze of limitation. We begin to experience the limitation of intellect. When we are overly controlled, regulated, and/or 'locked in' to a belief system, we begin to feel the pinch.

On our spiritual quest, it is the conditioning of Jupiter and Saturn that can also present the greatest barrier for us as individuals if we lock ourselves into a belief system too soon, before we have fully explored what may be next, beyond the level of thought.

Saturn, Lord of Karma

In the ancient wisdom teaching Saturn is known as both Lord of Karma and Lord of Time, which speaks to the connection between karma and time. To understand this we need to deeply understand what karma is. Simply put, karma can be thought of as repeating habits that are perpetuated over lifetimes, through our mental conditioning[147].

We can see the connection between karma and time: as time unfolds, through incarnation after incarnation, our ingrained habits become stronger, generating more and more karma, until we recognize the process and take steps to break the pattern and step off the cycle.

This 'wheel' of death and rebirth is known in many spiritual traditions as *samsara*[148] and is thought in Buddhism to be the main cause of our suffering. In short, our experience creates Karma over time: and the repetitious unfolding of events in time are known as samsara.

---

[147] See chapter nine, *Navigating The Depths of Karma*.

[148] See definition of samsara in footnotes for previous chapter.

Kalachakra: Time Cycles

In my work I often mention the great *Kalachakra masters*, especially in relation to their ability to study astrology without the use of telescopes. They use their clarity of mind to study the energy of the Universe, and are able to make predictions based on their deep understanding of the repeating cycles of time and the connection to karma. In fact the word kalachakra is Sanskrit for Time (kala) Cycles (chakra):

> "The Kālacakra tradition revolves around the concept of time (kāla) and cycles (chakra): from the cycles of the planets, to the cycles of human breathing, it teaches the practice of working with the most subtle energies within one's body on the path to enlightenment."
>
> - Wikipedia[149]

To understand how our actions create karma, how this keeps us stuck in a cycle of suffering, and what this has to do with Saturn, we need to refresh our understanding of conditioning, as we discussed right at the very beginning of *Soul Astrology*:

> "the two main factors that contribute to our state of illusion are:
> (a) social conditioning and
> (b) the way our human brain is wired to enable us to learn"
>
> - Chapter one, *Soul Astrology*[150]

Saturn and The Structure of Mind

Saturn is largely responsible for our conditioning. Like Mercury, we can look to Saturn for information about how our mind operates. However, whereas Mercury tells us about the movement of mind, Saturn tells us about the structure: how organized and focused we are, or not; where we have a sense of limitation (often self-imposed); where we have the potential for mastery by focused intent on a subject etc.

---

[149] *Kalachakra*. Online document found at https://en.wikipedia.org/wiki/Kalachakra Accessed December 10th 2019.

[150] Hadikin, R. (2016) *Soul Astrology: How Your Rising Sign Reveals Your Soul Path and Life Purpose.* Ruth Hadikin Associates. Order online at https://soulastrologybook.com

According to Esoteric Astrologer Alan Oken, Saturn rules the 'structure of mind'. Now let's pause there for a moment and clarify what may be meant by 'mind' in this context. For the majority of people 'mind' means thinking, but this is not the view of mind taken in some spiritual traditions. For example in the Buddhist tradition mind is considered to be your entire inner experience including thoughts, feelings, emotions, etc. Indeed any and all information that you are receiving through your five senses: sight, sound (to include thought), touch, taste, and smell (sense perceptions). From this perspective, how you relate to your experience is your mind, and any predisposition you may have to favor one sense-perception over another, would be part of the 'structure' of your mind.

Also remember that we can think about planetary dynamics as having a lower fear-based vibration and a higher love-based expression. The great sage Ramana Maharshi once said,

"there are no levels of reality,
only levels of experience for the experiencer".

So when we speak of mind, we are really speaking about the way we, as individuals, experience our reality. Which makes perfect sense when we are speaking of Saturn. Saturn at the lower-fear-based level brings limitation. Containment. Bumping up against our own limitations, restrictions, fears. As we grow in our awareness we realize just how much of this limitation is actually created by, and held in place by, our own mind. As our capacity for consciousness increases, and we experience more of the higher love-based expression, our mind opens up. Saturn then brings authenticity: a capacity to be authentic in our self-expression as fully self-realized beings. With a more evolved consciousness, Saturn brings us the ultimate reality check: the reality of our own true nature.

Saturn, Control and Authority

Saturn is also associated with authority. The fact that prescriptive ideas of 'how we ought to be' are held in the collective 'mind' of society, and imposed upon it's members, is a fear-based Saturnine theme. This includes the idea that the 'masses' need to be strictly controlled, limited, and regulated by rigid legislature lest anarchy should prevail. As part of the 'socialization' process (where we are conditioned into the behavior of the society), groups, organizations, corporations and societies apply both formal and informal sanctions (mechanisms of social control) to keep members in line. The creation of laws, their enforcement, policing, authority and the application of sanctions all are part of the domain of Saturn.

Saturn and Liberation

Yet esoterically (and somewhat ironically) Saturn is also considered to be associated with liberation. How so? Because with evolved consciousness we realize that *anything imprinted into our mind from outside of ourselves, is not an inherent part of who we really are.* Anything learned (conditioned) can also be unlearned. The highest octave of Saturn brings us to this highest reality check!

We can think of Mercury and Saturn as both being associated with lower mind. Saturn influences your ability to think methodically, plan and organize your thoughts, your brain wiring, and plays a role in building your belief system, while Mercury rules the movement of mind (the thoughts themselves and the repeating cycles and patterns of those thoughts). Alan Oken uses the analogy of a bee hive where Saturn is the structure (the structure of the hive and the honeycombs) and Mercury is the movement of the bees themselves going about their daily business!

Saturn and Your Brain Wiring

Saturn rules our established brain wiring, the neural networks through which our thoughts are created and experienced, but when it comes to re-wiring our brain (changing our neural networks so something can be experienced differently) then Mercury and Saturn work together. Esoterically Mercury is said to be responsible for creating the antahkarana or rainbow bridge between lower and higher mind. One thing we know about mind is that it is changeable. If it weren't we could never learn and grow and this changeability, this capacity to learn, comes under Mercury's domain.

Much of our mind works by association. If you have been watching your mind closely you will see this. On a daily basis we associate certain experiences people, thoughts, feelings and memories, like movies and popcorn or even having sugar and cream in our coffee. Earlier we mentioned neuroscientist Dr. Joe Dispenza who explains how "nerve cells that fire together, wire together". These associations become our brain wiring. It's like that game where one person says a word and you say the first thing that comes into your mind. The first thought that comes is likely to be one that is currently 'wired' to the other word, for example 'coffee' and 'cream'.

Three Planets of Mind: Mercury, Saturn and Uranus

On a daily basis we tend to unconsciously follow the habitual patterns of our brain wiring. This is partly the result of our following the movement of Mercury and the 'monkey-mind', but we can also see that Saturn is involved, because Saturn is laying down and holding the neural network in place. All that needs to happen for that to change, is for us to stop following our thoughts. Once we no longer energize the neural networks with our thoughts, they actually shrivel up and die, and our thoughts seek out new neural pathways. Mercury will seek out alternative pathways (change and learning) and then Saturn will create neural networks so we can easily remember and take our new path.

Mercury is able to create the Rainbow Bridge from lower to Higher Mind because Mercury can help us to change habit patterns that have us stuck, and allow us to step into new ways of being. However, we also need consciousness otherwise we can simply substitute one habit for another, which keeps us equally stuck. This is where Uranus comes into the picture.

Uranus is the planet of intuition and is associated with Higher Mind. Uranus is associated with electricity, lightening, and flashes of insight. It used to be thought that our nervous system was one continuous, unbroken, network like a railway track upon which our thoughts run like trains (a train of thought)! However, modern science and high-powered electron microscopes tell a different story. We explore Uranus in more depth in a later chapter but for now it is enough to see the connection between the three planets of 'mind': Mercury (movement), Saturn (structure) and Uranus (intuitive mind).

Saturn: The Grim Reaper

Saturn is all about limits. Boundaries. What is realistic. Method. What we can feasibly achieve with our given finite resources, within a given time.

Traditionally Saturn is the embodiment of limitation. This present lifetime is finite. The image of "Father Time" is Saturn personified. We are on a cycle that will end. Another Saturnian personification is the "Grim Reaper". Before Pluto was discovered Saturn was traditionally the planet of death, symbolizing the end of a cycle. Time running out. Saturn reminds us of what is realistic to expect, and to achieve. Causing us to ask again and again, "what is really, real?" Death is certain. So in a very real sense, Saturn brings us the ultimate reality check: what can we or will we do... before we run out of time?

Saturn: The Malefic

So we have seen how Saturn has a strong association with karma and, indeed, death. Little wonder then that Saturn in Vedic Astrology and mediaeval astrology was known as a malefic planet thought to bring misfortune and detrimental conditions. Because of Saturn's connection with the repeating cycles of time we know as karma, we can see how ancient people's connected Saturn to repeating patterns of unfavorable conditions.

So why would a 'malefic' planet be a sacred planet? Because Saturn can be a powerful catalyst: by drawing our attention to our repeating patterns, and giving us an opportunity to see how we play a part in their reinforcement and repetition (through our attachment and conditioning), Saturn takes on the role of the wise teacher or Master. We can't change what we can't see, and by giving us an opportunity to see and experience these repeating cycles, Saturn is delivering a lesson in self-awareness, and at the same time offering an opportunity to make different choices - whereby we can break the cycle. Remember Saturn is exalted in Libra: the sign of ethical choice.

Hearing The Call to Authentic Light

Melanie Reinhart proposes 'authenticity' as a higher vibration keyword for Saturn, and that is a key to understanding the highest potential of Saturn. Saturn is calling us to be ever more deeply authentic. In the limitations and challenges that Saturn brings at the personality level, we have a catalyst that can potentially catapult us to our highest authentic light. Our *real* light. The key is to remain wide awake, and highly self-aware, in our experiences.

Saturn: Storehouse of Ancient Wisdom

Karma doesn't just mean negativity, it refers to everything in your mindstream (your energy field): good and bad. So because of the connection with karma, Saturn can also indicate where you have your own personal treasure-trove of wisdom that you have carried over from past lives. If you feel as though you missed the boat when talent was being given out, look to where Saturn is in your chart.

Although it might be bringing you difficulties in your present life, they will be of a specific nature, that are waking you up to talents that you already have and are not recognizing, or that you created in a past life, and that you can perfect in this one. Wherever Saturn falls in your chart is an area of potential mastery for you.

Saturn: Catalyst for Self-Mastery

We briefly mentioned above that Saturn is a powerful catalyst, but this point deserves deeper contemplation. First, what exactly is a catalyst? In chemistry, some compounds remain inactive, or dormant, until they come into contact with another chemical or substance. That chemical or substance, which has the power to activate another, is known as a catalyst. Saturn does exactly that.

Saturn can awaken latent or dormant qualities in you that you never knew you had. There is an axiom that sounds something like: "You never know how strong you are until you need to be strong". This is the kind of catalyst that Saturn is.

You may not choose the challenges that Saturn presents in your life, but by dealing with them, you are developing skill, capacity, and strength that will be a great support for you later in your journey.

Under the tutelage of Saturn you can master areas of self-awareness, self-discipline and self-mastery that you never knew you had. People with Saturn well-placed in their charts are usually very capable individuals.

The sign in which Saturn is placed can indicate the nature of the mastery to be learned. According to Isabel Hickey:

- *Saturn in Aries* – brings the test of self-centeredness
- *Saturn in Taurus* – brings the test of ownership
- *Saturn in Gemini* – brings the test of faith and optimism in life
- *Saturn in Cancer* – brings the test of valuing responsibility and empathy
- *Saturn in Leo* – brings the test of true humility and lovingness
- *Saturn in Virgo* – brings the test of discrimination between what is important and what is not
- *Saturn in Libra* – brings the test of relatedness to life

- *Saturn in Scorpio* - brings the test of outgoing desire
- *Saturn in Sagittarius* - brings the test of understanding
- *Saturn in Capricorn* - brings the test of right use of power
- *Saturn in Aquarius* - brings the test of responsibility
- *Saturn in Pisces* - brings the test of release and letting go

- Isabel Hickey, Astrology: A Cosmic Science.

Esoterically Saturn denotes where we may manifest a degree of mastery, and also where we may be a teacher to others: the sign placement will show the nature of such mastery while the house placement indicates the life area it shows up in.

Saturn and Capricorn

"in Capricorn, the will nature arrives at fulfillment and a visioned goal is reached. In Capricorn, the man reaches either the height of personal ambition or he becomes the initiate, attaining his spiritual objective."

- The Tibetan, *Esoteric Astrology*

Saturn is both the personality and Soul ruler of Capricorn. It is said of Capricorn that it is both the most materialistic and the most spiritual sign at one and the same time.

"Saturn's power is completely ended and his work accomplished when man (the spiritual man) has freed himself from Karma and from the power of the two Crosses – the Common [Mutable] and the Fixed. Esoterically, Saturn cannot follow man on to the Cardinal Cross"

- The Tibetan, *Esoteric Astrology*

Saturn, God of Liberation

The Romans thought of Saturn not only as a God of agriculture and time, but also as a God of liberation, and there is also a key here to the higher purpose of Saturn and Capricorn. The Soul in Capricorn has to journey up the mountain from the very depths of humanity to the very heights of Christ Consciousness, and this is no small task.

The higher purpose of Capricorn involves choosing a spiritual path and understanding the laws of creation so that we may create heaven on Earth.

Capricorn rules the knees and this symbology is important in understanding the Soul's journey through Capricorn. It is Saturn's job, at personality level, to bring Capricorn to his knees so he develops insight, humility, and turns his attention away from the trappings and excesses of materialism that would keep him trapped in ego.

> *"...only when the Capricornian subject learns to kneel in all humility and with his knees upon the rocky mountain top to offer his heart and life to the Soul and to human service, can he be permitted to pass through the door of initiation and be entrusted with the secrets of life. Only on his knees can he go through that door."*
>
> *- The Tibetan, Esoteric Astrology*

Saturn is a wise teacher bringing important lessons and guidance to support us in making choices that align with our highest good. The word creation comes from the Latin *creō* which means *to create, make, produce, beget, give birth to, prepare, cause or choose*. So in creating heaven on Earth, there is an element of choice: it is through our choices and actions that we create heaven on Earth, or not. It may be Saturn that brings the Capricorn personality to his knees, but it is equally Saturn that invites renunciation of material ambition so the individual may walk the steady path of discipleship to the spiritual mountain-top.

Saturn and Aquarius

Saturn was traditionally considered to be the planetary ruler of Aquarius, and to many people still would be. The conditions mentioned above pertaining to Saturn and Capricorn, also relate to Aquarius when humanity is largely personality-centered and driven by fear and attachment.

Once the Soul has completed the stage of development in Capricorn, and has accessed Christ Consciousness, it no longer is limited by the constraints of Saturn and comes under the custodianship (planetary rulership) of Uranus:

> "On the reversed wheel[151] the Saturnian influence exhausts itself in Capricorn and the man is then set free from karma and needs no presentation of opportunity for he stands a free initiate ... and can proceed with world service undeterred and held back by no thought of self or selfish desire"
>
> - The Tibetan, *Esoteric Astrology*

Saturn and Libra

Much of what we have said about Saturn seems pretty grim, yet nothing is set in stone. Your horoscope is not a sentence, a burden that you must carry like a millstone around your neck, although it may feel like it at times. The reason that Saturn is exalted in Libra, is because Libra holds the key to your liberty: your self-liberation. As mentioned at the beginning, Saturn is also the hierarchical ruler of Libra, which means there is a deep esoteric connection between Libra and Saturn that we would be wise to meditate upon. It is through the Libra art of making conscious, ethical, choices that you can break free from the habit of degenerative repeating karmic cycles, and step off the samsaric wheel of death and rebirth.

> "An authentic man does not live by rules, maxims, commandments. That's the way of the pseudo-man. The authentic man simply lives."
>
> - OSHO

Saturn as Personality and Soul Ruler

As you read on, take note if you have Capricorn or Aquarius Rising. If so Saturn is your Personality Ruler and the condition of Saturn by sign, house and aspect will be playing a particularly significant role in your life, by bringing you people and circumstances that have the potential to bring your karmic conditioning into your awareness, for healing, transformation, and release.

If you do have Capricorn Rising know that Saturn is also your chart ruler at Soul level, so the condition of Saturn in your chart deserves some deeper, ongoing, study and contemplation to develop deeper understandings of your Soul's journey and the unfolding process of personality-Soul fusion.

---

[151] See *The Reversed Wheel* in chapter twenty-four.

Saturn Through The Signs

At it's highest vibration Saturn brings the ultimate 'reality-check', causing us to recognize that which is authentic and real.

Saturn in Aries - Fall

Individuals with Saturn in Aries tend to be a law unto themselves. Saturn is said to 'fall' in Aries, which means his energy is somewhat repressed and unable to flow freely. Unless offset by other chart factors, the structuring, orderly, and organizing energy of Saturn can be misdirected for personal use, which means the individual can become authoritarian with a desire to control others. This person may live by their own rules, which can also be projected onto others. When afflicted this can be a self-centered, righteous, and/or controlling individual. When well-placed this position can bring great concentration, focus and self-discipline.

On a Soul level this placement is excellent for making steady spiritual progress. Saturn helps to stabilize the 'monkey-mind' and brings a quality of self-discipline that is very beneficial when following a spiritual path. A dedicated practice of self-questioning, combined with cultivating compassion, will ameliorate the tendency for self-centeredness inherent in this placement.

Saturn in Taurus

Individuals with Saturn in Taurus are often patient, determined, steadfast and unrelenting in the pursuit of their goals. They often have great vitality, which brings a capacity for endurance and resilience. They can be formidable in getting what they want. Unless mitigated by other chart factors, there can be too much focus on strategizing for future material gain, to the point where the person misses out on the present moment. When afflicted there can be excessive possessiveness and jealousy.

On a Soul level, if the individual is spiritually inclined, this is an excellent placement for making steady progress on one's chosen spiritual path. The highest vibration of Saturn is authenticity, which causes us to question what is really real? Steady progress along this line of spiritual inquiry and practice can lead to deep, authentic, realizations of the true nature of reality for this individual.

Saturn in Gemini

Individuals with Saturn in Gemini tend to structure the mind through intellectual pursuits. Saturn in this position can steady the Gemini mind, bringing a power of concentration that can support greater depth of study than Gemini is naturally inclined to. Depending upon the aspects to Saturn, this may be experienced as beneficial or as a sense of limitation, by the individual. When afflicted the individual may somehow be limited in their communication.

On a Soul level this is another placement where, if well-placed, Saturn can help to tame the 'monkey-mind': bringing progress and deep insights through one's meditation or spiritual path.

Saturn in Cancer - detriment

Individuals with Saturn in Cancer may experience some kind of limitation in their home life. Saturn is said to be in detriment in Cancer, meaning his energy is weakened and his power is minimized. Unless mitigated by other chart factors, this individual may not have experienced a nurturing environment in childhood, and consequently may be limited in their own capacity to nurture. There may have been excessive authority or structure, where the home life may have been organized like a school or military environment. The individual may continue this pattern in adulthood and their own domestic life may be tinged with authoritarianism, or run like a self-imposed school timetable. Alternatively, this could equally be someone who totally rebels against authority and limitation, and rejects self-discipline. Either way, there can be a strong sense of restriction that the individual is either embracing or rebelling against.

On a Soul level this placement calls for active engagement in relationship as a spiritual path. The individual may incline toward a hermit lifestyle to avoid the difficulties of human relating, but this would not necessarily support the individual in cultivating compassion and empathy. The highest vibration of Saturn in Cancer is the realization of the authenticity of love. There would be great benefit in using the discipline of Saturn to diligently pursue a devotional path, where empathy and compassion can be cultivated, and where love may be experienced as real.

Saturn in Leo - detriment

Individuals with Saturn in Leo tend to be autocratic and follow their own rules. Saturn is said to be in detriment in Leo, meaning his energy is weakened and his power is minimized. Unless mitigated by other chart factors individuals with this placement may experience difficulties and limitation with regard to romance, and children because they may find it hard to be cooperative and their attitude can be too authoritarian. When afflicted there can be excessive egotism and a desire to control others.

On a Soul level Saturn in Leo is calling for the discipline of the heart-path. If strong egotism can be overcome, the discipline of Saturn can be used to follow the path of the heart until there is real, authentic, spiritual experience. Leo is the sign of the heart, and Saturn's highest vibration is authenticity, so this placement can be utilized to attain the deepest realizations of the true power of the heart.

Saturn in Virgo

Individuals with Saturn in Virgo tend to have a methodical, analytical mind and may be oriented towards perfectionism. Unless mitigated by other chart factors they have a good eye for detail, and can make excellent researchers. When afflicted they can be overly critical of others and may have trouble discriminating between what is important and what is unimportant. Sometimes an afflicted Saturn in Virgo can limit one's ability to be practical and/or technical. There can also be a tendency to obsess over minor details.

On a Soul level even a well-placed Saturn in Virgo can bring challenges to the spiritual path by keeping the individual going around in analytical circles. This keeps their attention focused in the intellectual stage of development, instead of opening up to the intuitive stage. This individual would be well served to develop a regular meditative practice where they become familiar with the activity of mind through observation, without 'following' every thought that passes through.

Saturn in Libra - exalted

Individuals with Saturn in Libra tend to take relationships seriously, with a sense of responsibility. In Libra Saturn is said to be exalted, which means his energy is most active and able to flow freely. There can be a sense of limitation in relating, which becomes a catalyst for the individual to develop mastery in the art of relationship. When afflicted the challenge of relationships may be too complex and/or overwhelming, and the individual may withdraw from human interaction entirely, preferring a 'hermit' lifestyle!

On a Soul level this can be an excellent placement for approaching relationship as a spiritual path. Individuals with this placement often have an innate sense of the sacredness of relationship, and an intuitive knowing that through the art of relating: cooperation, collaboration, communication and harmony, one can develop one's own higher qualities of love, compassion and empathy.

Saturn in Scorpio

Individuals with Saturn in Scorpio tend to have an intense, focused, relentless mind. Unless mitigated by other chart factors they usually have great mental endurance and a capacity to penetrate deeply and unceasingly into whatever interests them. There can be a tendency to be intransigent. If afflicted there can be a ruthless streak: they may lack empathy and use their deep understanding of a situation to control events and other people for their own gain.

On a Soul level this can be an excellent placement for spiritual progress if controlling, self-centered, tendencies can be overcome. There is usually a great capacity for focused attention, which can be put to great use in shamatha and analytical meditation. The highest octave of Saturn brings us to the highest reality check: our own true nature. With Saturn in Scorpio there is the powerful opportunity to elevate this dynamic to it's highest expression, by utilizing the self-discipline of Saturn to 'regulate' the passion (desire) of Scorpio so that the energy can be re-focused and transformed into tangible spiritual energy, which leads to higher consciousness, higher love and the highest 'passion', which is compassion.

Saturn in Sagittarius

Individuals with Saturn in Sagittarius take a serious and responsible approach to higher learning and or/philosophy. This can show up in either formal education, or as learning through travel, spiritual and/or religious experiences. Unless mitigated by other chart factors this is someone who will take life seriously, and view all life experiences as opportunities for learning and forming one's own personal philosophy of life. If afflicted there can be a tendency for one's beliefs and/or opinions to form dogma, which is then projected onto others.

On a Soul level this is an excellent placement for understanding higher truth through personal spiritual experiences. Care must be taken not to fixate on mental conceptions and form them into a 'philosophy' or new religion at the expense of spiritual reality. With

Saturn in Sagittarius a good motto to adopt would be "I see a boundary, I go beyond that boundary, and then I see another". Keep "going beyond".

Saturn in Capricorn - dignity

Individuals with Saturn in Capricorn tend to take a serious, responsible, approach to whatever they put their minds to. Saturn is said to be in dignity in Capricorn meaning his energy flows well and he is most free and uninhibited in his effects. If unmitigated by other chart factors there can be ambition and great potential for material gain and success through applied effort, determination and endurance. There can be a tendency to value people and things only in terms of their 'usefulness' and to disregard that which is considered not useful. When afflicted there can be ruthless materialism and a disregard for others that can border on cruelty.

On a Soul level this is an excellent placement for steady, diligent, spiritual progress if the individual has an interest. Unless offset by other chart factors there could be excessive focus on material gain and a denial of spiritual experience. If this individual is inclined to pursue a spiritual path, they can make great headway, because their responsible, focused and dedicated approach will take them far. Saturn in Capricorn is the sign of the diligent disciple.

Saturn in Aquarius - dignity

Individuals with Saturn in Aquarius tend to take their idealism seriously and responsibly. Saturn is said to be in dignity in Aquarius meaning his energy flows well and he is most free and uninhibited in his effects. Saturn can bring focus, discipline and organizational ability to the idealistic humanitarian vision of Aquarius, contributing to the success of one's individual and shared goals. When well-placed this is someone who has a big vision and can materialize it, for the improvement of society. Not only would they have the capacity, they would feel it is their responsibility to do so. However, Aquarius is the fixed air sign so, if unmitigated by other chart factors, Saturn can bring even more rigidity to an already rigid mind. If afflicted, pathological stubbornness and an unwillingness to consider other people's ideas can bring limitation and obstacles to progress.

On a Soul level this can be a challenge to spiritual progress due to the individual's possible inflexible mind, and attachment to their own mental constructs. The ancient Chinese saying, "Empty your cup" refers to the idea that you cannot fill a cup that is already full. In other words, you need to empty your mind of your already preconceived ideas in order to fill it with true wisdom. There is great potential to make progress through Zen and the concentration paths, by applying the innate capacity to focus inherent in this placement. But first one must develop humility, and be prepared to let go of what you already *think* you know.

Saturn in Pisces

Individuals with Saturn in Pisces have a tendency to structure the abstract. If they do this successfully they may be gifted at math or music, where structured concepts and patterns can repeat infinitely. However there is equally a chance that any sense of structure dissolves in Pisces and they may lack the necessary self-discipline to succeed in their chosen field. There can be a tendency to dwell on the past and one of the major lessons of Saturn in Pisces is letting go.

On a Soul level this can be an excellent placement for spiritual progress by experiencing the vastness of mind. The challenge is to learn the art of letting go while at the same time, cultivating the self-discipline needed to stay with the process until spiritual awakening is experienced.

Saturn in The Houses

Saturn in a house shows an area where the individual may feel bound by 'rules', responsibilities, limitation, duty or obligations until they have transcended that boundary and liberated that specific aspect of mental conditioning.

Saturn in the First House brings a sense of responsibility, authenticity and potential mastery to the sense of self. There can be early disappointments with life, and/or with oneself, that cause the individual to rise up and overcome their challenges. Can lead to a greater sense of self-worth later in life, through one's own efforts to develop a realistic sense of self.

Saturn in the Second House brings a sense of responsibility, authenticity and potential mastery to the area of one's inner and outer resources: including material possessions, income, finances and one's inner values and talents. There can be concerns over finances: either through limited finances or concern over how best to manage finances and material resources.

Saturn in the Third House brings a sense of responsibility, authenticity and potential mastery to the processes of communication, thinking and learning. Formal education can be limited, restricted and/or interrupted in some way. However an individual with Saturn in the third often develops mastery in the art of 'self-learning', which becomes a lifelong support.

Saturn in the Fourth House brings a sense of responsibility, authenticity and potential mastery to the area of home and family. The individual may feel bound to or limited by their home, or family traditions in some way. It may even indicate someone who is housebound. The opportunity for mastery lies in transcending the traditional view of home, family and ancestry, and realizing the spiritual truth of our connection as one human family.

Saturn in the Fifth House brings a sense of responsibility, authenticity and potential mastery to the area of self-expression and creativity. Creative self-expression may be restricted, inhibited, or limited in some way. There may be a lack of children, or the joy of parenting may be dampened by being too strict, serious and/or severe in one's approach. The opportunity for mastery lies in learning not to take oneself too seriously, and learning to experience the unbounded joy of an awakened heart.

Saturn in the Sixth House brings a sense of responsibility, authenticity and potential mastery to the area of one's work, health, and responsibilities. The 'duty' of hard work seems unavoidable, whether imposed by oneself or others. Apparently simple jobs can become weighted down with tasks, get out of hand and/or quickly become burdensome projects. Health can suffer due to overwork. The opportunity for mastery here lies in both work/life balance, and in a healthy balancing of self-care and responsibilities towards one's job and/or dependents.

Saturn in the Seventh House brings a sense of responsibility, authenticity and potential mastery to the area of one's partnerships and relationships. Relationships take on a serious tone. Marriage can be late, if at all. However when these individuals do commit, they often take their partnerships very seriously indeed, and may remain in relationship for the long haul as they progress in their mastery. Not usually a good placement for business partnerships: depending upon other chart factors, this person may prefer to live and work alone. The opportunity for mastery lies in the entire spectrum of relating: from communication and cooperative skills, to emotional, social and spiritual intelligence.

Saturn in the Eighth House brings a sense of responsibility, authenticity and potential mastery to the area of other people's money, personal transformation and healing. In contrast to the seventh house of marriage and partnerships, the eighth house is more about our deeper, intimate connections with others, and so is usually associated with sex, death and other people's money. Taxes, insurance and inheritance are all eighth house themes. Saturn's challenges in this area of life may therefore come in the form of limitation in the area of sex: too much or too little; and/or there could be an inheritance that either fails to materialize or becomes a burden in some way; and/or the person may have fears and obsessions over death, for example. There can be a tendency to desire power and control in any or all these areas, which comes from a deep-rooted fear of loss. The mastery that is required here is to deepen an authentic spiritual connection until an inner trust in the cycles of life arises. Then one can relax into one's own true nature, and as a result become the wise master who supports others in managing their resources.

Saturn in the Ninth House brings a sense of responsibility, authenticity and potential mastery to the area of higher learning, higher education and religion, and the deeper search for meaning. There can be a tendency to be dogmatic and/or feel limited by, one's religion or philosophy. This can be a good position for focusing the mind on one's spiritual path, provided such dogma can be avoided. The opportunity for mastery here lies in going beyond conventional ideas about truth and allowing the expansion of one's mind to higher spiritual realizations of truth.

Saturn in the Tenth House brings a sense of responsibility, authenticity and potential mastery to the area of one's achievements, career, public standing or worldly position. There can be a tendency to have strong ambition yet feel thwarted or unfulfilled. Success may come later in life through patience and consistently applied effort. The opportunity for mastery lies in the right use of power. Any abuse of power for self-interest is likely to result in a downfall for this individual until they learn to use power wisely and appropriately for the good of all.

Saturn in the Eleventh House brings a sense of responsibility, authenticity and potential mastery to the area of groups, societies, friends, community, and shared goals. There can be a sense of limitation or 'burden' in terms of friendships and group activities: either friends are not helpful and may prove a hindrance or burden somehow, or the individual attracts few friends due to an attitude of only seeking out people because of how they may prove useful. The individual may be given too many responsibilities in communal projects and develop an aversion to them. The opportunity for mastery lies in cultivating an attitude of appreciation for friends and community, and in developing discrimination and personal boundaries, to support healthy, balanced, friendships.

Saturn in the Twelfth House brings a sense of responsibility, authenticity and potential mastery to the area of one's inner world. In astrology the twelfth house conventionally rules prisons, monasteries and/or institutions. With this placement there can be a confinement of sorts: real or felt, that can thwart this individual in terms of their ambitions and personal goals. There can be a limited imagination that prevents them from developing ambitious goals, and/or there can be a self-repression due to hidden / unconscious fears. The opportunity here is for mastery over one's own mind, to make the unconscious conscious, and become familiar with the inner workings of one's own mind, so that one can transcend unconscious fears and shift to self-liberation.

The development of intellect, through the expansion and open-mindedness of Jupiter combined with the disciplined methodology of Saturn - concentration meditation - sets the foundation for us to step through the portal of love-wisdom into the heart where we begin our journey through the intuitive stage of human spiritual development and evolution.

Our spirit wants to soar. We urge to break free from the social conditioning and restrictions of Jupiter and Saturn, and we sense that there must be something 'beyond this'. That feeling propels us into the intuitive level, where the freedom of Uranus awaits us.

Suggested Fieldwork

- Deeper Self-observation. Take out your own horoscope (natal chart) and make a note in your journal of the sign and house position of Saturn. Then read the descriptions above and make a note of any ideas and insights that come to you. Meditate on how Saturn might be showing up in your life. Record your impressions and insights in your reflective journal.

- Further Reading: *Soul Centered Astrology: A Key to Your Expanding Self*, by Alan Oken, refer to the appropriate section for more information on Saturn. Read about Saturn in chapter five of *Soul Astrology*.

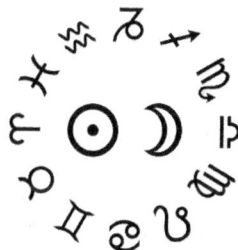

20. The Dweller on The Threshold

At The Threshold

As we leave Saturn and prepare to meet Uranus, we find ourselves at a threshold.

Until the discovery of Uranus by William Herschel in 1871, for hundreds of years Saturn had represented the limit of our knowledge: the farthest boundary of the known Universe. Following the discovery of Uranus, we were required to release old ideas and begin to consider what lay beyond. Humanity had entered a new era.

In our exploration of the deeper meaning of the planets, we now also find ourselves at a threshold: a portal between the past and the future. Let's pause there for a moment, and explore this word 'threshold'. Originally a threshold was a wooden sill, at the bottom of the front door of a house. During the harvest, grain crops were traditionally 'threshed'. Threshing was a practice of separating the grain from the stalks by beating the cut and dried crop on the floor. The grain could then be used to make flour, while the stalks could be gathered up for cattle fodder and bedding. This process naturally generated a lot of dust that you wouldn't want inside your house. The "thresh hold" was there to hold back the waste material from entering your home during threshing time.

As we pause at this threshold, there is a sense that we are about to pass through a portal where we leave behind that which is not needed, that which is impure, and that which could hinder us in our future growth. We cross the threshold, pass through a portal, and in a clearer, purer, state of consciousness, we are ready for the next stage of our journey.

Planetary Spaceholders

In chapter six we discussed how the planets embody energy and as a result are therefore able to hold a certain vibrational tone:

> *"planets are formed from consciousness itself, and therefore must by nature contain the consciousness that they emerged from. Each planet is therefore a formation of energy that holds a unique field of consciousness.*
>
> *Planets are embodied consciousness: holding a specific vibration, frequency, or field of awareness."*[152]

The natural tendency for each planetary body to hold it's own vibrational 'tone' or frequency, is what allows it to make its unique contribution to our Universal eco-system. Just as each plant, tree or bird has a unique 'tone' that contributes to the overall 'atmosphere' of the forest, so each planet emanates a unique tone that contributes to the conditions for our growth and development.

A planetary ruler is therefore not something or someone that has power over us, like a king, but rather something that contributes to the conditions that support us in our growth: much like a loving gardener who knows exactly what conditions are necessary not only for plants to survive but to thrive and reach their highest potential. In this sense the planetary 'ruler' is more like a guardian, or custodian. It is therefore more useful to think of planetary rulers as spaceholders, providing the necessary vital conditions for specific stages of our individual Soul's growth and our collective evolutionary unfoldment.

So far we have discussed the personal planets that are spaceholders for the development of instinct (Sun, Moon, Mercury, Venus and Mars). We have explored the social planets that are the spaceholders for the development of intellect (Jupiter and Saturn)

The next stage of our evolutionary journey is the development of

---

[152] See chapter six: *The Planets*

intuition, and the planetary spaceholder for this stage is Uranus. But before we can fully embrace the energy of Uranus and understand his role in the evolution of human consciousness, we need to shift our perception.

Fields of Consciousness

It's important to be clear on what we mean by the term *Planetary Spaceholders*. As we study astrology and become increasingly familiar with astrological language, it can be tempting to think that Mars, Jupiter and Saturn are gods, sitting up in the heavens, dispensing good luck or misery upon humanity at their every whim. In Ancient Greece and Rome that is exactly what people believed. If you wanted benefits you prayed and made offerings to Venus or Jupiter. If you wanted relief from some misfortune that had befallen you, you prayed and made offerings to Mars, or Saturn.

At the instinct and intellect levels of our development, we tend to project ourselves outwardly. This results in the creation of gods that have similar qualities to ourselves: anger, lust, jealousy etc. Astrology is a language of archetypes. An archetype is a blueprint of sorts, a 'type' or 'model' that we can use to quickly convey an image, or state of mind. Therefore, if we say someone is "Saturnian" for instance (and we know our astrological archetypes), this immediately conveys an image of someone who is strategic, serious, structure-oriented, and stays focused on the task at hand.

When we apply the astrological archetypes to the planets, we are not talking about actual physical gods as the ancient Greeks and Romans would have done. Rather we are referring to a field of consciousness. Ultimately there is only ONE field of consciousness, but within that are many different frequencies. Just you may only see one rainbow but it has many colors within it. This Universal Consciousness can express itself in a myriad of ways, resulting in myriad worlds.

When I say for instance, 'we need to go beyond the Saturn-bound' intellect, I am speaking metaphorically not literally. There is no god called Saturn that is holding you prisoner. Saturn is symbolic of the limitations of intellect. It is your own intellect that 'binds' you, through your conditioning, keeping you in the illusion that you are separate, and preventing you from directly perceiving reality[153]. This imprisonment of our consciousness in our own intellect, and it's

---

[153] Read more about how we are conditioned to see illusion in chapter one of *Soul Astrology*.

subsequent release, is perhaps what The Tibetan is referring to when he said:

> *"Saturn's power is completely ended and his work accomplished when man (the spiritual man) has freed himself from Karma and from the power of the two Crosses –*
> *the Common [Mutable] and the Fixed. Esoterically, Saturn cannot follow man on to the Cardinal Cross"*
>
> - The Tibetan, *Esoteric Astrology*

In our evolutionary journey to this point, we have created an important foundation, which we can now use as a springboard to spiritual awakening. Our journey is summed up in psychologist Abraham Maslow's[154] *Hierarchy of Human Need*.

First we had to establish ourselves in terms of survival and safety, so our time energy and attention isn't spent in foraging for food, and protecting ourselves to survive. Once we have our foundation we can turn our attention to self-exploration: the search for our own true nature.

The Dweller On The Threshold

In *Esoteric Astrology* the Tibetan made reference to the *Dweller on the Threshold*, but who is the dweller and what is the threshold?

> *"Saturn is one of the most potent of the four Lords of Karma and forces man to face up to the past, and in the present to prepare for the future. Such is the intention and purpose of karmic opportunity. From certain angles, Saturn can be regarded as the planetary Dweller on the Threshold, for humanity as a whole has to face that Dweller as well as the Angel of the Presence, and in so doing discover that both the Dweller and the Angel are that complex duality which is the human family."*
>
> - The Tibetan, *Esoteric Astrology*

---

[154] Maslow's hierarchy of needs, is often represented as a pyramid with the more basic needs at the bottom, see *Maslow's hierarchy of needs*, online article at https://en.wikipedia.org/wiki/Maslow%27s_hierarchy_of_needs Accessed December 2nd 2019.

In the above quote it is clear that the Tibetan is speaking of *The Dweller* both in terms of an association with Saturn, and as an aspect of human duality. We can therefore think of the Dweller on The Threshold as *that aspect of ourselves that has reached the limitation of intellect and is now ready to go beyond*. When we hear the call of Uranus it is time to go beyond the limitation of intellect, symbolized by Saturn, and to walk the path of intuition with the Angel of our own Presence.

Going Beyond

The concept of *going beyond* is present in many spiritual traditions. The following mantra comes from a Buddhist scripture called The Heart Sutra[155]:

> *"Gate Gate Paragate, Parasamgate Bodhi Svaha"*

Roughly translated it means:

> *"Gone, gone, beyond. Gone altogether beyond.*
> *Oh what an awakening."*
>
> - commentary on The Heart Sutra

We can see that spiritual teachers and yogis through the ages have pointed to a reality that lies beyond ordinary experience. Not only do they say that it is possible for us to 'awaken' to this reality, but they themselves are living examples of 'spiritual awakening', and they have given us the tools and methods they used to get there.

Earlier we mentioned consciousness researcher Steve Taylor who explains how our current everyday state of consciousness is in fact itself a kind of sleep[156]. He compares this to higher states of consciousness and peak experiences.

We can therefore think of going beyond the limitations of Saturn, as going beyond our everyday mind, so that we begin to directly perceive the true nature of reality as those higher states of consciousness that lie beyond.

---

[155] *The Heart Sutra Mantra*. Online document at http://visiblemantra.org/heart.html Accessed December 2nd 2019.

[156] See *Spiritual Awakening and The Mind* in chapter fifteen.

The Angel of The Presence

> *"Upon the mental plane*
> *the Angel of the Presence and*
> *the Dweller on the Threshold*
> *are brought face to face.*
> *Their synthesis is brought about*
> *upon the Path of Initiation."*
>
> - The Tibetan, *Esoteric Astrology*

In relation to the *Dweller on The Threshold*, The Tibetan also mentions the *Angel of the Presence*. Both the "Dweller" and "The Angel" are aspects of us. When we are solely personality centered, our attention and energy is continually projected outside of us trying to meet the needs of the personality. Once we begin to awaken, we might still be mainly personality-driven, but we also experience the stirrings of Soul awakening. Once we are ready to go beyond the intellect, in recognition that there is more to us than meets the eye, we are The Dweller on the Threshold. By keeping our attention fully in the moment, we realize a constant, aware, presence that has never left us. This is The Angel of the Presence, and it is us.

Contemporary spiritual teachers have also commented on the power of presence, or present-moment awareness. The most notable of these is probably Eckhart Tolle[157]. Whilst we can have an intellectual understanding of the power of presencing, we won't really know the deeper insights for ourselves, until we have our own experience.

When we fully and sincerely practice present-moment awareness we undergo a powerful transformative process whereby we can access higher truth. We begin to widen our perceptive capacity and can recognize the inner gateways to the Universe through our own intuition. These inner doors, sometimes referred to by mystics as the 'Bhagavat in the ten directions', are our gateway to the Universe through inner space. We have access to ultimate truth because we are not separate from it. We can expand our capacity to reach the place where, as the Tibetan said, 'The will of God is known'.

Once we go deeper with our experience of self-observation, we realize that there is much more than merely observing. There is what

---

[157] Tolle, E. (2004) *The Power of Now: A Guide to Spiritual Enlightenment.* New World Library.

the mystics referred to as opening the "inner doors". We experience some very deep realizations about the nature of reality, and who we are within it. Our capacity for directly perceiving energy increases. This opens and expands our intuitive capacity. We become more skilled at focusing our attention, or to be more precise, at bringing our awareness to something. We realize that the quality of awareness that we bring to something, can change it.

> *"Once your awareness becomes a flame,*
> *it burns up the whole slavery that the mind has created."*
>
> - OSHO

Insight meditation teacher Jack Kornfield[158] describes how we can heal ourselves by looking directly at our physical, emotional, and psychological pain and simply bringing our *loving awareness* to it. This isn't a metaphor it is a very real, tangible, and powerful process.

When we have cultivated our perception to this degree we realize how our own awareness has the power to transform energy, not through anything we are doing, but simply by *bringing loving awareness to it*.

The Path of Intuition: Remembering

We don't just wake up one day, crystal clear, and fully present in the stage of intuition. Pure crystal, clear, awakened heart-mind is something that comes in a later stage of our journey. First we must get there, and to do that, we must walk the path of intuition.

At the beginning, when intuition is just starting to awaken, we begin remembering. We don't necessarily recognize this as memory in the way we usually experience memories. We might experience visions, sense perceptions, sounds, sensations, emotions, thoughts, and certainly personality traits, patterns and tendencies that are remnants from past lives.

It's like when you finally put the light on in a room that has been dark for many years, and you get to see just how much dust has accumulated in the dark corners!

---

[158] Kornfield, J. (1993) *A Path with Heart: A Guide Through the Perils and Promises of Spiritual Life.* Bantam.

"From ancient recesses of the memory, from a deeply rooted past which is definitely recalled, and from the racial and the individual subconscious (or founded and established thought reservoirs and desires, inherited and inherent) there emerges from individual past lives and experience that which is the sum total of all instinctual tendencies, of all inherited glamours and of all phases of wrong mental attitudes; to these (as they constitute a blended whole) we give the name of the Dweller on the Threshold.

This Dweller is the sum total of all the personality characteristics which have remained unconquered and unsubdued and which must be finally overcome before initiation can be taken. Each life sees some progress made; some personality defects straightened out and some real advance effected. But the unconquered residue and the ancient liabilities are numerous and excessively potent and—when soul contact is adequately established—there eventuates a life wherein the highly developed and powerful personality becomes, in itself, the Dweller on the Threshold.

Then the Angel of the Presence and the Dweller stand face to face and something must then be done. Eventually, the light of the personal self fades out and wanes in the blaze of glory which emanates from the Angel."

- The Tibetan, *Esoteric Astrology*

My mentor Anya Sophia Mann[159] often says, *that which is not you comes up into the light for healing*. Habitual, conditioned, reactive ways of living and being, rooted in fear and negative emotions, cannot remain in the light of your awareness. The more you remain fully present to you, the more you will become aware of just how much of your behavior is the result of lifetimes of conditioning. Layer by layer you will let them all arise and release them.

Meditation: The Path of Self Knowing

"Know thyself. If thou canst learn the true nature of thine own self, thou wilt know the reality of the Universe"

- Swami Abhedananda

---

[159] Https://AnyaSophiaMann.com

Simply put, meditation is a path of self-knowing. Up to now, on our journey through the personal and social planets, we have gathered strength and resources from without - partner, friends, family and society: from here on we will depend upon our own inner resources. In order to 'go beyond' Saturn we need an inner shift in perception. Our intellect is the foundation for the next stage, but we must not be attached to it. We need to apply our intellect, in order to go beyond it. And the way we do that is through a range of contemplative practices for observing and exploring our inner world. This range of techniques and practices (of which there are many) are grouped together under the general term of 'meditation'.

*"Habit kills intuition, because habit prevents
living experience, direct perception."*

- Lama Anagarika Govinda[160]

It is our conditioning: our repetitive thoughts, words and actions, that create karma and prevent us from accessing higher states of consciousness. Without meditation, or some kind of contemplative 'presencing' or mindfulness practice, astrology remains just an intellectual exercise and the deeper insights remain lost to us. Indeed this is where the danger of astrology lies: without the realizations that meditation brings through practice and experience, astrology could keep you stuck at the intellect stage of development. It is the contemplative component that sets Soul Astrology apart from other forms of astrology, and leads to deeper insights.

Meditation is the only valid tool for exploring the true nature of your Self. It cannot be done from the outside. The only way to discover your true nature, is to go within. Be still and, once all the noise subsides, notice the simple truth of who you are, underneath all the ideas and labels.

"when you are tied by ideas and the sense world, instead of stressing out, stop your sense perception and silently watch your mind. Try to be totally awake instead of obsessed with just one atom. Feel totality instead of particulars."

- Lama Thubten Yeshe[161]

---

[160] Govinda, A. (1976) *Creative Meditation and Multi Dimensional Consciousness* Theosophical Publishing House.

Intellect separates and polarizes: good-bad; light-dark etc. To arrive at our true nature it is necessary to go beyond the intellect, beyond ideas, thoughts, thinking, and cognitions, and simply rest in beingness. There you will find your Self.

> *"Far beyond ideas of wrong-doing,*
> *and right-doing, there is a field.*
> *I'll meet you there"*

- Rumi

Silence and The Brain

> *"an answer from the silent mind is always better than too many words. There are so many views and philosophies; instead of helping, they sometimes cause more confusion."*

- Lama Thubten Yeshe

Science is only just beginning to understand the importance of silence for our brain's health and development. Recent studies[162] show that when our mind is quiet, our brains actually begin to repair and regenerate themselves.

Spending twenty to forty minutes each day in silence is actually good for your brain health and, even more importantly, it is vitally important for releasing habitual conditioning and revealing your own true nature. It is in silence that you have deeper insights. It is in pure silence that you can recognize your own essence, without layers of conditioning and distorted ideas.

It is in silence that The Dweller on The Threshold, meets the Angel of the Presence. In other words, it is in silence that you eventually meet your Self. Silence is vital to your process of spiritual awakening.

---

[161] Yeshe, T. (2004) *The Peaceful Stillness of Silent Mind.* Lama Yeshe Wisdom Archive. PDF version available for free download at http://www.lamayeshe.com/sites/default/files/pdf/139_pdf.pdf

[162] *Science Says Silence Is Much More Important To Our Brains Than We Think.* Online document at https://www.lifehack.org/377243/science-says-silence-much-more-important-our-brains-than-thought Accessed December 2nd 2019.

The Deepest Purpose of Meditation

> *"Meditation is not evasion;*
> *it is a serene encounter with reality."*
>
> – Thich Nhat Hanh

People meditate for so many reasons these days: to reduce stress, feel calmer, have better health and so forth. These are all wonderful reasons to meditate, however, the real purpose of meditation, and the one that we are most interested in here, is self-exploration. This is important to remember when choosing which type of meditation to practice regularly.

Some contemporary guided visualizations can be relaxing, but will not support you in quieting the mind, or going to the deeper realizations beyond. An effective meditation method provides the opportunity for you to recognize for yourself: that who you are, at the very core of your being IS consciousness; to give yourself time for the usual mental activity to subside - to quieten or slow enough so that you can recognize the consciousness that IS you[163].

Briefly, meditation can be placed in two categories: *vipassana* (open) and *shamatha* (concentration)[164]. It is wise to combine the two for the best results. Meditation in some form is essential for self-discovery: to recognize your true nature, and the true nature of reality. No one has ever had a true spiritual awakening without it.

> *"Know thyself.*
> *If thou canst learn the true nature*
> *of thine own self,*
> *thou wilt know the reality*
> *of the Universe"*
>
> - Swami Abhedananda

---

[163] *Is The World An Illusion?* Rupert Spira discusses the nature of self and consciousness. YouTube video at
https://www.youtube.com/watch?v=IIqqxzT_aQvI

[164] Hadikin, R. (2015) *Learn To Meditate: A quick start guide to meditation for beginners.* Kindle Edition. Ruth Hadikin Associates.

Go Beyond

From a new perspective, in present-moment awareness, with a developed capacity for direct perception, we are ready to meet Uranus, and walk the path of intuition...

Suggested Fieldwork

• Deeper Self-observation. If you don't already have a regular meditative or contemplative practice, it is a good idea to make a regular commitment to your Self and build this into your daily routine. Just sitting quietly in nature for twenty minutes, and allowing your mind to settle, is enough to expand your awareness.

• Further Study: *The Peaceful Stillness of Silent Mind*, by Lama Thubten Yeshe, especially chapter three: *Experiencing Silent Wisdom*. In *Soul Astrology* study and contemplate chapter five: *The Planetary Spaceholders;* and chapter six: *Self-Awareness: The Science of Your Soul*. Online document: *Science Says Silence Is Much More Important To Our Brains Than We Think*[165] VIDEO: *Is The World An Illusion*[166] Excellent discussion on the true nature of consciousness and reality with Rupert Spira (15:34 minutes).

---

[165] *Science Says Silence Is Much More Important To Our Brains Than We Think.* Online document at https://www.lifehack.org/377243/science-says-silence-much-more-important-our-brains-than-thought Accessed December 2nd 2019.

[166] *Is The World An Illusion?* Rupert Spira discusses the nature of self and consciousness. YouTube video at https://www.youtube.com/watch?v=HqqxzT_aQvI

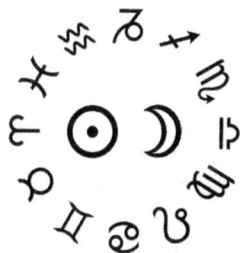

21. Uranus, A Sacred Rebellion

Planets of Transformation

Having journeyed through the levels of instinct and intellect under the custodianship of the personal and social planets we now arrive at the planets of transformation, to provide the conditions for the next stages of our evolutionary journey of spiritual awakening: intuition, illumination and emptiness.

The slowest moving planets, Uranus, Neptune and Pluto have been called the *planets of transformation*[167] because of the powerful impact they have in our chart, by natal position and by transit. Because they move so slowly they spend a long time in one area of our chart (meaning they have a prolonged effect in one area of our life) and they cannot possibly cross our whole chart in one lifetime (except for a few individuals who are blessed to live to be eighty-four years or older, so they experience a 'Uranus Return'). Looking at the specific areas of our lives where they transit, throughout our whole life, can tell us much about what we are here to change, learn, heal, and transform in our lifetime.

They help us to see our role in the world as part of our generation and Soul Group (by which sign they are in), and to understand our individual Soul's development more clearly (by which houses they

---

[167] *Astrology, Karma & Transformation: The Inner Dimensions of The Birth Chart.* Arroyo, S. (1992) CRCS Publications.

occupy in our natal chart and by which houses they transit throughout our life). They can also help us to understand why we have some of the challenges that we do at the level of our personality, if we understand some of the subtle (and not so subtle) waves they are making in our lives in order to wake us up!

There is a golden rule in Soul Astrology: that which the personality (or ego) generally thinks of as a 'bad' thing (sudden change, loss, upheaval) is always beneficial to our Soul's growth on a deeper level. So what might appear to be 'negative' conditions in conventional astrology, are always positive in Soul Astrology. This is because ultimately we are moving towards living in wholeness and unity consciousness, which eventually means letting go of the illusion of being a separate ego. And to the ego, letting go can be painful.

The planets of transformation are a case in point. By nature they make life difficult for the ego. Look on the internet on any given day and you will see people lamenting 'transits' of Uranus, Neptune and Pluto. When they travel through (transit) a particular area of our chart (which represents of an area of our real life) they really stir things up. I mean, they really, REALLY, stir things up!

Slow moving planets are generational in nature, for example most people born between 1939 and 1957 had Pluto in Leo, so that tells us something about what that generation is here to do as a Soul Group. To see where they have a more personal impact on your life, you can look to see where they are in your natal chart, meaning in which house.

What is The Farthest Point of Consciousness?

Have you ever thought about it? How far can you go in expanding YOUR mind, YOUR consciousness, YOUR awareness? In conventional astrology Saturn is considered to be the planet of limitation because it rules the structure of mind, and as we saw previously it is those same mental structures that limit our perception.

Our brain loves to 'learn', and we get through our everyday existence because we have learned so much: walking, talking, reading, writing, driving and so on. There is nothing wrong with learning, but the very way that the brain functions also keeps us in illusion. Neuroscience is discovering what ancient yogis and spiritual teachers have taught for centuries, which is that each of us is actually living in a world created by our brain. We don't experience reality 'as it is' at all. What we experience as reality is actually a projection from our brain based on past experience. Our whole neurological wiring - and the projections that result from it - come under the realm of Saturn.

When *Esoteric Astrology* was first published in 1951 it said that humanity didn't yet have the consciousness to perceive the subtle energies of the outer planets on an individual level. Which is why we largely consider them to be generational in nature. However, that is changing... fast.

Evolutionary Shifts in Consciousness

We have been through evolutionary waves in human consciousness throughout the 1960's, 70's, 80's, 90's, 2000's and beyond - until here we are now in the present year. We have experienced the whole transcendental meditation movement, experiments with mind-altering substances such as LSD, not to mention the influx of eastern spiritual practices like yoga, which were relatively unheard of in the 1950's and are now sweeping the planet. All this has led to experiences beyond our conventional mind. Beyond Saturn.

So do we have the same consciousness that we had in 1951? No. You can see this on an everyday level. It is now much more acceptable (at least in Western Societies) to talk about spirituality and different spiritual traditions than it was in the 1950's. It is much more acceptable to connect with people outside of our own culture and traditions. Collectively we have made a huge shift beyond the confines of Saturn and I believe a substantial group of people is now able to perceive the subtler levels of consciousness that go beyond Saturn's mental structures.

Clear Light Mind

The Tibetan Dzogchen tradition specifically talks about an ability to 'go beyond' everyday mind (Saturn) to experience the 'clear light mind' beyond. Consciousness itself is not limited by human brain wiring.

With practice, we can cultivate an ability to go beyond our own mental structures, to take our conscious awareness beyond the limitations of our own brain wiring, and experience the vastness of our own being in the unbounded 'clear light mind' beyond!

The Role of The Outer Planets

Realizing clear light mind is a process that involves the outer planets (beyond Saturn) working on an individual level...

First *Uranus* opens our intuitive capacity. This awakens perception so we are able to be receptive to the higher subtler energies, which allows us to welcome Neptune. Uranus brings us an experience of great clarity.

Then *Neptune* 'spiritualizes' what it touches, bringing great illumination. Through the experience of Neptune we are able to perceive and utilize higher frequencies without being 'blinded' by the light.

Once we have been illuminated by Neptune, we become receptive to *Pluto* where we can realize the highest wisdom of all, which is the wisdom realizing emptiness:

> *"You live in illusion and the appearance of things.*
> *There is a reality, but you do not know this.*
> *When you understand this, you will see that you are nothing,*
> *and being nothing you are everything.*
> *That is all."*
>
> *- Kalu Rinpoche*

In short:

- *Uranus* brings great clarity,
- *Neptune* brings great illumination (light), and
- *Pluto* brings great wisdom (specifically the 'wisdom realizing emptiness').

Liberate Your Mind

Even this is only the beginning of our exploration of consciousness! We cannot comprehend any farther because we have reached the limit of our current understanding, the current limit of human consciousness. It's like when you're hiking and you can't see how much farther until you get around the next bend in the trail!

One thing we do know is that it doesn't end here... there are frontiers beyond frontiers ... and once we get beyond our own Saturnian limitation, our consciousness is free to explore.

You are here to set yourself free. To liberate your mind so that you can experience the natural state of your own expanded consciousness. If you're wanting to progress to understanding Soul Astrology at an advanced level it is vital that you open up your doors of perception to cultivate your awareness of subtler and subtler vibrations of energy.

Uranus and The Evolution of Consciousness

Remember that as we evolve through the levels of instinct > intellect > intuition > illumination and emptiness, each stage is necessary. It's not that we 'lose' our instincts and intellect, as we move into intuition, but rather that each stage is a vital foundation for what comes next. So by the time we reach the level of the wisdom realizing emptiness, we also realize that we are also all of it. We are everything that has gone before. We don't 'transcend' instinct by 'getting rid of it' but rather it becomes integrated into our whole being.

After the confinement, limitation and restriction of Saturn along comes The Rebel, Uranus, to turn the tables. In our journey toward ultimate truth we need to go way beyond the mental constructs of Saturn and the first energy that clears the way ahead is Uranus. The conditions created by Uranus clear the path, remove obstacles, and give us higher perception and clarity. The tool that we need for the next phase in our journey, is intuition, and we develop intuition as a result of our experiences under the conditions of Uranus.

Uranus is associated with sudden change, upheaval and even rebellion. Esoterically Uranus is the planet of intuition. In our personal chart it shows the area of life where we are awakening: becoming more aware, more intuitive, and also that area of life that will bring us the people, situations and circumstances that cause us to wake up. Wherever Uranus falls in your chart shows an area where you may even be called upon to rebel, to make a stand by standing in the truth of your experience.

A Very Sacred Rebellion

> *"[A rebel] lives individually – not as a cog in the wheel, but as an organic unity. His life is not decided by anybody else, but by his own intelligence. The very fragrance of his life is that of freedom –*
> *not only that he lives in freedom,*
> *he allows everybody else also to live in freedom.*

> *He does not allow anybody to interfere in his life; neither does he interfere in anybody else's life. To him, life is so sacred – and freedom is the ultimate value – that he can sacrifice everything for it: respectability, status, even life itself."*
>
> — OSHO

The kind of rebellion demanded by Uranus is a sacred rebellion. It is not a rebellion against anything or anybody, but rather an awakening to one's own true nature, and a commitment to live out that expression in one's life. Intuition has been described as *"our ability to perceive the quality of energy"*[168] so ultimately Uranus is expanding our capacity for perception, thus awakening our ability to perceive energy.

The Gap Between Your Thoughts

Our nervous system is a network of individual nerve cells that appear to be connected but if we look closely there is a gap between each one called a synapse. As thoughts pass through our nervous system, they actually leap across this synaptic gap in the form of an electrical charge. If you could see your brain at microscopic level while you are thinking, it looks like a lightning storm. Uranus rules lightning and electricity, so if the gap between our thoughts is electrical in nature (like lightening), then it comes under the rulership of Uranus.

Three Planets of Mind

There are three planets associated with mind: Mercury, Saturn and Uranus. Mercury rules the movement of mind (the thoughts themselves), Saturn rules the structure of mind (our neural network), and Uranus rules higher mind: the gap between our thoughts.

The gap between thoughts, or beyond thinking, is where we experience deep insight and intuition. It is in the space between our thoughts that we are able to access higher perception and discern a higher reality beyond the normal limitations of our senses and our brain wiring (Saturn). Hence the association of Uranus with electricity, lightning, and intuition.

---

[168] Oken, A. (2008) *Soul-Centered Astrology: A Key to Your Expanding Self.* Ibis Press.

What is intuition?

Intuition has been described as our ability:

> *"to acquire knowledge without proof, evidence, or conscious reasoning, or without understanding how the knowledge was acquired."*[169]

We can immediately see that, when we are using intuition, we have gone beyond thought. We have gone beyond the cognitive part of our brain that is responsible for thinking, logic, and reason. When we are using intuition we are tapping into another capacity beyond thinking. This is sometimes describes as sensing, and sometimes described as clear knowing. When we tap into intuition we are beginning to become aware of awareness itself. We are beginning to wake up to the fact that we are aware, and in that awareness there is knowledge.

Master Astrologer Alan Oken describes intuition as:

> *"The ability to perceive that quality of energy, the true essence of meaning, within any form of expression"*

It is Mercury that governs the bridge between lower and higher mind because Mercury rules the movement of mind: thought, and thoughts are a 'vehicle' for our consciousness.

When we follow our thoughts, we are actually giving our attention to them. We are allowing our consciousness to follow the thoughts. But when an individual thought leaps into the gap in-between thoughts it enters the realm of Uranus.

Then, for the very briefest of moments, we have an opportunity to drop the thought, get off the train, release the vehicle, and experience pure perception: pure consciousness itself, uncontaminated by thoughts, ideas and concepts. It is in that moment that we can 'wake up' and directly perceive our true nature as spiritual beings without the contaminating distortion of thoughts and ideas.

---

[169] *Intuition*, online document at https://en.wikipedia.org/wiki/Intuition Accessed December 10th 2019.

> *"There may come to you an awakening of the intuition*
> *which will translate modern astrology*
> *into something of real moment*
> *and significance to the world"*
>
> — The Tibetan, *Esoteric Astrology*

Direct Perception

It is this capacity for direct perception, without any thoughts or concepts clouding our experience, that we call intuition. As long as our awareness remains in that gap between thoughts (the synapse) we are free. We have access to the entire Universe through Universal Mind, free from the conditioning of our brain wiring. It is from here that we are truly 'awake' and all can be known. This is why meditation is so important. It is through some form of meditative practice (basically observing ourselves and how our mind works) that we are able to cultivate the ability to remain in the gap between our thoughts for longer and longer periods.

It is though direct perception that the ancient Kalachakra Masters were able to practice astrology without telescopes, tables, or ephemerides. In other words, they were able to directly perceive the entire workings of the Universe through their intuition. You have this potential, the key is to jump into the gap between your thoughts and stay there for as long as you can. Then you too may discover that the Universe lies in the gap between your thoughts!

The Discovery of Uranus: A Leap In Consciousness

The planet Uranus was discovered by the German-born British astronomer William Herschel on March 13th 1781. In *Esoteric Astrology* The Tibetan suggests that humanity discovers planets (and all phenomena) when our consciousness has evolved to the point where we have the capacity to perceive them and respond appropriately to their energy.

The discovery of Uranus was a momentous occasion: it was the first time that a planet had been discovered since ancient times. Indeed it was technology in the form of more highly refined telescopes that allowed for the discovery of Uranus.

Herschel himself was a maker of advanced telescopes. Even though the name Uranus was not fully adopted until many years later (Herschel had originally named the planet after King George III of

England) his epitaph[170] reflected the enormous sense of having gone beyond:

Coelorum perrupit claustra
(He broke through the barriers of the heavens)

As we saw previously, prior to the discovery of Uranus it was a long-held belief that Saturn marked the outer limit of our Solar System. So Uranus became the planet of 'going beyond our limits and boundaries'. Certainly the main themes that were rippling through the consciousness of humanity at the time, are the very Uranian themes of rebellion, revolution, and new technology.

The American War of Independence was at its height and the development of technology (leading to the industrial revolution and the subsequent mechanization of agriculture and labor) was barely getting started. Humanity was on the threshold of a new era as people were required to move beyond their boundaries, to leave their homelands, villages and families and for the first time move en masse to large cities (which grew exponentially) in order to find work in the newly-forming factories.

Technology and Revolution

The development of technology and the seeds of revolution went together hand in hand as people were able to congregate in larger masses then ever before in the fast-growing cities. Developments in printing technology in the early 1800's allowed for mass printing of flyers that could be distributed swiftly among the people. The new ability to mass-produce books and written materials greatly accelerated the literacy rates in common people who, until now, had been largely illiterate.

The Conditions for Rebellion

The conditions were in place for people to rise up against oppression for the first time and seek individual freedom. The discovery of Uranus heralded a wave of revolutions that spread like wildfire across Europe and European-held territories as people could now meet, spread information, rally together, and organize themselves on

---

[170] William Herschel online document at https://en.wikipedia.org/wiki/William_Herschel Accessed December 10th 2019.

an unprecedented scale. The first eighty-four year cycle of Uranus (1781 - 1865) saw a wave of unprecedented revolutions that completely transformed the face of the Earth, and advanced human consciousness:

- American Revolutionary War (Britain) 1775 - 1783
- French Revolution 1789 - 1799
- Haiti (France)1791-1804
- Ireland 1798
- Serbian Revolution 1804-1835
- Spanish America 1810-1825
- Spain, Portugal, Russia, Italy, Greece 1820
- Brazil (Portugal) 1821-1824
- Netherlands, Poland, Switzerland 1830
- The "Revolutionary Year" Austria, Hungary, Denmark, Poland, Netherlands, France, Germany, Italy 1848
- Colombia (Spain) 1851-1885

Freedom and The Father of Archetypes

Esoterically Uranus is known as *the father of archetypes*[171] and so conditions were lining up for the 'birth' of a new human archetype: one who was more individualized and 'free' than had ever been known before on Earth. Free from being tied to one's birthplace, and free from oppressive regimes. Never before had there been mass revolution on a global scale, which continues to this day, as people are still rising up against oppressive regimes in many parts of the world. The connection between Uranian-ruled technology and revolution also continues as people now use the internet and social media to share information for setting themselves free.

Freedom is a vital precursor to the development of intuition. If we are living under oppression it keeps us stuck in the former stages of consciousness: instinct and intellect. As long as anyone has control over us we use our instincts to survive, and remain focused in our intellect to plan our 'escape' strategy, negotiate for better conditions, or take up some form of study to gain a better position in the society.

---

[171] Dictionary definition of archetype: *"[1] the original pattern or model from which all things of the same kind are copied or on which they are based; a model or first form; prototype. [2] (in Jungian psychology) a collectively inherited unconscious idea, pattern of thought, image, etc., universally present in individual psyches."* From https://www.dictionary.com/browse/archetype

Planning, organizing, strategizing, and studying, all keep us engaged at the level of intellect.

The Mind's True Liberation

To liberate our minds and experience intuition, we must set ourselves free from intellect too, but this is a delicate path to walk. Setting ourselves free from intellect is not the same as under-developing our intellect. If we simply become 'anti-intellect' we may just remain dull and stupid, and lack understanding of spiritual awakening. This is a risk that comes with revolution, when simple people gain too much power too soon, without the development of intellect. Many revolutions end up as oppressive as the regimes they were intended to replace. Keeping people in ignorance through propaganda, misinformation and disinformation, is not freedom. In fact the reverse is true, it reinforces conditioning. Remember each stage in the evolution of consciousness is a foundation for the next stage. If we don't develop our intellect at all, we remain at the animalistic level of instinct and do not grow into our intuition.

The key is to develop the intellect in order to use it to study altruism and spiritual matters, and then know when to let go. Many great spiritual masters were former scholars who then turned their attention to their spiritual path. For example Rumi was a great scholar and university teacher until he met his spiritual teacher Shams Tabriz, whereupon he relinquished his former life and went off into the desert with him.

Uranus The Sky God

In Ancient Greece, Uranus (Ouranus) was known as the sky-god. Occasionally he was personified, whereupon he was referred to as though 'he' was a person, but for the most part the name of Uranus simply referred to the sky. This is in contrast to the Roman idea of Jupiter as a sky-god. Whereas the Roman Jupiter was thought of as the god of the sky (with very human-like qualities), Uranus was the sky itself. This symbolizes both the vastness and the transpersonal nature of Uranus.

Sky Gazing

In chapter fourteen, in the section on *The Seven Rays*, we discussed how the practice of sky-gazing is used to help spiritual practitioners attune to subtler levels of conscious light and energy. In this practice one gazes softly towards the sky (not grasping at it visually) and practices what are known as the four chozhags (let-be's): the body is left as it is; the eyes are left seeing whatever; the mind rests in clarity, allowing mental events to be; and the entire field of one's sensory awareness is simply left *as it is*. Practicing this form of meditation is thought to be important for expanding one's consciousness and bringing great spiritual realizations.

"Everything is like the sky - this is what I have to realize"

- Shantideva

We can see the individualistic, unique and even eccentric influence of Uranus at work in our journey to spiritual awakening. Because it is individuals who awaken, not societies, Uranus creates the conditions for us to go beyond the boundaries (Saturn) of the society into which we were born, so we may discover our uniqueness. This begins the search for the true 'me' and it is in this search for Self that we expand our consciousness, and realize intuition.

Uranus and Aquarius

Uranus, together with Saturn, is one of the personality rulers of Aquarius. In Astrology it is often said that there are two types of Aquarian personality: the Saturnian type, who is concerned more with tradition, method, strategy and structure; and the Uranian type, who is more future oriented with a facility for (if not a love of) technology. Because of the fixed energy of Aquarius, either type can find themselves bound in the past, re-living karmic cycles of ego-personality. The solution is to tap into the energy of Uranus and spend more time in the gap between thoughts, where intuition can be accessed.

Uranus and Libra

Uranus is the Soul Ruler of Libra. If you have Libra Rising pay particular attention to where Uranus is in your chart by sign, and by house. The condition of Uranus in your chart will indicate where your Soul is calling you to awaken and deserves deeper contemplation.

Uranus Through The Signs

Uranus in Aries (1927 to 1934; 2010-2018)

If you were born when Uranus was in Aries you are part of a soul group who 'rebels' by seeding new archetypes for the future of humanity. This generation plants the seeds of ideas for future generations to carry forward.

Uranus in Taurus - Fall (1934-1942; 2019-2025)

If you were born when Uranus was in Taurus you are part of a soul group whose rebellion is one of releasing attachment to form and perceiving the light within the form.

Uranus in Gemini (1942-1949; 2025-2032)

If you were born when Uranus was in Gemini you are part of a soul group that is experiencing a rebellion of the mind and communication. This is a generation that seeks to expand awareness of communication, ultimately leading to communion with your higher self.

Uranus in Cancer (1949-1956)

If you were born with Uranus in Cancer yours is a quiet yet powerful rebellion of compassion that takes place within the home and family. This soul group awakens us to the truth of our connectedness and, by transforming our ideas of family, evolves us from tribal thinking to the realization that we really are one human family.

Uranus in Leo - Detriment (1956-1962)

If you were born with Uranus in Leo you are part of a soul group that values individuality, and your 'rebellion' is one of individual creative expression awakening you to your own true nature as a spiritual being. This is a generation that walks the path of self-realization: you are here to transcend the ego and become aware of your Soul.

Uranus in Virgo (1962-1969)

If you were born with Uranus in Virgo you are part of a soul group whose 'rebellion' is to transform attitudes to health and wellness. This is a generation that is waking up to the truth that our physical body and our soul are not separate and that the physical is also sacred. This generation is active in the drive towards alternative and complementary therapies.

Uranus in Libra (1968-1975)

If you were born with Uranus in Libra your soul group is leading a 'rebellion' of peace, harmony and love! Uranus is the Soul-centered 'ruler' of Libra, and Libra is associated with law, equality and ethics. During the era from 1968-1975 there was a worldwide transformation in equal rights legislation and this generation continues to spearhead a global 'rebellion' towards equality, peace and harmony.

Uranus in Scorpio - exaltation (1975-1981)

If you were born when Uranus was in Scorpio you are part of a soul group whose 'rebellion' is one of personal power. This is a generation who is learning important lessons around the right use of personal power, including sexual power, and is spearheading a personal and global 'rebellion' of self-empowerment.

Uranus in Sagittarius (1981-1988)

If you were born when Uranus was in Sagittarius you are part of a soul group of 'teachers' who have come to bring higher degrees of wisdom onto the planet. Your 'rebellion' will be one of education: transforming outdated and outmoded philosophies and knowledge systems and spearheading a 'rebellion' towards Soul-Centered wisdom.

Uranus in Capricorn (1988-1995)

If you were born when Uranus was in Capricorn you are part of a soul group that is transforming the distribution of resources on the planet. Yours is a 'rebellion' of resources, institutions, and financial systems. Your generation will spearhead a 'rebellion' towards right-use of resources.

Uranus in Aquarius - dignity (1996-2003)

If you were born when Uranus was in Aquarius you are part of a soul group that is ushering in the Aquarian age. Yours is a rebellion of consciousness: collectively you will be making the transition from separation to fully awakened group consciousness. Technology is a stepping-stone on your journey. The current social media is cultivating your awareness of group consciousness and eventually you will realize your innate telepathic abilities, and know your ultimate connection doesn't require technology!

Uranus in Pisces (1920-1927; 2003-2011)

If you were born when Uranus was in Pisces you are part of a soul group whose 'rebellion' is one of Universal Love. You are here to transcend suffering and usher in an era of heart-centered living, leading to the ultimate awakening of the sacred heart of humanity: where all hearts beat as one!

Uranus in The Houses

With all the slow-moving planets there is always a generational 'soul group' transformation happening, that ultimately is guiding the evolution of human consciousness. Yet there is also, always, a very personal awakening happening at the same time: for it is the individuals within the soul-group that drive the collective awakening through their own personal awakening. It is vital to remember this very important point - it is always individuals who awaken, not the group. The personal meaning of the planets of transformation for you can be determined by looking at their placement in the houses of your natal chart, and their aspects to other planets.

Your natal chart is a symbol of your personal energy field - your mandala. So when you look at your natal chart you are looking at a symbol of your energy matrix: a pictorial representation of your real energy field. It is always important to remember that, so you remain aware that you are not looking at something outside of you.

When we talk about the 'houses' of your chart, we are talking about twelve areas of life where your energy may be expressed during the course of your lifetime, similar to a 'wheel of life'. The twelve houses represent areas such as your sense of self and identity; your income and personal resources; mental processing, thinking and learning; your home and family; your creativity; your health, well-being and personal growth; your relationships and so on.

Now back to Uranus. There is a sudden, unexpected, quality to Uranian energy that is in the nature of a 'short, sharp, shock'. Yet there is also clarity and greater awareness. Spiritual teacher Tenzin Wangyal Rinpoche suggests that when something startles us, we should pay attention and try to remain in that state of alertness as long as we can because we have just been catapulted into a different state of consciousness. It is a great opportunity for awakening that is to be welcomed!

Remembering that Uranus is the planet of intuition and awakening, we can now look to see where in your chart Uranus may be raising your consciousness, developing your intuition, and bringing you the necessary 'surprises' that cause you to 'wake up' in your life:

Uranus in the First House

If you have Uranus in your First House you are waking up to the reality of your own existence. To be aware of your own beingness, and the sacred nature of that. You may go through many identity crises at personality level, as you explore your own uniqueness and individuality, and bump up against society's ideas of how you ought to be, vs. your own sense of who you really are. Ultimately you are waking up to your own existence.

Uranus in the Second House

If you have Uranus in the second house you are waking up to your own sense of value and self-worth. At personality level this is connected to finances, income and your own resources, which may be erratic as you explore your own unique ways of generating income. Ultimately you are waking up to your own innate and inherent value simply as a spiritual being.

Uranus in the Third House

If you have Uranus in the third house you are waking up to the scope of your own mind. At the personality level you may process information, think, and learn, in unique, unusual, and highly individualistic ways. You can have flashes of insight that can seem like eccentricity and/or genius. Ultimately you are being awakened to the higher dimensions of mind, and your own ability to connect and commune with your higher self.

Uranus in the Fourth House

If you have Uranus in the fourth house you are waking up to the true meaning of home. Home is where the heart is, and Uranus in the Fourth House initiates a heart awakening[172], because an awakened heart is the doorway to intuition. At personality level you may go

---

[172] In the buddhist tradition the awakened heart is called *bodhicitta* and is cultivated by practising a positive attitude and through acts of compassion and kindness. See *Bodhicitta: The Excellence of Awakened Heart*. Online document at https://www.lionsroar.com/bodhichitta-the-excellence-of-awakened-heart/ Accessed December 2nd 2019.

through many sudden and unexpected changes of residence, and/or as a child perhaps your family moved home a lot. You may have times where you are challenged by sudden and unexpected 'uprooting' and moving. Ultimately you are being called upon to redefine home and to realize that, as a spiritual being, your only true 'home' is the one within your own heart, and you carry that wherever you go.

Uranus in the Fifth House

If you have Uranus in the fifth house you are waking up to your uniqueness as a creative being. At the personality level you may explore unique and highly individualistic forms of creative self-expression, as you seek to understand your own true nature. You may be tempted to take risks, and/or be attracted to adventurous or dangerous sports, as you explore just how far you can go in exercising your own power as a co-creative individual. Ultimately you are being called to the path of Self-realization where you realize your own true nature as a spiritual being.

Uranus in the Sixth House

If you have Uranus in the sixth house you are waking up to the true meaning of health and well being. In *Esoteric Astrology* The Tibetan tells us that all dis-ease results from separation. At the personality level you may experience suddenly becoming dependent upon others to care for you, or alternately you may find yourself suddenly caring for dependents. You may be attracted to radically unique and different forms of healthcare, and take a unique approach to your personal development. Ultimately you are being awakened to the truth of our interdependence and the holistic nature of reality.

Uranus in the Seventh House

If you have Uranus in the seventh house you are waking up to the nature of right relationship. On the personality level you may be attracted to unique and innovative people and/or they may be attracted to you. Ultimately you are awakening to the truth that we are all reflections of ourselves in each other, which begins the process of personality and soul fusion.

Uranus in the Eighth House

If you have Uranus in the eighth house you are waking up to the nature of spiritual energy as a transformational power. On a personal level you may experience sudden and unexpected gains and/or losses in terms of join finances and resources. Ultimately you are being awakened to the fact that you are your own best resource, and that all personal and group resources are ultimately spiritual resources.

Uranus in the Ninth House

If you have Uranus in the ninth house you are waking up to higher wisdom. On a personality level you may feel moved to rebel against conventional wisdom, you may attract unusual and innovative teachers with connections to higher knowledge paths and/or you may receive wisdom from contact with foreign lands and/or people. You may receive clear and sharp flashes of intuition that reveal wisdom to you. Ultimately you are being awakened to cosmic law and higher wisdom.

Uranus in the Tenth House

If you have Uranus in the tenth house you are waking up to the path of discipleship and spiritual ambition. On a personality level you may choose an unusual, unique or highly individualized career path. You may also experience sudden and unexpected changes in your career, status or worldly position. Ultimately you are being awakened to the truth that your true 'vocation', or purpose in the world, is to follow your spiritual path.

Uranus in the Eleventh House

If you have Uranus in the eleventh house you are waking up to the nature of group purpose and service to humanity. On a personality level you may find that you can gain or lose friends suddenly and that friendships can change form unexpectedly. You may enjoy unique, innovative and/or even eccentric friends. You may also enjoy being with groups of like-mined people who share your ideals and visions. Ultimately you are being awakened to the nature of group consciousness and group service to humanity.

Uranus in the Twelfth House

If you have Uranus in the twelfth house you are waking up to the nature of oneness, or unity consciousness. At the personality level the twelfth house can symbolize our unconscious mind. So you may experience sudden and unexpected events that cause you to wake up to your own unconscious behavior. You may experience people and situations that challenge your beliefs and assumptions and cause you to change your thinking. Ultimately you are being awakened to higher states of consciousness and ultimately, unity consciousness: the personal experience of oneness.

First Uranus brings freedom from oppression, so that we are free to explore our individuality. Then through exploring our individuality we discover our intuition and prepare ourselves for the illumination stage of our development. However, we have also seen so far, how it is possible to become 'stuck' at any one of these stages. This is why humanity has not yet awakened 'en masse'.

At this moment in time we are all at various stages in terms of our spiritual development. At the level of intuition we can become attached to our freedom, our individuality, and the idea that there is a 'me' in here who is 'the intuitive one'.

We can also remain stuck at the level of revolution - seeing ourselves as the freedom fighter and not exploring the greater awareness that our newly found freedom is inviting us to explore. Once free from our oppressors we can easily go off the rails by simply following the desires of our own ego, which becomes our new tyrant.

It might seem like a long haul, but that is how the planets of transformation (Uranus, Neptune, Pluto), work: slowly, over time. We are currently experiencing a global spiritual revolution, where spirituality and spiritual paths can (in most free countries) be spoken of freely and explored in unprecedented ways.

The revolutions of Uranus have paved the way for a great spiritual revolution that can be experienced by humanity as a whole. It is the gateway of intuition that allows us to perceive the higher transcendent states of consciousness that are the realm of Neptune.

Uranus sets you free. If your perception, intuition, self-awareness and clarity are increasing, then Uranus has done his job and you are ready for the illumination of Neptune. When the student is ready, the teacher will appear...

We can see that throughout humanity, the conditions for human advancement into freedom and individuality are created by the activities of Uranus: the spaceholder for the intuitive level of our development.

Suggested Fieldwork

• Deeper Self-observation. Take out your own horoscope (natal chart) and make a note in your journal of the sign and house position of Uranus. Then read the descriptions above and make a note of any ideas and insights that come to you. Meditate on how Uranus might be showing up in your life. Record your impressions and insights in your reflective journal.

• Further Reading: *Soul Centered Astrology: A Key to Your Expanding Self*, by Alan Oken, refer to the appropriate section for more information on Uranus. Read about Uranus in chapter five of *Soul Astrology*[173].

---

[173] Hadikin, R. (2016) *Soul Astrology: How Your Rising Sign Reveals Your Soul Path and Life Purpose.* Ruth Hadikin Associates. Order online at https://soulastrologybook.com

22. Neptune, The Luminous Nature of Being

As we continue our deep exploration of the planets, and their role in the evolution of consciousness, we arrive at the stage of illumination. Remember that as we evolve through the levels of instinct > intellect > intuition > illumination and emptiness, each stage is necessary. It's not that we 'lose' our instinct, intellect and intuition, as we move into illumination, but rather that each stage is a vital foundation for what comes next. So by the time we reach the level of the wisdom realizing emptiness (clear light mind), we also realize that we are also all of it. We are everything that has gone before. We don't 'transcend' instinct by 'getting rid of it' but rather it becomes integrated into our whole being.

Neptune, God of The Ocean

In Roman Times Neptune was considered to be the God of freshwater, and the oceans. He was also associated with horses, which symbolize power. In terms of Soul Astrology then, we can think of Neptune in association with the power of oceanic consciousness: the crystal clear expansive vastness of being that awaits us once we have transcended our conditioned mind. According to spiritual masters and yogis throughout the ages, once we realize this transcendental consciousness, we become aware that it's nature is also luminous. In other words the true nature of our being is light. So from an esoteric and Soul Astrology perspective, we also associate Neptune with illumination.

Neptune and Illumination

Illumination in the modern sense can often mean explaining something in terms of giving more information or knowledge to "shed light" on a subject, but when we use the word illumination in this sense we are speaking figuratively. We are not literally shining actual light on a subject as though we had a flashlight! In the sense of the evolution of consciousness, when the Tibetan spoke of the illumination stage, he was speaking literally. He was speaking of the stage of spiritual enlightenment when our body, mind, and spirit, becomes filled with actual light that we experience and perceive.

Neptune is the planetary spaceholder for the 'illumination' stage of human evolution. In his book Buddhist Astrology, Buddhist astrologer Jampa Shaneman describes Neptune as the *spiritualizing pole*. Neptune spiritualizes what it touches, because Neptune dissolves everything into the ocean of conscious light. The Universe is of the nature of conscious light, and everything in the known (and unknown) Universe: you, me, Mother Earth and all her vast forests, landscapes, oceans, deserts, and creatures, have emerged from this conscious light and will return to this conscious light.

The Discovery of Neptune

Neptune was discovered in 1846 by Urbain Le Verrier and Johann Gottfried Galle. We could therefore say that the spiritual enlightenment of humanity started in 1846, yet if this is the case, how can it be that there is still so much turmoil, unrest, violence and war on the planet? Neptune is a slow moving planet and actually takes about 165 years to complete one orbit around the Sun, or one complete cycle through each of the twelve zodiac signs. According to the tropical zodiac Neptune was at 25° Aquarius when it was discovered, and completed one cycle by February 10th 2010.

A Three-Step Process: Illusion, Disillusion and Illumination

It is important to understand how Neptune 'spiritualizes' through a three-step process of illusion, disillusion, and finally illumination. Before we arrive at the exalted state of spiritual illumination and bliss, we have to navigate a long unfolding process of illusion and disillusion. Collectively, humanity experienced a great deal of Neptunian crises in the 165 years between 1846 and 2010 leading to confusion, illusion, deception, and the emergence and expansion of chemical and drug use and abuse (both commercially and illicitly).

We may not yet be spiritually enlightened, but collectively we are becoming increasingly aware of deception as we have become aware of fraudulent schemes and 'scams'. We have access to more information, and are both more street-wise and cynical than people of the 1840's. We also have access to more 'tools' of fantasy, addiction, and escapism: drugs, sex, movies, internet, computer games, fantasy games etc. Our capacity to become lost in our own imaginations and delude ourselves, becoming even more detached from reality, has also increased.

From Illusion to Disillusionment

It seems that this first cycle of Neptune has led us from illusion into a necessary 'disillusionment' with our leaders, our religions, our societal and governmental structures, so that we will wake up and question what is the real point of our being here at all. Although it might seem far from our spiritual journey, the experiences that Neptune brings are actually an inherent part of it.

Now let's go a bit deeper into how Neptune transforms through this three-step process of illusion, disillusionment and finally illumination. We mentioned above that Neptune is said to 'dissolve' what it touches, and that Buddhist Astrologer Jhampa Shaneman describes Neptune as the 'spiritualizing pole' precisely because of this 'dissolution'. It is the process of dissolution that eventually leads to illumination. This happens because, by dissolving the structures of mind and limiting beliefs that are in our way, Neptune can reveal the clear light beyond, leading to greater illumination.

Illusion

Before we can experience spiritual bliss, nirvana, and enlightenment, we need to wake up to the reality of our own mind and see what keeps us from it. It is through our own attachments and addictions that we keep ourselves 'locked' into repeating habits of behavior that block our ability to receive and perceive spiritual light. In the early stages of our Neptune experience, Neptune shines a light on how we delude ourselves and block our ability to access the highest vibrations of Neptune: great compassion, unconditional love, and Divine bliss.

One of the most notable examples of our capacity for self-delusion happened exactly at the time of Neptune's discovery in 1846. *The Great Famine* in Ireland, during which around 1,000,000 people died and the population of Ireland dropped by 20%[174], was notable because of the indifference and lack of help on the part of those in power. The worst winter was 1846-1847 (Neptune was discovered in September 1846). Measures that could have been taken weren't, as the British Prime Minister of the time, Sir Robert Peel, deluded himself in a very Neptunian way that this was "Divine" intervention, and that the Irish were "exaggerating". This illustrates our great capacity to delude ourselves that we are doing "God's work" while ignoring the suffering of our human family.

The lower expressions of Neptune - delusion and false belief (illusion) - prevented access to the highest expressions of Neptune: compassion, love, and spiritual nourishment. The great nourishing capacity of spiritual love and compassion is why Neptune is exalted in Cancer. Approximately one million lives were lost because those in power were unable to access simple human compassion.

Whereas previous famines in history could be conveniently forgotten about, the rise in technology meant that news could spread: so the Irish famine, and the prevailing attitude of the government at the time, has been 'illuminated' - brought to light, and future generations can see the circumstances and brutish attitudes that made a bad situation disastrous. This leads to disillusionment with those to whom we have given power.

Disillusionment

The next stage in the Neptune three-stage process is disillusionment: a necessary disillusionment whereby we lose our 'illusions'. Although disillusionment is uncomfortable for our ego, it is a necessary stage on our spiritual journey.

We have to divest ourselves of false beliefs and illusions so that we can begin to recognize spiritual truth. Truth in this sense doesn't mean whether a mental concept or idea is 'true' or 'false' but rather the truth of our reality as spiritual beings and our connectedness as one human family. This means being able to recognize and perceive our inner light.

---

[174] *"It is estimated that at least one million people died from starvation and its attendant diseases, whilst a further one million emigrated during the famine years. The population of the island dropped from over 8 million in 1845 to about 6 million in 1850."* - https://www.quora.com/How-many-people-died-in-the-Great-Famine-aka-Irish-Potato-Famine

Illumination

Finally Neptune illuminates or, rather, provides those conditions whereby we are finally able to perceive our pre-existing light. We are already beings of light, and as we divest ourselves of our conditioned behaviors and limiting mental concepts, our light magnifies to the point where it may even become visible to the naked eye. This is an advanced stage of spiritual development and it is why great saints and yogis are often depicted with halos, because people have witnessed actual light emanating from their bodies. These are not one-off occurrences that only happened hundreds of years ago. Although rare, this advanced stage of spiritual development is still possible today for those who devote themselves to the spiritual path.

A real-life example was recently documented by Catholic priest Father Francis Tiso, who describes actual light emanating from advanced Buddhist practitioner Lama A Chö:

> "He showed us two photographs taken of him in the dark, and in these photographs his body radiated rays of light."
>
> - Fr. Francis Tiso[175]

Scientists have also been able to photograph people in a dark room, using special cameras that can operate in very low light levels, and even ordinary people have been shown to be emanating some degree of light[176].

We Are Light

We are light, and (in astrological terms) it is under the Neptunian stage of our spiritual development (illumination) that we are able to perceive it, and when that happens our light magnifies and grows even stronger. Our bodies become filled with light, and eventually become light. Along with this process can come a feeling of great

---

[175] Tiso, F. V. (2016) *Rainbow Body and Resurrection: Spiritual Attainment, the Dissolution of the Material Body, and the Case of Khenpo A Chö.* North Atlantic Books.

[176] Choi, C.Q. (2009) *Strange! Humans Glow in Visible Light.* Online document at https://www.livescience.com/7799-strange-humans-glow-visible-light.html Accessed December 10th 2019.

bliss or Divine Rapture. Spiritual masters often caution against getting 'lost' in the bliss. Remember it is possible to get 'stuck' at any stage of our spiritual development, and we can easily become attached to bliss, which then hinders our progress to the next stage of our spiritual development.

Indeed it is attachment to bliss that can keep us stuck at the lower level of our Neptune experience. If we continually chase after alcohol, drugs and other addictions, purely for the experience of bliss itself, this itself becomes a form of conditioning that keeps us seeking things outside of ourselves, and blocks our spiritual development[177].

Awakening Heart Intelligence

Although Neptune and Uranus are both waking us up, they do so in very different ways. Where Uranus is awakening our intuition it is still working on the level of mind, albeit higher mind, by bringing us intuition, flashes of insight, and deeper knowing.

Neptune continues the process of awakening that begins with Uranus, by taking our intuition and developing it even further by awakening our heart. The highest vibration of Neptune is compassion, so where Uranus awakens Higher Mind, Neptune awakens Heart Intelligence. Both are needed if we are to be whole and fully, spiritually, awake.

Through heart intelligence Neptune awakens us to a sensing capacity where we are able to sense the quality of energy in all aspects of our being: the physical body, the energy body, the mental body, the intuitive body, the bliss body and, ultimately, Universal Mind. This sensing capacity, through great empathy, initially alerts us to the presence of suffering which, in turn, ignites great compassion and the wish to be of benefit to others.

Neptune is associated with illusion and on the path of Neptune it seems that we get caught in our illusions and delusions, only to experience a necessary disillusionment, which catalyses us to continue our deeper search for that which is real, true, and meaningful.

---

[177] There is a distinction between chemically-induced states of bliss and true spiritual experience, which is described beautifully in Steve Taylor's book: *Waking from Sleep*.

The ultimate purpose of Neptune is that once we are more receptive to it's energy, through conscious awareness, it has the potential to awaken great compassion in us.

Neptune and The Veil

In order to really appreciate what Neptune is trying to teach us we have to understand a little bit about states of consciousness. Neptune opens us up to subtle realms of existence and is said to be associated with 'the veil'. Ironically wherever Neptune is in our chart, is also where we are most likely to delude ourselves. Neptune brings a subtle and nebulous quality to our awareness as he awakens us to different states of consciousness.

What is actually happening is that as we open ourselves up and become more receptive to the energies of Neptune, we first become aware of our own limitation. We become aware of the 'veil'. The veil of which we speak here is a boundary, a limitation on our consciousness that prevents us from seeing subtler realms 'beyond the veil'.

People who have psychic and clairvoyant abilities are said to be able to 'see beyond the veil' because their consciousness has expanded to be able to perceive the subtle realms. This 'veil' is actually created by our own mind, by our own subconscious. It is a result of focusing solely on our intellect and being centered in our heads instead of our hearts. Having said that the 'veil' is very real. It is like a magnetic field generated by the cumulative mental energy of the 7 billion or so human beings on this planet! Much like an invisible web that is spun around the world by the collective 'mind' of humanity!

As we become attuned to the energy of Neptune we become aware of the nature of this mental 'veil' and as we become more heart-centered, our intuitive capacity increases and we become aware of more subtle realms 'beyond the veil'. Opening the heart center is the key to the working with the nature of Neptune and which is why Neptune is also considered the planet of great compassion. As our consciousness expands, under the influence of Neptune, we become aware of subtler and subtler aspects of our own being.

Patanjali's Five Energy Bodies

Patanjali, one of the founders of modern Yoga described the physical (earth) body, the energy (fire) body, the mental (water) body, the intuitive (air) body, and the bliss (ether) body[178]. Our journey is one of awareness as we awaken to the existence and nature of these layers of our being. And, although we may enjoy it, bliss is not the end result! We go beyond bliss and eventually our consciousness opens up into what Patanjali called 'Universal Mind' (this is also analogous with the Clear Light Mind in the Tibetan tradition). Yet at the personality level we can get 'caught' at any one of these stages, which is why we are all at different stages on our spiritual journey. We're all working our way through one of these stages to get to the next.

The whole purpose of our spiritual journey is to awaken us to these subtle aspects of our being, and in astrology that is Neptune's role. Neptune awakens our senses through increasingly subtle and often pleasurable feeling states, to draw these energies to our attention.

We can clearly see the spiritual potential and also the dangers of walking the path of Neptune. When we start to pursue a feeling state for it's own sake, rather than as a stage on our spiritual journey, that's where we can go wrong and get caught in drug, sex or alcohol-induced states without spiritual awareness.

Transpersonal States of Awareness

Yes we have the potential to awaken to higher, transpersonal, states of awareness and yet there is also the potential for us to delude ourselves: to get caught in an individual or collective trance and/or get lost in bliss along the way. Not because Neptune is 'doing' anything to us, but because of the nature of the energy involved and our own tendency at the personality level towards attachment: wanting to seek out and 'hold on' to any of these particular states of consciousness rather than simply enjoying them and allowing them to pass as we continue on our way.

This is why, on our spiritual journey, it is important to move towards greater and greater states of clarity. To navigate our way through these nebulous waters without getting caught in addictive states, we need to stay fully present to our own experience and remain crystal clear. Then Neptune becomes a planet of illumination that supports us in opening our consciousness to Universal Mind, which is where we experience Universal (Divine) Love.

---

[178] Also see *The Five Bodies* in chapter sixteen.

Neptune and Pisces

Neptune is co-ruler of Pisces with Jupiter at the personality level. Whereas Jupiter's role is to expand the sense of self beyond the individual, Neptune brings awareness of the nature of suffering, which ignites Universal Compassion. Neptune has the potential to bring oceanic consciousness, the awareness of the vastness of our true being, but first Neptune illuminates our delusions and shows us where we can be caught in the illusion of our own beliefs. If you have Pisces Rising, then Neptune is your chart ruler at the personality level, and the position and condition of Neptune in your chart, by sign, house and aspects, will be showing you where you have limiting beliefs that can keep you caught in illusion at the personality level. Your challenge is to transcend these beliefs so that you may experience the expansiveness of your true nature.

Neptune and Cancer

Neptune is the Soul Ruler of Cancer. If you have Cancer Rising Neptune, is the Soul Ruler of your chart and the position and condition of Neptune by sign, house, and aspect is very important and deserves deep contemplation. This is the area of your life where your Cancer Soul is calling you to release lower ego-driven behaviors so that you can step more fully into Universal Compassion, and realize your Soul's Purpose.

Neptune Through The Signs

Neptune takes about 165 years to make one complete orbit of the Sun so not many people live to see a 'Neptune' return in their charts! Because it is a slow-moving planet whole generations have Neptune in the same sign, so we can see that there is a generational and cyclical quality to the process of heart awakening for the whole of humanity.

Let's see how this unfolds with Neptune through the signs, as each generation builds on the one before, continuing this ongoing process of awakening to heart intelligence and compassion:

Neptune in Aries (1862-1875, 2025-2039)

This placement combines Neptune's imaginative, glamorous idealism, with Aries urge to initiate new beginnings with boldness and courage.

Aries begins all new cycles, and sows the seeds of ideas for future generations to follow. The Soul-centered purpose of Aries is to inspire others with Divine ideas. As this generation reached their 20's some Neptunian 'seed ideas' were being sown that would grow throughout the next 165 years: electricity was being introduced as a source of illumination in new homes; the first motion pictures were created from still images, connecting humanity in a way never done before by creating the illusion that we now know as 'movies'; and the emergence of the first automobiles opened up worlds of connection by allowing the masses to travel further distances through which we began understanding cultures different from our own.

There were also widespread calls for social reform to improve the health and well-being of the poor: with the introduction of widespread strategies for heath, welfare and education. These are some early indications of a more 'humane' heart-centered humanity that was emerging.

Neptune in Taurus (1875-1888, 2039-2052)

This placement combines Neptune's illusory nature with Taurus' desire for security, in particular financial security.

The Soul-centered purpose of Taurus is spiritual illumination through the release of personal desire and attachment. As this generation reached their 20's there had been a series of financial 'booms' and subsequent 'busts' in the stock market - early precursors of the major stock-market crash of 1929 which led to the great 1930's depression. During this earlier period bankers and investors (previously caught up in the glamour of boom and unbridled financial gain) were alerted to the rhythms of gain and loss, and began trying to put safeguards in place to protect themselves from future losses.

These are the early lessons of Neptune in Taurus: that our deepest sense of security cannot come from the illusory nature of money. The highest potential of this placement (which may be realized by the next Neptune in Taurus generation) is the opening of the third eye, spiritual illumination, and the realization that all is light.

This is an excellent placement for a generation of enlightened human beings!

Neptune in Gemini (1888-1902, 2052-2065)

This placement combines Neptune's dreamy idealism with Gemini's talent for connection and disseminating information.
The Soul-centered purpose of Gemini is to teach right human relationship: to 'marry' the head-mind and the heart-mind. The challenge for this generation is one of delusion through misinformation. Note that Adolf Hitler had this placement and his generation was the first to use propaganda on a large scale: the intentional use of misinformation to spread fear and control the masses. The highest potential of this placement is deep communion through a real heart-centered connection with Divinity.

Neptune in Cancer - exaltation (1902-1916)

This placement combines Neptune's idealism with Cancer's urge for safety and security. Neptune is exalted in Cancer which means its energy is at it's most potent.

This may not always be positive because it can lead to excess and extremism. The Soul-centered purpose of Cancer is to flow more compassion into the world. The challenge for this generation is not to succumb to illusory fears, which can become magnified. Cancer rules the Nursing profession and during this period the nursing professions were establishing ideal (Neptune) 'standards' for professional practice to ensure the safety (Cancer) and well-being of patients.

Neptune in Leo (1915-1929)

This placement combined Neptune's illusory nature with Leo's orientation to individuality and the search for Self.

The Soul-centered purpose of Leo is heart-centered leadership through becoming an individual expression if Divine Will. The challenge for this generation is self-delusion. By the time this generation reached their 20's tensions were building up to World War II as encroaching dictatorial regimes such as fascism and communism threatened to diminish the rights of the individual.

This generation was catalyzed by world events into standing for their rights as individuals. This is a powerful placement for self-realization and self-illumination once we transcend our lower ego-challenges.

Neptune in Virgo - detriment (1929-1943)

This placement combines Neptune's idealism with Virgo's practical systems-oriented approach towards healthier ways of living and being.

The Soul-centered purpose of Virgo is to flow Divine Love into the world through one's work. Virgo is a sign of heart and mind. The challenge for this generation was in the illusion that physically-oriented health systems alone could succeed without a deeper energetic heart connection.

By the time this generation were reaching their 20's science was coming into it's own as the 'savior' of humanity. Not only had antibiotics and vaccines been invented but also they were being distributed to the masses by the introduction of new 'idealized' global systems of healthcare and the World Health Organization.

There is now a necessary disillusionment with systemic approaches to healthcare, but it cannot be forgotten that the changes introduced by this generation brought health and well-being to a new level, eradicated many diseases of the day, and reached people on a global scale never before seen in the world. These were important stepping-stones in our collective learning process that, combined with our disillusionment, have now become a catalyst fueling our current movement towards more holistic approaches to health.

Neptune in Libra (1943-1957)

This placement combines Neptune's dreamy idealism with Libra's desire for harmonious relationship.

It gave birth to the original hippy generation who just wanted peace and love, man, "Why can't we all just get along?" The Soul-centered purpose of Libra is to bring greater degrees of harmony and balance into the world through right relationship. The challenge for this generation has been not to get lost in a dreamy "Pollyanna" version of reality, deluding themselves that all is well.

Their necessary disillusionment with the world, and with idealized forms of relationship, has been a catalyst for many to enter the spiritual path, seeking deeper, more meaningful, spiritual connection. This is a powerful placement for true peace and harmony through deeper spiritual connection and right relationship with oneself.

Neptune in Scorpio (1956-1970)

This placement has Neptune's dreamy, illusory, call to escapism and fantasy combined with the Scorpionic desire for intensity in experience.

Not surprising then that this spawned a generation of 'addicts' on all levels: from television, movies, tobacco and alcohol to sex and drugs. The Soul-centered purpose of Scorpio is to transform darkness into light, and the Soul-centered purpose of this Neptune placement is to enter the darkness to really understand the magnetic pull of temptation from an experiential perspective.

This is a powerful placement for regeneration and healing, and this generation also has birthed many healers who support others through the experiential knowledge gained from wrestling their own demons and walking their own personal path of transformation and healing.

Neptune in Sagittarius (1970-1984)

This placement combines Neptune's dreamy, fantasy-oriented, idealism with Sagittarius' search for freedom, truth and higher meaning.

The Soul-centered purpose of Sagittarius is to uplift humanity through the revelation of truth and wisdom. The challenge is that wisdom and beliefs are not the same thing. This generation can get caught in man-made ideals and mental concepts of 'truth' at the expense of deeper spiritual truth. They can also delude themselves that they are following 'truth' when in fact they are justifying their ego and their desire to do things their own way. This is a powerful placement for cultivating genuine heart-wisdom, and intelligence once this generation learns to distinguish real spiritual truth and experience from man-made beliefs and philosophies.

Neptune in Capricorn - fall (1984-1998)

This placement combines Neptune's dreamy, illusory-like, glamour with Capricorn's urge for right-use of resources.

The Soul-centered purpose of Capricorn is to create heaven on earth through right use of our individual and collective, physical, mental, emotional and spiritual resources. The highest capacity of Capricorn is to be an engineer of light - building structures of light on the etheric planes that will support the evolving consciousness of humanity. The challenge for this generation is to overcome the temptation to usurp collective resources for personal gain.

There is the danger of deluding themselves that they are acting for the greater good when indeed they are still being driven by the same ego-centered materialism as their forefathers, albeit in a new form.
This is a powerful placement for creating the discipline and focus necessary to persevere with meditative spiritual practice and by doing so activate the true intelligence of the heart.

Neptune in Aquarius (1998-2012)

This placement combines Neptune's dreamy, fantasy-oriented, idealism with Aquarius' humanitarian ideals.

The Soul-centered purpose of Aquarius is to flow the dual waters of 'love and life' in ways that benefit humanity. The challenge is to overcome the power of the mind. Aquarius is a very 'mental' sign and the temptation for this generation will be to delude themselves that they are building an 'ideal' society based on mental concepts alone. This can lead to overly idealized futures where the individual is lost to the needs of the society.

This is where communism went wrong. Societies cannot be created by mental ideals alone, but depend on the awakened hearts of the individuals within. This is a powerful placement for heart opening, and learning to flow real spiritual energy through the heart, which will ultimately benefit humanity.

Neptune in Pisces - dignity (2012-2026)

This placement combines Neptune's illusory yet illuminating nature with Pisces sensitivity to human suffering and tendency towards compassion. Neptune is in dignity in Pisces where its energies are powerful.

This is a generation that has the potential to realize fully awakened heart intelligence: access Universal Love (Divine, unconditional love and compassion) and flow it through the heart - inaugurating the sacred heart of humanity. The sacred heart of humanity is where all hearts beat as one, and the consciousness of the collective is embodied through the heart chakra of humanity.

The challenge will be to not get lost in all forms of escapism, which disconnects them from their own hearts, and those of their fellow human beings. We can already see the potential for this as this generation, who are only toddlers at present, are born into a world where 'social technology' reigns. This generation is likely to become disillusioned with the 'illusion' of connection through social media and seek a truer, more meaningful, heart-based connection, which gives birth to compassion and Universal Love.

We can see that even though we might succumb to the illusions that Neptune can generate, at the end of any particular cycle of Neptune we are also catalyzed to rise above the delusion and move closer toward our heart intelligence.

Neptune in The Houses - This Time It's Personal

What makes Neptune personal and unique to you is the placement in your chart by house, by it's relationship to your personal planets, and by 'rulership'. For example if you have Pisces Rising or Pisces Sun (because Neptune rules Pisces) the condition of Neptune will take on a more personal note, and/or you have Cancer Rising, the placement and condition of Neptune becomes very important because Neptune is the Soul-Centered ruler of Cancer.

First a brief recap of the main points to bear in mind:
- Neptune is sometimes called the 'spiritualizing pole': it spiritualizes what it touches.
- Wherever Neptune is in your chart, that part of your life is being 'spiritualized' by awakening your innate heart intelligence.
- Neptune works in a three-step process of illusion - disillusion - illumination.

That said, let's now see where in your life Neptune might be calling you to wake up to the intelligence of your heart!

Neptune in the First House

If you have Neptune in your First House you are being called to wake up to the spiritual reality of your own being.

Early in life you may get caught in the illusion of self, believing yourself to be all the labels that others impose upon you. At some point in your life you will become disillusioned with this. You may question yourself, begin asking 'who am I?', and even question the very nature of existence. You may experience an existential crisis where you ask 'what is the point of it all?' Eventually as you continue your process, you will begin experiencing illumination, where you begin to experience and understand the deeper truths of your own reality, and your own existence as a spiritual being.

Neptune in the Second House

If you have Neptune in the second house you are waking up to your own sense of spiritual values, and to value of yourself as a spiritual being.

Early in life you may get caught in the illusion of materialism. In other words the society tells you that your value or worth is based on how much you can earn or acquire, and/or how well you can provide for yourself and others. At some point in your life you may become disillusioned with this. You may have been successful in generating wealth, and begin questioning the point, wondering what it's all about and what you are really working for, or you may have had other experiences which cause you to question and explore your own sense of self-worth.

Eventually as you continue your process, you will begin experiencing illumination, where you realize that your prana, or life-force energy, is meant for something other than just working to earn money, but is there to support your spiritual growth. As a result of your spiritual experiences you begin recognizing your inherent value as a spiritual being.

Neptune in the Third House

If you have Neptune in the third house you are being awakened to the spiritual nature of your own mind.

Early in life you may get caught in the illusion of mental activity and learning. You may believe what you are taught at school, and view the world in an idealistic way. At some point in your life you may become disillusioned with this as you begin to see underneath conventional learning. You may experience disenchantment as you see how much of our thinking is 'programmed by mass media' communications.

Eventually as you continue your process, you will begin experiencing illumination, where you realize the real spiritual power of your own mind, which goes beyond any programming.

Neptune in the Fourth House

If you have Neptune in the fourth house you are being called to anchor yourself within your spiritual heart, as your true home.

Early in life you may get caught in the illusion of home and family. You may have ideas of how an ideal home and family ought to be.
At some point in your life you may become disillusioned with this as you realize that real-life families are far from ideal and come with many problems and challenges. Eventually as you continue your process, you will begin experiencing illumination, where you recognize your spiritual home within, at your heart center, and as you move towards oneness and unconditional love, you realize that the whole world is your family.

Neptune in the Fifth House

If you have Neptune in the Fifth House you are being awakened to your spiritual power as a creator being.

Early in life you may get caught in the illusion of your creative self. In exploring who you are and your own power, you may get caught in the trap of seeking yourself through fleeting sensory pleasures that can lead to addictions. At some point in your life you may become disillusioned with this, once again questioning what is it all about. You realize through experience that chasing after sense-pleasures only leads to the desire for more (hence addiction) and any happiness that comes as a result, is fleeting and temporary. Eventually as you continue your process, you will begin experiencing illumination, where you recognize that what you are really searching for was within you all along. You begin to identify with your Soul rather than anything outside yourself, and realize that permanent lasting happiness comes from a deep Soul connection.

Neptune in the Sixth House

If you have Neptune in the sixth house you are being awakened to the sacredness of health and well-being as a spiritual path.

Early in life you may get caught in the illusion of service. You may have been told that you have to deny yourself in order to be of service to others, and that meeting your own needs would be 'selfish'. At some point in your life you may become disillusioned with this. You may experience burnout from many years of trying to give to others while denying your own needs, or you may experience co-dependency, or you may simply discover that however much you try, you cannot really help others: they need to find it within themselves to help themselves.

Eventually as you continue your process, you will begin experiencing illumination, where you realize that true service comes from a deeper connection within yourself, and that the best way to 'serve' others is by standing fully in your own spiritual power, which serves as an inspiration and encouragement for others to find their own self-empowerment.

Neptune in the Seventh House

If you have Neptune in the seventh house you are being awakened to the sacredness of right relationship as a spiritual path.

Early in life you may get caught in the illusion of relationship. You may have been hooked on the idea of romance and/or finding your ideal partner. At some point in your life you may become disillusioned with this as you realize that the 'ideal' relationship that is portrayed through romantic novels and movies is actually a fantasy. Eventually as you continue your process, you will begin experiencing illumination, where you recognize that the key to deep meaningful relationship and love is to have a deep, spiritual connection within yourself. Then you do not need others to fulfill you, and you are able to make a valuable contribution in relationship.

Neptune in the Eighth House

If you have Neptune in the eighth house you are being awakened to the sacredness of spiritual energy (including sexual energy) as a spiritual path.

Early in life you may get caught in the illusion of sex and money, which is really the illusion of power. You may experience abuses of power in intimate relationships, and possibly deception around sex and/or shared resources (loans/debt/taxes etc.) At some point in your life you may become disillusioned with this, which causes you to look within for your own power. Eventually as you continue your process, you will begin experiencing illumination, where your journey within leads you to the discovery of spiritual power and you are able to transmute the energy of desire into spiritual energy which you are able to focus for the higher good.

Neptune in the Ninth House

If you have Neptune in the ninth house you are being awakened to higher knowledge, sacred wisdom, and deep spiritual truth.

Early in life you may get caught in the illusion of knowledge. You may seek learning and/or education only to become disappointed as you realize it didn't have the deeper more meaningful answers that you were looking for. At some point in your life you may become disillusioned with this and begin looking elsewhere, deepening your search into spiritual traditions.

Eventually as you continue your process, you will begin experiencing illumination, where your spiritual path leads you to higher wisdom through your own experience and you begin to realize the deeper spiritual wisdom that lies beyond words and information systems.

Neptune in the Tenth House

If you have Neptune in the tenth house you are being awakened to the sacred path of discipleship and a spiritual path as a way of life.

Early in life you may get caught in the illusion of worldly success and ambition. You may have been told that the key to success was to climb the ladder, work hard, and secure your position in the world. At some point in your life you may become disillusioned with this. You may have worked very hard only to find it didn't bring the promised rewards, or you may have a successful position yet still feel empty inside because it didn't bring you fulfillment.

Eventually as you continue your process, you will begin experiencing illumination, where you discover the true path of discipleship. You realize through your experience that there is a deeper spiritual purpose, and that the deeper fulfillment you are looking for, can be found by applying yourself diligently to a spiritual path or tradition.

Neptune in the Eleventh House

If you have Neptune in the eleventh house you are being awakened to the sacredness of humanity and group service as a spiritual path.

Early in life you may get caught in the illusion of friends and group conformity. You may have humanitarian ideals that you share with groups of like-minded people, and work together to improve society. At some point in your life you may become disillusioned with this, either because your shared ideals don't come to fruition, or you become disillusioned somehow with the group process. You may lose yourself in the group and begin wondering what it was all about.

Eventually as you continue your process, you will begin experiencing illumination, where you deepen your own individual path and realize that the way to connect with the collective consciousness is to first have a deep connection within yourself.

When you discover your true spiritual power as an individual you will have a deeper understanding of group service that goes beyond mental ideals.

Neptune in the Twelfth House

If you have Neptune in the twelfth house you are being awakened to the sacred nature of oneness, and the power of Universal Love flowing through your own heart-center.

Early in life you may get caught in the illusions of your own subconscious. You may have psychic experiences or meaningful dreams which open you up to exploring the subconscious realms. At some point in your life you may become disillusioned with this, either because you are afraid of your experiences, don't understand them, or feel that there is something more that you can't quite grasp.

Eventually as you continue your process, you will begin experiencing illumination, where your consciousness becomes expanded and you have access to higher levels of consciousness beyond psychic impressions. Ultimately you may experience oneness and Universal Love.

Bliss is not the end result. It is merely a side-effect of illumination, as our body fills with light and prepares us for the next stage of our spiritual development: emptiness.

We can see that throughout humanity, the conditions for human advancement into illumination and light are held in place by the activities of Neptune: the spaceholder for the illumination level of our development.

Suggested Fieldwork

- Deeper Self-observation. Take out your own horoscope (natal chart) and make a note in your journal of the sign and house position of Neptune. Then read the descriptions above and make a note of any ideas and insights that come to you. Meditate on how Neptune might be showing up in your life. Record your impressions and insights in your reflective journal.

- Further Reading: *Soul Centered Astrology: A Key to Your Expanding Self*, by Alan Oken, refer to the appropriate section for more information on Neptune. Read about Neptune in chapter five of *Soul Astrology*.

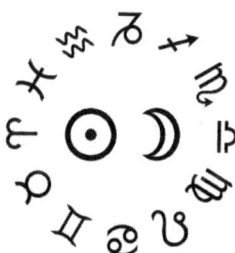

23. Pluto, Emptiness and Clear Light Wisdom

As we conclude this section on the planets and their role in the evolution of consciousness we arrive at the final stage of emptiness. Remember that as we evolve through the levels of instinct > intellect > intuition > illumination and emptiness, each stage is necessary. It's not that we 'lose' our instinct, intellect, intuition and illumination, as we move into emptiness, but rather that each stage is a vital foundation for what comes next. So by the time we reach the level of the wisdom realizing emptiness, we also realize that we are also all of it. We are everything that has gone before. We don't 'transcend' instinct by 'getting rid of it' but rather it becomes integrated into our whole being.

Pluto, The Power of Transformation

Pluto is a planet of major transformation. He is associated with death and re-birth and is possibly associated with transformation more than any other planet. The power of destruction and re-generation. Astrologer Melanie Reinhart suggests a higher vibrational keyword for Pluto is *emptiness*[179]. In many Buddhist traditions the highest wisdom possible is considered to be the wisdom realizing emptiness. This reminds us that: everything is one ongoing dance of interrelated energy; that nothing is permanent; and that nothing exists independently from everything else.

---

[179] Reinhart, M. (2010) *Chiron and the Healing Journey.* Starwalker Press.

Understanding Emptiness

Emptiness is quite a difficult concept to grasp, so first we will spend some time exploring what it means so we may at least have some intellectual understanding. That said, it is also very important to bear in mind that it really is not possible to understand emptiness completely from the intellect! Emptiness can really only be understood from personal experience of this higher state of consciousness. Emptiness is such an advanced state of consciousness that The Tibetan did not mention it at all in *Esoteric Astrology*. His teaching stopped at the level of illumination. This is most likely because humanity did not have the consciousness to comprehend emptiness at that time (indeed the majority of people have difficulty understanding emptiness now, let alone have the ability to recognize it in practice).

It is only when we explore the Tibetan system in more depth, that we find the 'ultimate', final, or highest state of consciousness is actually emptiness. Buddhahood (or full enlightenment) is where we abide in a permanent state of 'emptiness' without faltering even for a second. As we shall see, it makes perfect sense that Pluto would be the planetary spaceholder for the 'emptiness' stage of human evolution.

So what exactly do we mean by emptiness? In the Tibetan tradition the 'wisdom realizing emptiness' is considered the highest wisdom of all, beyond intellect, intuition and even beyond illumination. It is often said that we cannot understand emptiness with our ordinary mind and for this reason it was among the most secret or esoteric of all teachings in Buddhism.

It is only in very recent times that the emptiness teachings have been made available to wider audiences, including Westerners. Not all Buddhist teachers thought this was a good idea, because of the enormous potential for misinterpretation and misunderstanding[180].

What Is Emptiness?

The English word emptiness is commonly used to translate the original Sanskrit term *shunyata*. But in English, emptiness implies a void: nothing. Yet the Tibetan definition *tak ché dang dralwa*,

---

[180] Richmond, L. (2013) Emptiness: The Most Misunderstood Word in Buddhism. Online document at https://www.huffpost.com/entry/emptiness-most-misunderstood-word-in-buddhism_b_2769189 Accessed December 11th 2019

translates as: *free from permanence and [free from] non-existence.*[181] This is the true nature of reality, and the whole purpose of our spiritual journey is to realize this for ourselves, through heightened awareness and our own experience.

It doesn't sound very exciting to realize that our true nature is impermanent, but as we shall see, there is so much more to emptiness than this dry 'intellectual' definition would imply. When people experience emptiness on a personal level for the first time, they often describe it as a profound spiritual experience, with a deep presence of universal love, compassion, union, deep insight, wisdom, awareness, oneness, clarity and/or deep peace.

> *"Till that moment in my life I always thought this is me and that's somebody else and something else. But for the first time I did not know which is me and which is not me. Suddenly, what was me was just all over the place.*
>
> *The very rock on which I was sitting, the air that I breathe, the very atmosphere around me, I had just exploded into everything. That sounds like utter insanity.*
>
> *This, I thought it lasted for ten to fifteen minutes but when I came back to my normal consciousness, it was about four-and-a-half-hours I was sitting there, fully conscious, eyes open, but time had just flipped."*
>
> — Sadhguru Jaggi Vasudev

You Are Nothing, And Everything

In all true experiences of emptiness the two defining qualities are clarity and awareness. We might say wide awake and free from thoughts of self. As in the example of Sadhguru above, we experience a complete loss of 'ego', becoming 'empty' of any sense of a permanent 'me' or 'self' that could exist as a separate entity within the Universe. Indeed in emptiness we realize that we ARE the Universe, having a momentary expression as us. Ironically there is a fullness in emptiness where we realize that we are not 'nothing', but we are everything.

---

[181] Emptiness. Online document at
http://www.rigpawiki.org/index.php?title=Emptiness Accessed December 11th 2019.

*"You live in illusion and the appearance of things.
There is a reality, but you do not know this.
When you understand this,
you will see that you are nothing,
and being nothing you are everything.
That is all."*

- Kalu Rinpoche

The Discovery of Pluto

The Planet Pluto was discovered on February 18th 1930 by Clyde Tombaugh. At the time of its discovery, according to the Tropical Zodiac, it was at 17° of Cancer. Pluto is a very slow moving planet, spending from 13 to 32 years in each sign and taking about 248 years to complete one cycle through the zodiac (one complete orbit around the Sun). At 20° Capricorn Pluto is opposite it's discovery position right now (2019), about halfway through a cycle, and will have completed a full cycle by the year 2175!

Pluto and The Underworld

In Greek mythology Pluto was the Lord of the Underworld where Souls go after death. The Tibetan equivalent Yama, is a Lord of death who is also a protector of the spiritual path. So here we can see Pluto's connection with protecting or guiding Souls after the death of the physical body.

Pluto also rules wealth or *buried treasure*, because wealthy minerals such as gold, silver, and precious gems, come from under the ground. Therefore on a Soul level *Pluto can also be said to reveal our greatest and most precious inner treasure*.

Pluto and Power

Pluto also symbolizes great power and in modern astrology is associated with nuclear power, in particular the element plutonium, which was named after the planet. For this reason we can see how Pluto is also associated with death and destruction.

How can Pluto be associated with death, destruction, and also the greatest revelation, or enlightenment? Anything that can be destroyed is impermanent. By showing us that which can be destroyed, Pluto reveals that which can never be destroyed: awareness itself.

Indestructible Consciousness

The biggest lesson that Pluto teaches us is that no matter what we do to each other, our basic conscious awareness remains. When we are happy, we are aware that we are happy. When we are sad, we are aware that we are sad. Even though our experiences change, the awareness of those experiences remains the same. When we place our attention on awareness itself, rather than the experiences that arise in our awareness, we are on the path to emptiness and oceanic consciousness. No accident that Pluto is the Soul Ruler of Pisces: the sign of Universal Love and Oceanic Consciousness. When we deeply experience emptiness we lose all sense of self, often accompanied by a sense of great clarity and peace. In this 'destruction' of ego we realize that consciousness survives and is actually indestructible, as in the above example of Sadhguru where he says "I had just exploded into everything".

So how has Pluto been pointing to this Universal Truth since it's discovery in 1930? The years that followed Pluto's discovery, with the creation of atomic weapons and the increased mechanization of warfare, have been the most destructive in human history, and the most devastating for our planet Earth. There is no continent that has not escaped the ravages of war, with death, devastation and genocide on an unimaginable scale. There is great wealth associated with warfare (the Plutonic theme of wealth from darkness) as the weapons industry, and it's investors, stand to gain a great deal from every human conflict. Yet there is only so much humanity can stand. There is only so much destruction our planet can stand. So eventually, we will be forced to wake up and see what we have done to each other, and our Earth home by following our darker desires for wealth, power, and greed. We cannot 'uninvent' atomic weapons. For the first time in history, we are living under constant threat of annihilation. We must find a way to work together, or face wiping out the human race and our Earth Mother completely.

"The 20th century witnessed the greatest suffering, with the greatest number of lives lost at the hands of other humans, in the entire history of the species."

- Gregg Braden[182]

---

[182] Braden, G. (2009) *Fractal Time: The Secret of 2012 and A New World Age*. Hay House

Transforming Darkness Into Light

As one of the most important of the planets of transformation, Pluto is the great revealer. Pluto reveals that which is hidden, lurking beneath the surface, the darker side of our own nature. In this way Pluto show us what we have to change if we are to transform darkness into light. This is not a case of pointing out others' faults and seeing how 'they' need to change. When it comes to the lessons of Pluto, we are each called up to look deep inside our own hearts. To work with our own demons, and to transform the darkness within ourselves. Only by changing ourselves will we change the world. This is why every spiritual master advises us to first and foremost work on changing ourselves.

> *"Just as in counting to a million one must begin at the number one, so to benefit society, one must begin by working on oneself."*
>
> - Chögyal Namkhai Norbu

Your Core Power

Pluto teaches us to recognize that we are not perfect, we are not enlightened, and yet we do have that innate potential within us. By showing us our own darkness, Pluto not only shows us how to bring that darkness to the light - but also that you, and only you, have the power. Just like an atomic weapon, your power lies hidden at your core, it is not outside of you, yet you have to go deep, through many layers, to discover your real hidden treasure. You can only transform your own darkness by first acknowledging it.

At Your Core You Are Pure Light

Through deep meditative practice, whereby we recognize and remain in a state of 'emptiness' for longer and longer periods, we begin to see for ourselves a deep spiritual truth: that we are not our darkness, but we are actually light. Our 'darkness', all our negative emotions, rage, anger, jealousy, hatred, greed, and any ensuing actions such as violence, war, and killing, is the result of our distorted thinking.

All our darkness and negativity is the result of conditioning, and when we release the conditioning, underneath we clearly see that pure light, pure loving awareness, is who we really are. Once we go beyond the conditioning of our everyday mind, we have access to the clear light mind beyond, and recognize that as our true nature.

As we continue going deeper, we realize that even Neptunian experiences of bliss and illumination are not who we really are, and that there is a deeper truth: the truth of the highest wisdom, the emptiness of clear light mind and clear light wisdom:

> *"While meditating this way, experiences of bliss, luminosity,*
> *and nonconceptuality can dawn in your mind,*
> *but these experiences actually are on a coarse level*
> *and are not of the most subtle level,*
> *as if they cover over and obstruct innermost awareness,*
> *like a husk over a seed."*
>
> - HH the fourteenth Dalai Lama[183]

Remember it is possible to get stuck at any stage in our journey, especially the Neptunian stage of illumination because of the great bliss that is experienced. When bliss arises it is a good sign, it shows you're making progress, yet great care must also be taken in meditation to remain very present and aware.

> *"It is not sufficient just to keep your mind from diffusing and*
> *scattering. Even if bliss, clarity, and nonconceptuality dawn in*
> *meditative experience, these interfere with being introduced to and*
> *identifying naturally arisen innermost awareness.*
> *You need to avoid even bliss, clarity, and nonconceptuality.*
> *You have to get beyond all of these."*
>
> - HH the fourteenth Dalai Lama

Pluto and Personal Transformation

Of all the planets of transformation (Uranus, Neptune, Pluto) Pluto is the one that is most closely associated with personal transformation. Wherever and whenever we are touched by Pluto we are always transformed in one way or another. We always experience a "death" of sorts, and a subsequent regeneration, or resurrection.

So while Pluto is associated with death and destruction, remember that this is only in the context of nature's cycles, which free up energy for new life forms to manifest. So, unlike man-made

---

[183] Gyatso, T; Hopkins, J. (2016) *The Heart of Meditation: Discovering Innermost Awareness.* Shambhala.

destruction (which is often mindless and senseless) nature's destruction is actually part of an ongoing cycle of life. For example, in winter the energy of deciduous trees is focused underground (at the roots) in preparation for the bursting forth of life in spring. Likewise, Pluto brings our attention underground, to the root of the matter.

Also, in terms of our soul's evolution and our spiritual journey, Pluto teaches us that no matter how many physical forms 'die' and are reborn, consciousness never dies. Pluto teaches one of the highest spiritual lessons: *that consciousness itself is indestructible*.

Pluto, The Great Revealer

Pluto has the unenviable reputation of being associated with all forms of power, abuses of power, death and destruction. And while this is true, Pluto also brings us some of the deepest teachings of our soul journey. As we have seen so far, each of the planets of transformation awakens us in a different way. Pluto is associated with the underworld, underground, that which is hidden or in the dark, and awakens us by bringing to the light issues that we may previously have been unaware of. Hence, Pluto is known as the great revealer. Pluto transforms by revealing that which is hidden, and by destroying that which is no longer necessary for, and indeed may have become a hindrance to, the evolution of consciousness.

Pluto and Self-Empowerment

Although it may be painful at first to face the truth, Pluto brings us the gift of self empowerment, for it is only in truth that we stand in our true power. In fall, the leaves drop from the trees, fall to the Earth, and decompose, nourishing the Earth and thereby creating space for new life to emerge in the spring. Likewise Pluto destroys that which has ended its life-cycle and creates space for new life to begin. So Pluto is a planet of revelation, destruction, power, regeneration, and rebirth.

Pluto and Scorpio

Pluto, along with Mars, is one of the co-rulers of Scorpio at the personality level. If you have Scorpio Rising the conditions of Pluto and Mars by sign, house and aspect will show you where you are experiencing personality challenges that are calling you up to walk more in alignment with your Soul Purpose. In the case of Pluto these are likely to be in the nature of power and destruction, as aspects of your ego-personality are brought into the light of your awareness for conscious de-construction, so you may let go of egoic patterns and experience the self-empowerment of your own inner light. If you are experiencing painful challenges in this area, look to see where you might be trying to cling on to old identities and beliefs about yourself that no longer reflect the truth of your being. Like a caterpillar turning into a butterfly, it is better to relax into your transformation and enjoy the ride.

Pluto and Pisces

Pluto is the Soul Ruler of Pisces. If you have Pisces Rising the position and condition of Pluto by sign, house, and aspect is very important and deserves deep contemplation. This is the area of your life where your Pisces Soul is calling you to release lower ego-driven behaviors so that you can go deeper into Universal Love, ignite your Sacred Heart Center and fully realize your Soul's Purpose.

Since Pisces is the sign of the ocean, and oceanic consciousness, Pluto's role as the Soul Ruler of Pisces reminds us that the only thing in the whole of existence that is truly indestructible, is consciousness itself.

Pluto Through The Signs

Pluto is also a slow-moving planet, taking about 248 years to orbit the Sun, and is therefore known as a "generational planet". Because Pluto stays in the same sign for over 20 years, whole generations will have Pluto in the same sign. Pluto becomes more personal to you as a result of its house placement and aspects in your natal chart.

Pluto in Aries - dignity (1823-1852)

As the first sign of the Zodiac, part of the soul-purpose for Aries is to create the physical space for the manifestation, or incarnation, of existence. Pluto in Aries brings power challenges on our very right to exist as an individual in our own right, with our own 'space'. During this period the slavery movement was being challenged.

Pluto in Taurus - detriment (1852-1884)

The highest soul purpose of Taurus is the release of personal attachment. Pluto in Taurus brings power challenges over 'possessions' and ownership, ultimately awakening us to the deep spiritual truth that ultimately in the Universe nothing is 'owned' by anybody. During this time many indigenous lands were encroached and 'possessed' by expanding 'nations' and , as today, wars were fought and lost over the land boundaries of 'nations'.

Pluto in Gemini (1884-1914)

The highest soul purpose of Gemini is higher communication and 'right human relations'. Pluto in Gemini brings the power of voice to the brotherhood/sisterhood of humanity. During this time the trade union movement grew as ordinary people campaigned for their right to 'have a voice' and restore 'right relationship'.

Pluto in Cancer (1912-1939)

The highest soul-purpose of Cancer is compassion and unconditional love. Pluto in Cancer brings to our awareness where we are not treating our human family with empathy, compassion and unconditional love. This period in history brought two world wars that revealed undercurrents of power, and were ultimately to bring us one step closer together as one human family. Those born in this generation experienced first-hand undercurrents and abuses of power that can happen within a family, and have an opportunity for healing and regeneration.

Pluto in Leo - fall (1937-1958)

This generation is walking a path of self-realization through individuality and self-empowerment. Divine Will is expressed through the power of individuals and this generation has been (and still is) very active in asserting the rights of individuals. As this generation reached voting age and began realizing their personal power a whole movement of civil rights and human rights began that is still currently sweeping the planet.

Pluto in Virgo (1958-1972)

This generation is active in the transformation of techniques for health and healing. Building on the previous generations established foundation of the importance of the individual, this generation was now able to question approaches to health and healing. Alternative approaches to healing were embraced that shifted the focus from 'curing' people, to the body's own power to heal and regenerate itself.

Pluto in Libra - detriment (1971-1984)

This generation is active in the transformation of relationships: including our relationships with each other and our relationships with Mother Earth and her creatures. During the lifetime of this generation there will be a breaking down of old patterns of relationship that do not support the life of Humanity and Planet Earth as one. Man-made laws that are not congruent with spiritual law will be broken down so that there can be balancing and a regeneration of right relationship to sustain life on Earth for future generations.

Pluto in Scorpio - dignity (1982-1995)

This generation is active in the transformation of personal spiritual experience. Pluto is one of the co-rulers of Scorpio at the personality level and creates those trials and tribulations that lead to the 'death' of ego-driven desires that feed the illusion of separation, so the individual may come to know Divinity through their own depth of personal experience, and transform emotional energy into spiritual energy. This is the process of personality-soul fusion. During this generation's lifetime there will be a great shift in planetary consciousness and spiritual awakening, as individuals recognize and acknowledge their own inner spiritual experience.

Pluto in Sagittarius (1995-2008)

This generation is active in the transformation of education and wisdom. Building upon the previous generations' depth of spiritual experience and knowledge, this generation will be active in how we approach education and develop schools of wisdom. Outdated educational systems that no longer support a spiritually awakened humanity will be dissolved to allow for the regeneration of wisdom schools that support the evolution of human consciousness.

Pluto in Capricorn (2008-2023)

This generation will become active in the transformation of the distribution of wealth and resources. As a regenerated spiritually-awakened humanity moves forward into the future, this generation of more spiritually aware humans will question any inequalities in the distribution of wealth and resources. Old institutions and political systems that foster inequality and separation will be dismantled so that there can be a regenerative approach to the distribution of resources on the planet for the whole of humanity.

Pluto in Aquarius - exaltation (2023-2043)

This generation will be active in the transformation of group consciousness, establishing a foundation for the Aquarian Age. Building on the foundations of previous generations, this generation will have an innate spiritual connection to the higher group consciousness of humanity and will seek to establish freedom and independence for all, in order to support the evolution of human consciousness.

Pluto in Pisces (2043-2063)

This generation will be active in the transformation of consciousness. Pluto is the Soul-ruler of Pisces and creates those conditions that dissolve ('destroy') all illusions of separation so that we may come to know the truth of our inherent connection. Individual experience is honored and recognized as vital for the evolution of consciousness, yet at the same time the heart of humanity as one being is also known and personally felt, as a deep spiritual truth. This generation will build on the experiences of previous generations so that through the depth of their own inner spiritual experience (gained in Scorpio), and their innate connection with the group consciousness of humanity (gained in Aquarius) they will now be able to move forward together as one body of humanity in which all hearts beat as one. This is the awakening of the sacred heart of humanity. There is the potential for a blossoming of human consciousness through which universal love becomes the driving force of future evolution for all humanity.

Pluto in The Houses

Wherever Pluto is in your chart you will experience Plutonic themes on a deep level: you may be having experiences that cause you to look deeply at the root of the matter, and/or that cause you to go 'underground' and illuminate what is there, bringing it to the light for healing. You may have experiences that cause you to look at issues around power: including uses and abuses of power; how you use your own personal power; and issues of self-empowerment.

Underpinning all of these Plutonic issues is the potential to recognize Divine Will and your own will as one. Ultimately, wherever Pluto is in your chart indicates where you have the power to either self-destruct or to step fully into your regenerative power for healing and enlightenment, depending upon how you focus your will.

Pluto in the First House

The First House is all about sense of self: self-development, how we form our self identity, and how we move forward into the world. If you have Pluto in the First House, you may experience many deep and transformational events in your lifetime. The ultimate lesson is that you cannot take your identity from any external forms that are constantly shifting and changing. The deepest lesson is that you ARE the indestructible consciousness, which sees all.

A major theme in your life will be transforming your self-identity. The First House shows how you experience yourself in the world. Pluto here is uprooting ideas and beliefs around the nature of your existence until you find deeper answers to the question "Who Am I?".

Pluto in the Second House

The second house is all about our resources, physical resources which include our finances and possessions but also our deepest inner resources: our spiritual strength and power. If you have Pluto in the second house you may experience many losses and gains in terms of your resources. This is bringing your attention to the fact that you are your own best resource. Pluto is teaching you self empowerment by drawing your attention to your deepest spiritual strength and power.

A major theme in your life will therefore be transforming your inner values and resources. Pluto here is uprooting all false ideas about what is of 'value', especially in terms of yourself. You may experience major changes and/or power struggles about your finances, possessions: what you own, what is yours, how you generate income. Pluto here is also uprooting false values until you find the deeper treasure of your own inner spiritual resources.

Pluto in the Third House

The third house is about mental processing: how we learn and communicate. If you have Pluto in the third house, you are transforming your mind. You may experience continual "death" and destruction of thought forms: ideas, opinions, beliefs etc. Pluto is teaching you the deeper lesson that all thoughts are transient and ever changing. The deepest lesson is that your real mind is the illumined consciousness from which all thought arises.

A major theme in your life will therefore be, transforming your thinking. The third house indicates your mind, mental processing, thinking, learning and communication. Pluto here is uprooting false beliefs, limited thinking and cultural conditioning to illuminate the true spiritual nature of mind as light.

Pluto in the Fourth House

The fourth house is about our home, family, and our psychological roots. On a soul level, it is about transforming your "Karma", which is your inherited, and learned (through many lifetimes), behavioral conditioning. With Pluto in this position you may experience many deep changes in your home and family situation, which cause you to develop a stronger sense of individuality, and also transform your ideas around family and belonging. The deepest lesson is that your home is within: it is your conscious awareness that you carry with you wherever you go.

A major theme in your life will therefore be transforming your roots. The fourth house indicates your familial and ancestral conditioning. Pluto here is uprooting and exposing negative patterns of conditioning that we specifically inherit through our family and ancestral lineage. Outdated patterns of behavioral conditioning are being uprooted and illuminated so that healthier, more appropriate roots can be set down that support you moving forward as an awakening spiritual being.

Pluto in the Fifth House

The fifth house is about self-expression, about how we express our individual innate creativity out into the world. On a personality level it is the house of fun: play, children, romance and lovers. If you have Pluto in this position may experience many changes in terms of romantic liaisons. The deepest lessons are about developing awareness, and correct use of, your own creative power.

A major theme in your life will therefore be transforming your creative self-expression. The Fifth House indicates your power to create as an individual, whether that be through creating a work of art, or having children. It is about how you express your individuality through fun, play, romance and creativity. It is about discovering and expressing your personal power. Pluto here will be uprooting and illuminating any limitations or distortions in your self-expression so you get to experience your true creative power as an individual.

Pluto in the Sixth House

The sixth house is about our health, work, and those that depend upon us. With Pluto in this position you may experience many job changes and/or uses and abuses of power in the workplace. You may also experience health issues that bring to your awareness the process of healing and regeneration. On a spiritual level you are now learning how to use your inner power to be of service to humanity.

A major theme in your life will therefore be transforming your approach to work, health and well-being. The sixth house indicates where we may be of service: including how we maintain our own 'fitness' to be of service to ourselves and those whom depend upon us, either as employers, family or even our pets.

The first five houses have been about personal development. In the sixth house we are beginning to shift our attention from our 'self' to see how we may fulfill our 'purpose' in our tribe or community. Pluto here can bring major changes in our attitudes towards health, work and fulfilling our obligations within our community.

Pluto here will also be uprooting and illuminating any distorted ideas we may have about servitude so we can become enlightened servers in true 'service' to humanity.

Pluto in the Seventh House

The seventh house is about marriage and partnerships. On a soul level it's about the "marriage" (or fusion) of personality and soul. With Pluto in this position you may experience intensity and power dynamics in personal relating, as Pluto brings about the "destruction" of all false ideas about what relationships ought to be. The ultimate lesson is that "me" and "you" are one.

A major theme in your life will therefore be transforming partnership. The seventh house indicates partnerships: including marriage, committed relationships, and business relationships.

Pluto here will be transforming your attitudes and approach to relationships, and 'equalizing' where there may be power imbalances.

Pluto here will also be revealing where there are any imbalances of power so that all your partnerships can be based on equality going forward. This may mean you learning new skills and techniques to remain in a balanced position in your relating.

Pluto in the Eighth House

The eighth house is about shared responsibility and resources. With Pluto in this position, on a personality level you may experience power dynamics in sexual relationships. On a soul level the ultimate lesson is about the transformation of dense energy into subtle energy, and the transformation of material resources into spiritual resources. It is a powerful position for healing and regeneration.

A major theme in your life will therefore be transforming power and trust in intimate relating. The eighth house reflects our deeper intimate connections with others whom we are required to trust, and/or who must trust us. These deeper issues of trust often arise in the context of sex and money. Pluto in this area may be throwing up challenges that reveal where you can trust and where you cannot trust, or where that trust has been betrayed. Are you trustworthy yourself? Pluto is bringing all these issues into the light for healing, so you can learn more about the power dynamics involved. You may be learning new skills around where you give away your power in certain situations, and where you can bring healing through your own self-empowerment.

Pluto in the Ninth House

The ninth house is about higher learning, philosophy and knowledge. On a personality level you may be transformed by educational or religious experiences, or by foreign travel. On a soul level the deepest lesson is about uprooting false knowledge systems, and revealing the truth of illumined wisdom.

A major theme in your life will therefore be transforming your wisdom. The ninth house includes higher education, religion, philosophy and higher knowledge. Pluto here may be uprooting and illuminating false beliefs, religious dogma, ideals and distorted knowledge, so that you are open to become aware of deeper spiritual truth and wisdom.

Pluto in the Tenth House

The tenth house is about our career and/or position in the world. Pluto in this position can bring many career changes that lead to renewal and regeneration of our goals and aspirations. On a soul level the deepest lesson here is about focusing on your spiritual aspirations and aligning with your spiritual journey. Esoterically the tenth house is the house of the Masters and with Pluto in this position, once you align with your soul path, you can access the support of your spiritual lineage.

A major theme in your life will therefore be transforming your career or vocation. In contrast to the sixth house, which is more about your 'job', the tenth house says more about your vocation, or the work you came to do in the world. (The distinction would be an actor who currently makes a living as a waiter: acting would be his tenth house calling, whereas waiting on tables would be his sixth house). Pluto here may be uprooting and illuminating ideas about who you are in the world: what you feel called to manifest in the world and/or what your position or status is within your community, society or company.

Pluto in the Eleventh House

The eleventh house is about higher group consciousness: the collective consciousness of humanity. With Pluto in this position you might experience many changes, renewals and 'regenerations' in your circles of friends, and groups you are associated with. The deepest spiritual lesson here is the continuous renewal of group activity until the highest group consciousness can be made manifest in reality.

A major theme in your life will therefore be transforming your role within groups and societies that you belong to. The eleventh house is also about kindred spirits: friends and groups that you belong to that have shared ideals and aspirations. Pluto here will be uprooting and illuminating group dynamics that no longer serve the highest and best good. You may be called upon to change your role within certain groups, or even leave and join new groups, so you may actively participate in groups that will evolve the collective consciousness of humanity.

Pluto in the Twelfth House

The twelfth house is about our subconscious, or unconscious world, and as such is the house of our hidden resources and talents. On a soul level it's about Universal Consciousness, which is Universal Love. Pluto in this position can bring you life experiences that reveal your hidden inner world. The deepest spiritual lesson here is to recognize that the deepest, most sacred, source of Universal Love, lies within you.

A major theme in your life will therefore be transforming your inner world. The twelfth house is known as the house of mystery and secrets. This includes your unconscious mind, but also is your gateway to higher consciousness through meditative and spiritual experiences that awaken you to higher dimensions of consciousness. Pluto here may be creating experiences in your life that bring your own unconscious behavior to the light of your own awareness for healing.

Where Are You Touched By Pluto?

Pluto is the slowest moving planet and will only cross some of the houses in your chart in this lifetime. So it is important to notice which areas of your life have been, and are being, 'touched' by Pluto because they will be the areas where you have possibly experienced the greatest challenges and the most personal transformation in your whole life. When Pluto makes his slow and laborious journey through an area of your life, you are never the same again. You will be changed. You can either resist the change, whereby it becomes a painful struggle, or you can embrace the change and recognize where your soul is calling upon you to grow, learn and awaken.

Be The Hundredth Monkey!

Even though world events seem dire, you still have the power to change everything, but only by changing your own inner world. This is the true power of Pluto, this is the true hidden gem: the power of your own light to transform the darkness. The Hundredth Monkey concept[184] suggests that once enough people have learned something, reached a certain skill or level of consciousness, then (because human minds want to synchronize with each other) we reach a tipping-point where the rest automatically tip over into that state.

The more people who recognize emptiness (inner awareness, calm mind) the easier it is for others to follow. This is the flowering of human consciousness and the fruition of Pluto's purpose. Concepts of 'self' dissolve and pure awareness remains: 'empty' of concepts, labels, and contrived states, humanity returns to its pure, natural state.

---

[184] The Hundredth Monkey Effect. Online document at https://en.wikipedia.org/wiki/Hundredth_monkey_effect Accessed December 11th 2019.

We can see that throughout humanity, the conditions for collective human advancement into emptiness and Universal Union are held in place by the activities of Pluto: the spaceholder for the emptiness level of our development.

Suggested Fieldwork

• Deeper Self-observation. Take out your own horoscope (natal chart) and make a note in your journal of the sign and house position of Pluto. Then read the descriptions above and make a note of any ideas and insights that come to you. Meditate on how Pluto might be showing up in your life. Record your impressions and insights in your reflective journal.

• Further Reading: *Soul Centered Astrology: A Key to Your Expanding Self*, by Alan Oken, refer to the appropriate section for more information on Pluto. Read about Pluto in chapter five of *Soul Astrology*.

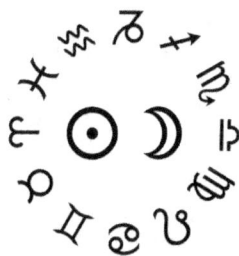

24. The Angel of Presence

The Final Installment

We have finally arrived at the final chapter in *The Foundations of Soul Astrology*. I trust you have enjoyed the ride and that you have found it to be both informative and transformative! Who knows where you are going. Who knows where you will end (if ever). Buddhist philosophy says you are an infinite stream of mental moments without beginning and without end.

It is my sincere wish that this book and newsletter series has been beneficial to you and that you recognize the magnificence of your own true nature as a Divine spiritual being and, if not, that you at least begin to catch a glimpse of your Divine nature. You are a being of love and light, anything less than that is a result of your karmic conditioning from this and past lifetimes. Any perceived flaws, failings and shortcomings in you, are not an inherent part of your true nature, but have simply been learned at some time. This means they can also be unlearned, so that your true nature can shine through. Soul Astrology is simply a tool that can help you to see these learned (karmic) patterns more clearly, so that you can finally let them go and rest, as you.

What's Next For Your Soul?

I'm often asked, What happens after the Soul completes its journey from Aries to Pisces? The truth? I don't really know. No-one knows for certain, unless you are a fully enlightened being like the Buddha!

What I will do though, is share some thoughts and ideas, based on my current understanding of this vast and complex subject. My best guess is that it begins again in Aries, on a higher turn of the spiral. This may be immediate if your mind-stream has the karma to propel itself forward, or it could be after some time spent resting in the light of pure consciousness (time being a relative thing at this level). I'll let you know for sure once I've been there and returned with enough clarity to remember the journey!

Your Soul May Not Be Permanent

In areas where I don't have personal experience, I usually defer to a wisdom greater than my own, more often than not this will be from the Buddhist tradition, because this would be in accord with the teaching of the Tibetan himself, given that he was a lama in a Tibetan Buddhist monastery.

The Buddha taught that nothing that exists is permanent; that every thing that we experience in manifest existence is *free from permanence and free from non-existence* (the exception to this would be consciousness itself, which is said to be infinite). This is where Buddhism differs from other faiths that teach that the Soul is eternal.

In a conversation about the permanence of *Atman*[185], the Hindu concept of core self, or soul, the Buddha is thought to have simply said "it's not like that". Indeed questions about self, and self-identity are among the questions that the Buddha said were unwise to contemplate[186] because they can lead to unhelpful beliefs and distract us from direct experience of our own true nature.

Your Soul's Journey

To the best of my understanding, in both *Esoteric Astrology* and especially in *The Labours of Hercules*[187], The Tibetan suggests that

---

[185] *Atman.* Online document **at** https://www.britannica.com/topic/atman Accessed December 12th 2019.

[186] *The Unanswered Questions.* Online document at https://en.wikipedia.org/wiki/The_unanswered_questions Accessed December 12th 2019.

[187] Bailey, A.A. (1974) *The Labours of Hercules: an astrological interpretation.* Lucis Press Ltd.

the Soul is going through developmental stages, which can be identified using the twelve zodiac signs from Aries through to Pisces. We mentioned earlier how some astrologers believe that the Soul spends up to eight lifetimes, or physical incarnations in each sign. This would be in accord with the Buddha's teaching that the soul is neither permanent, nor 'non-existing', but that it's essence has a starting point, passes through changes (stages) over time, and has a final 'destination' or end point.

Three Buddha Bodies: Dharmakaya, Sambhogakaya, Nirmanakaya

With up to eight lifetimes in each sign, and there being twelve signs, we might then deduce that a Soul is about eighty-four human lifetimes old! So the Soul seems to exist for a time, and then return to the light of consciousness, in contrast to pure consciousness itself, which is eternal. This makes sense from the Buddhist perspective of the three buddha 'bodies' of *dharmakaya*, *sambhogakaya* and *nirmanakaya*[188]. Before going further, it might also be helpful to remember what a 'buddha' actually is. Aside from the historical Buddha, Gautama[189], the word *buddha* itself is a Sanskrit term, which simply means *being awake*. So a buddha in a general sense is simply *one who is awake to their own true nature*.

Dharmakaya is the eternal light of pure consciousness. In Tibetan Buddhism it is said to be the primordial 'ground of all being', which is without beginning and without end. The *sambhogakaya* is said to be the first 'realm' of existence that emerges from the dharmakaya, and it is of the nature of light and energy. This is where we have a light body, rainbow body and/or energy body. In other words we have a 'body' of light and energy that is immaterial in nature and is known by many names in various traditions. It is the realm of holy beings, buddhas, bodhisattvas and angels. Indeed all forms of 'light beings' are said to inhabit this realm.

From the sambhogakaya emerges the *nirmanakaya*, or physical body. This is where a buddha has a physical body, as do you and I.

---

[188] O'Brien, B. (2018) *The Trikaya: The Three Bodies of Buddha*. Online document at https://www.learnreligions.com/trikaya-three-bodies-of-buddha-450016 Accessed December 12th 2019.

[189] O'Brien, B. (2018) *Who Was the Buddha?* Online document at https://www.lionsroar.com/who-was-the-buddha/ Accessed December 12th 2019.

The Journey of Your Soul IS Life's Greatest Adventure

So where does your Soul fit into this picture? What we call our Soul is likely to be our individual light body, or rainbow body, that emerges in the sambhogakaya realm, and from which emerge each of our physical bodies (for up to eighty-four lifetimes). The Tibetan seems to be pointing to the Soul as a body of Divine consciousness, energy, and light, that arises and passes through the specific developmental stages that we have discussed both here and in *Soul Astrology*[190], before returning to the light of pure consciousness in the dharmakaya realm. *In the dharmakaya realm consciousness itself is eternal*, and can arise again as another Soul, at another time.

What would be the purpose of this journey? So that we can simply experience the truth of life. So we can experience the beauty and magnificence of Divine Consciousness, Divine Presence, in physical form, as ourselves. Life itself gets to have the greatest adventure ever, as your Soul... and YOU! And those that recognize their true nature (in other words they remember who they are), can remind the rest of us, when we forget!

The Nature of Time

For the sake of simplicity, and to assist understanding, in this book we have spoken about time as though it is linear, because that is how we experience time in our daily lives. We wake up in the morning and time seems to pass in a linear fashion, until the sun sets and we go to bed at night. However, according to Albert Einstein, and contemporary scientific theory, time does not really exist like that at all! Scientists now believe what ancient spiritual masters have been saying for centuries: that everything already exists in the present moment. There is no past, present or future, but only an endless experiencing of now.

> *"the distinction between past, present, and future is only an illusion, however persistent"*
>
> - Albert Einstein[191]

---

[190] Hadikin, R. (2016) *Soul Astrology: How Your Rising Sign Reveals Your Soul Path and Life Purpose.* Ruth Hadikin Associates. Order online at https://soulastrologybook.com

[191] PBS documentary series: *The Fabric of The Cosmos.* Season 38 Episode 17: *The Illusion of Time.* Online streaming at https://www.pbs.org/video/nova-the-fabric-of-the-cosmos-the-illusion-of-time/ Accessed December 12th 2019.

This is important to bear in mind because when we study astrology, we are studying *cycles of time*. In astrology we observe how repeating patterns in nature are associated with stellar events. So if time is an illusion, how can we be experiencing repeating cycles? This is due to our karmic conditioning. It is our conditioning (karma) that keeps us repeating habitual cycles (patterns) of behavior throughout infinity until we step off the wheel of death and rebirth.

Beyond The Three Times

Many Buddhist scriptures refer to 'going beyond the *three times*'[192]. Once we become enlightened like the Buddha we are said to be free from the confines of the three times, but what does this mean? If we observe our thoughts for any length of time, we can see how we constantly experience thoughts of past, thoughts of the future or thoughts about the present moment. This constant engagement in thought is actually an obstacle, preventing us from experiencing this present moment directly.

> *" This fresh immediate awareness of the present moment,*
> *transcending all thoughts related to the three times,*
> *is itself that primordial awareness ...*
> *that is self-originated intrinsic Awareness.*
> *This is the direct introduction to one's own nature."*
>
> - Namkhai Norbu[193]

When we have the ability to rest continuously in our experience of the present moment, we are said to have gone beyond the three times.

The Reversed Wheel

In *Esoteric Astrology* the Tibetan refers to the returning (or reversed) wheel vs. the wheel of 'rebirth' or outgoing wheel. What does he mean by this? I believe he is talking about an advanced stage of

---

[192] A Buddha's Omniscience of the Three Times. Online document at https://studybuddhism.com/en/advanced-studies/abhidharma-tenet-systems/time-the-universe/a-buddha-s-knowledge-of-the-past-present-and-future/a-buddha-s-omniscience-of-the-three-times Accessed December 12th 2019.

[193] Namkhai, N. (1999) *The Crystal and the Way of Light: Sutra, Tantra, and Dzogchen.* Snow Lion.

spiritual development whereby we are no longer driven by the demands of the outside world, but neither are we lost in our inner world either. We have transcended the dualistic plane of 'inside and outside' and are now simply present, resting, awake and aware, in our own beingness. This is what the Tibetan Dzogchen tradition refers to as 'the natural state'. The 'wheel of rebirth' would refer to the wheel of death and rebirth, otherwise known as *samsara*[194].

In samsara we are driven by our karmic conditioning and therefore 'wander' unconsciously through repeating cycles of existence. According to Buddhist teaching this is normal everyday life for the majority of us, as we follow the habits and tendencies of our ordinary conditioned mind. When we are fully spiritually awake so that we are no longer driven by our unconscious habits, then we are in the process of returning to our natural unconditioned state and may be said to be on the reversed wheel.

Understanding our true nature, the natural state, and the real nature of time, is essential to really understanding what the Tibetan means when he talks about the 'reversed wheel'. We cannot grasp this from the intellect because mental concepts merely serve to add more confusion. Rather this is a state of conscious awareness that is to be perceived directly and fully experienced.

"The entire question of the revolving wheel ... must remain a difficult and abstruse problem until such time as astrologers have developed a four-dimensional consciousness and know the true meaning of the Biblical phrase: the "wheel turning upon itself."

In reality, the wheel does not turn like a wheel in a car either forward or the reverse. It turns every way and both ways simultaneously. This fact is, as yet, an impossible one for the human consciousness to grasp."

- The Tibetan, *Esoteric Astrology*

The Light of Astrology

"Astrology is the science of wholeness, unity, non-duality"

– OSHO

---

[194] See footnotes in chapter eighteen for a definition of samsara.

When we combine a deep understanding of our horoscope, together with deep spiritual practice (experiential knowing) astrology can help us to develop deeper awareness of our own karmic patterns. If you enjoy astrology, and this method resonates for you, you can use astrology to identify karmic patterns that are ready to be released, and to help understand your own true nature as a spiritual being.

Of course astrology can only ever be secondary: it is a tool that can help you shed light on your own conditioning, but it is not the goal. Nor is it suitable for everyone. If it is keeping you 'in your head', stuck at the intellect stage of your development, then you would be very wise to drop it and go meditate instead! As in the old Zen adage, astrology can be a 'finger pointing to the Moon' but it can never be the Moon itself!

To ensure you are using astrology wisely (and not becoming yet another deluded ego in the world) become a sincere practitioner of Soul Astrology. Practice mindfulness throughout your day, and become familiar with the patterns of your ego-personality (indicated by the personal planets), as they play out in the form of your daily habits, tendencies, predilections, attachments and defense mechanisms.

The Tibetan said the astrologers of the future would be intuitive. As we evolve through instinct > intellect > intuition and illumination to emptiness (clear light mind), astrology will naturally evolve into an astrology of nonduality. Eventually the astrologers of the future will be practicing from clear light mind, and their abilities will be equal to those of the great kalachakra masters[195].

Clear Light Mind

How can we ever recognize truth for ourselves? Anything we hear and understand with the intellect is speculation and hearsay. It's like a theory that hasn't been tested yet. What our spiritual journey calls for each of us to do, is to test these ideas from our own experience. In order to do that we have to be clear enough to perceive reality directly. At the moment we can't do that because our vision is clouded by our conditioning, our karmic mind. Once we are able to perceive reality directly, we go beyond the illusions of our conditioned mind and enter the clear light mind beyond. It is said

---

[195] For more about the kalachakra masters see chapter nineteen: *Saturn, Catalyst For Self-Mastery.*

that in clear light mind we can access what is called *clear light wisdom*.

From this higher perspective it is said that everything becomes clear and all can be known without doubt. It is like being able to reach a mountain top and suddenly being able to see all around. There is no more doubt, and no need for speculation, because you can see everything clearly, exactly as it is. This ability is called 'omniscience', or all-knowing. It is often spoken of in terms of the 'miracles' that manifest on the path to enlightenment, but great spiritual teachers, including Jesus Christ and Gautama the Buddha, were emphatic that we all have this potential, we only have to remove the obstacles of our karmic mind and recognize our own light.

Presence: Your True Nature

Your own true nature, and the true nature of reality are one and the same. This cannot be grasped intellectually, but can only be known through experience. The more you can sit in silence and be fully present and aware, the closer you will come to realizing this truth for yourself. This is what every great spiritual teacher has been pointing to. The Tibetan himself tells us that there is no separation. The very fabric of reality, and you, are one and the same. ...and the nature of that reality, the nature of existence, is consciousness. It is through your own awareness that you will fully know and understand the true nature of reality, because awareness (yours and everybody else's because they are not separate) IS reality.

> *"Beyond our ideas of right-doing and wrong-doing,*
> *there is a field. I'll meet you there.*
> *When the soul lies down in that grass,*
> *the world is too full to talk about.*
> *Ideas, language, even the phrase 'each other'*
> *doesn't make sense any more."*

- Rumi[196]

There is a field of pure consciousness (above we noted that Tibetan Buddhists call this field 'dharmakaya') and within this field of

---

[196] Translation by Coleman Barks, online at https://www.goodreads.com/quotes/538827-beyond-our-ideas-of-right-doing-and-wrong-doing-there-is-a Accessed December 12th 2019.

consciousness all that is known arises and falls, but never at any time is it separate from its original source. This source consciousness is alive, and aware.

> *"When our existing consciousness*
> *transforms into its essential wisdom nature,*
> *which is its sustaining basis,*
> *we see the world as sacred and divinely perfect*
> *just as it is.*
>
> *Our mandala of experience*
> *does not become a realm of blank emptiness.*
> *Rather it is seen as it has always been:*
> *a rich seamless web*
> *of relationships and luminous energies*
> *that delight the eye and*
> *inspire spontaneous joyful creativity.*
>
> *In this realm of infinite freedom,*
> *we discover that the woof and warp*
> *of those relationships*
> *are grounded in compassion and love,*
> *the mandala's pulse and lifeblood.*
>
> *We can enter this mandala*
> *through the wisdom path*
> *or through the path of unconditional love.*
> *The completion of either*
> *is the completion of both.*
>
> *Inspire yourself along this journey*
> *by opening your heart to love all beings and life.*
>
> *Delight yourself in nature's splendor*
> *and dance freely in the Clear Light*
> *of your own self-recognition*
> *from moment to moment."*
>
> — Jackson Peterson[197]

---

[197] Peterson, J. (2013) *The Natural Bliss of Being.* Createspace Independent Publishing Platform.

The Angel of Presence

> *"If there was a big bang in the beginning,*
> *you are not the result of the process...*
> *you are still the process.*
> *You are the original force of the Universe"*
>
> — Alan Watts[198]

When you live fully and completely in the light of your own awareness, you discover a presence that is not separate from you.

It IS you.

This is the true angel of presence,

and it is you.

---

[198] Alan Watts: You Are The Universe - The Nature of Consciousness. YouTube video online at https://www.youtube.com/watch?v=ZYffSEV7pdw Accessed December 12th 2019.

Further Reading and Study

- Download and read *Your Essential Guide to Soul Astrology*[199] (if you haven't read it for a while, read it again to refresh your memory).

- Get two notebooks. Use one for your study notes (what you are learning about astrology); and use the other as a reflective journal where you write your deeper insights, self-observations and realizations about YOU that arise from your studies, your observations of and insights about your zodiac signs, your mindfulness practice and your meditation.

- Deeper Self-observation. If you don't do so already, begin a daily meditative practice. Sitting at the same time each day is helpful: it helps the mind to 'learn' to be still for a short time. Take the benefits with you throughout your day. Practice mindful presence in your daily activities.

   Familiarize yourself with your horoscope. Notice any repeating behavior patterns that are characteristic of your personality signs. Keep recording your impressions and insights in your reflective journal, on an ongoing basis.

VIDEOS:

- The Illusion of Time. PBS documentary series: *The Fabric of The Cosmos*. Season 38 Episode 17: *The Illusion of Time*. Online streaming at https://www.pbs.org/video/nova-the-fabric-of-the-cosmos-the-illusion-of-time/

- Alan Watts: You Are The Universe. On YouTube at https://www.youtube.com/watch?v=ZYffSEV7pdw

- The Yogis of Tibet DVD. Available from https://tibetspirit.com/the-yogis-of-tibet-dvd/

---

[199] *Your Essential Guide to Soul Astrology*. Free download available from https://ruthhadikin.com

AUDIO:

- *The Flowering of Human Consciousness: Everyone's Life Purpose.* Audiobook by Eckhart Tolle available at https://www.amazon.co.uk/Flowering-Human-Consciousness-Everyones-Purpose/dp/B00TIWFO16

HIGHLY RECOMMENDED - FREE .PDF BOOK:

- *The Peaceful Stillness of The Silent Mind*, by Lama Thubten Yeshe. Available for free download at http://www.lamayeshe.com/sites/default/files/pdf/139_pdf.pdf

I highly recommend that you download this free book, study it, and revise the contents often to deepen your understanding of your true nature.

BOOKS:

Astrology: A Cosmic Science, by Isabel Hickey

Astrology, Karma and Transformation, by Stephen Arroyo

Astrology: Superstition, Blind Faith, or a Door to The Essential? by OSHO

A Path With Heart: A Guide Through The Perils and Promises of A Spiritual Life, by Jack Kornfield

Awakening The Sacred Body, by Tenzin Wangyal Rinpoche

Breaking The Habit of Being Yourself: How to Lose Your Mind and Create a New One, by Dr. Joe Dispenza

Buddhist Astrology, by Jhampa Shaneman

Chart Interpretation Handbook, by Stephen Arroyo

Esoteric Astrology, by Alice Bailey

Esoteric Astrology: The Journey Of The Soul, by Candy Hillenbrand[200]

Learn To Meditate: A quick start guide to meditation for beginners by Ruth Hadikin

---

[200] Hillenbrand, C. *Esoteric Astrology – The Journey of the Soul.* Online document at http://www.aplaceinspace.net/Pages/CandyJourneyoftheSoul.html

Mahamudra: How To Discover Our True Nature, by Lama Thubten Yeshe

Power vs. Force: The Hidden Determinants of Human Behavior, by Dr David Hawkins

Soul Astrology: How Your Rising Sign Reveals Your Soul Path and Life Purpose, by Ruth Hadikin

Soul Centered Astrology: A Key to Your Expanding Self, by Alan Oken

The Arkana Dictionary of Astrology, by Fred Gettings

The Astrological Houses: The Spectrum of Individual Experience, by Dane Rudhyar

The Crystal and The Way of Light, by Chögyal Namkhai Norbu

The Labours of Hercules: An Astrological Interpretation, by Alice Bailey

The Natural Bliss of Being, by Jackson Peterson

Transpersonal Astrology: The Astrology of Purpose, by Errol Weiner

Waking From Sleep: Why Awakening Experiences Occur and How to Make them Permanent, by Steve Taylor

Your Essential Guide To Soul Astrology, by Ruth Hadikin. Free ebook available for download at https://RuthHadikin.com

Index

A

Air 14, 15, 26, 37, 38, 39, 40, 42, 44, 47, 49, 52, 55, 116, 127, 217, 223, 235, 245, 283, 328, 343
Alan Oken v, 8, 9, 31, 33, 35, 78, 112, 135, 141, 163, 176, 183, 185, 186, 187, 188, 189, 192, 195, 198, 200, 202, 212, 228, 246, 265, 271, 272, 288, 307, 320, 340, 359, 373
Alan Watts 370, 371
Albert Einstein 180, 364
Alice Bailey 11, 35, 80, 140, 168, 372, 373, 387, 388
Angel of Presence .... viii, 361, 370
Anger 10
Anya Sophia Mann ....v, 296
Aquarius 11, 14, 15, 16, 20, 26, 31, 32, 44, 49, 50, 52, 69, 104, 105, 128, 143, 149, 151, 189, 193, 208, 225, 241, 242, 247, 256, 261, 267, 276, 277, 278, 283, 312, 314, 322, 334, 352.
AQUARIUS SOUL 26
Aries x, 3, 11, 13, 14, 15, 16, 19, 24, 29, 32, 44, 46, 48, 50, 52, 63, 65, 95, 96, 126, 147, 150, 177, 186, 193, 203, 221, 232, 233, 234, 236, 239, 256, 275, 279, 312, 329, 330, 349, 361, 362, 363,
ARIES SOUL 24
Ascendant x, 8, 23, 52, 63, 75, 91, 117, 118, 137, 139, 140, 144, 145, 235, 254
Aspects ......vii, 126, 134, 157, 158, 159
Autumn 14, 48, 50
Awakened heart 190, 191, 285, 295, 316, 334
Awareness 1, 5, 12, 16, 21, 24, 30, 37, 38, 39, 42, 43, 47, 52, 55, 56, 58, 63, 65, 69, 74, 76, 79, 83, 86, 87, 89, 90, 95, 96, 97, 102, 107, 108, 109, 110, 111, 114, 115, 122, 125, 127, 128, 130, 131, 134, 142, 149, 156, 163, 166, 167, 169, 170, 172, 178, 179, 188, 190, 193, 195, 197, 198, 199, 200, 202, 205, 206, 207, 209, 210, 218, 219, 220, 221, 222, 223, 231, 234, 247, 253, 254, 255, 256, 257, 260, 261, 271, 274, 275, 278, 290, 294, 295, 296,

(awareness, contd.) 300, 302, 303, 305, 307, 308, 312, 313, 314, 315, 319, 327, 328, 329, 343, 344, 345, 346, 347, 349, 350, 354, 355, 358, 365, 366, 367, 368, 370

B

Bhuddism 1
Birth chart v, x, 2, 5, 34, 52, 159, 161, 301
Blended Six 15
Blending of opposites 16
Bodhicitta 316
Bodhisattva 125, 225, 241, 261
Bön 169, 170
Brain 12, 17, 18, 43, 85, 166, 196, 200, 201, 202, 270, 272, 273, 298, 302, 303, 306, 307, 308
Buddha v 1, 37, 165, 204, 212, 361, 362, 363, 365, 368

C

Cancer x, 3, 11, 14, 15, 16, 20, 24, 27, 29, 32, 44, 49, 50, 52, 63, 66, 98, 124, 127, 144, 148, 151, 176, 187, 205, 222, 237, 248, 254, 258, 275, 280, 313, 324, 329, 331, 335, 344, 350, See Cancer, See Cancer, See Cancer, See Cancer, See Cancer
CANCER SOUL 24
Candy Hillenbrand .... v, 372
Capricorn 11, 14, 15, 16, 18, 20, 26, 31, 32, 44, 49, 50, 52, 68, 103, 104, 128, 149, 151, 176, 188, 208, 209, 217, 224, 225, 233, 240, 241, 246, 251, 259, 260, 267, 276, 277, 278, 283, 314, 333, 344, 351.
CAPRICORN SOUL 26
Cardinal 13, 14, 47, 48, 49, 50, 73, 74, 222
Career 3, 46, 110, 130, 179, 211, 227, 245, 264, 286, 318, 356, 357
Chögyal Namkhai Norbu 88, 167, 346, 373
Chogyam Trungpa Rinpoche .. 184, 185
Clear Light viii, 155, 156, 303, 328, 341, 367, 369
Clear Wisdom 10, 12
Compassion 10, 12, 66, 76, 124, 329
Conditioning 12, 17, 43, 60, 81, 84, 85,

(conditioning contd.) 86, 87, 90, 91, 93, 94, 108, 113, 116, 118, 119, 120, 140, 141, 143, 154, 173, 174, 190, 196, 202, 219, 220, 234, 246, 247, 254, 256, 264, 265, 268, 269, 270, 274, 278, 284, 287, 291, 296, 297, 298, 308, 311, 326, 346, 354, 361, 365, 366, 367

Consciousness xii, 9, 10, 12, 16, 18, 19, 20, 27, 31, 37, 38, 45, 46, 55, 56, 57, 59, 60, 69, 73, 77, 81, 89, 90, 91, 93, 94, 98, 105, 110, 111, 113, 117, 118, 119, 125, 131, 134, 140, 141, 143, 144, 145, 154, 168, 169, 172, 173, 175, 185, 186, 187, 191, 193, 199, 200, 201, 202, 205, 207, 209, 214, 215, 216, 218, 219, 222, 223, 224, 229, 248, 252, 254, 257, 258, 260, 261, 271, 272, 273, 282, 290, 291, 293, 297, 299, 300, 302, 303, 304, 305, 307, 308, 309, 310, 311, 312, 314, 315, 316, 318, 319, 321, 322, 327, 328, 329, 333, 334, 339, 340, 341, 342, 343, 345, 348, 349, 351, 352, 353, 357, 358, 362, 363, 364, 366, 368, 369

Contents vii
Conventional truth 56
Core energy 5
Cosmic law 1, 318
Crisis 29, 30, 31, 188, 189, 233, 335
Custodian 31, 32, 58, 191, 290

D

Dane Rudhyar 73, 74, 78, 131, 135, 373
Detriment 95, 104, 207, 221, 223, 236, 239, 257, 258, 280, 331, 349, 351
Dharma 1, 2, 3, 141, 176
Dharmakaya 37, 363, 364, 368
Dignity 99, 204, 206, 221, 223, 236, 239, 260, 261, 283, 314, 334, 349, 351
Divine Intelligence 63
Divine love 25, 128, 214, 215
Divine Will 2, 25, 57, 67, 76, 96, 108, 110, 189, 190, 331, 350, 352
Dr. David Hawkins 10, 199, 373
Dr. Noel Huntly 18, 19
Dualistic mind 10, 11
Duality 17, 58, 73, 172, 200, 219, 261, 292, 293, 366
Dzogchen . 38, 39, 40, 54, 92, 152, 169, (dzogchen contd.) 261, 303, 365, 366

E

Earth 13, 14, 18, 20, 37, 38, 39, 42, 44, 46, 48, 49, 52, 55, 68, 115, 183, 194, 206, 217, 222, 223, 232, 235, 246, 249, 253, 268, 327, 333
Eckhart Tolle 294, 372
Ego-mind 45, 46
Ego-personality 5, 15, 18, 43, 44, 45, 64, 90, 94, 103, 108, 140, 183, 218, 251, 312, 349, 367
Electric 15, 51, 52, 53, 54, 229
Element vii, 14, 15, 37, 38, 39, 40, 41, 42, 44, 45, 46, 47, 48, 126, 215, 234, 241, 277, 344
Emptiness viii, 42, 57, 58, 59, 92, 117, 172, 216, 229, 248, 267, 268, 301, 304, 305, 321, 340, 341, 342, 343, 345, 346, 347, 358, 359, 367, 369
Energy vii, x, 37, 38, 39, 40, 48, 54, 86, 158, 162, 183, 238, 327
Enlightenment 24, 66, 87, 132, 143, 151, 155, 199, 204, 223, 240, 241, 252, 270, 322, 323, 342, 344, 352, 368
Errol Weiner 373
Esoteric Astrology vii, x, 10, 11, 13, 16, 21, 27, 37, 45, 57, 65, 69, 73, 80, 85, 137, 138, 145, 157, 161, 165, 166, 168, 170, 171, 172, 173, 174, 175, 176, 180, 181, 182, 185, 191, 193, 202, 215, 216, 217, 219, 220, 232, 233, 234, 247, 253, 254, 267, 276, 277, 278, 292, 294, 296, 303, 308, 317, 342, 362, 365, 366, 372, 387, 388
Evolution 31, 45, 48, 57, 59, 60, 69, 77, 90, 92, 111, 117, 119, 133, 138, 172, 175, 185, 191, 216, 229, 233, 234, 246, 249, 268, 287, 291, 311, 315, 321, 322, 341, 342, 348, 351, 352
Exaltation 208
Exploration xii, 12, 16, 128, 191, 229, 230, 246, 259, 267, 289, 304, 321

F

Fall 78, 95, 101, 205, 209, 222, 230, 237, 243, 260, 279, 333, 348, 350
Fear to love 10, 64
Fire 13, 14, 37, 38, 39, 40, 42, 44, 45, 46, 48, 52, 54, 55, 201, 217, 235, 272, 327

Five disturbing emotions 38
Five lights 170
Five senses 45, 215, 271
Five wisdoms 38
Fixed 13, 14, 15, 26, 47, 48, 49, 50, 73, 74, 148, 185, 198, 199, 209, 253, 283, 312
Fred Gettings 373
Fusion in consciousness 16

G

Gautama 363, 368
Gemini 2, 11, 14, 15, 16, 20, 24, 27, 29, 32, 33, 35, 44, 49, 50, 52, 66, 94, 97, 127, 143, 145, 148, 150, 186, 193, 204, 217, 219, 220, 221, 222, 234, 237, 257, 259, 275, 280, 313, 330, 331, 350,
GEMINI SOUL 24
Generosity 10, 12, 252
God Consciousness .... vii, 247
Greed 10
Gregg Braden 345
Guardian 32, 58, 231, 233, 290
Gustav Holst 61

H

H.P. Blavatsky 8, 17, 167, 168
Healing 3, 16, 74, 77, 100, 102, 109, 115, 116, 118, 122, 124, 125, 126, 127, 128, 130, 142, 147, 153, 177, 187, 211, 220, 227, 234, 239, 240, 244, 256, 260, 263, 278, 286, 296, 333, 350, 352, 355, 356, 358
Hinduism 1
Holistic 12, 317, 332
Hologram 12
Horoscope ix, x, 2, 4, 14, 31, 33, 60, 61, 65, 70, 71, 78, 79, 84, 87, 89, 112, 113, 124, 126, 134, 152, 156, 163, 176, 184, 192, 194, 203, 212, 220, 228, 235, 246, 256, 257, 265, 278, 287, 320, 340, 359, 367, 371, 388
Houses ix, 3, 4, 9, 71, 72, 73, 74, 75, 78, 79, 106, 107, 147, 152, 156, 160, 163, 185, 186, 301, 302, 315, 355, 358

I

Ignorance 10
illumination 24, 57, 58, 59, 60, 66, 117, 172, 191, 204, 216, 229, 248, 267, 301, 304, 305, 319, 321, 322, 323, 325, 328, 330, 331, 335, 336, 337, 338, 339, 340, 341, 342, 347, 367
Illusion 12, 16, 43, 45, 60, 73, 78, 93, 185, 251, 270, 291, 302, 304, 322, 323, 324, 326, 329, 330, 332, 334, 335, 336, 337, 338, 339, 344, 351, 364, 365, 371
Incarnation ix, 30, 75, 113, 176, 188, 232, 253, 269, 349, 388
Innate core essence 5
Inner nature 5
Inner treasure 12, 75, 344
Instinct 45, 57, 58, 117, 124, 172, 175, 214, 216, 229, 230, 245, 246, 247, 248, 250, 267, 268, 290, 291, 301, 305, 310, 311, 321, 341, 367
Integrated 15, 19, 41, 64, 70, 73, 152, 156, 173, 204, 207, 216, 233, 234, 248, 268, 305, 321, 341
Intellect xi, 38, 45, 56, 57, 58, 90, 117, 153, 154, 169, 172, 173, 175, 191, 216, 219, 221, 229, 246, 247, 248, 249, 251, 254, 257, 259, 265, 267, 268, 269, 287, 290, 291, 293, 294, 297, 298, 301, 305, 310, 311, 321, 327, 341, 342, 366, 367
Intuition xii, 16, 24, 38, 42, 45, 57, 58, 60, 61, 72, 78, 117, 126, 128, 140, 145, 146, 147, 156, 172, 173, 175, 177, 185, 186, 191, 201, 202, 203, 206, 209, 215, 216, 219, 229, 248, 256, 267,

(intuition contd.) 273, 291, 293, 294, 295, 297, 300, 301, 305, 306, 307, 308, 310, 311, 312, 315, 316, 318, 319, 321, 326, 341, 342, 367, 390
Intuitive 72, 78, 96, 145, 162, 190, 203, 206, 208, 217, 273, 281, 282, 287, 295, 304, 305, 319, 326, 327, 328, 367
Isabel Hickey 107, 112, 163, 275, 276, 372

J

Jack Kornfield 295, 372
Jackson Peterson 369, 373
Jealousy 10
Jesus Christ 368
Jhampa Shaneman 204, 323, 372

Joe Dispenza 88, 201, 272, 372
Jupiter vii, 32, 34, 52, 57, 59, 60, 83, 160, 174, 182, 213, 214, 216, 247, 248, 249, 250, 251, 252, 253, 254, 255, 256, 257, 258, 259, 260, 261, 262, 263, 264, 265, 267, 268, 269, 287, 290, 291, 311, 329

K

Kalachakra Masters 168, 203, 308
Karma vii, 1, 5, 59, 79, 80, 81, 82, 83, 84, 85, 86, 90, 111, 119, 120, 141, 162, 176, 211, 252, 269, 270, 274, 276, 278, 292, 297, 301, 354, 362, 365, 372
Karmic mind 86, 140, 166, 367, 368

L

Lama Anagarika Govinda 17, 297
Lama Thubten Yeshe 146, 200, 297, 298, 300, 372, 373
Law of Attraction .... vii, 213
Laziness 10
Leo 2, 3, 11, 14, 15, 16, 20, 25, 27, 30, 31, 32, 44, 46, 48, 50, 52, 56, 67, 99, 116, 123, 127, 143, 144, 149, 151, 187, 205, 206, 222, 238, 254, 258, 275, 280, 281, 302, 313, 331, 350
LEO SOUL 25
Libra 2, 11, 14, 15, 16, 19, 25, 30, 31, 32, 44, 49, 50, 52, 58, 67, 101, 127, 147, 150, 187, 206, 217, 218, 219, 220, 222, 223, 233, 239, 259, 267, 268, 274, 275, 278, 281, 312, 314, 332, 351
LIBRA SOUL 25
Life Purpose ix, 1, 4, 61, 73, 110, 134, 139, 270, 320, 364, 373, 387, 388
Life's Greatest Adventure .... ix, xi, 5
Light x, 7, 8, 9, 11, 12, 13, 17, 18, 20, 24, 25, 26, 28, 30, 31, 33, 37, 41, 42, 48, 56, 58, 60, 65, 68, 81, 89, 90, 93, 94, 96, 97, 99, 105, 107, 114, 115, 119, 120, 121, 122, 124, 128, 132, 140, 156, 158, 159, 166, 168, 169, 170, 172, 176, 177, 178, 181, 184, 191, 195, 196, 197, 198, 203, 204, 205, 206, 207, 208, 209, 216, 217, 221, 229, 232, 233, 252, 253, 261, 274, 295, 296, 298, 303, 304, 311, 313, 321, 322, 323, 324, 325, 330, 333, 340, 346, 347, 348, 349, 352, 354, 356, 358, 361, 362, 363, 364,

(light contd.) 367, 368, 370
Love 10, 12, 20, 57, 66, 67, 68, 69, 76, 78, 87, 106, 120, 145, 170, 177, 178, 189, 214, 215, 217, 219, 220, 221, 225, 228, 243, 247, 253, 315, 328, 332, 334, 340, 345, 349, 357
Luminous Nature viii
Lunar Nodal Axis 4
Lunation Cycle 126, 131, 135

M

Magnetic 15, 21, 51, 52, 53, 59, 85, 86, 102, 118, 119, 170, 213, 217, 219, 225, 226, 227, 228, 229, 230, 327, 333
Mahayana 56
Mars vii, 32, 34, 52, 57, 58, 59, 60, 65, 70, 83, 87, 160, 174, 188, 214, 216, 229, 230, 231, 232, 233, 234, 235, 236, 237, 238, 239, 240, 241, 242, 243, 244, 245, 246, 248, 290, 291, 348
Mass consciousness 24, 98, 119
Masters and guides 3
MC 3, 4, 52, 157
Meditation 5, 12, 21, 27, 49, 53, 54, 56, 61, 65, 70, 86, 87, 91, 92, 94, 107, 111, 140, 143, 149, 155, 170, 186, 195, 196, 199, 202, 205, 207, 208, 209, 212, 221, 223, 257, 258, 259, 280, 282, 287, 295, 297, 299, 303, 308, 312, 347, 371, 372, 389, 390
Mercury vii, 32, 33, 34, 35, 52, 57, 59, 65, 70, 83, 87, 108, 145, 174, 180, 181, 193, 194, 195, 196, 197, 198, 199, 200, 201, 202, 203, 204, 205, 206, 207, 208, 209, 210, 211, 212, 214, 216, 219, 233, 234, 246, 248, 250, 270, 272, 273, 290, 306, 307
Midheaven 3, 4, 161
Mindfulness 41, 45, 46, 84, 85, 116, 155, 197, 297, 367, 371
Modality .... vii, 14, 15, 37, 48
Moon vii, ix, x, 2, 4, 8, 12, 13, 16, 17, 18, 19, 20, 21, 27, 31, 32, 34, 44, 52, 55, 56, 57, 59, 61, 63, 65, 70, 83, 87, 89, 90, 93, 94, 112, 113, 114, 115, 116, 117, 118, 119, 120, 121, 122, 123, 124, 125, 126, 128, 129, 130, 131, 132, 133, 134, 135, 137, 138, 139, 140, 141, 144, 147, 153, 155, 156, 160, 163, 174, 175, 194, 216, 219, 246, 248, 290, 367

Index **381**

Moon's Nodes ....vii, 137, 138, 140
Motivation 29, 84, 86, 189, 232, 235, 237
Mutable .14, 47, 48, 49, 50, 73, 74, 253

N

Natal chart x, 12, 33, 43, 44, 61, 70, 78, 87, 89, 90, 91, 112, 132, 134, 143, 156, 163, 176, 192, 212, 228, 246, 265, 287, 302, 315, 320, 340, 349, 359
Natural state 305, 358, 366
Nature of Time 364
Negative 12, 13, 14, 15, 17, 38, 51, 52, 53, 82, 84, 85, 95, 116, 121, 159, 264, 296, 302, 346, 354
Neptune viii, 32, 34, 57, 59, 60, 83, 174, 180, 216, 255, 301, 302, 304, 319, 321, 322, 323, 324, 325, 326, 327, 328, 329, 330, 331, 332, 333, 334, 335, 336, 337, 338, 339, 340, 347
Ngönshes 166, 170
Nirmanakaya...............................37, 363
North Node 4, 138, 141, 142, 143, 144, 145, 146, 147, 148, 149, 150, 151, 153, 154, 155, 156

O

Openness...10, 12
Opposite signs 17
OSHO ..43, 44, 278, 295, 306, 366, 372

P

Patanjali 45, 90, 217, 218, 232, 261, 327, 328
Peacefulness 10, 12
Personality ix, 7, 8, 9, 11, 12, 15, 16, 19, 24, 27, 31, 33, 34, 42, 43, 46, 64, 65, 69, 73, 74, 85, 90, 91, 94, 101, 102, 110, 114, 117, 122, 124, 125, 138, 139, 140, 144, 145, 146, 147, 152, 155, 156, 159, 160, 183, 185, 193, 198, 204, 206, 207, 208, 214, 217, 219, 220, 226, 232, 233, 234, 247, 251, 252, 254, 255, 256, 258, 259, 267, 274, 276, 277, 278, 294, 295, 296, 302, 312, 316, 317, 318, 328, 329, 348, 351, 354, 355, 356, 371
Personality-Soul Fusion vii, 7, 12, 15, 19, 139, 185, 253

Pisces x, 11, 13, 14, 15, 16, 20, 26, 31, 32, 44, 49, 50, 51, 52, 65, 69, 105, 106, 121, 128, 142, 143, 149, 151, 155, 189, 209, 215, 217, 225, 242, 247, 255, 256, 261, 276, 284, 315, 329, 334, 335, 345, 349, 352, 361, 363
PISCES SOUL 26
Planets vii, ix, x, 4, 9, 33, 34, 44, 46, 52, 53, 55, 57, 58, 59, 60, 61, 63, 64, 65, 70, 71, 74, 78, 79, 83, 87, 90, 95, 99, 116, 125, 145, 157, 159, 160, 161, 162, 163, 165, 171, 173, 174, 181, 191, 194, 199, 200, 204, 215, 216, 229, 232, 236, 246, 247, 248, 251, 270, 273, 289, 290, 291, 297, 301, 302, 303, 304, 306, 308, 315, 319, 321, 335, 341, 346, 347, 348, 367
Pluto viii, 32, 34, 57, 59, 60, 61, 83, 174, 188, 216, 233, 255, 273, 301, 302, 304, 319, 341, 342, 344, 345, 346, 347, 348, 349, 350, 351, 352, 353, 354, 355, 356, 357, 358, 359
Polarities 11, 16, 51, 52, 66, 148, 152, 159
Polarity vii, 14, 15, 17, 18, 19, 20, 37, 51, 52, 152, 156, 200, 219
Portal .... x, 287, 289
Positive 12, 13, 14, 15, 17, 38, 51, 52, 53, 82, 95, 116, 121, 159, 230, 302, 316, 331
Power vs. Force.......................... 10, 199
Preparation 29, 30, 31, 348
Pride 10
Public image 4
Pythagoras..................... 40, 41, 56, 57

R

Rainbow Bridge vii, 76, 108, 193, 199, 201, 273
Reality 10, 12, 20, 21, 23, 38, 39, 43, 52, 56, 74, 84, 86, 87, 92, 120, 125, 128, 146, 151, 169, 170, 172, 182, 191, 200, 202, 207, 211, 223, 250, 251, 255, 257, 261, 267, 271, 272, 274, 279, 282, 291, 293, 295, 296, 299, 300, 303, 304, 306, 316, 317, 323, 324, 332, 335, 343, 344, 357, 366, 367, 368
Returning (or reversed) wheel 365
Right living 1

Rising Sign ix, x, 1, 2, 4, 12, 13, 18, 20, 23, 24, 27, 29, 31, 32, 33, 34, 35, 61, 63, 64, 65, 70, 73, 75, 79, 81, 114, 117, 118, 139, 160, 175, 178, 254, 270, 320, 364, 373
Rulership 31, 58, 99, 202, 204, 206, 217, 277, 306, 335
Ruling planet 31

S

Sacred Rebellion .... viii, 301, 305
Sagittarius 11, 14, 15, 16, 20, 26, 31, 32, 44, 46, 48, 50, 52, 68, 103, 121, 128, 143, 148, 150, 188, 192, 207, 208, 224, 240, 247, 254, 255, 256, 260, 261, 276, 282, 283, 314, 333, 351
SAGITTARIUS SOUL 26
Sambhogakaya 37, 363, 364
Samsara 252, 269, 366
Sanskrit 1
Saturn vii, 32, 34, 52, 57, 59, 60, 74, 83, 160, 174, 195, 200, 201, 202, 216, 248, 259, 267, 268, 269, 270, 271, 272, 273, 274, 275, 276, 277, 278, 279, 280, 281, 282, 283, 284, 285, 286, 287, 288, 289, 290, 291, 292, 293, 297, 302, 303, 304, 305, 306, 309, 312, 367
Scorpio 3, 11, 14, 15, 16, 20, 25, 30, 31, 32, 44, 49, 50, 52, 68, 102, 127, 148, 150, 188, 207, 223, 224, 233, 234, 239, 240, 259, 276, 282, 314, 332, 333, 348, 351, 352
SCORPIO SOUL 25
Season 14, 50
Seeds 9, 11, 12, 82, 83, 84, 309, 313, 330
Self-discovery 29, 41, 299
Self-exploration ix, x, 35, 41, 54, 56, 121, 181, 197, 240, 292, 299
Self-Mastery .... vii, 267, 275, 367
Self-observation 1, 5, 21, 29, 39, 41, 52, 61, 69, 70, 78, 86, 87, 112, 134, 156, 157, 163, 192, 212, 228, 246, 265, 287, 294, 300, 320, 340, 359, 371
Separation 7, 9, 10, 11, 12, 16, 17, 19, 90, 132, 154, 219, 314, 317, 351, 352, 368
Service 25, 29, 31, 76, 100, 109, 110, 111, 129, 141, 153, 154, 155, 176, 177, 178, 179, 186, 189, 190, 228,

(service contd.) 238, 251, 263, 277, 278, 318, 337, 339, 340, 355
Shamatha 208, 209, 282, 299
Six Lokas 10, 11
Sixth House 3, 76, 109, 129, 179, 190, 210, 226, 244, 251, 258, 263, 285, 317, 337, 355
Sky-gazing 170, 311
Soul x, 5, 8, 9, 23, 31, 34, 41, 362, 363, 364
Soul Astrology i, iii, vii, ix, xi, xii, 1, 4, 5, 7, 12, 13, 16, 17, 33, 34, 35, 42, 51, 61, 64, 65, 70, 73, 75, 78, 79, 80, 81, 82, 84, 88, 92, 93, 94, 110, 112, 117, 119, 134, 137, 138, 139, 140, 141, 145, 152, 156, 158, 165, 169, 178, 185, 192, 212, 228, 230, 243, 246, 265, 270, 288, 291, 297, 300, 302, 305, 320, 321, 340, 359, 361, 364, 367, 371, 373, 387, 388, 389, 390
Soul fusion 7, 12, 16, 138, 152, 234, 256, 278
Soul Path ix, 1, 4, 61, 73, 139, 270, 320, 364, 373, 387, 388
Soul's Purpose vii, 13, 23, 91, 96, 97, 98, 99, 100, 101, 102, 103, 104, 105, 106, 117, 329, 349
Soul's journey ix
Space 38
Spaceholder 59, 89, 291, 319, 322, 340, 342, 359
Spectrum of Consciousness 10
Spectrum of vibration 10, 11
Spiritual awakening iii, ix, x, xii, 5, 54, 56, 57, 59, 60, 65, 66, 73, 74, 75, 117, 143, 144, 147, 152, 155, 165, 166, 170, 173, 181, 184, 185, 191, 193, 199, 200, 212, 215, 216, 218, 219, 220, 221, 252, 253, 284, 292, 293, 298, 299, 301, 311, 312, 351, 389, 390
Spiritual development 3, 76, 95, 117, 120, 142, 146, 174, 204, 208, 229, 230, 231, 236, 238, 239, 251, 253, 257, 287, 319, 325, 326, 340, 366
Spiritual energy 5, 26, 67, 69, 75, 104, 148, 149, 175, 177, 225, 233, 240, 242, 261, 282, 317, 334, 338, 351
Spiritual lineage 3, 77, 191, 357
Spiritual masters xii, 40, 166, 167, 311, 321, 364, 388
Spiritual Path vii, 1, 5, 30, 76, 94, 109,

(spiritual path contd.) 110, 115, 134, 144, 150, 155, 179, 194, 196, 198, 208, 209, 218, 224, 236, 237, 238, 240, 242, 251, 257, 259, 260, 264, 277, 279, 280, 281, 282, 283, 286, 311, 318, 325, 332, 337, 338, 339, 344
Spring 14, 47, 50, 51, 348
Stephen Arroyo 42, 163, 372
Steve Taylor 199, 293, 326, 373
Summer 14, 47, 50
Sun vii, ix, x, 2, 4, 8, 12, 13, 16, 17, 18, 19, 20, 21, 27, 29, 31, 32, 34, 40, 44, 52, 57, 59, 61, 65, 70, 83, 87, 89, 90, 91, 92, 93, 94, 95, 96, 97, 98, 99, 100, 101, 102, 103, 104, 105, 106, 107, 108, 109, 110, 111, 112, 114, 115, 116, 117, 118, 120, 121, 122, 123, 132, 133, 134, 135, 137, 138, 160, 163, 174, 175, 176, 178, 180, 181, 184, 187, 189, 194, 205, 214, 216, 219, 229, 235, 246, 248, 290, 322, 329, 335, 344, 349
Sun-gazing 170

T

Taurus 3, 11, 13, 14, 15, 16, 20, 24, 29, 32, 44, 48, 50, 52, 66, 96, 97, 126, 148, 150, 185, 186, 188, 192, 203, 204, 205, 217, 218, 220, 221, 222, 223, 236, 239, 257, 275, 279, 313, 330, 349
TAURUS SOUL 24
Tenth House 3, 77, 110, 130, 179, 191, 211, 227, 245, 264, 286, 318, 339, 356
Tenzin Wangyal Rinpoche 11, 38, 39, 54, 315, 372
The Dweller on The Thresholdviii, 289, 298
The Planets Suite 61
The Pulse of Life .... vii, 229
The three times 365
The Tibetan 11, 73, 168, 388
Tibetan xii, 10, 11, 15, 16, 20, 21, 23, 27, 29, 31, 37, 38, 39, 40, 44, 54, 55, 56, 57, 58, 69, 73, 79, 80, 82, 85, 86, 92, 119, 120, 137, 138, 140, 146, 152, 157, 161, 162, 165, 166, 167, 168, 169, 170, 171, 172, 173, 174, 175, 176, 181, 182, 183, 184, 185, 202, 215, 216, 219, 220, 232, 233, 252, 253, 254, 276, 277, 278, 292,

(tibetan contd.) 293, 294, 296, 303, 308, 317, 322, 328, 342, 344, 362, 363, 364, 365, 366, 367, 368, 387, 388
Transformation 3, 31, 68, 77, 102, 106, 109, 130, 177, 179, 190, 191, 211, 220, 227, 234, 240, 242, 244, 256, 263, 278, 286, 301, 302, 314, 315, 319, 333, 341, 346, 347, 348, 349, 350, 351, 352, 356, 358
True nature 5, 41, 46, 67, 86, 87, 93, 94, 97, 99, 107, 111, 140, 143, 145, 150, 156, 169, 184, 200, 202, 222, 223, 228, 238, 251, 258, 260, 267, 271, 279, 282, 286, 292, 293, 296, 297, 298, 299, 300, 306, 307, 313, 317, 321, 329, 343, 346, 361, 362, 363, 364, 366, 367, 368, 372
Two truths 56

U

Ultimate truth 56, 57, 294, 305
Unconscious habits 84, 85, 366
Unity 17, 302, 305, 318, 319, 366
Uranus viii, 32, 34, 57, 59, 60, 71, 83, 174, 180, 188, 195, 200, 201, 202, 216, 256, 273, 277, 287, 289, 291, 293, 300, 301, 302, 304, 305, 306, 307, 308, 309, 310, 311, 312, 313, 314, 315, 316, 317, 318, 319, 320, 326, 347

V

Venus vii, 32, 34, 52, 57, 58, 59, 60, 65, 70, 83, 87, 145, 160, 174, 180, 213, 214, 215, 216, 217, 218, 219, 220, 221, 222, 223, 224, 225, 226, 227, 228, 229, 230, 231, 246, 248, 251, 253, 290, 291
Vipassana 208, 209, 221, 299
Virgo 11, 14, 15, 16, 20, 25, 30, 31, 32, 33, 35, 44, 48, 50, 52, 67, 100, 124, 127, 142, 143, 149, 152, 155, 187, 193, 206, 222, 223, 238, 258, 260, 275, 281, 313, 331, 332, 350
VIRGO SOUL 25
Vocation 3, 26, 179, 318, 357
Vulcan 34, 165, 174, 180, 181, 182, 183, 184, 185, 186, 187, 188, 189, 190, 191, 192

W

Water . 9, 14, 15, 37, 38, 39, 40, 42, 44,

(water contd.) 47, 49, 52, 55, 158, 213, 217, 235, 238, 327
Western Astrology 13, 71, 137, 139, 175, 185, 213
Wholeness 15, 16, 18, 19, 152, 184, 302, 366
Winter 14, 50, 51, 324, 348

Z

Zodiac Signs vii, x, 13, 15, 17, 29, 50, 64, 65, 70, 94, 152, 232
Zodiakos 13

About The Author

Ruth Hadikin BSc. graduated with a first class honors degree (summa cum laude) in midwifery. She has studied spiritual and esoteric subjects since she was 19 years of age, integrating her wisdom with experience gained from her own spiritual practice, and worldwide travel.

As a professional astrologer, her defining talent is bringing deep insight, clarity and simplicity to complex subjects: in particular *Esoteric Astrology* and the teachings of The Tibetan through the work of Alice Bailey.

Ruth has traveled extensively in the UK, Ireland, Spain, USA, Australia, Kenya, Egypt, India, Nepal and Tibet. She has lived in England, Scotland, Spain and the USA.

She specializes in supporting you on your own greatest adventure: using Soul Astrology to explore your Soul Path and Life Purpose.

Web: **https://RuthHadikin.com https://Astrology-Symbols.com**

eMail: **Ruth@RuthHadikin.com**

Get *Your Essential Guide To Soul Astrology* free when you subscribe to Ruth's weekly newsletter *Life's Greatest Adventure* at https://RuthHadikin.com

Twitter: @SoulAstrologer @RuthHadikin
Facebook: https://www.facebook.com/SoulAstrologer

More by This Author

Soul Astrology by Ruth Hadikin

This amazingly simple method from a Tibetan Master unlocks the secrets of your Soul - revealing your Soul Path and life purpose for this incarnation. A potentially mind-blowing read, Soul Astrology can help you to get clear on *WHAT* you came here to do AND *HOW* you'll do it!

What you can learn in Soul Astrology:
* WHAT you came here to do
* HOW you'll do it
* BLOCKS that are in your way
* HOW to REMOVE them
* HOW to FIND your SOUL PATH in YOUR HOROSCOPE
* Your INNATE MASTERY and GIFTS that you brought with you that will accomplish your life purpose

During the early twentieth century a Tibetan Master who simply called himself "The Tibetan" transmitted a body of work known as *A Treatise On The Seven Rays*, to an Englishwoman named Alice Bailey. Part of that work was the volume known as Esoteric Astrology. Many have studied Esoteric Astrology and found the work to be complex in its presentation.

In Soul Astrology Ruth Hadikin cuts through the complexity so you can easily access the essential wisdom of the Tibetan Master DK. This amazingly simple (yet deeply profound) approach to your birth chart shows you how to easily identify your Soul's Path and determine your life purpose for this incarnation.

"Who am I?" and "Why am I here?" are the biggest questions that you will ever ask yourself as you walk though this journey of life. The answers are hiding in plain sight and can easily be revealed through your horoscope. You just need to know how to look, and this book is about to tell you...

Drawing upon Esoteric Astrology, the Greek myth of Hercules, and ancient principles from spiritual masters, Ruth Hadikin describes the journey of your Soul through the twelve signs of the Zodiac. Your Soul's Path and your life purpose will become crystal clear to you.

For spiritual seekers and lovers of astrology alike, Soul Astrology is a powerful addition to your toolbox for your ongoing journey of spiritual awakening.

Full details online at https://SoulAstrologyBook.com

Your Soul Sign by Ruth Hadikin

A series of Kindle short reads - one for each Soul Sign. The section on your Soul Sign is adapted from Chapter Three of Soul Astrology.

If you've read Soul Astrology the Soul Sign description is the same, however the following will be new to you:

- Personality and Soul
- Soul Recognition
- Personality and Soul Expressions of your Soul Sign
- Your Unique Soul Meditation

Even if you have read Soul Astrology, you might find this handy Kindle short read to be a useful reference guide - especially your unique Soul Sign meditation!

See full details at
https://ruthhadikin.com/books/soul-sign-books.html

Your Soul Sign Video

Soul Astrologer Ruth Hadikin reads about each Soul Sign and gives additional commentary.

Watch the trailer at https://ruthhadikin.com/videos.html

Learn to Meditate by Ruth Hadikin

Meditation is an essential foundation for Soul Astrology. Through meditation you will awaken higher intuition and gain deeper insights into your Soul's journey.

In this short book, Ruth introduces different meditations, some active, some sitting, and a quick-start meditation, so everyone can practice this ancient art of spiritual awakening.

Available in Kindle or .pdf versions. Full details online at: https://ruthhadikin.com/books/ebooks/learn-to-meditate.htm

Your Essential Guide To Soul Astrology
by Ruth Hadikin

This short pdf eBook is a companion volume to **Soul Astrology**.

Get it free when you sign up for Ruth's free newsletter at:

https://RuthHadikin.com

www.ingramcontent.com/pod-product-compliance
Lightning Source LLC
Chambersburg PA
CBHW051624230426
43669CB00013B/2170